The Gospel among the Nations

American Society of Missiology Series, No. 46

THE GOSPEL AMONG THE NATIONS

A Documentary History of Inculturation

ROBERT A. HUNT

ORBIS BOOKS

Maryknoll, New York 10545

Library of Congress Cataloging in Publication Data

Hunt, Robert A.
   The Gospel among the nations : a documentary history of inculturation / Robert A. Hunt.
      p. cm.
   Includes bibliographical references.
   ISBN 978-1-57075-874-4 (pbk.)
   1. Christianity and culture—History. 2. Missions. 3. Intercultural communication—Religious aspects—Christianity. I. Title.
   BR115.C8H86 2010
   266.009—dc22
                                          2009041064

Contents

PART 1
INTRODUCING CHRISTIANITY AND ITS
BOUNDARY CROSSING HISTORY

Preface to the American Society of Missiology Series

The purpose of the American Society of Missiology Series is to publish—without regard for disciplinary, national, or denominational boundaries—scholarly works of high quality and wide interest on missiological themes from the entire spectrum of scholarly pursuits relevant to Christian mission, which is always the focus of books in the Series.

By *mission* is meant the effort to effect passage over the boundary between faith in Jesus Christ and its absence. In this understanding of mission, the basic functions of Christian proclamation, dialogue, witness, service, worship, liberation, and nurture are of special concern. And in that context questions arise, including, How does the transition from one cultural context to another influence the shape and interaction between these dynamic functions, especially in regard to the cultural and religious plurality that comprises the global context of Christian life and mission.

The promotion of scholarly dialogue among missiologists, and among missiologists and scholars in other fields of inquiry, may involve the publication of views that some missiologists cannot accept, and with which members of the Editorial Committee themselves do not agree. Manuscripts published in the Series, accordingly, reflect the opinions of their authors and are not understood to represent the position of the American Society of Missiology or of the Editorial Committee. Selection is guided by such criteria as intrinsic worth, readability, coherence, and accessibility to a range of interested persons and not merely to experts or specialists.

The ASM Series, in collaboration with Orbis Books, seeks to publish scholarly works of high merit and wide interest on numerous aspects of missiology—the scholarly study of mission. Able presentations on new and creative approaches to the practice and understanding of mission will receive close attention.

The ASM Series Committee
Jonathan J. Bonk
Angelyn Dries, O.S.F.
Scott W. Sunquist

Preface

This book explores the ways Christians have engaged and can engage a pluralistic world with the gospel. It aims to highlight the various ways Christians have understood what that engagement means and how it should take place. The book is structured in such a way as to encourage students to begin reflecting critically on the three basic theological (and to my mind missiological questions) suggested by Charles Wood: Is a particular Christian presentation of the gospel authentically Christian? Is it intelligible and true? And is it fittingly enacted? (Wood 1985, 36-55). The foundation for answering the first and third of these questions is laid in the first chapter, which describes briefly the basis in the New Testament for understanding the Christian gospel, with which the church in mission engages the Christianly understood world. The second of these questions, regarding intelligibility and truth, is less central to this book but clearly cannot be answered without reference to the first and third.

Numerous terms have been used to characterize Christian engagement with the non-Christian world. Preaching, proclamation, witness are prominent in the New Testament and remain so today, although the meaning of these words in English doesn't necessarily correspond directly to their Aramaic, Greek, and Latin antecedents. In the last five hundred years the term *mission* has been most commonly used for Christian engagement with the non-Christian world, but it is a term with multiple meanings shaped in new contexts. Donal Dorr, in his work *Mission in Today's World*, focuses on mission as dialogue. He also points out that mission has been seen as evangelism or evangelization, inculturation, the struggle for liberation, reconciliation, taking the side of the poor, and manifesting the power of the spirit (Dorr 2000). David Bosch, in his massive historical survey *Transforming Mission* speaks of *paradigms* of mission and the multiple paradigms that have emerged in the last half century of Christian history, including those noted by Dorr as well as others (Bosch 1991). In less theologically informed discussions of mission many Christians simply distinguish between seeking conversion of non-Christians to Christianity and providing charity or social services. In its second, third, and fourth chapters, this book will introduce students to ways of thinking about Christian engagement with the non-Christian world through an overview of the history of Christian mission. This overview invites a critique of the authenticity, intelligibility, and fittingness of Christian mission in various periods of history.

Complementing this overview, the remaining chapters of the book offer readings from both primary sources and secondary analyses intended to engage the student further in his or her own critical reflection on Christian mission both historically and, more importantly, in the contemporary church.

The conviction of this book is that the gospel expressed normatively in the New Testament comprehends not only the gospel as good news of God's reign and Jesus as the Christ of that reign, but also the value in the diversity of cultures and religions to which he relates as such. An authentic representation of the gospel in mission is contextual not only in order to be fittingly enacted, but in order to be authentic. Contextualization is not just a strategy for mission, it is an ever-present critique of all attempts to bind the meaning of the gospel and the reign of Christ to a single cultural context. Such attempts rob the gospel of its fullness by defining the reign of God in terms of the demands for submissive uniformity found in human kingdoms and empires rather than in the light of God's self-emptying of all imperial claims with the death of Jesus on the cross. The eschatological openness of God's reign as found in the Revelation of John (21:25-26), coupled with the self-emptying of God in Christ (Philippians 2:6-8), is the sign that God's transcendence does not negate the diversity of God's immanence, nor does it suppress the immediate fecundity of God's Word. The Christian witness to the gospel affirms both the reign of the One God incarnate in Jesus Christ, and the constantly renewed plurality of ways of being human toward and within that reign.

Acknowledgments

I would like to thank my colleagues at Perkins School of Theology, particularly Ruben Habito and Charles Wood for their patience and encouragement, and Bill Burrows of Orbis Books for the help and guidance in preparing this work. Bill has played every part in the birthing of books from matchmaking to midwifery, playing no small role in neonatal care as well. His literary godchildren are many, and a legacy for us all.

I have received gratefully the work of many, some unknown or unnamed, who originally collected, preserved, translated, or published the works used in this book. I acknowledge with gratitude the following who have given permission to use their materials in this book: The Society of Biblical Literature for permission to reprint excerpts from *The Acts of Mār Mārī the Apostle*, by Amir Harrack; The State University of New York Press for permission to reprint excerpts from *The History of the Armenians/ Agathangelos*, translated with commentary by R. W. Thomson; Slavic Publications for permission to reprint excerpts from *Medieval Slavic Lives of Saints and Princes*, edited and translated with commentary by Marvin Kantor; The Medieval Academy of America for permission to reprint excerpts from *The Russian Primary Chronicle: The Laurentian Texts*, translated by Samuel Hazzard Cross and Olgerd P. Sherbowitz-Wetzov; Oxford University Press for permission to reprint excerpts from *The Helian: The Saxon Gospel*, translated by G. Ronald Murphy; Orbis Books for permission to reprint excerpts from *Transforming Mission* by David Bosch; Banning Press and Jasper Hopkins for permission to reprint excerpts from volume 1 of *Complete Philosophical and Theological Treatises of Nicholas of Cusa*, translated by Jasper Hopkins; The Ricci Institute for Chinese-Western Cultural History, University of San Francisco Center for the Pacific Rim, for permission to reprint excerpts from *100 Roman Documents Concerning the Chinese Rites Controversy (1645-1941)*, translated by Donald F. St. Sure, edited with introductions by Ray Noll; Baker Publishing Group for permission to reprint excerpts from *Wake Up or Blow Up* by Frank C. Laubach; *Missiology: An International Review* for permission to reprint "Black Consciousness and the Black Church in America," by Eric Lincoln; Gerald Anderson for permission to reprint introductions to works originally published in *Mission Trends*, edited by Gerald Anderson and Thomas Stransky; The United Methodist Church Board of Church and Society for permission to reprint "The Search for Freedom, Justice, and Fulfillment," by Samuel Escobar in *Engage/Social Action*; Bishop Manas Buthelezi for permission to reprint "Change in the Church"; Libreria Editrice Vaticana for permission to reprint excerpts from Decree on the Missionary Activity of the Church (*Ad Gentes*), Declaration on the Unicity and Salvific Universality of Jesus Christ and the Church (*Dominus Iesus*), and Proclamation on the Vocation and Mission of the Lay Faithful in the Church and the World (*Christifideles Laici*), John Paul II, December 30, 1988; *Christian Century* for permission to reprint "Christian Missions and the Western Missionary Guilt Complex," by Lamin Sanneh; The World Council of Churches for permission to reprint excerpts from "The Universal Claims of Orthodoxy and the Particularity of Its Witness in a Pluralistic World," by Petros Vassiliadis in *The Orthodox Churches in a Pluralistic World*, as well as "The Evangelistic Witness of Orthodoxy Today," "Encyclical Letter of the Patriarch of Constantinople, Joachim III, 1902," "Encyclical of the Patriarch of Constantinople, 1920,"

"Churches throughout the World," and "The Evangelistic Witness of Orthodoxy Today, Bucharest 1974," in *The Orthodox Churches in the Ecumenical Movement: Documents and Statements, 1902-1975,* edited by Constantine G. Patelos; The Lausanne Movement for permission to reprint excerpts from the "Lausanne Covenant" (1974).

PART ONE

Introducing Christianity and Its Boundary Crossing History

1

The Formation of the Church and Its Witness in a Pluralistic World

The Mission of Jesus—Proclaiming the Good News That God's Reign Is Near

The term *mission*, both in its Latin roots and in its mundane secular meaning, refers to the sending of a person or persons as agents of another charged with a specific task. Although the New Testament does not use the term *mission* with regard to Jesus, it does tell us that Jesus is sent from God to proclaim the good news that God's reign is near (Mark 1:14-15). Thus Jesus may be regarded as having a *mission* (Larkin and Williams 1998, 30-31).

This mission does not consist, however, of mere words. Jesus engages individuals and communities with the nearness of God's reign by enacting that reign in both words and deeds. God's reign involves forgiveness of sins, good news for the poor, freedom for prisoners, healing for the sick, sight for the blind, deliverance for the oppressed and demon possessed, and justice for all. Luke 4:16-19 is more than an announcement of Jesus' mission; it introduces Luke's account of Jesus' ministry. Following his announcement of his mission Jesus realizes all the signs of God's reign in both his actions and his words. Thus his declaration that God's reign is near is demonstrated as he makes the characteristics of that reign manifest through the faith that people and communities place in God, the freedom they experience from all oppressive forces, and the blessings they receive from God.

Beyond the announcement and enacting of the nearness of God's reign through works of love and justice, the gospels also tell us that Jesus' mission is fulfilled in his death on the cross and resurrection.

These events effect a real change in the relationship between the reign of God and the powers of the world, a change confirmed by the descent of the Holy Spirit at Pentecost. It becomes possible for those who put their faith in the resurrected Christ to not only experience signs of the nearness of God's reign, but to live within that reign by their participation in the life of the Body of Christ, the Church. They become a forgiven people, reconciled to God through Christ.

Beyond this the gospels, and the whole New Testament, affirm that the mission of Jesus will finally be completed with his eschatological return and final submission of all those powers opposed to God's reign. The mission of Jesus can be summarized as the announcement and enactment of God's reign, the creation of a human community whose participants experience life in that reign, and the eschatological fulfillment of all human destinies within God's reign.

The Mission of the Apostles— Enacting the Lordship of Jesus Christ

In the gospel accounts, particularly Luke's, Jesus charges the apostles to continue engaging the world with the good news that God's reign is near through their own preaching, teaching, and works of justice and deliverance (Luke 9:1-6; 10:1-20). They do not undertake this mission on their own authority, however, or even on the authority of the God of Israel. They are authorized by Jesus. Thus they preach, teach, and heal "in his name" (Mark

9:37-39). The fullness of what his name means is revealed in his death and resurrection. He is the Lord of the reign of God, the Son of God. The power that makes present his reign is his own Spirit living in and through their community. Only when the apostles acknowledge that Jesus is the Christ and are filled with his Spirit can they fully engage in and continue the mission of Jesus; a mission not only to announce and enact God's reign, but to invite those outside that reign to live within it through the fellowship of the Church, and place their hope in Christ's final fulfillment of his mission through the coming of all to his Reign (Acts 1:4-8).

Thus the apostolic mission involves more than enacting the nearness of God's reign by working in the power of God's Spirit to free people from all forms of oppression and bring to them all the blessings God has for God's people. It also involves inviting them to participate in the worship of Jesus as Christ, the Lord; for worship is the only appropriate behavior of any person in the presence of God. Those who once kneeled or bowed down in the presence of one whom they respected as a man now know that these were precursors to their worship of him as God's Son.

Several titles are used for Jesus after his resurrection, including "Lord," "Messiah," and "Christ." In the complex cultural background to which the apostles directed their witness, these terms, although uniformly exalted, did not mean precisely the same thing. Moreover they were in some tension with the ignominious death of Jesus on the cross. The relationship between the lordship of the resurrected Christ and the revelation of his self-emptying love constitutes not only a theological problem, but one for the apostolic mission as well. His death and resurrection both modify just what it means to call Jesus "Lord," and the understanding of the nature of his reign. Throughout the history of mission, as will be seen, it has been difficult for Christians to let the life and teaching of Jesus define what it means to reign rather than letting the culturally accepted prerogatives and behaviors of political rulers define the lordship of Jesus.

Related to the invitation to worship, and thus to join those acknowledging God's reign as a present reality in their community, the apostolic mission also involves the making of disciples of Jesus

(Matt. 28:19). Specifically it involves "teaching them all that I have commanded you," a reference in Matthew to that whole body of Jesus' teaching found in his gospel, and particularly Jesus' Sermon on the Mount. This sermon, like its archetype in the book of Exodus, instructs the people of God in how to be God's Holy People. Thus the mission to carry on Jesus' work of engaging the world with the nearness of God's reign involves the worship of Jesus as Lord, the making of disciples for the Lord, and enacting the nearness of God's reign in words and deeds of forgiveness, healing, restoration, freedom, and justice. The credibility of each part of this mission relies on the others—as Paul's letters, for example, make clear. Paul's concern for righteousness within and among Christians is not a new form of legalistic concern for salvation through obedience to the law, but with the witness of their behavior to the claim of Christ on their lives. It is not credible to state that God's reign is near in Jesus Christ if God in Christ is not worshiped by those who declare it. It is not credible to proclaim that God's reign is near if God in Christ is worshiped but God's liberating power is absent in the life and work of their communities. Nor is it credible that God's reign is near if God in Christ does not transform the individual lives of those who make that claim. Thus the coherence of the life of the church with its mission is, like that of Jesus with his mission, integral to its intelligibility and truthfulness.

The Context of the Apostolic Mission

In the New Testament accounts of his life not only does Jesus charge the apostles to continue his work, he characterizes those whom they will engage with the gospel in terms explicitly taken from the Jewish Scriptures as interpreted by his own teaching. Initially they are to go to "the lost sheep of Israel" (Matt. 10:6), a term reminiscent of Jeremiah 50:6. After his resurrection he directs them specifically to go "to the nations" with the good news. A Christian understanding of the mission of the church in a religiously plural environment must thus inquire into how Jesus and his apostles understood both "the lost sheep of Israel" and "the nations" as the context of their work engaging the world with the gospel.

The Lost Sheep in the Teaching of Jesus

The image of Israel as a flock of sheep is found in Jeremiah 50:6:

> My people have been lost sheep; their shepherds have led them astray and caused them to roam on the mountains. They wandered over mountain and hill and forgot their own resting place. Whoever found them devoured them; their enemies said, "We are not guilty, for they sinned against the LORD, their verdant pasture, the LORD, the hope of their ancestors." (50:6-7, NIV)

Here it is their earthly shepherds who have led them astray, while the Lord is understood to be their "verdant pasture." Jesus' teaching builds on this image as his disciples recall Israel to God's reign (Matt. 10:7). In the context of Jesus' ongoing disputes with the religious authorities in Matthew this recollection also reminds the reader that in part the lost sheep are those who have been marginalized and excluded by the imposition of impossible legalism. The lost sheep are not wicked, although they may be forced to live beyond the moral conventions of their religious community. And they are sinners only insofar as this is a pejorative term applied by religious authorities to those incapable of conventional righteousness because of their personal or social situation. Like the lost sheep of Jeremiah they are being devoured by a foreign empire, but they were as much driven from the Lord's pastures as seized and taken into exile. In Matthew 15:24-28 we also see that a return to God's pastures is not only for Israel, but extends to others suffering from the oppression of wandering beyond God's rule, in this case a Canaanite woman whose daughter is possessed by demons.

Finally in Luke 15:4-6 we have a parable that speaks of a single lost sheep, one now isolated from the flock and sought out by a shepherd who will not suffer even one person to be lost. It is important for understanding these images of lost sheep that they not be conflated one with the other, or with images of sheep and the good shepherd in the gospel of John. Jesus' mission to the "lost sheep" of Israel cannot be reduced to the seeking out of individuals who have fallen out of the community. It must include an overthrow of structures of teaching and authority that restrict the mercy of God and exclude those whom God loves from the nourishing fellowship of God's reign.[1]

The Nations in the Jewish Scripture

It has been the tendency of Christians to characterize "the nations" as a realm of sin, idolatry, and ignorance, particularly insofar as the lives of the nations are understood primarily in terms of the fall of Adam and, consequently, the human race. Yet while the Jewish scripture characterizes the nations as falling under God's judgment for all of these things, it is also the case that Israel falls equally under God's judgment. And in the Jewish scripture the nations are equally portrayed as places where righteousness, true worship, and wisdom are found. The Jewish scripture, in other words, has a more nuanced understanding of the nations than is found in a mere dichotomy between sinful and righteous, fallen and saved (Cracknell 2005, 8-28).

This is equally true of the New Testament characterization of the nations. Like all humanity, the life of the nations is dominated by sin and ignorance. Yet in New Testament accounts Jesus also finds righteousness, faith, and insight outside of Israel, as does Paul and presumably the authors and editors of the New Testament responsible for making the tradition of Jesus and the apostles available to the church. This isn't surprising since their own understanding, like that of the apostles, was almost certainly shaped by Jewish scripture.

This more nuanced understanding of the

---

1. Given the interpretation I have offered for the "lost sheep" in these passages it is not possible to identify them with the Jews as such after the Christian community has been effectively separated from the Jewish community. Jesus sought to restore the lost sheep to the community from which they had been excluded, not to drive or lure them into an entirely new community. Jesus did not teach, nor did the apostles, that the reign of God was the exclusive provenance of his followers even if he alone is its Lord.

nations begins with the assertion of the Jewish Bible that the nations have a God-given purpose and live under a God-given covenant. Genesis 1-11 establishes both the purpose God has for the nations through Adam and his descendants ("be fruitful and multiply and spread across the face of the earth") as well as the covenant that not only guides them in that purpose but also assures them of God's continued providential care.

> "As for you, be fruitful and increase in number; multiply on the earth and increase upon it." Then God said to Noah and to his sons with him: "I now establish my covenant with you and with your descendants after you and with every living creature that was with you—the birds, the livestock and all the wild animals, all those that came out of the ark with you—every living creature on earth." (Gen. 9:7-11, NIV)

The prophets affirm this purpose and covenant, and going further, look forward to the final unity of all God's peoples in recognizing God as the source of purpose and their blessings. All, according to Psalm 87, will discover that they are citizens of Zion, of the reign of God, by birth. All, according to Isaiah, will find their way to Zion (Isa. 60).

This is likewise confirmed in the teaching of Jesus, and later Paul. Both of them find faith and righteousness outside of Israel, in the nations to whom they bring the gospel (Luke 7:9-10, for example). This expectation of finding faith and righteousness strongly colors the apostolic mission, so that whether it is Philip meeting the Ethiopian eunuch (Acts 8), Paul and Barnabas meeting the unsophisticated idol worshippers of Lystra (Acts 14), or Paul meeting the philosophers in Athens (Acts 17), the starting point for proclaiming and enacting the gospel is reminding people of what they have already known and experienced of God's grace and mercy. The apostles understand that followers of Jesus are not the only witnesses to God's providence and grace.

Also coloring that encounter is the apostolic understanding of the relationship of individuals, families, and social groups to the gospel. Briefly we find in the Jewish Bible and the New Testament that there is a recognition of both the importance of the individual's relationship with God and the importance of fellowship in enabling or hindering that relationship. Particularly in Paul's letters the church is a witness with its life and within its life to Jesus Christ and God's reign. No one finally stands alone before God, even if each will be judged for his or her own deeds.[2] This complex interplay between individual and communal faith and responsibility is not surprising given the Jewish antecedents of Jesus' teaching and Paul's instructions to his congregations. The particular form of individualism found in the contemporary Western society was unknown in their cultural and religious context.

Engaging the Nations in the Early Church

The New Testament depicts a multifaceted engagement by the apostles with the persons and societies that they encounter among the nations. They preached, they instructed, they healed, they exorcised demons, they raised people from the dead, and they confronted those who claim to possess power and authority that by right belongs to Christ alone. As importantly, they founded communities that manifested in life together the same outpouring of Christ's Spirit that fell on the first believers at Pentecost, while maintaining a plurality of forms and structures arising from the plurality of social and cultural situations in which they arose. These Christian communities gradually developed an identity that gave what had been the movement initiated by Jesus a sense of unity based on the continuity of its mission with that of the apostles as articulated in the gospels, the apostolic letters, and finally a New Testament whose books were presumed to have been authored by the apostles (Lar-

---

2. Of several relevant passages from Paul's letters, 2 Corinthians 5:1-6, speaking of being "clothed over with a tent from the heavens" captures this idea. Clothing, in this case the body, is intensely personal while the tent in Israel's worship and history is communal. Similarly the image of the body in Paul refers to both the individual's body and the "body" of all believers of which each individual is only a part.

kin and Williams 1998). The mission of the church in continuity with this early church is no different from that of the apostles, for it is the Christian communities founded by the apostles (directly or indirectly) that carried on their work in their absence, and it is these communities together which constitute the Body of Christ in the world.[3] And like the apostles, these communities, these churches manifest a plurality of forms and structures even as they are engaged with a plurality of cultures and religions.[4]

The New Testament witness to those communities does not idealize them, but it is didactic: with an intention to instruct their successors on how they should, and should not, live their newfound faith in Christ. One of the most important lessons the New Testament teaches in this regard is the wideness of God's mercy—the decision of God to include all the nations in the salvation won by Jesus Christ. Initially this meant the Greeks, or more broadly those whose lives had been shaped by Hellenism. Yet in principle it included all the peoples of the world, all the different nations with their differences. Indeed the Christian fellowship was to embrace people not only of different national and ethnic cultures, but of different social classes and genders as well (Gal. 3:28-29). The vision of Revelation 21, in which all the nations of the earth are coming into the New Jerusalem complements and extends the images in the Jewish Bible cited earlier. In this regard it is significant that the New Testament was written in *koinē* Greek, the language of intercultural relationships, whether political, commercial, or religious, in the lands to which the Christian apostles were dispersed and in which the first Christian communities were founded.[5]

The creation of such fellowships as a sign of God's reign posed, and still poses, distinct challenges for the church. On one hand the fellowship is a counterculture to those aspects of any culture that deny God's purposes for God's creation. So, for example, it stands against the folly of idolatry and the subservience to demonic power that idolatry often hides (1 Cor. 8-10). It can even stand against its parent Jewish culture to the extent that this culture hinders the gospel (Tit. 1:10-16). It acknowledges that God's righteousness is also found among the nations and is welcome whatever its cultural garb. Paul freely quotes what are known as the Hellenistic "household codes" in his letters to Timothy and Titus, and admonishes his churches that everything God created is good and is not to be rejected if it is received with thanksgiving and consecrated with the Word of God and prayer (1 Tim. 4:4-5).

---

3. The question of what constitutes the church has been the subject of intense debate in the last century with the rise of the Protestant ecumenical movement and the continued insistence by the Roman Catholic Church that it alone possesses all those things that constitute the true church of Jesus Christ. It is sufficient for this essay that readers understand that the definition of *church* above is essentially Protestant, in that it focuses on the task of carrying on the apostolic mission rather than on a succession of charisms passed on through the laying on of hands. It understands the worship of Jesus as Christ in terms of obedience to his command that the bread be broken and the cup shared in his name rather than specifically as the Mass presided over by a priest ordained in the so-called apostolic succession. This said, Protestants, Catholics, and Orthodox agree that the mission of the church is the continuation of the mandate placed by Jesus on his apostles.

4. While it is useful to distinguish the apostolic mission from that of the earliest congregations, it should not be thought that somehow the apostles acted independently of the support and concerns of these congregations. It is clear not only that Peter, Paul, Barnabas, and others worked out of the supportive environment of those early churches, but also that the concerns of those churches (in relationship to the role of the Jewish Torah, for example) and the witness of those churches and their members was integral to the apostolic mission.

5. The image found in Revelation 21 of the nations and their kings entering into the New Jerusalem both plays off of and subverts existing understandings of what it means to exalt Jesus as Lord of God's reign. Unlike the kings and nations that under compulsion brought tribute to Rome, those entering the new Jerusalem come freely. And instead of finding an emperor upon his throne they find the Lamb of God and the river of the water of life. This image complements Paul's image in 2 Corinthians 2:14 of Christians being led as captives in a triumphal procession of Christ. He apparently imagines Christians as an aromatic sacrifice that pleases God, but more importantly spreads to bear the gospel to others.

The challenge of the church to be at once a distinct human community (and thus one that possesses its own culture) while affirming God's universal providence for and presence among the nations, and then living as a sign of God's intention that all humans be gathered into the reign of Christ, can be seen as the key theme of early church history. Paul understands righteousness as something that sets the Christian community apart and yet also links it to God's universal providence for human well-being. Righteousness doesn't limit the Christian community to those who have received the Torah, but rather expands it to include all those whose lives are transformed by the presence of Christ. We also find in Paul's writings about the Eucharistic meal in 1 Corinthians 8-11 indications of how a distinctive cultic meal must be both exclusive (for one cannot participate in that meal and also the cultic meals with demons) and inclusive (for one cannot partake of the meal apart from fellowship with those of all genders, classes, and ethnicities). The use of fictive kinship in which all members of the Christian community bear the same responsibility for one another as parents, children, brothers, and sisters also created a community that, like all families, was bounded (keeping specific lists of widows, orphans, and others entitled to its care) while also open to all those who fell outside the care and concern of the larger society and who thus needed a family (Larkin and Williams 1998, 58).

None of these principles, or the others found in the New Testament, was easily implemented as Christian communities grew and Christianity spread into new cultural and social realms. The early correspondence of post-apostolic church leaders, the theological reflections of the so-called church fathers, and even the physical remnants of Christian places of worship and homes give witness to a vibrant and conflict-filled effort to faithfully engage the nations with the gospel of Jesus Christ. This engagement included efforts to explain within a Hellenistic worldview just who Jesus was and how he related to both God and humanity—the stuff of the doctrinal controversies leading to the great church councils and their creeds. It also included questions about lifestyle that went beyond the problems confronted in the New Testament and would lead to a plethora of ways of living Christianly, including those of hermits, monks, nuns, and forms of religious fellowships other than normal family life. And it included the appropriate hierarchical organization of Christian communities and their relationships with one another, as well as divisions over just how those hierarchies would function and who would control them.

2

Post-apostolic Evangelism
in a Pluralistic World

The reports we have of the work of the great evangelists of this early period continue in the tradition of preaching, exorcism, healing, and teaching associated with the apostles. In those contexts these were all comprehensible ways of inviting people to new communal and spiritual allegiances for they were religiously little different from the environment of the communities addressed by the apostles. The challenge for the churches was how to live as communal signs of God's reign in new and changing social and cultural circumstances. What would emerge were churches increasingly shaped in their doctrine and worldview by Hellenism and in their organization by social structures of the Roman Empire. These developments are neither particularly surprising nor necessarily negative. To the extent that the gospel would be intellectually credible, and the church a sign of God's righteousness expressed in terms of the orderliness, peace, and mutual concern valued by Romans, then the churches would have to conform visibly to the culture in which they found themselves. The challenge posed by that conformity would be to exclude the values (and forms of social organization that manifested them) that were contrary to the Good News entrusted to those churches by the apostles.

The evidence in this regard is complex. It can be argued that with regard to the freedom and role of women, for example, the early churches soon betrayed the promise of their apostolic roots—gradually excluding women from the leadership they had earlier enjoyed (Bassler 2003). Similarly associating Christ with Hellenistic and Roman concepts of kingship can be argued to have led to distortions in the understanding of who he is and intends to be for his human followers (Rieger 2007, 80-84). Yet there is also evidence that both the care they showed for their own members and the ways in which they cared for the sick and destitute in society more generally were not only faithful to the mission of Jesus, but appealed to and manifested Roman ideals. Romans became Christian in part because the churches exemplified a social righteousness that Romans regarded as culturally their own, even if it was rarely manifest (Stark 1996). The periodic persecution of Christians and their willingness to endure martyrdom rather than conform to the expectations of their cultural context demonstrated (at least to those not inured to blood and death) that Christianity remained a countercultural institution even if it didn't counter every aspect of culture opposed by the teaching of Jesus.[1]

---

1. It should be noted that while the text below speaks broadly of imperial Christianity and imperial missions, the concept of empire and emperor was in a state of flux over the entire Roman period, notably between the principate and dominate emperors. Thus the association of God's reign and Jesus as Christ with empire was likewise changing. The broad strokes with which the relation of mission to context is being sketched here should not mislead the reader into ignoring those smaller-scale changes that influenced the practice of mission.

The Rise of Imperial Christianity

The Association of Christianity with Religion

The question of whether Christian mission both authentically and fittingly engaged the Roman world with the gospel is brought sharply into focus with the association of Christianity and Rome after the conversion of Constantine after 312 C.E. As within the boundaries of the Roman Empire, Christian communities became Roman, and eventually Christianity became the official religion of the Roman Empire—so its language of God's reign and Christ as Lord of that reign took on new meaning. After Constantine began integrating Christianity into Roman imperial life, Christian understandings of the role of how the Roman Empire fit into God's plan of salvation changed. The Empire now had responsibility for representing God's reign and engaging the world with the gospel. And Christian communities now saw themselves as participating in a *religion* in the Roman sense of a hierarchically organized cult responsible for relationships within the spiritual realm parallel to the responsibility of the emperor and his government for the earthly realm. Religions were not, and were not allowed to be, countercultural institutions in the Roman worldview. Quite to the contrary. To render unto Caesar taxes paid with the denarii bearing his imprint is very different from giving him advice from one's own spiritual treasure stores, particularly if it was expected he would receive that advice. Bishops might presume to tell emperors how to behave, as many did, but this only indicates that they now saw themselves as part of the same cultural coin. They had become leaders of a state religion whose role was little different from that of their predecessors who read the entrails of sheep, however more sophisticated they might have regarded both their revelation and its exegesis (Bosch 1991, 193).

The Association of Christianity with Civilization

By the fourth century, when Constantine had his vision to conquer under the sign of the cross, Christianity had already become an urban movement, and thus already identified with the "civic" aspects of civilization. Once it identified with the Roman city as such, and ultimately with Rome as an imperial city, its character was transformed. Christian communities identified the characteristics of Roman civilization with the reign of God. The city that had been the whore of Babylon now became the New Jerusalem, and Jesus the Messiah became Jesus Pantocrator—an imperial figure whose iconic representation gazed with distant authority as his earthly servants offered him churches as the tithe from the spoils of wars launched under his banner and in his name. It was an ambiguous image, linking Jesus to both scriptural claims that he is the Christ of God's Reign and mundane models of imperial hierarchy and rule. So close was the identification of the church with Roman civilization that when the city of Rome first fell to the barbarians in 410 it sparked a theological crisis. Augustine of Hippo was obliged to lead the church into tortured reflections on the difference between the City of God and the human city (Bosch 1991, 220-21).

Had he witnessed Rome's fall, John of Patmos might have been amazed that the successors of his seven churches would mourn the fall of the beast, or justify her defense. Yet times had changed, as had attitudes toward the value of Rome. After all, Christians were no longer persecuted and the imperial example, imperial infrastructure, and imperial conquests were allowing for the unprecedented spread of the gospel. So long as the church had to be *in* the world—even if events like the fall of Rome reminded Christians they should not be too much *of* it—at least some Christian communities concluded that Rome's now-friendly civilization could even be a sign of God's reign, a witness in itself. Moreover the claims of the bishop of Rome to primacy over all other bishops rested in part on those claims. Leo X, for example, pointed to God's providential placing of Peter at the center of the Roman Empire, a city in which all the nations of the earth met. Rome, for Leo, was the place of a new kind of Pentecost (Kidd 1920, 314).

The Christian Counterculture

Yet there also arose an important Christian counterculture within Roman civilization. The earliest origins of monasticism may have been Christians fleeing Roman persecution in the reign of Diocletian in the late third century. Yet following the example and leadership of men like Anthony the Great in Egypt and his successors among the desert fathers, individual Christians and later Christian communities lived in a witness to God's reign less entangled with Roman culture while still confronting those spiritual forces widely believed to dominate human life. The earliest hermits and monks were revered as men and women who, by their solitary lives in the wilderness, placed themselves in direct confrontation with the demonic, and whose triumph over those powers made them channels for the healing power and wisdom of Christ. Under the leadership of Martin of Tours and John Cassian, monastic communities were also established in Gaul. These communities, with their emphasis on poverty, spiritual practice, self-sufficiency, and charitable works promised a witness to a gospel free from the political and economic ambitions characteristic of imperial Christianity. And they offered a place to those not only in physical want, but desiring a less attenuated encounter with God's reign. With the widespread adaptation of the Benedictine Rule in the sixth and seventh centuries, as well as the formation of new monastic communities in Ireland, England, and across the eastern Roman Empire, monasticism became a distinctive type of witness to the gospel. The monk or nun sought to be a fit vessel for the gospel against a corrosive civilization, and would eventually become the bearer of many aspects of that civilization when the world fell into barbarism (Bevans and Schroeder 2004, 119-26).

Rome and the Nations

Post-Constantinian Christians were also re-evaluating "the nations" to whom the church was sent. If Christian Rome was civilized, indeed *the* civilization, then the hostile nations that surrounded it must be *barbarians*. And since Rome possessed the only true religion, those nations beyond its borders were by definition *heathen*, rustic possessors of mere superstition and idolatry (Bosch 1991, 193).

These attitudes were complemented by an increasingly complex, but consistent, understanding of the role of the church in salvation. The Christian churches were no longer a scattered fellowship of believers, but institutions with their own cultures of sacramental worship maintained by priests, bishops, and patriarchs. Although these cultures maintained distinct liturgical traditions and spiritual outlooks for many centuries, they were also converging into a single church that excluded certain types of nonconformists as heretics. This church saw itself as the only culture (within the only civilization) that stood as both a sign of God's reign in Jesus Christ and a participant in that reign. Insofar as entering into the life-giving power of God's reign was possible, it was possible only by entering the church through baptism (Bosch 1991, 218-19). This emphasis on the need for a single community, and thus a single witness to God's reign, may be understood as itself a way of addressing the particular cultural context of the Roman Empire, although it was also driven by more mundane concerns for consolidating political power and influence. Hierarchical ordering, even of diverse local church cultures, could be seen as a sign of God's reign overcoming the chaos of a divisive and conflict-filled world. The relationship between unity and uniformity is understood differently in different cultures, particularly when the source and end of that unity is acknowledged to be transcendent.

In Rome the emergence of a single distinctly Roman church changed the nature of Christian engagement with the nations. Hellenistic culture had been recognized early on as a realm within which the gospel could be fully understood and articulated. The culture and civilization of Rome eventually enjoyed equal legitimacy in the eyes of the church. Yet while the preaching of Christian evangelists and the stories of Jesus might be contextualized, respect equal to that of Greece and Rome was not to be accorded to the barbarian lifeways. With few exceptions Christian missionaries regarded them as neither cultured nor civilized.

Even after the fall of Rome the way in which the gospel was commonly presented was the power encounter in which Jesus triumphed over and destroyed the demons with their shrines and sacrifices, replacing them with his churches, his priests, and his sacrifice on the cross. Imperial missions were born.

Imperial Missions

Mission as the Extension of the Church

Imperial missions were not simple, and indeed were as complex as Rome's relationships with the barbarians. In some respects it is this complexity that sets them apart from earlier missionary efforts. Demonstrating through miraculous deeds that the claims of the church about Jesus were credible was nothing new. Demonstrating the power of Jesus the Christ over all other spiritual forces had also been the stock in trade of the apostles and early missionaries. Even failure and martyrdom was a witness to faith in the resurrection. Such a witness certainly continued into the imperial era and beyond. Patrick and other Celtic missionaries continued the pattern of wandering evangelists who learned by hard experience to speak the gospel in comprehensible terms, to challenge forces of oppression in the name of Jesus Christ, and yet remain dependent on and vulnerable to people in those societies. But after Constantine the spread of the gospel increasingly meant the spread of the church as an institution, and that could only happen through the same complex strategies of political, social, spiritual, and cultural engagement that characterized imperial diplomacy. Missionaries were no longer personal emissaries of a transcendent Lord; they represented a host of earthly powers as well (Fletcher 1998, 193-227).

This is not to say that individual missionaries or missions were entirely compromised in either their intentions or their actions. It simply places them in their proper context, whether it was the context of Orthodox engagement with the nations that surrounded the eastern part of the Roman Empire or the context of the Roman church engaging the tribes of northern Europe.

Ordered communities of monks, who were often the first Christians in a given area, presented such a witness to the reign of God. They were preachers of Jesus and his power to save people from their sin. They were also representatives of a way of life far different from that of the peoples that surrounded them. It was a settled life of agriculture, building, reading, regular work and worship, and written laws and order. It was a sign of civilization in the classic Roman sense. Yet it was also a life of constant prayer, liturgical and sacramental worship, and withdrawal from the entanglements of social and political obligations. In this the monastery represented the City of God distinct from a human city. It represented a religion that transcended human culture and civilization. Joining the religion of the monks was an initiation into a new form of understanding human possibilities in relation to both society and God. Eventually, of course, some of these monastic communities became centers of political power in their own right. They became players in power struggles of emerging Christian Europe. Yet there were also recurring efforts over a thousand years to return monastic life to its original witness; whether through movements like the Cistercians or through the mendicant orders that sought to imitate evangelistic witness of the apostles. At least some Christian leaders realized that both Christian Europe and even the church itself constantly needed to be engaged anew with the gospel. The "lost sheep" of a church that understood itself to be the successor of Israel (and some of its failings) were ever present for mission. The question, which led to intense conflict during the Reformation, was just who had led them astray and where they might find pasture.

Other missions were more directly imperial in their nature. Bishops like Ambrose of Milan had urged Constantine and his successors to Christianize their empire, and the emperors responded, when it was politically feasible, with both the forced conversion of pagans within the empire and the sending of clergy to their frontiers. So by the seventh century, Rome was the center of Western Catholicism. Yet realistically it was no longer a Roman Empire as had existed under Constantine. The city of Rome was the center of a petty Italian state, and power in Europe has shifted to one rather large Christian Frankish kingdom, consolidated by Charlemagne, and numerous smaller political entities involving a variety of ethno-linguistic groups. All of these kingdoms (to use the term loosely) were based on a social order in which religious solidarity was essential, at least at a public level. The conversion of a king to Christianity was thus an important key to the conversion of the people, and sometimes an absolute prerequisite. As a result Christian missionaries were involved in complex diplomatic missions that required not only convincing leaders to become Christian but accounting for the mutual obligations of other nobility, the sentiments of their retainers and peasants, and the interests of the nascent Holy Roman Empire of Charlemagne's successors (Fletcher 1998, 192).

This in turn demanded different strategies in mission. Where there was a local ruler who could impose Christianity on his people, missionaries could encourage him to physically destroy the vestiges of indigenous religion. Without that support, missionaries were forced to adopt less confrontational methods, baptizing indigenous practices and beliefs as a prelude to a long period of instruction and conversion. There is evidence that in both cases some people experienced a real change of mind and heart by which they joyfully gave themselves over to God's reign and Jesus as Lord. Yet just how many were converted and what that meant is open to question. Pre-Christian religious practices were still extant in Europe centuries later. As James Russell has shown, in the end many aspects of medieval Catholicism—even at the fundamental level of understandings of the atonement—owed more to German culture than to Latin and Greek Christian teaching (Russell 1994, 209). In any case the missionary intention was a Christian community completely integrated into, if not entirely dominating, existing social and political structures. The reign of God as a counterculture and its citizens a people with no other Lord but Jesus were sometimes forgotten ideals. In the Europe of the medieval period the peasant, merchant, or warrior who folded his hands in prayer before God on Sunday might fold them into the hands of his liege lord on Monday with scant idea where the authority of one ended and the other began.

Orthodox mission was somewhat different from that of the Roman West, in part because the eastern half of the empire didn't fall to foreign powers for several hundred years, and in part because the church was even more closely related to imperial power. In the East the emperor was the head of the church and all missions were thus imperial by definition. The Christianization of any group had to meet imperial needs and proceed with imperial warrant (Bosch 1991, 205). This didn't mean an end to missions, but even more than in the West it meant an end to idiosyncratic missionaries. The days of individual preachers and miracle workers like Mār Mārī or Gregory Thaumaturgus were waning. Mission meant engaging non-Christians with the claims of both Christ *and* the emperor, for to submit to the former was by definition to in some way submit to the latter. It is no surprise, therefore, that Orthodox missions were for centuries carried out through delegations to the barbarian courts on the fringes of the empire (Fletcher 1998, 341-42). Those delegations sought to offer all that Christ had offered, but now the idea of God's reign was refracted through the lens of Byzantium and colored by the worldly splendors of its court and the rich dignity and formality of the Orthodox liturgy. Whether this authentically represented the gospel of God's reign come close to the poor and marginalized remains in question.

Mission without Empire

Until recently in Christian history the Roman and the Orthodox missions could have stood for the whole of Christian engagement with the world in the first thousand years. Now, however, there has been a reassessment of the Christian communities of Asia, and particularly of Nestorian Christianity, and there is a new willingness to see them and their missions as genuinely Christian (Moffett 1992, 175-77). These missions are significant, for the Nestorians carried them out not as representatives of an empire, but as members of a minority religion that sometimes faced persecution for participating in the religion of Rome—an enemy of the empires in which the Nestorians found their home. The Nestorians were closely enough related to the Orthodoxy of Rome to be both anathematized by it, *and* accused of representing its imperial interests (Moffett 1992, 137-45).

Nestorian engagement with non-Christians occurred in at least two ways. Commercial travelers moving eastward into modern India and Southeast Asia shared the gospel with their business partners and contacts. Where they settled they established churches and Christian communities, some of which exist to this day, thoroughly integrated into the local culture (Moffett 1992, 266-70).

A different example is the Nestorian mission to China. It was a mission founded on the idea that witness to the gospel was best carried out by a worshiping community. Much as early Roman Catholic missions presented the reign of God represented in the ordering power of civilization found in a monastery, so the Orthodox, including the Nestorians, presented the reign of God through a community that brought together God's reign and human reality in a rich liturgical setting. After all, both along the Silk Road and in China the Nestorians were not dealing with barbarians, but with civilizations as old as or older than Greece and Rome (Moffett 1992, 288-314).

And their engagement was at least in part successful. Their monastery in China was built in local architectural styles. Its community life resembled that of already established Buddhist and Taoist monasteries, and the monks pioneered a language for communicating the key ideas of the gospel that placed it in the context of the Chinese worldview and language. Chinese became Christians, and Christianity became for a time a Chinese religion. Finally, however, the Christian community disappeared after the mid-ninth century when nationalist reaction led to the suppression of all foreign religions. Like Buddhism, Christianity remained linked with traders from the West whose activities were suspected of undermining the Chinese culture and social solidarity. More importantly, like Buddhism it never succeeded in integrating itself into the Confucian system of imagining social relationships in China. Christian communities were seen, perhaps accurately, as being in competition with the Chinese family under its head: the emperor and his ances-tors back to Shang Ti, the ultimate ancestor of all Chinese (Gernet 1982, 291-96). Although they participated in the rich variety of philosophical and religious ideas found in Chinese society they apparently were not regarded as an authentically Chinese religion, one which almost by definition accepts a plurality of religions under a single political and cultural head as the social and cultural norm. This issue remains alive today.[2]

The T'ang dynasty persecution of the Nestorian community in China was not the only instance of ecclesial life and mission carried out under the pressure of non-Christian empires. Persian emperors, no less than Constantine, believed that imperial order demanded religious uniformity, or at least submission. Under the reign of Shapur II in the fourth century, Christians were persecuted as part of a long-standing conflict with what had become Christian Rome, a persecution carried out under the aegis of restoring purified Zoroastrianism as the official religion of Persia (Moffett 1992, 137-45).

Beginning in the seventh century, the Muslim invasions of Christian lands, and the establishment of Muslim empires within which large numbers of Christians lived provided new challenges in mission. Islam recognized the legitimacy of Christianity as a monotheistic religion, and Muslims were in theory obliged to tolerate and protect Christian communities in their midst. Still, because of both social pressures and increasing anti-Christian apologetics there were growing numbers of converts from Christianity to Islam from the eighth century onward; this spurred Christian apologists, writing in Arabic, to both defend their faith and sometimes quite virulently attack Islam (Samir and Nielsen 1994). Moreover, in an era when religious affiliation was associated with political loyalty, Christian leaders were called upon by Muslim leaders to give account of their beliefs about Islam and Muhammad and justify the legitimacy of a Christian presence in Muslim lands. Eventually

---

2. Until today the Chinese government will not allow Christians to participate in structures of governance and accountability beyond the boundaries of China. Roman Catholics in China cannot recognize the pope. Protestants must participate in the China Christian Council, under indigenous leadership, if they are to be recognized by the government.

Christian confrontations with Islam gave way to relatively stable multireligious societies in which Muslims dominated politically and in all matters of public religious observance. Christian mission, Christian witness to the reign of God, could take place only in the language of Orthodox liturgy and the quiet living of Christ-like lives (Moffett 1992, 360-61). It was the mission of a church that recognized that religious pluralism was not only socially and culturally acceptable, but was demanded by the dominant religion of Islam. Imperial Islam brooked no challenges to the universality of its understanding of religion and society. The question raised by this experience is whether the gospel claims that Jesus is the Christ can be appropriately put forward with less than a continual public challenge to all competing claims.

3

New Encounters with the Nations

The period of mission dominated by the imposition of norms assumed by Christians to stem from Roman civilization had a long, slow end as developments in Europe from the ninth century onward gradually gave birth to contemporary European civilization, as well as its offspring in the Americas. Quite different but equally consequential for imperial missions was the gradual fall of eastern Roman lands to Muslim armies until finally Constantinople itself fell in the fourteenth century. Orthodox mission would not completely end, for the emergent Christian empire of Russia would carry its own imperial mission to the peoples on its eastern and southern borders. Moreover there remained unconverted groups even in the Balkans. Yet by and large the ancient Orthodox churches found themselves isolated and sometimes beleaguered communities in the midst of a succession of Islamic empires and states, forced to consider how the church could be in mission while having neither political power nor access to geographical and religious frontiers.

The Western church did not face these limitations, and at least three interrelated movements in European history have shaped Christian engagement with non-Christians in the last six hundred years. One was the cultural and intellectual movement called the Renaissance, as well as its successors. It was more than the rebirth of classical culture in Europe; it was also a new way of understanding history that unveiled some of the processes of cultural change. As they became increasingly aware of cultural change Renaissance scholars were awakened to the reality that across Europe much of what was accepted as Christian was a holdover of pre-Christian religious practices. Christianization

could be seen as a process that was far from complete, not just because of human sinfulness, but because of the persistence of pre-Christian cultures (Fletcher 1998, 509). The Spanish and Portuguese voyages of discovery likewise provided a new sense of perspective on the world, and the place of Christianity within it, through encounters with peoples and cultures that were dramatically different from one another and from Europeans. And finally the rise of colonialism and seaborne empires provided the overarching political and economic context within which the Christian engagement with culture would proceed.

Re-engaging Europe with the Gospel

By the fifteenth century some European church leaders believed that many, if not most, Europeans had only a tenuous grasp on Christian faith (Fletcher 1998, 508-10). Yet they also assumed that they were in Christian Europe, and that although people might be uninstructed, uncouth, and immoral they were not pagan in the sense of the Germanic tribes or Norse raiders of half a millennium earlier. Reformers, Puritans, Anabaptists, Moravians, and others thought of themselves primarily as renewing the original Christianity of the apostles. Yet there were also signs that Christians recognized the changes in their cultural environment, and were responding by engaging their world in new ways with the gospel. For example, the movement called *Devotio Moderna* in the fourteenth and fifteenth centuries understood itself to be uniquely "contemporary," a self-identified product of its time. And it was. Its focus on personal devotion fit well the rising sense of individualism found among the rising merchant class in urban northern Europe, while its role in education and the publication and dissemination of Christian literature addressed the values of that same class. That the virtual handbook of this movement, Thomas à Kempis's *Imitation of Christ,* remains a best seller even today suggests just how closely this movement engaged modern people with the gospel. The Reformation emphasis on the Word, both read (often in personally owned Bibles, something unheard of in earlier generations) and preached, engaged a culture that increasingly understood the self and its relationship with God as dwelling within the individual heart and mind rather than in great communal spaces and shared rituals. Such an understanding would become the foundation for the acceptance of a new Christian pluralism, and a plurality of witnesses to Christ matching the variety of human responses to Christ's reign. The question of whether such pluralism represented a return to the appropriate representation of the gospel or a deviation from it remained a matter of bitter contention.

The European Encounter with Other Civilizations and Religions

Beyond Europe, the age of discovery led to a renewed and greatly enlarged expansion of Christian engagement with non-Christian cultures. In the Americas, Spanish missions most frequently took place within two settings, either an *encomienda* (a Spanish settlement) or a *convento* (where missionaries, a few Spanish families, and a much larger group of indigenous people would live together in a Christian village) (Bevans and Schroeder 2004, 176-77). In both cases indigenous persons were taken out of their own social environment in order to become part of the Spanish or Portuguese economic, cultural, and religious system. Most missionaries assumed that the indigenous people were a *tabula rasa* possessing neither culture nor religion worth respecting. Hence Christian mission was an extension, forcible, of both true religion and real civilization. Yet there were also those such as Bartholomé de Las Casas who valued indigenous peoples and culture. And

as Bevans and Schroeder point out, the *convento* system could be seen as a return to a pristine Christian community built on indigenous social solidarity (Bevans and Schroeder 2004, 183, 201). Yet ultimately these voices were overwhelmed by the dominant confidence in the superiority of Spanish Christian culture and its right to engage non-Christians with the gospel by replacing their cultures. Mission attentive to engaging a culture was largely overwhelmed by a new type of imperial mission that sought to destroy and replace such cultures.

The result of this engagement was not entirely determined by Christian missionaries. There were ways in which those forcibly converted managed to retain their own identity and change the church to fit their culture. The way in which Christianity was *received* could also determine its character. In 1531, less than a decade after the Spanish conquest of the Aztec capital of Tenochtitlan, a newly baptized Christian named Juan Diego had a vision of a dark-skinned woman who called herself Mary, the mother of Christ. She instructed him to report this vision to the bishop. When he came to the bishop with roses that had bloomed out of season, his tunic was miraculously imprinted with the image of the Virgin, now famous as the Virgin of Guadalupe. She is surrounded by symbols that, although now interpreted in terms of Catholic doctrine by the church hierarchy, may also be associated with the indigenous Aztec religion. The bishop agreed to build a chapel to her on the hill where this miracle occurred, the same hill that was the site of an earlier shrine to the Aztec goddess of the earth the same bishop had earlier caused to be destroyed. Today devotion to the Virgin of Guadalupe is ubiquitous with Latin American spirituality and infuses it deeply with indigenous elements which initially were neither recognized nor valued by most Catholic missionaries. Similar examples of indigenous receptions and reformulations of the way in which peoples related to God through the gospel can be found across Latin America and in the Philippines (Nesvig 2006).

The first missionary to Asia, Francis Xavier, sailed from Lisbon in 1541. While he despised the brutality and immorality of the Portuguese and Spanish colonizers, he also had little respect for the cultures and religions he met in his journeys until he arrived in Japan (Bevans and Schroeder 2004, 185). His letter to Ignatius Loyola concerning the character of the Japanese is richly revealing as to what he found he could value in a culture (Bevans and Schroeder 2004, 185). His emphasis was on the willingness of the Japanese to be convinced by *reasoning*. This for the Jesuit was the mark of civilization. And this is also a further indication of how European culture was changing under the influence of the Renaissance. At least in Japan, Xavier's understanding of how to share the faith was different from that of evangelists in earlier centuries who had relied on the power of miracles and concepts of fealty and social solidarity to engage non-Christians with the gospel. Xavier's successors in China and Japan would likewise find much to admire in Japanese and Chinese culture. They would find among the scholars—both Buddhist and Confucian—those with whom they could reason and who understood the technical and scientific knowledge of the missionaries (Gernet 1982, 448-54). Matteo Ricci, the best-known missionary to China of this era, adopted the lifestyle and dress of the Chinese *literati* and allowed those who converted to continue practicing the ancestor rituals, which educated Confucians regarded as affirmations of social solidarity rather than spiritual exchanges. This was possible because Ricci could make a distinction easily recognized by modern Westerners, but not so self-evident at earlier periods of Christian history: the distinction between personal piety and belief and ritual recognition of the invisible but important sources of social solidarity. And it was a distinction the Chinese *literati* themselves recognized as appropriate for their culture and religion. In the presence of what were clearly both real civilizations and religions, Christians could only engage others with the gospel by leaving behind some of their imperial hubris.

Whether this approach authentically represented the gospel and fittingly applied it to the Chinese was soon questioned in what would become known as the Rites Controversy. The seventeenth-century influx of missionary orders into Asia brought political rivalries and new experiences of indigenous cultures to bear on the issue of contextualization. Missionaries such as Juan Bautista de Morales condemned Ricci's method as accepting what amounted to idol worship (Bevans and Schroeder 2004, 193).

Perhaps the most charitable interpretation of the attitudes of those who opposed Ricci is that they worked primarily among people who were not *literati* and for whom belief, ritual, and culture were inseparably intertwined. In de Morales we also see how the European experience of religion and culture at home was being translated into an interpretation of religion and culture in Asia. As early as the twelfth and thirteenth centuries, there was a growing consciousness among some Roman Catholic leaders that much of the European countryside was effectively non-Christian or sub-Christian. And Catholic religious orders like the Dominicans to which de Morales belonged were actively trying to Christianize rural Europe in the same period that they were evangelizing the Chinese (Bevans and Schroeder 2004, 137-68). Thus they were quite sensitive to anything that appeared syncretistic. Moreover, with the onset of the Reformation, Christianity in Europe was becoming more plural and to some dangerously fissiparous. Powerful forces in the church resisted the Renaissance style of humanism that seemed to lead to cultural relativism, and insisted at home, and abroad, on conformity to practices and lifestyles approved by the church hierarchy.

The dispute over Christian participation in traditional Chinese rites went on from 1645 to 1715, with regular delegations appearing before different popes for rulings. In the midst of the controversy the Chinese emperor declared in 1700 that the ancestor rites were civil rather than religious in nature. Then in 1704 he responded to Pope Clement XI's condemnation of missionary "accommodation" in China by declaring that missionaries must follow the methods of Ricci if they were to remain in China. In 1715 the pope officially forbade the methods of de Nobili and Ricci and their successors. Two years later the Chinese emperor forbade Christianity, closed all the churches, and expelled all missionaries. European Christianity had met a society that was amenable to reason, but that also possessed sufficient unity and power to reject the imposition of European judgments on the meaning of its cultural forms. In eighteenth- and nineteenth-century China there was no room for two empires. And in eighteenth- and nineteenth century Rome there was no room for rival claims to know and interpret the social and religious setting of any land. Catholic Christianity and China parted company (Moffett 1998, 130).

Christian Responsibility for New Worlds

Whatever the Roman Catholic verdict on the cultures of Asia and Latin America, the church continued to understand Christian engagement with the non-Christian world in terms of planting the church, represented at first by small religious communities in non-Christian lands. Only such communities had both the Mass as a necessary witness to Christ's presence and the fellowship, representing the social aspect of God's reign. That the church should thus spread worldwide was understood to be self-evident, quite apart from imperial or colonial impetus. It is important to remember when evaluating Catholic missions that the Vatican was its own nation, independent of and, in its own view, above mere states and sovereigns. Their colonial endeavors did not necessarily determine its mission, however much they might be drawn into its service or draw it into theirs.

Protestant responses to the discovery of "new worlds" were shaped by their very different social context. Protestant churches in Europe were almost all national churches, associated with and limited by the colonial endeavors of those nations. Nor was it self-evident, particularly among those Protestants influenced by the doctrine of predestination, that the church should follow burgeoning imperial adventures with the gospel. In the late eighteenth century William Carey had to argue stridently with his British Baptist colleagues before they would accept the need to "convert the heathens."

In the established churches there was a question about just who was responsible for these missions. Lutheran, Anglican, and Presbyterian Churches as institutions took responsibility for sending chaplains to accompany colonial and commercial "missions" into new lands. However, where engaging indigenous peoples with the gospel might harm those political and economic missions, evangelism was frequently forbidden. At least initially commercial and political goals were regarded as paramount by those most directly engaged with non-Christian cultures. In Protestant lands there was tension between the limited spiritual domains of national churches, their responsibility within the expanding political and economic interests of their nations, and a growing conviction that there were souls to save beyond the boundaries of Christendom.

Mission beyond the borders of Christian nations began to take place in part because churches that were not associated with governments, such as the Baptist churches in England, could pursue, if interested, evangelistic activities to the extent allowed by colonial and local governments. Moreover there was a growing sense of personal responsibility for the gospel among Christians whose understanding of self was shaped by the emerging Enlightenment worldview. For these Christians the apostolic task belonged not to the church at large but to individuals who were so called. Peter, Paul, and John were no longer seen as the predecessors of bishops and founders of Episcopal sees but as examples of faithful personal discipleship. Within both non-state-related churches and state churches, private societies that reflected these personal religious interests and spiritual inclinations of like-minded individuals were emerging. Christians increasingly saw their religion in terms of personal faith and commitment to mission. Groups such as the Society for the Propagation of the Gospel (1701), the Dutch Halle Mission (1704), the Society for the Promoting of Christian Knowledge (1698), the German Moravians (1731), the London Mission Society (1795), and the American Board of the Commissioners of Foreign Mission (1810) pioneered what were private Christian missions, albeit with links to state churches and free church organizations.

As pioneers these mission societies pursued a wide range of organizational styles and methods. Some funded chaplaincies that were also to act as missions. Others began by coordinating what had been individual or congregation-based initiatives. Some provided substantial support for missionaries while others encouraged missionaries to support their calling by some type of work. What they all had in common was a fundamental emphasis on personal evangelism. They all participated in what David Bosch calls the Enlightenment paradigm of mission (Bosch 1991, 274). In that paradigm the gospel primarily engages individual persons who respond by placing their personal faith in Jesus and conforming their behavior to what are assumed to be Christian norms. The nations as cultural realms became less important than the nations as homes to individual sinners in need of God's saving grace through personal faith in Jesus Christ.

Missionaries realized very early, however, that merely preaching to non-Christians in lands outside Europe was relatively fruitless. The personal faith that Protestant missionaries valued so highly required an infrastructure that they took for granted in Europe: places to meet, existing believers who could nurture converts, readily available Bibles and other catechetical materials, and the literacy to make use of these materials. These basic forms of the infrastructure for personal faith were complemented by more complex social structures. The town and city environments of Europe, particularly in the early industrial age, provided individuals and families the freedom and to some extent the anonymity to pursue their religious beliefs, even if they were somewhat at odds with the prevailing community beliefs. This wasn't necessarily true elsewhere. Even in an urban environment like Serampore, India, where William Carey began his pioneering mission, individuals were caught up in social networks of caste, profession, and family, which were in turn intimately related to Hindu belief and ritual. In villages these connections were even more intense. In some cultures, indeed most, European-style individualism simply didn't exist. The idea of "personal faith" made no sense to potential converts, or was understood in terms the missionaries could not countenance (such as accruing a new form of spiritual power to be used over rivals) (Walls 2002, 127). For most of the nineteenth and twentieth centuries the twin demands to personally evangelize potential converts and to create the social infrastructure within which personal faith could exist and thrive existed side by side. The need for many of these missions to also generate revenue to support themselves could fit well with demands for infrastructure. Early missionaries were pioneers in education, agricultural development, and creating small industries (often around printing and publishing) because these were both necessary to create an environment in which converts could survive, and because they helped fund the mission. This created tension as missionaries found themselves distracted from what they regarded as their primary evangelistic task in order to care for infrastructure development. It also meant that missionaries were being drawn into the colonial enterprise, which likewise needed an infrastructure of literacy, access to local printing facilities, and most importantly individuals at least partially freed from local social ties so that they could loyally serve colonial governments and businesses (Hunt 1991).

Imperialism, Colonialism, and Mission

The initial missionary contacts with non-Christians had come about because Europeans had sought alternative routes to the sources of valued goods from Asia. If that were all they had discovered, and if new trade networks were all they had established, then Christianity might well have simply gone through a second phase of moving into trading communities outside Europe, as it did when early Christians established themselves along the Silk Road and in the coastal communities of India and Southeast Asia. Yet the voyages of discovery were about more than trade routes. European rulers continued to dream of creating empires. The impulse for conquest, riches, power, and prestige that are at the center of the imperial quest particularly motivated nations like Spain, Portugal, the Netherlands, and England whose prospects for forming empires in continental Europe were dim, but who had ready access to the sea and increasingly sophisticated and powerful sailing vessels.[1] One result was the rapid conquest and destruction

---

1. It is important to put the impulse toward empire in its historical and social context. For several millennia a basic assumption of societies worldwide, so far as we can tell, was to expand their political and economic influence. The motivations for such expansion were complex. Most obviously, societies that drew on a wider range of economic resources were more secure than those with limited resources. However, it was also assumed that the governance of such societies depended on the prestige of their rulers, with prestige acting as a symbol of their power to control those resources. As a result empire building involved not only establishing political control, but accumulating wealth at the center of the empire. Such wealth was necessary to pay the military forces that maintained political control and to create the prestige

of indigenous civilizations in the Americas and the looting of their treasures. Initially unable to participate directly in this looting of South and Central America, and controlling lands in North America with no such obvious treasure hordes, the English and Dutch engaged in piracy, which is the logical complement of imperialism in that it consists of simply looting another person's goods for the sake of wealth, power, and prestige. Similar patterns occurred in Africa, India, Southeast Asia, and Asia. Where Europeans were able they conquered territory and removed whatever was of value for use in Europe. When they couldn't they stole from one another. When necessary they entered into alliances with one another and local rulers for the longer-term exploitation of the lands they had discovered. Since at this stage in the development of global transportation the only ships available to missionaries were those dedicated to the imperial enterprise, and because these carried Christian chaplains in any case, Christian mission was closely associated with imperial exploitation. Sometimes, as in the case of de Las Casas and Francis Xavier, this was regretted. In other cases it was embraced by missionaries who saw imperialism as a force for spreading civilization.

It is longer-term exploitation that might appropriately be called colonialism. In Europe from the seventeenth century onward new economic systems were gradually developing. It was being realized that wealth could be created, rather than simply being extracted from the land in the form of agriculture or acquired through trade or conquest. The mechanisms for this were not well understood even after the publication of Adam Smith's *The Wealth of Nations* in 1776, and even today nations continue to experiment with how best to create and distribute wealth. What was clearer to

European imperial powers was that a long-term presence in the lands they conquered, as well as long-term structural changes in the societies of those lands, would be necessary in order to use them to increase wealth in Europe. Just how this would take place varied with the situation. In the Americas large numbers of Europeans formed permanent settlements, sometimes to manage indigenous or imported slave labor and sometimes in order to themselves pursue farming, exploration, and trade. In Africa and Asia the "colonies" had a smaller European presence, albeit with strong military backing, to discover and manage economic interests. Whatever the pattern, the desired result was the same—to draw local indigenous resources and industry into worldwide patterns of trade in such a way as to increase European wealth. The economic, if not necessarily moral, justification for this was that Europeans added value with their "civilization," whether in the form of management of trade, industry, or more efficient forms of resource exploitation. Supporting that assertion were two closely related moral claims, that European civilization was essentially better for human flourishing than the civilizations (or barbarisms) it replaced and that Europeans were intrinsically better people than those they conquered, and thus deserved a greater share of the wealth generated in the colonial systems. This latter claim was tied to claims of class within Europe—where it was assumed that lower classes could be exploited for their labor as readily as indigenous Americans, Asians, and Africans. And it was tied to claims of race both inside and outside Europe, with a growing sense of racial superiority by Europeans and European Americans throughout the eighteenth to twentieth century.

Missionaries were not unaware of the moral and

projects that glorified the ruler or ruling family and symbolized political power. This transfer of wealth was also accompanied by the humiliation of those who opposed the ruler, so as to establish negatively the power differential. Empire building thus involved a near-constant engagement in warfare, not only because the imperial power was constantly threatened by rival empires without and rival rulers within, but because the wealth necessary to maintain the empire could never be generated by the relatively static agrarian economies of that time. The result was that there were groups in societies worldwide for whom martial values, ostentatious prestige, and the accumulation of wealth were unquestioned values. There were also groups with other values—for whom free and peaceful trade, for example, or mere peace, were primary. And of course there were dominated groups upon whose labor wealth ultimately rested. The shift in political power between these classes has dominated European political history for the last five hundred years.

practical implications of being so closely related to the colonial enterprise, whether they represented private missions or were more closely linked to colonial governments. Catholic missionaries, if independently responsible to Rome, were also closely linked to colonial governments. In Catholic Europe the state and Roman Catholic establishment were closely related up to the mid-twentieth century, and excluded all private religious enterprise. Protestants often had looser relationships with their governments, but were still dependent on the colonial enterprise. Missionaries like Robert Morrison, who worked for an opium trader in order to gain access to China and prepare a Chinese Bible, understood the moral ambiguity of their position but believed that the benefits of reaching non-Christians with the gospel outweighed the risks. One hundred years later, when many Christian schools in Asia were funded through taxes levied on the opium trade, missionaries opposed to that trade found it hard to participate in one part of the colonial scheme and not the whole (Hunt 1991). Many missionaries, like the pioneer David Livingstone, embraced colonialism believing that "Christianity, Commerce, and Civilization" constituted a package that would "lift up" lives trapped in supposed darkness. And in general, although missionaries might be more sanguine than Livingstone about some of the benefits of commerce in the nineteenth and twentieth centuries they accepted the proposition that Western civilization and Christian faith together represented what humankind needed (Walls 2002, 183). They rarely questioned whether the civilization they brought was a fitting expression of Christ's message, or colonialism a fit means of enacting it.

Less clear to missionaries was the place of indigenous Christian communities in the overall structure of the Christian church. Despite divisions between different national churches, between

Catholic, Protestant, and Reformed churches, and between officially supported and free churches in European Christianity, missionaries had a concern for unity at least within their own churches. Still, some pioneers such as Henry Venn (secretary of the Church Missionary Society from 1841 to 1873) believed that indigenous churches could and should become fully self-governed and self-supporting, whatever their ongoing ecclesial ties with their mother church. For him only such communities could fully witness to God's reign. Missionaries were to be tutors who would create independent churches and then move on to other work. Militating against this idea were several factors. One was practical and economic. Missions frequently owned property and businesses (such as schools, plantations, and publishing houses) on which they depended financially and which they were reluctant to hand over to local church leaders.[2] In many places the Christian *church* was much more than just Christian *congregations*. Some mission churches were part of a national church structure back in Europe, as was the case with Anglicans, Lutherans, Reformed churches, and Methodists. Mission congregations were thus part of a structure of ecclesial authority centered in a Western country. Perhaps most importantly, by the time Venn put forward his proposals European and American missionaries were becoming convinced that it would take decades or longer before indigenous church leaders were capable of working independently. A sense of their own superiority, rising educational standards in their home countries, an increasing emphasis on doctrinal purity and fear of syncretism, and even the prospect of losing their own sense of purpose led most missions and missionaries to keep indigenous churches in a state of dependence (Walls 2002, 162-64). Missions within colonial empires had become colonial missions within ecclesial empires.

---

2. In the author's personal experience this reluctance endures to the present and has been witnessed in such diverse environments as Malaysia and Zimbabwe.

4

Disentangling the Gospel from Empire and Colonialism

A number of factors led to the slow disentangling of the Christian engagement of the world with the gospel from the colonial engagement of the world with Western civilization.

Indigenous Christian Movements

Indigenous Christians, who were frustrated with continued missionary control of their ministry and the suppression of indigenous spiritual needs, began to form Christian movements outside the church.

One example from Java is Sadrach (originally named Radin Abas). He was a product of Javanese Islamic schools who converted to Christianity in 1866 after making contact with a local Christian evangelist. After several years working within the framework of the Dutch mission as an evangelist, Sadrach moved to central Java and began working autonomously. Over a period from 1870 to 1900 he converted several Muslim religious leaders and founded dozens of Christian communities, frequently converting entire villages to Christianity. Sadrach adopted a number of characteristics of Javanese religion. He presented himself as a *kiayi*, or *guru ngelmu*: a teacher of esoteric religious knowledge who had been especially called by God to teach people in central Java. He gathered *murid* or disciples who maintained a close personal relationship with him. They were not merely students, but his "children" whom he guided in all spiritual matters. And they in turn were gurus to their Christian followers in the villages where they taught. Sadrach proclaimed the Jesus was the *ratu adil* or "just king" promised in Javanese eschatological thinking, and that Jesus was the *panutun* or "perfect example." Worship in Sadrach's communities was flexible, following typical Javanese patterns of song, prayer, and exhortation. Javanese customs and rituals related to pregnancy, childbirth, circumcision, marriage, death, land cultivation, farming, harvesting, and inheritance were accepted and "Christianized." Sadrach recognized, like some earlier Dutch missionaries, that there could be no "individual" Christian in Javanese society. The web of *adat* or customary law did not allow for autonomous religious belief. Thus Sadrach initiated Christian villages, or converted whole villages by convincing the local religious leader to embrace Christianity. He was also declared a heretic by the Dutch Reformed Mission, and his congregations were suppressed when possible (Partonadi 1990).

In Africa a number of indigenous Christian leaders either broke from established missions or were expelled and formed what are now known as African Independent Churches, African Initiated Churches, or African Indigenous Churches. One example is William Harris, a Methodist who broke from the church around 1910, adopted striking new dress styles of indigenous origin, and began to travel across Liberia, Sierra Leone, and Ghana. Having earlier participated in rebellions against the existing Liberian government, he began to preach a gospel of Christ's triumph over all spiritual forces and encourage peaceful living, sobriety, and fidelity. He was accompanied by two women who sang and played gourd shakers, and he encouraged indigenous forms of prayer, praise, ecstatic worship, prophecies, and miraculous healings and exorcisms. He allowed polygamous marriage. Ultimately he sparked a mass revival movement that radically transformed a large swath of West Africa and gave Protestant Christianity, and in particular Methodism, its first real impetus there. Many of his followers were absorbed into the Methodist Church, and at the end of his life he encouraged his followers to come under Methodist discipline and instruction. Yet many objected, in particular because the Methodist Church forbade polygamy and paid its pastors, two practices that seemed the opposite of Biblical precedent. Independent churches that trace their founding to Harris remain today (Shank 1986).

Similar movements arose in India, the Philippines, China, and Latin America when local Christian evangelists and teachers broke from existing missions that failed to address concerns within the indigenous worldview or use indigenous resources for worship. These movements created tensions with missionary-led churches, but also alerted sympathetic missionaries to the reality that indigenous Christian movements might arise outside colonial structures.

Missionary Objections to the Influence of Colonialism

Many missionaries themselves eventually became disenchanted with these colonial structures, both external to and internal to their own mission organization, when they worked against the gospel. In Southeast Asia, for example, where the Methodist mission was heavily involved in the development of large rubber plantations, missionaries protested that they had not come to minister to trees, but to people. Others objected to the promulgation of English-language rather than indigenous-language education, the former clearly serving colonial interests while the latter preserved local cultures and social networks. And both were thought inimical to the goal of personal evangelism, which represented the missionary ideal of a fitting enactment of the gospel. And as already mentioned, many missionaries objected to the way in which their endeavors were co-opted by the trade in opium (Hunt 1991).

The Rise of Ecumenism

A third factor in allowing missionaries and indigenous Christians to begin to distinguish between the gospel and colonialism was the movement of denominational cooperation that would eventually give rise to the ecumenical movement. As Christians working outside the West realized the need to cooperate, given the vastness of the un-evangelized world, they also had to distinguish the gospel from their denominational and national interests. Changes in Europe also affected this cooperation. Napoleon's early nineteenth-century conquests in Europe extended the French policy of freedom of religion to countries such as the Netherlands, and thus to the colonies that had been previously closed to outside missions. The treaty of Berlin in 1878 brought freedom of religion to all the lands and colonies of the signatories. Missionaries quickly followed, until every mission "field" had a number of different national and denominational missions. By the turn of the century, missionaries were realizing that with Christianity they were also bringing divisions that related far more to the history of political and economic struggles in the West than to the gospel. The early regional missionary conferences, and in particular the worldwide mission conference in Edinburgh in 1910, represented the first efforts to establish a common understanding of the gospel apart from other interests, so that work could be shared rather than duplicated (Latourette 1975, 1342-45).

Missional cooperation was not the only reason for an interest in intra-Christian relationships. Freedom of religion in colonized lands also opened the door to Protestants in lands formerly dominated by Catholics and vice versa. Particularly in Eastern Europe and the Middle East (but Northern Africa and India as well) both Protestants and Catholics gained increasing access to lands where Orthodoxy was the primary form of Christianity. Conflicts were inevitable, and some remain until the present day. Yet positively, greatly increased interaction among Christians led to a growing concern for ecumenism as Protestants, Catholics, and Orthodox sought, as they continue to seek, ways of not only construing non-Christians and non-Western cultures, but one another as well.

The growing recognition in the late nineteenth and early twentieth centuries that the gospel was ill-served by its colonial ties did not mean that missionaries or indeed indigenous church leaders were necessarily prepared to distinguish the gospel from the "civilizing" work that had become so central to Christian mission. Indeed, while the Edinburgh conference took the first steps toward valuing non-Christian religions and cultures it was still assumed that they were a preparation for understanding the gospel, and had value only insofar as their values pre-figured those in the West. What demanded a more serious critique of the association between Western civilization and Christianity was the First World War, although this affected European missions more than those of the United States. The devastation of internecine conflict in Europe made Western claims of moral superiority suspect, even in Europe, and made both Christians and non-Christians outside Europe more conscious of the disjunction between the professed values of European Christendom and the treatment of those who lived in European colonies. Around the world the supposed beneficiaries of colonialism began to see themselves as victims. Christians began to realize, albeit slowly, that they would need to distinguish between the gospel of Jesus Christ and not only colonialism, but the *culture* of the West.

The worldwide mission conferences of 1928 in Jerusalem and 1936 in Tambaran became forums in which indigenous Christian leaders increasingly spoke out for both independence from colonial missions and the recognition of their own cultural values. They found some sympathy with missionaries who saw in non-Western cultures a bulwark against the rising tide of modernism and theological liberalism. More common, however, were missionary fears that *without* Western culture and civilization the gospel would be distorted by syncretism. Hendrick Kraemer's influence on this latter conference was substantial, because he argued, persuasively to many, that the gospel transcended and must transform *all* cultures. All forms of religion fell short of authentic faith in Christ. While Kraemer's critique was intended to

be even-handed it could also be a justification for maintaining the imperfect status quo of Christianity in the garb of colonial culture. Moreover by essentially dismissing non-Christian religions as purely human phenomenon he left little room for a flourishing theological exploration of how other cultures and forms of religious expression were part of God's plan for the nations. Instead the study of non-Christian religions in relation to the gospel was treated, as it still is in some missionary circles, as primarily *instrumental*, a means of discovering better ways in which to undermine or overthrow those religions with the gospel. Others at Tambaran opposed Kraemer, notably A. G. Hogg. In their view Christians might expect to find, beyond the bounds of Christianity, other intimations and understandings of God's reign (Eck 1988).

Other questions were raised by a massive study of Christian mission, published in 1932, entitled *The Laymen's Inquiry*. It suggested that in the end economic and social development were more important forms of Christian mission than conversion of non-Christians to Christianity. *The Laymen's Inquiry* was a particularly American document, reflecting the hubris of a nation that did not believe itself caught up in the failures of either imperialism or colonialism. Thus it could imagine Christian missionaries bestowing the blessings of Western education and economic development quite apart from political domination. In some ways it laid the groundwork for what would be called neo-colonialism: cultural and economic domination hidden behind the mask of political self-determination and economic development (Laymen's Foreign Missions Inquiry, Commission of Appraisal, and Hocking 1932).

World War I brought into question, at least in Europe and its colonies, the association between colonialism and engaging the non-Christian world with the gospel. The Second World War effectively brought an end to colonialism as a respectable pursuit of nations and legitimate framework for Christian missions. Nationalist movements were afoot around the world, and between 1946 and 1970 virtually all of Europe's colonies became independent nations. As traumatic as this political process proved to be, its ecclesial equivalent was even more fraught with difficulty. The church was supposed to be universal, its fellowship unhindered by national boundaries. For many Christians, both mission-aries and indigenous leaders, the formation of national churches in these new nations seemed to oppose half a century of increasing Christian ecumenism. For others, however, it was the only opportunity to finally free the gospel from the con-straints of ecclesial colonialism and discover just what it meant to engage non-Christians with the good news of God's reign unencumbered by pan-dering to Western political and economic interests, not to mention Western cultural forms.

In the end there was no single pattern of church relations in the post-colonial world. Apart from China, where the communist government insisted that Catholics break all ties with the Vatican, the structure of Roman Catholicism remained the same. In China, Protestant churches were likewise forcibly separated from their founding denomi-nations and placed in a single ecumenical body. Other worldwide churches, such as Lutherans, Methodists, Presbyterians, and Anglicans some-times formed independent churches and some-times remained connected to their denominational structures. In churches that had no such clear hier-archical structure local churches sometimes broke free, forming, for example, independent Bap-tist conventions. In other cases foreign missions retained control of both property and ministries in newly independent nations, and thus effectively continued to control the churches formed in an earlier era.

While patterns of post-colonial church rela-tionships varied, what did not change was the widespread dependence of non-Western churches on Western money and, to an extent, missionary expertise and leadership. As a result Christian engagement of non-Christians with the gospel con-tinued to be shaped by the often conflicting views of indigenous and Western Christians, resulting in a plurality of understandings and approaches. Still, by the 1950s a significant change was underway in Christian engagement of the non-Christian world. It was no longer an engagement that depended on creating a Western political, economic, and cul-tural framework for the gospel. Indeed Christian engagement with the non-Christian world often challenged that framework as part of Christian wit-ness, and affirmed the value of indigenous societies and cultures. *Inculturation* and *contextualization*

were becoming central to any fitting representation of the gospel (Bosch 1991, 447-57).

Comparing Cultures and Religions

Discussions of inculturation and contextualization were possible not only because churches outside the West were asserting the value and indeed neces-sity of working within their cultural contexts, but because a new framework for understanding cul-ture and religion had been emerging since Europe-ans first came into contact with the cultures of Asia and the New World. As in the Rites Controversy, it was becoming possible and necessary to identify aspects of non-European cultures as specifically religious because of their apparent similarity with those beliefs and practices that in Christendom were associated with religious (as opposed to secu-lar) belief and practice. These could include moral codes, various types of ritual directed toward what were considered spirits or spiritual forces, and beliefs about those spirits and forces. Although these newly identified religions were defined in terms of their relationship with Christianity, and were generally considered as lesser or deficient forms of religion, the groundwork was laid for the comparative study of religion.

The results were twofold. As noted in the next section, such comparative studies would eventually call into question the whole project of Christian mission as the superseding of supposedly lesser religions with Christianity. More immediately with the comparative study of religions was the development of the social sciences whose meth-odologies would make possible more systematic and consistent study of religion, culture, and social behavior generally. In particular the nineteenth-century growth of anthropology and sociology had an influence on missionaries who had struggled to understand the people and societies whom they were engaging with the gospel. Now missionaries had new tools for understanding cultures different from their own, and how effectively to communi-cate the gospel in those cultures. Rather than sim-ply assuming that all persons had the same needs and desires as the missionaries themselves, these new sciences augmented theological assessments of non-Christian humanity and promised to give missionaries a glimpse into the world of indigenous understanding (Hiebert 1996). Differing cultures could thus be "targeted" more effectively to use the militaristic language that still pervaded much missionary discourse in the early twentieth century.

Later, as the rise of indigenous Christian leadership demanded new understandings of mutuality, partnership, and respect for indigenous cultures, the social sciences could be bent to the task of adapting the gospel to new cultural settings. They could help missionaries and local church leaders map the cultural terrain in which the gospel was being shared. Then evangelists could help appropriately apply theological criteria to local belief and practice in order to discern just what properly could belong to a Christian expression of the gospel. Not surprisingly these analyses of culture and religion based on Western social sciences were soon turned on the cultures of their first practitioners. As early as the Jerusalem conferences in 1928 Chinese church leaders were pointing out the inconsistencies of Western Christian cultures by using the same tools with which missionaries were analyzing Chinese culture. By the end of the century, and sometimes much earlier, even more conservative and theologically oriented missionaries were using the social sciences to analyze their own culture, as well as applying these sciences to an understanding of the New Testament. Both Biblical studies and mission to Christendom's "lost sheep" could benefit from their insights. There remained limits, however, among Christians who reserved for a revelation-based theology the task of inquiry into God and the human condition. For them the social sciences have remained primarily tools at the service of mission rather than a complement to theology for inquiry into the human condition.[1]

Beyond new forms of understanding culture and human society there emerged in the twentieth century new analyses of the reasons for poverty, political oppression, and other social woes. Social scientists and theologians alike, along with missionaries and indigenous Christian leaders were beginning to recognize that colonialism and cultural imperialism were only the surface manifestations of deeper structures of inequality and exploitation in the modern world. Christian mission, if it was to engage the world with the gospel, would need to understand and confront these. Acknowledging that people are victims not just of personal sin, but of worldwide political, economic, and cultural structures that are manifestly un-Christian has become a central theme of Christian missions. Serious attention to context has been understood to demand mission as *solidarity* with the poor and marginalized, as well as *liberation* from oppressive powers (Bosch 1991, 432). Social analysis became a partner with mission not only in discerning fitting representations of the gospel, but the appropriate understanding of its central meaning as well. Moreover they became a distinctly modern way to address the question of the truth of the gospel in terms of its consistency and coherence with universal human experience.

Post-colonial Engagement

In looking at the post-colonial era in Christian mission it must first be noted that there is no agreement among Christians about how non-Christians should be engaged with the gospel. Indeed, the most common word associated with mission from the late 1960s to the early 1980s was *crisis*. The old order in which Christian missions had located itself seemed irrevocably past, while despite the work of the Second Vatican Council, the World Council of Churches, and the International Congresses on World Evangelization no strong new framework

---

1. The work of late-twentieth-century Christian social scientists Paul Hiebert and Charles Kraft is illustrative of highly sophisticated versions of this basic approach. In the view of this author, both Kraft and Hiebert are quite aware that the gospel is bound to culture. Yet both maintain that God, and in particular God's revealed Word in the Bible are supracultural and transcultural. The social sciences may serve the mission of the church but may not undermine the basis of its claim to ultimacy through an alternative form of knowing the world. The larger debate over science and religion is also a debate between social science and mission (Kraft 2005).

or common understanding of Christian mission emerged in these years. Throughout the colonial era there had been missionaries, and not only from the West, who saw the human situation not so much in terms of politics, economics, culture, and worldview as in terms of personal human sinfulness being addressed by divine forgiveness in Jesus Christ. From this perspective the admonition of James to make sure that people are fed and cared for is an essential *accompaniment of witness*, and is to be taken seriously (Jas. 2:17). But such efforts are at any level merely a prologue to the preaching of Jesus as Savior from human sin and the power of death. This missional focus continues today within the World Evangelical Fellowship and similar organizations. The WEF and associated missionaries often have a sophisticated analysis of how human sin is manifest in sinful social, political, and economic structures, yet they tend to use the social sciences instrumentally to communicate the gospel of personal salvation more than to understand the nature of the oppression that God's reign confronts. Personal salvation through individual faith remains paramount in the documents of the Lausanne consultations.

In the colonial era there were also missionaries, both indigenous and coming from the U.S. Pentecostal movement, that placed engaging the world with the gospel in terms of what is commonly called "spiritual warfare," or mission in the power of the Spirit. Evangelists such as John Sung in the first half of the twentieth century offered the power of Jesus as Lord not only against personal sin, but against the demonic forces that most people outside the West assumed were active in destroying human life. The precise focus on spiritual warfare as the engagement of the non-Christian world with the gospel varies from place to place and culture to culture. Many Pentecostal evangelists closely linked the power of the demonic with the failure of personal holiness and preached that Christ's gospel offers forgiveness and freedom only when his followers adopt a holy lifestyle. Thus the gospel is said to demand temperance, fidelity, self-discipline, and gainful employment if its power is to be effective. Such a message is not so different from that of John Wesley, although its bearers may offer more flamboyant proofs of the miracle of Christ's power over demons and disease.

At the other extreme there arose in the early twentieth century proponents of a gospel of positive thinking such as Norman Vincent Peale. Faith in God's desire that the faithful enjoy happy, healthy lives became central to their message, and they became the predecessors of contemporary preachers dedicated to the so-called health and wealth gospel. They understand spiritual oppression primarily in terms of sickness and poverty and the promise that in following Christ people will discover the power to overcome disease and gain wealth. It is not unusual for these preachers to have followers both from among the poor who do not understand the origins of their misery to be oppressive social structures, and the very wealthy whose lifestyle is lifted up as a sign of blessing.

A third strand of missionary engagement of the non-Christian world with the gospel is implacably opposed to this affirmation of wealth and its assertion that poverty is primarily a spiritual problem of the poor. A wide range of Christian missionaries struggle to understand the complex relationship of poverty and injustice with personal sin, trans-human spiritual powers, and local and global economic, political, and cultural structures. What they have in common is a conviction that the gospel engages not just individual sinners or unseen spiritual forces, but all of those human-built structures that challenge the Lordship of Jesus Christ and his work of freeing the oppressed. Such a conviction arises out of, and requires, a careful analysis of the human problem engaged by the gospel, and a methodology that exposes all forms of sin and oppression.

No single rubric covers all the ways in which contemporary Christian theologians and missionaries of this third type attempt to fully understand the nature of the human problem and how it is addressed by the gospel. There are, however, some commonalities among them. First there is a conviction that the gospel, while universal, is first and foremost good news to those who are powerless and marginalized in human society. Liberation theologians speak of "God's preferential option for the poor" without necessarily defining poverty in purely economic terms. People can also be marginalized on the basis of gender, race, class, political ideology, religion, and even worldview.

Second, there is a conviction that the social

structures that oppress individuals and groups include, but are more subtle than, mere economic, class, political, or even religious systems. There is in particular a recognition that language plays a strong role in structuring the ways in which humans think about human relations, and thus in perpetuating oppressive systems. And this problem of language is not limited to gender, race, or class inclusivity. It includes all the ways those in power characterize events and relationships to either misrepresent them or create a sense of inevitability about them. Thus missionaries must be vigilant about engaging the world with a gospel that challenges all structures of oppression, including those woven into the use of language to talk about both God's reign and the power structures which it challenges.

Such a task would be impossible except for the third conviction of theologians and missionaries: that those who are oppressed must be allowed to speak for themselves. It is they who, given the time and liberty, will best understand and articulate the nature of their oppression and what it means that God's reign confronts that oppression in Jesus Christ. Mission must be a dialogue with the poor and oppressed, whatever their religion.

The primary role of the marginalized in speaking for themselves notwithstanding, these postcolonial missionaries tend to make use of the social sciences to explore, understand, and explain the oppressive structures within human life. As a result there is a tension in the post-colonial mission partnership between intellectuals and those marginalized peoples with no opportunity for academic study. There is no single solution to this problem, just as there is no single solution to the problem of the continuing power imbalance between Western and two-thirds-world churches. There is, however, recognition that partnership and solidarity are the necessary ingredients of mission, to the extent that the recipient plays a role equal to or greater than that of the giver, and the giver becomes the recipient of a deeper understanding of the dimensions of God's graciousness in Jesus Christ. The task of the missionary evangelist is not so much to proclaim the gospel as to discover it by living in solidarity with those to whom it is addressed by God. This requires a delicate balance within the constant tension between a meta-analysis of global structures of economic and political oppression and attentiveness to the integrity and difference of distinctive cultures and situations. In the end both the authenticity of any articulation of the gospel and the appropriate means of enacting it must arise out of a partnership between the missionary and those being engaged with the gospel.

Religious Pluralism and the Future of Christian Mission

This introduction has spoken of Christian mission primarily in dialectical terms: that of a Christian gospel presented to a non-Christian world. For most of Christian history missionaries have assumed that this dialectic is fundamental and that in the long run this dialectic will be resolved when all the nations have been engaged with the gospel and either accept it or face God's judgment. Such a view need not be culturally imperialistic. Missionaries have found positive value in non-Christian religious cultures that could be divorced from their strictly religious context to continue even after a people became Christian. Such values, and some forms of non-Christian religious practice, could even be resources for new Christian communities, making their new faith "at home" in the culture. Such resources might even positively shape the Christian faith in the same way that a fruit tree, transplanted to new soil, bears fruit that is potentially different in flavor from that of its sister trees in other soils. Still, it would be a Christian fruit.

In addition to the possibilities it offers for understanding enculturation, the rise of comparative religions has proven troubling to the concept of Christian mission. As early as the late nineteenth century, scholars and some missionaries would question whether Christianity was in any way superior to religions such as Islam, Hinduism, and Buddhism. And just as World War I called into question the moral superiority of Western civilization it called into question the claim of Christianity to represent the pinnacle of religion. There are those engaged in Christian mission who have come to the conviction that religious pluralism is not only an inevitable part of human life, but a desirable reflection of the richness of God's grace. Looking back over the history of Christian mission they see an unfolding realization that God has blessed many civilizations, cultures, peoples, and ultimately religions. For them this realization is the ultimate antidote to imperialism and colonialism. They imagine a time when all religious people will recognize that they possess cultural variants on a single theme of humanity in relationship with the Divine. And thus different religions will enrich one another through dialogue rather than having Christianity dominate them through proclamation of the gospel. The theological underpinnings of this conviction are well articulated by contemporary theologians such as Paul Knitter, Peter Phan, Mark Heim, and Kenneth Cracknell (Heim 1995; Knitter 2002; Phan 2004; Cracknell 2005).

Whether or not they embrace a pluralist theology of religions, having recognized the dangers of colonialism, and how it undermines the liberating claims of the gospel, the last thing Christian missionaries should want is to begin witnessing with an attitude of cultural superiority. Moreover religious conflict is at the heart of many political conflicts. Exacerbating those conflicts hardly seems consistent with witness to God's reign of peace. As a result, a wide spectrum of missionaries and missiologists have recognized that *interreligious dialogue* is central to Christian mission. Such dialogue can take place at many levels and has many forms, as identified by recent Roman Catholic and World Council of Churches documents. Essential to all of them is the concept of equality among participants, a willingness to listen to and to learn from others, as well as speaking and acting honestly. Yet engaging in interreligious dialogue, however well articulated the forms and ground rules, is not without challenges.

One is finding a common subject for dialogue. Apparently similar categories of religious thought and activity such as revelation, sin, forgiveness, redemption, worship, and so on are often found on closer examination to be quite different. So, for example, not only are Hindu and Christian scriptures different, the entire concept of scripture and its role in the religion is different. The same can be said of other apparent commonalities with other religions. There are social scientists who regard the very concept of "religion" as the imposition of an alien category on forms of human behavior and self-understanding found outside the Christian West. Even without spiraling into complete deconstruction of all categories of religious experience and behavior, both missionaries and their dialogue partners often find it hard to agree on topics for mutual discussion and enrichment, particularly in the realm of theology and spirituality. The shared challenges of daily life in a shared political, economic, and social situation are often more readily accessible meeting points for dialogue than religious beliefs.

More difficult than finding the common topic necessary for real dialogue is the problem of the absolute and ultimate claims found in all global religions. Christians have typically claimed that there is only one, God-ordained, standard for human relationships and that ultimately there will be only one human end: the gathering of the nations into the New Jerusalem to worship God and Christ. The Buddha, Mohammad, or the Vedas may be granted as some penultimate value, but eventually they will fade in the light of Christ. Muslims likewise, while acknowledging a plurality of revelations, regard the Qur'an as both the source and end of all such revelations and the balance in which they are judged. For Muslims, the original religion of humankind and the one to which all will return is Islam. Similar claims can be found among Buddhists and Hindus, for each religion claims to encompass and ultimately transcend all other religious options. The Hindu may tell the story of how a group of blind men feeling different parts of the same elephant come to different conclusions about its form. Yet the telling of the story is an assertion that there is a whole that the storyteller alone clearly sees. One of the greatest struggles of interreligious dialogue is finding a shared basis for theological reflection, something that in the end may require participants in all religions to give up both explicit and implicit claims that the transcendent source of their revelation of the truth gives *them* a transcendent perspective from which to judge all other religious truth. In this author's view, disallowing any human claim to such a transcendent perspective does not negate the possibility of revelation, and honors the prerogative that—according to Christian belief—belongs only to God.

So long as a common theological perspective remains out of reach, there is nonetheless at least one common concern that transcends the individual and collective interests of humans: the well-being of planet earth. Whether or not we can agree about the nature of the source and end of all creation, we can agree that we are of the earth, to it our bodies will return, and whatever else we have in common we pursue our religious ends embodied, and thus related to the fragile environment of our home planet. *Dialogue with and for creation* is part of mission, and "Thy will be done, on earth as it is in heaven" is also a mandate for mission, albeit one that focuses on the penultimate rather than ultimate context of that mission. It reminds us that the first concern given to the entire human family is the care of earth, and that it is through the earth's care for us that God has most universally revealed God's grace and love to all peoples over the entire span of human history. The nearness of God's reign with which we as Christians engage the world is not merely an eschatological claim. It is a statement of faith that God's Spirit has accompanied humanity throughout its journey in the blessings bestowed by seedtime and harvest and the rains in due season (Gen. 9). To preserve and extend those blessings may be, in our time, the greatest witness to the gospel.

Bibliography for Part One

Bassler, J. M. 2003. "Grace: Probing the Limits." *Interpretation* 57, no. 1: 24.

Bevans, S. B., and R. Schroeder. 2004. *Constants in Context: A Theology of Mission for Today.* Maryknoll, N.Y.: Orbis Books.

Bosch, D. J. 1991. *Transforming Mission: Paradigm Shifts in Theology of Mission.* Maryknoll, N.Y.: Orbis Books.

Cracknell, K. 2005. *In Good and Generous Faith: Christian Responses to Religious Pluralism.* London: Epworth.

Dorr, D. 2000. *Mission in Today's World.* Maryknoll, N.Y.: Orbis Books.

Eck, D. L. 1988. "The Religions and Tambaram: 1938-1988." *International Review of Mission* 77: 375.

Fletcher, R. A. 1998. *The Barbarian Conversion: From Paganism to Christianity.* New York: H. Holt.

Gernet, J. 1982. *A History of Chinese Civilization.* Cambridge [Cambridgeshire]/New York: Cambridge University Press.

Heim, S. M. 1995. *Salvations: Truth and Difference in Religion.* Maryknoll, N.Y.: Orbis Books.

Hiebert, P. 1996. "Critical Issues for Social Sciences and their Implications for Mission Studies." *Missiology* 24, no. 1: 65-82.

Hunt, R. A. 1991. "Have You Not Seen a Vain Vision: The Marginalization of the Methodist Church in Malaysian Society." *Asia Journal of Theology* 5: 410.

Kidd, B. J. 1920. *Documents Illustrative of the History of the Church.* London: Society for Promoting Christian Knowledge.

Knitter, P. F. 2002. *Introducing Theologies of Religions.* Maryknoll, N.Y.: Orbis Books.

Kraft, C. H. 2005. *Christianity in Culture: A Study in Dynamic Biblical Theologizing in Cross-Cultural Perspective.* Maryknoll, N.Y.: Orbis Books.

Larkin, W. J., and J. F. Williams. 1998. *Mission in the New Testament: An Evangelical Approach.* Maryknoll, N.Y.: Orbis Books.

Latourette, K. S. 1975. *A History of Christianity.* New York: Harper & Row.

Laymen's Foreign Missions Inquiry, Commission of Appraisal, and W. E. Hocking. 1932. *Rethinking Missions; A Laymen's Inquiry after One Hundred Years.* New York/London: Harper & Brothers.

Moffett, S. H. 1992. *A History of Christianity in Asia.* San Francisco: HarperSanFrancisco.

———. 1998. *A History of Christianity in Asia.* Maryknoll, N.Y.: Orbis Books.

Nesvig, M. A. 2006. *Local Religion in Colonial Mexico.* Albuquerque: University of New Mexico.

Partonadi, S. S. 1990. *Sadrach's Community and Its Contextual Roots.* Amsterdam: Rodopi.

Phan, P. C. 2004. *Being Religious Interreligiously: Asian Perspectives on Interfaith Dialogue.* Maryknoll, N.Y.: Orbis Books.

Rieger, J. 2007. *Christ and Empire: From Paul to Postcolonial Times.* Minneapolis: Fortress Press.

Russell, J. C. 1994. *The Germanization of Early Medieval Christianity: A Sociohistorical Approach to Religious Transformation.* New York: Oxford University Press.

Samir, K., and J. S. Nielsen. 1994. *Christian Arabic Apologetics during the Abbasid Period, 750-1258.* New York: E.J. Brill.

Shank, D. A. 1986. "The Legacy of William Waddy Harris." *International Bulletin of Missionary Research* 10, no. 4: 170.

Stark, R. 1996. *The Rise of Christianity: A Sociologist Reconsiders History.* Princeton, N.J.: Princeton University Press.

Walls, A. F. 2002. *The Cross-cultural Process in Christian History: Studies in the Transmission and Appropriation of Faith.* Maryknoll, N.Y.: Orbis Books.

Wood, C. M. 1985. *Vision and Discernment: An Orientation in Theological Study.* Decatur, Ga.: Scholars Press.

PART TWO

5

Readings Related to the Founding of the Church and Its Witness in a Plurality of Cultures

The earliest documents indicating the understanding of the church and its witness to a religiously and culturally plural world are found in the New Testament and are readily available to the reader. By the second century Greek culture was no longer merely being addressed by Christian evangelists. It had become a source of theological insight as Christians reflected on the meaning of their faith. This raised the question, answered rather differently by Justin and Tertullian, of both the relation of non-Christian learning to Christian understandings of the gospel, and the responsibility of ordinary believers to examine carefully the cultural influences on their faith.

1. *Apology II, xiii–*, by Justin Martyr

Justin Martyr was one of the early apologists for Christianity, engaging in particular the intellectual elite of his time with the claims of the gospel. In this brief excerpt we see how he accounts for both the validity of pre-Christian philosophy and the Christian claim upon it. The Apology dates from the first half of the second century.

The Light That Lighteth Every Man

[§ 1] For I myself, when I discovered the evil disguise that was thrown around the divine doctrines of Christians by the evil demons, to deter others from them, laughed, both at the authors of these falsehoods, and their disguise, and the popular opinion; [§ 2] and I confess that I both prayed, and strove with all my might, to be found a Christian; not because the doctrines of Plato are entirely different from those of Christ, but because they are not in all respects like them; no more, in fact, are those of the others, the Stoics, for example, and poets and prose-writers. [§ 3] For each, seeing through a part of the Seminal Divine Word, that which was kindred to those, discoursed rightly. But they who contradict them on more important points, appear not to have possessed the hidden wisdom and the knowledge which cannot be spoken against. [§ 4] Whatever all men have uttered aright, then, belongs to us Christians; for we worship and love, next to God, the Word which is from the Unbegotten and Ineffable God: for it was even for us that He was made man, that He might be a partaker of our very sufferings, and bring us healing. [§ 5] For all writers through the engrafted seed of the Word, which was planted in them, were able to see the truth darkly; [§ 6] for the seed and imitation of a thing, which is given according to capability, is one thing, and the thing itself, of which the communication and imitation are given according to His grace, is another.—*L.F.* xl. 68.

(Source: *Documents Illustrative of the History*

of the Early Church, vol. 1, ed. B. J. Kidd [London: SPCK, 1938].)

2. *The Prescription against Heretics (Excerpts), by Tertullian*

Tertullian, writing in the late second and early third period, could observe firsthand how Christian thought was being influenced by Greek philosophy. The result in his mind was heresy that contradicted the revelation of Jesus Christ and scripture. The result of his reasoning on Christianity in a pluralistic intellectual environment can be read below.

Chapter VII.—Pagan Philosophy the Parent of Heresies. The Connection between Deflections from Christian Faith and the Old Systems of Pagan Philosophy

These are "the doctrines" of men and "of demons" produced for itching ears of the spirit of this world's wisdom: this the Lord called "foolishness," and "chose the foolish things of the world" to confound even philosophy itself. For (philosophy) it is which is the material of the world's wisdom, the rash interpreter of the nature and the dispensation of God. Indeed heresies are themselves instigated by philosophy. From this source came the Æons, and I known not what infinite forms, and the trinity of man in the system of Valentinus, who was of Plato's school. From the same source came Marcion's better god, with all his tranquility; he came of the Stoics. Then, again, the opinion that the soul dies is held by the Epicureans; while the denial of the restoration of the body is taken from the aggregate school of all the philosophers; also, when matter is made equal to God, then you have the teaching of Zeno; and when any doctrine is alleged touching a god of fire, then Heraclitus comes in. The same subject-matter is discussed over and over again by the heretics and the philosophers; the same arguments are involved. Whence comes evil? Why is it permitted? What is the origin of man? and in what way does he come? Besides the question which Valentinus has very lately proposed—Whence

comes God? Which he settles with the answer: From *enthymesis* and *ectroma*. Unhappy Aristotle! who invented for these men dialectics, the art of building up and pulling down; an art so evasive in its propositions, so far-fetched in its conjectures, so harsh in its arguments, so productive of contentions—embarrassing even to itself, retracting everything, and really treating of nothing! Whence spring those "fables and endless genealogies," and "unprofitable questions," and "words which spread like a cancer"? From all these, when the apostle would restrain us, he expressly names *philosophy* as that which he would have us be on our guard against. Writing to the Colossians, he says, "See that no one beguile you through philosophy and vain deceit, after the tradition of men, and contrary to the wisdom of the Holy Ghost." He had been at Athens, and had in his interviews (with its philosophers) become acquainted with that human wisdom which pretends to know the truth, whilst it only corrupts it, and is itself divided into its own manifold heresies, by the variety of its mutually repugnant sects. What indeed has Athens to do with Jerusalem? What concord is there between the Academy and the Church? what between heretics and Christians? Our instruction comes from "the porch of Solomon," who had himself taught that "the Lord should be sought in simplicity of heart." Away with all attempts to produce a mottled Christianity of Stoic, Platonic, and dialectic composition! We want no curious disputation after possessing Christ Jesus, no inquisition after enjoying the gospel! With our faith, we desire no further belief. For this is our palmary faith, that there is nothing which we ought to believe besides.

Chapter XXI.—All Doctrine True Which Comes through the Church from the Apostles, Who Were Taught by God through Christ. All Opinion Which Has No Such Divine Origin and Apostolic Tradition to Show, Is Ipso Facto False

From this, therefore, do we draw up our rule. Since the Lord Jesus Christ sent the apostles to preach, (our rule is) that no others ought to be received as preachers than those whom Christ appointed;

for "no man knoweth the Father save the Son, and he to whomsoever the Son will reveal Him." Nor does the Son seem to have revealed Him to any other than the apostles, whom He sent forth to preach—that, of course, which He revealed to them. Now, what that was which they preached—in other words, what it was which Christ revealed to them—can, as I must here likewise prescribe, properly be proved in no other way than by those very churches which the apostles founded in person, by declaring the gospel to them directly themselves, both *viva voce*, as the phrase is, and subsequently by their epistles. If, then, these things are so, it is in the same degree manifest that all doctrine which agrees with the apostolic churches—those moulds and original sources of the faith must be reckoned for truth, as undoubtedly containing that which the (said) churches received from the apostles, the apostles from Christ, Christ from God. Whereas all doctrine must be prejudged as false which savours of contrariety to the truth of the churches and apostles of Christ and God. It remains, then, that we demonstrate whether this doctrine of ours, of which we have now given the rule, has its origin in the tradition of the apostles, and whether all other *doctrines* do not *ipso facto* proceed from falsehood. We hold communion with the apostolic churches because our doctrine is in no respect different *from theirs*. This is *our* witness of truth.

(Source: *The Ante-Nicene Fathers: Translations of the Writings of the Fathers down to* A.D. *325*, ed. Alexander Roberts and James Donaldson [New York: Charles Scribner's Sons, 1903].)

3. *The Apology of Aristides, 125, cc. xv., xvi*

This brief excerpt from a document entitled "The History of Barlaam and Josaphat" has complex origins, and the historicity of the description of events within it must be questioned. It represents another way in which Christians presented their claims around the middle of the second century.

[c. xv.] Now the Christians trace their origin from the Lord Jesus Christ. And He is acknowledged by the Holy Spirit to be the Son of the Most High God, who came down from heaven for the salvation of men. And being born of a pure virgin, unbegotten and immaculate, He assumed flesh and revealed Himself among men that He might recall them to Himself from their wandering after many gods. And having accomplished His wonderful dispensation, by a voluntary choice He tasted death on the Cross, fulfilling an august dispensation. And after three days He came to life again, and ascended into heaven. And if you would read, O King, you may judge the glory of His presence from the holy Gospel writing, as it is called among themselves. He had twelve disciples who, after His ascension to heaven, went forth into the provinces of the whole world, and declared His greatness. As for instance one of them traversed the countries about us, proclaiming the doctrine of the truth. From this it is, that they who still observe the righteousness enjoined by their preaching are called Christians.

And these are they who more than all the nations on the earth have found the truth. For they know God, the Creator and Fashioner of all things through the only-begotten Son and the Holy Spirit; and beside Him they worship no other God. They have the commands of the Lord Jesus Christ Himself graven upon their hearts; and they observe them, looking forward to the resurrection of the dead and life in the world to come. They do not commit adultery nor fornication, nor bear false witness, nor covet the things of others; they honour father and mother, and love their neighbours; they judge justly, and they never do to others what they would not wish to happen to themselves; they appeal to those who injure them, and try to win them as friends; they are eager to do good to their enemies; they are gentle and easy to be entreated; they abstain from all unlawful conversation and from all impurity; they despise not the widow, nor oppress the orphan; and he that has, gives ungrudgingly for the maintenance of him who has not.

If they see a stranger, they take him under their roof, and rejoice over him as over a very brother; for they call themselves brethren not after the flesh but after the Spirit.

And they are ready to sacrifice their lives for the sake of Christ; for they observe His commandments without swerving, and live holy and just lives, as the Lord God enjoined upon them.

And they give thanks unto Him every hour, for all meat and drink and other blessings.

[c. xvi.] Verily then this is the Way of the truth which leads those who travel therein to the everlasting kingdom promised through Christ in the life to come. And that you may know, O King, that in saying these things I do not speak at my own instance, if you deign to look into the writings of the Christians, you will find that I state nothing beyond the truth. Rightly then did thy son apprehend, and justly was he taught to serve the living God and to be saved for the age that is destined to come upon us. For great and wonderful are the sayings and deeds of the Christians; for they speak not the words of men but those of God. But the rest of the nations go astray and deceive themselves; for they walk in darkness and bruise themselves like drunken men.—W. D. M. Kay, in A.-N.C.L., additional volume, ed. A. Menzies, 276 sqq.

(Source: *Documents Illustrative of the History of the Early Church*, vol. 1, ed. B. J. Kidd, SPCK, London.)

4. *The Story of Mār Mārī the Apostle*

This excerpt from the beginning of the Story of Mār Mārī may surprise the student with its assertions concerning an early statue of Jesus and the role it played in evangelism. It illustrates well both the wonder-working aspects of early evangelism and the focus on the conversion of royalty in societies outside of Rome. Historically the document has doubtful elements. More certain is that Edessa became Christian in the middle of the second century. The story is reported by Eusebius in the fourth century, but this document comes from an earlier period.

1 Through the divine power, we are writing the story of Mār Mārī the Apostle, one of the seventy (disciples): Our Lord, help me! Amen!

Fifteen years after Tiberius Caesar began to reign, and when the three years of the ministry of our Lord Jesus Christ among humans had come to their virtuous conclusion, the salvation of all people, those in heaven and on earth, was accomplished at that time. And at the time when the purpose of the Savior's plan of salvation was about to come to fruition, the good news of that divine plan spread rapidly not only among the Jews but also among the Gentiles. They came to our Lord, receiving life, for he was proclaiming to them the hope of the world to come. This they recognized not through mere words but also through deeds. They left him refreshed, since they received from him solutions to their problems and forgiveness of their sins.

For this reason, they truly depicted the image and likeness of our adored Lord in various ways, as one of those who put God on themselves shows, (saying): "When I went some time ago to Caesarea Philippi, I saw there the image of our Savior Christ in body. On the gate of the house of the woman about whom it was written in the Gospel that her blood ran for twelve years, I saw a bronze statue (of the woman) standing on a high stone, her knees bent and her arms stretched forth, begging, as if in reality. Another bronze statue of a man clothed with a cloak stood opposite her, stretching his hand toward this woman. This statue is the likeness of our Savior, as all those who were assisted by our Lord and Savior testified": They fashioned his image in every place with the finest pigments! (These images) stand until now, for at the beginning, the pagans used to honor them simply in this form and in like manner, as if it were a savior. The Good Message of the heavenly kingdom flew not only to the common people but also to royalty, according to what we have learned from old stories.

2 During the time in which the ministry of the Savior took place, the news of the healing power of our Savior Christ spread to Abgar, the lord of the city of Edessa. This one had a serious illness that was constantly tormenting him—gout in the feet. He heard that our Savior was performing signs and miracles, wrote to him a letter, and dispatched to him envoys and messengers, so that he might come to him and perform healing on him. This is what he wrote to him in his letter: "Abgar Ukkama, lord of the land, to Jesus the Savior, peace! I heard that you cleanse lepers, expel impure spirits, and exorcise devils, and I believe that you are God and the Son of God, who came down to heal the creation. I have a serious illness and am asking you to come

to me to treat this illness. I also heard that the Jews among your people hate you and seek to do you harm. If you desire it—I have a small city that is suitable for you and me; it would be sufficient for both of us, and we would be at rest in it."

The messengers arrived and entered Jerusalem on the twelfth in the month of *Nīsān* (April). They found Jesus in the house of a high priest of the Jews, and the letter was read before him. But our Lord was not in a position to send him messengers, nor was he of the opinion that his Good News should reach the nations before his resurrection. Because of this, he did not send envoys, but made a reply, sending Abgar greetings as follows: "It is written concerning me: Blessed are those who did not see me but believed in me. As for now, I am seeking to complete the work of the One who has sent me, but after my resurrection, and after I have ascended to heaven, I will send you one of my disciples who will heal you from your illness and will even grant you and those who are with you life. And your city will be blessed, and no enemy will overpower it."

3 The letter came to Abgar the king, and he received it with great joy. When they related to him the wonders that were performed by Jesus in the land of Judea, he admired and was amazed by the might of God. Since he was not worthy of seeing these things, he experienced great difficulty. But what did king Abgar do? He found skilled painters and ordered them to accompany his messengers, depict the face of our Lord, and bring the depiction, so as to rejoice with his image as it would be if he encountered him. The painters arrived with the messengers of the king, but they were not able to depict the Lord's admirable human appearance. When our Lord realized through his divine understanding the love of Abgar for him, and as he saw the painters who endeavored to find the image to depict him as he was, but failed, he took a cloth and imprinted on it his face, which gives life to the world, and the image looked like him as he was. The cloth was brought and was placed in the church of Edessa, where it still remains as a source of all kinds of help.

4 . . . Thereafter, Addai placed his hand on Abgar, and all his illnesses were healed through the power of Jesus. Abgar was astonished and even stunned, as Addai performed upon him the won-derful sign—healing from the illness in the feet that is called gout. He also healed one of his servants, whose name was ʿEbed son of ʿAbdū, from an illness that he had. He too got up and then fell down on the feet of the blessed Addai, paying him homage. He also healed their other citizens.

5 When the king and his nobility realized the signs that Addai performed, they began telling him: "We beg you to tell us: Jesus, who was he? What did he teach? What did he do?" Addai said to the king: "Time now is late, but if you want, let me tell you: Send out and call upon all your forces and I will come in the morning to relate to you the story of Jesus." The king accepted his order happily and sent to gather all his nobles. Addai came in the morning and started to talk about the divine economy and how (God) created the universe and fashioned human nature and the kinds of promises that he had made to the old generations; about the advent of the prophets and the coming of Christ and the signs that he performed; and about the resurrection and ascension of Christ to heaven and the authorization that he gave to the prophets and the disciples to preach in the nations. And as the Apostle said: The king praised his speech, and the Holy Spirit confirmed his words by the performance of signs. Immediately the city and its suburbs converted on account of the signs that occurred at the hands of Mār Addai. After a short while, the whole of Mesopotamia was drawn to faith in Christ. Many among those who accepted the faith strove to virtuous conduct. After he had built the church in Edessa, equipped it with whatever it deserved, and appointed priests and deacons in the city and in its suburbs, Addai the Apostle left this world in peace on Thursday, the fourteenth of the month of Iyyār (May), ending his lovely contests with the trophy of victory.

6 So far were (the stories) about the conversion of Mesopotamia. Let us now turn our attention to show how the fear of God moved from there to our own territories. Because this story is not told clearly, I am putting into writing the old tradition that is transmitted in the books, as follows.

Before the blessed Addai died, he selected one of his disciples named Mārī, who was living in the love of God and was adorned with virtuous manners. He placed his right hand on Mārī, as conferred to him by our Lord Jesus Christ, and sent him to the eastern region, to the land of Babylonia, ordering him to go and preach there the word of our Lord.

7 The blessed Mār Mārī left Edessa to begin preaching until he reached the city of Nisibis. After the blessed one converted the city of Nisibis, planted in it the truth of the true faith, overthrew its idols, and shattered its statues, he built in it churches and monasteries and set teachers and a school. From there, he moved to the land of Arzen, with Anasimos the priest who came with him from Edessa, along with Philippus, Malkīšōᶜ, and Addā—his disciples—as well as with many other people. He dispatched one of the latter—Philippus by name—to Qardu.

When the blessed one reached the city of Arzen, he converted many people through the mighty acts that he was performing. Now the king of Arzen was stricken by the disease called gout. When he heard about the miracles and healings that took place at the hands of the blessed one, with great eagerness he ordered that they should bring the blessed one before him. When Mār Mārī came and went into the presence of the king, the latter greatly rejoiced in him, because the blessed one bowed down happily before him. And when the king heard the word of the blessed one, he held him in increasing honor, because of his gentleness, humbleness, and joyful countenance—for Mār Mārī was very meek and very kind toward everyone, and in him jealousy and anger had no place whatsoever. The king said to him: "Tell me! What is your religion? For I believe you are a god!" Then the blessed Mār

Mārī answered and said to the king: "God forbid! I am not God, O my lord the king, but I am a man, servant of the Living God. My religion is Christianity, and I believe in Christ, the Son of God, who descended at the end of times from heaven, and turned the world away from the deception of the demons by which it was seized. I confess this One, O my lord the king, I perform these things in his name, bringing erring people (to God and) to the faith." The king answered and said to him: "According to your claim, can your Lord, therefore, heal this illness with which I have been stricken for a long time?" The blessed one said to him: "If you believe in him, your requests will be answered."

Immediately, the king kneeled and bowed down before the blessed one, begging and saying: "My Lord, I believe! Help me!" At this point the blessed one came close and placed his hand on the spot, saying: "In the name of our Lord Jesus Christ, whom the Jews crucified in Jerusalem, get up on your feet!" Concomitant with the word of the blessed one, the king was healed, and was baptized along with the members of his house. When the entire city realized that the king was healed, they too came to the blessed one, and he healed their bruises. He thus converted the whole city, built in it a church, and appointed over it priests and deacons.

(Source: *The Acts of Mār Mārī the Apostle*, translated with introduction and notes by Amir Harrak [Atlanta: Society of Biblical Literature, 2005], 1-17.)

6

Readings Related to the Pluralistic World in an Age of Empire

Letters from the Emperor Constantine

The following letters indicate how Constantine, once he had converted to Christianity, rapidly involved the Roman government in its support, and in suppressing its rivals. These letters date from 313 and 319 C.E.

5. Constantine to Cæcilian, Bishop of Carthage, Making a Grant of Money to the Catholic Clergy of Africa and Numidia, 313

[§ 1] Constantine Augustus to Cæcilianus, bishop of Carthage. Since it is our pleasure that something should be granted, in all the provinces of Africa and Numidia and Mauretania, to certain ministers of the legitimate and most holy Catholic Religion, to defray their expenses, I have written to Ursus, the illustrious finance-minister of Africa, and have directed him to make provision to pay to thy Firmness three thousand folles. [§ 2] Do thou, therefore, when thou hast received the above sum of money, command that it be distributed among all those mentioned above, according to the brief sent to thee by Hosius. [§ 3] But if thou shouldest find that anything is wanting for the fulfilment of this purpose of mine in regard to all of them, thou shalt demand without hesitation from Herællides, our treasurer, whatever thou findest to be necessary. For I commanded him, when he was present, that if thy Firmness should ask him for any money, he should see to it that it be paid without delay. [§ 4] And since I have learned that some men of unset-

tled mind wish to turn the people from the most holy and Catholic Church by a certain method of shameful corruption, do thou know that I gave command to Anulinus the proconsul, and also to Patricius, Vicar of the Prefects, when they were present, that they should give proper attention not only to other matters but also above all to this, and that they should not overlook such a thing when it happened. [§ 5] Wherefore, if thou shouldest see any such men continuing in this madness, do thou without delay go to the above-mentioned judges and report the matter to them; that they may correct them as I commanded them when they were present. The Divinity of the great God preserve thee for many years.—*N. & P.-N.F. i. 382.*

(Source: *Documents Illustrative of the History of the Early Church*, vol. 1, ed. B. J. Kidd [London: SPCK, 1938.])

6. Constantine to Anulinus, Proconsul of Africa, 313, on Exemptions for the Catholic Clergy

[§ 1] Greeting to thee, our most esteemed Anulinus. Since it appears from many circumstances that when that religion is despised, in which is preserved the chief reverence for the most holy celestial Power, great dangers are brought upon public affairs; but that, when legally adopted and observed, it affords the most signal prosperity to the Roman name and remarkable felicity to all the affairs of men, through the divine beneficence—it has seemed good to me, most esteemed Anulinus, that those men who give their services with due sanctity and with constant observance of this law, to the worship of the divine religion, should receive recompense for their labours.

[§ 2] Wherefore it is my will that those within the province entrusted to thee, in the Catholic Church, over which Cæcilianus presides, who give their services to this holy religion, and who are commonly called clergymen, be entirely exempted from all public duties, that they may not by any error or sacrilegious negligence be drawn away from the service due to the Deity, but may devote themselves without any hindrance to their own law. For it seems that, when they show greatest reverence to the Deity, the greatest benefits accrue to the State. Farewell, our most esteemed and beloved Anulinus.—*N. & P.-N.F. i. 383.*

(Source: *Documents Illustrative of the History of the Early Church*, vol. 1, ed. B. J. Kidd [London: SPCK, 1938].)

7. *Constantine's Suppression of Private Divination, February 1, 319, the Emperor Constantine Augustus to Maximus [Prefect of the City]*

Let no soothsayer approach the threshold of his neighbour, not even for some other cause [than that of soothsaying]; but let friendship, however long-standing, with men of this class be put away. Let the soothsayer who approaches his neighbour's house be burnt; and let him who invites him, whether by persuasion or offer of reward, be deprived of his goods and banished to an island. Those, who desire to follow their own superstition, will be at liberty to practise the rites proper to it in public. He who accuses a man of this offence is, in our judgment, no informer. On the contrary, he is one who deserves a reward. Given at Rome, on the first of February in the consulate of Constantine Augustus (his fifth) and Licinius Qesar.

(Source: *Documents Illustrative of the History of the Early Church*, vol. 1, ed. B. J. Kidd [London: SPCK, 1938].)

Christianity at the Boundaries of Rome

8. *The History of the Armenians*

This selection from a partially legendary account of the conversion of Armenia indicates both the diverse paths by which Christianity had come to Armenia from Rome without becoming the official religion of the kingdom, and the types of miraculous interventions by which Christians in the fifth and sixth centuries believed that God engaged stubborn paganism. The reader may wish to note what seems necessary to constitute the preconditions for baptism and thus the understanding of what represents the full "evangel" given to the Armenians through Gregory.

[This episode takes place during the period

in which Diocletian was persecuting Christians (304-311). It begins with a letter from Diocletian to Trdat, the ruler of the Armenians. In the letter Diocletian asks that Trdat return to him a Christian woman who, with her retinue, fled to Armenia to escape marrying Diocletian. At this time Gregory is already in prison as part of an earlier persecution of Christians who refused to worship the god Anahit.]

180. While saint Rhipsimē was offering all these prayers to God, king Trdat entered the chamber where she had been shut up. Now when he came in, all the populace, some outside the palace, others in the streets, and others inside (the city), all together struck up songs [cf. 3 Macc. 6:23] and

dancing. Some filled the citadel, others the center of the town, with merry-making. They all intended to celebrate the wedding with dancing. But the Lord God looked down on his beloved Rhipsimē in order to save her, lest the treasure she had preserved so carefully be lost [cf. 2 Tim. 1:12], and he heard her prayers and fortified her like Jael and like Deborah [cf. Judges 4]. He strengthened her to be saved from the impious tyrant's grasp.

181. When the king entered, he seized her in order to work his lustful desires. But she, strengthened by the holy Spirit, struggled like a beast and fought like a man. They fought from the third hour until the tenth and she vanquished the king who was renowned for his incredible strength. While he was in the Greek empire he had shown such bodily strength that everyone had been amazed; and in his own realm, when he had returned to his native land, he had shown there too many deeds of mighty valor. And he, who was so famous in every respect, now was vanquished and worsted by a single girl through the will and power of Christ.

[Because Rhipsimē refused to yield to the king and her retinue would not encourage her to do so she and many of them were killed.]

198. Then they stripped from her the torn clothing which was around her. And they fixed four stakes in the ground, two for her feet and two for her hands, and tied her to them. And they applied the torches to her for a long time, burning and roasting her flesh with their fire. . . .

199. And there were other saints, men and women, who had come with them, more than seventy people. But of those who came there at that time and who sought to wrap and bury their bodies, they put to the sword and killed thirty-two.

211. The king spent six days in profound grief and deep mourning because of his passionate love for the beautiful Rhipsimē. Then afterwards he arranged to go hunting; he had his soldiers gather the pack of hounds, the beaters scattered, the nets fixed, and the traps set; then he went out to hunt in the plain of P'arakan Shemak.

212. But when the king, having mounted his chariot, was about to leave the city, then suddenly there fell on him punishment from the Lord. An impure demon struck the king and knocked him

down from his chariot. Then he began to rave and to eat his own flesh. And in the likeness of Nebuchadnezzar, king of Babylon, he lost his human nature for the likeness of wild pigs and went about like them and dwelt among them [cf. Dan. 4:12-13]. Then entering a reedy place, in senseless abandon he pastured on grass, and wallowed naked in the plain. For although they wished to restrain him in the city, they were unable to do so, partly because of his natural strength and partly because of the force of the demons who had possessed him.

213. Likewise all the populace in the city went mad through similar demon-possession. And terrible ruin fell upon the country. All the king's household, including slaves and servants, were afflicted with torments. And there was terrible mourning on account of these afflictions.

214. Then there appeared a vision from God to the king's sister, whose name was Khosrovidukht. So she came to speak with the people and related the vision, saying: "A vision appeared to me this night. A man in the likeness of light came and told me 'there is no other cure for these torments that have come upon you, unless you send to the city of Artashat and bring thence the prisoner Gregory. When he comes he will teach you the remedy for your ills.'"

[Gregory is brought forth from prison and, after first seeing that the bodies of the martyrs are properly prepared for burial, he spends a night praying for the conversion of the Armenians. They then beg him to forgive their crimes against him and plead with God so that they do not perish. Gregory then preaches a sermon to the assembled crowd, instructing them for sixty-six days.]

226. Then the prisoner Gregory began to speak: "The one you call 'your God' is God and creator, who in his almighty benevolence has brought material creatures into being from immaterial nothing. The same ordered the earth to be established by his essential power from uncircumscribed, boundless nothing. He who created everything is the almighty, all-creative and all-loving God. Recognize him, in order that your pains from the punishment of your crimes may be healed. . . ."

227. "The true Son of God considers it no shame to call his brothers those who will turn to

the worship of the Father. And the holy Spirit will grant you the pledge of his love, and awaken your hearts to the joy that passes not away. But only if you turn and walk according to his desires will he give you eternal life. . . ."

[Gregory's sermon concludes with a call that chapels be built in order to put the martyrs to rest, and three such chapels are built immediately, with Gregory acting as the architect. Once the king and people construct these chapels, properly bury the dead martyrs, and build a shrine to honor visions that Gregory has seen, they are healed. Following this they receive further instruction from Gregory and, on his instructions, now overthrow all the pagan shrines "to suppress them entirely lest there be henceforth an obstacle to anyone or a stumbling block . . ." (para. 777). This, like the building of the chapels for the martyrs, is accompanied by miraculous signs.]

788. While he [Gregory] was so acting there with the support of all, he fulfilled all things necessary for preaching the gospel. He did not at all rely on the awe and authority of the king in order to persuade everyone; nor merely by words but also by signs and miracles and various kinds of healings the holy name of Christ was made glorious. . . .

794. . . . There appeared a wonderful vision from God to the king; he saw the angel of God speaking to him and saying: "You must without delay have Gregory ordained to the high priesthood, so that he may illuminate you by baptism." . . .

[The king then assembles all the princes of the Armenians and sends them, with Gregory, to the Archbishop of Caesarea for ordination. Once ordained Gregory returns with holy relics and a group of monks. After the miraculous destruction of mountain altars, Gregory builds the first church on the same site.]

814. . . . He erected an altar to the name of the Holy Trinity and arranged a baptismal font. First he illuminated with baptism those great princes who were with him and had traveled with him to the city of Caesarea, and then the people of the province, the inhabitants of the land. . . . He erected an altar in the chapel of repose of the saints which he had built, and he offered the saving liturgy, and distributed there the life-giving body and blood of Christ.

(Source: *Agathangelos/History of the Armenians,* translation and commentary by R. W. Thomson [Albany: State University of New York Press, 1976], 189, 191, 217, 219, 227, 229, 327, 329, 333, 353.)

9. *The Evangelization of Nubia,* by John of Ephesus, *Ecclesiastical History*

In this brief excerpt we find how a mix of imperial and confessional rivalries were transposed onto the Christian mission to the Nubians. For both Theodora and her husband, Justinian, it was not enough to convert the Nubians, but to convert them to the proper kind of Christianity. According to the account, the Nubians embraced non-Chalcedonian Christianity and remained faithful to Bishop (styled Pope by his followers) Theodosius, who had been ejected from the state church after Chalcedon.

Among the clergy in attendance upon Pope Theodosius was a presbyter named Julian, an old man of great worth, who conceived an earnest spiritual desire to christianize the wandering people who dwell on the eastern borders of the Thebais [a region of upper Egypt], beyond Egypt, and who are not only not subject to the authority of the Roman empire, but even receive a subsidy on condition that they do not enter nor pillage Egypt. The blessed Julian, therefore, being full of anxiety for this people, went and spoke about them to the late queen Theodora, in the hope of awakening in her a similar desire for their conversion; and as the queen was fervent in zeal for God, she received the proposal with joy, and promised to do everything in her power for the conversion of these tribes from the errors of idolatry. In her joy, therefore, she informed the victorious king Justinian of the purposed undertaking, and promised and anxiously desired to send the blessed Julian thither. But when the king heard that the person she intended to send was opposed to the council of Chalcedon, he was not pleased, and determined to write to the bishops of his own side in the Thebais, with orders for them to proceed thither and instruct them, and plant among them the name of the synod. And as he entered upon the matter with great zeal, he sent thither, without a moment's delay, ambassadors with gold and baptismal robes, and gifts of honor for the king of that people, and letters for the duke of the Thebais, enjoining him to take every care of the embassy, and escort them to the territories of the Nobadae [i.e., the people of Nobatia, one of the Nubian kingdoms]. When, however, the queen learnt these things, she quickly, with much cunning, wrote letters to the duke of the Thebais, and sent a mandatory of her court to carry them to him; and which were as follows: "Inasmuch as both his majesty and myself have purposed to send an embassy to the people of the Nobadae, and I am now despatching a blessed man named Julian; and further my will is, that my ambassador should arrive at the aforesaid people before his majesty's; be warned, that if you permit his ambassador to arrive there before mine, and do not hinder him by various pretexts until mine shall have reached you, and have passed through your province, and arrived at his destination, your life shall answer for it; for I will immediately send and take off your head." Soon after the receipt of this letter the king's ambassador also came, and the duke said to him, "You must wait a little, while we look out and procure beasts of burden, and men who know the deserts; and then you will be able to proceed." And thus he delayed him until the arrival of the merciful queen's embassy, who found horses and guides in waiting, and the same day, without loss of time, under a show of doing it by violence, they laid hands upon them, and were the first to proceed. As for the duke, he made his excuses to the king's ambassador, saying, "Lo! when I had made my preparations, and was desirous of sending you onward, ambassadors from the queen arrived, and fell upon me with violence, and took away the beasts of burden I had got ready, and have passed onward. And I am too well acquainted with the fear in which the queen is held, to venture to oppose them. But abide still with me, until I can make fresh preparations for you, and then you also shall go in peace." And when he heard these things, he rent his garments, and threatened him terribly, and reviled him; and after some time he also was able to proceed, and followed the other's track, with-

out being aware of the fraud which had been practiced upon him.

(Source: *The Third Part of the Ecclesiastical History of John Bishop of Ephesus*, trans. R. Payne Smith [Oxford: Oxford University Press, 1860], 251-57, 315-16, 319-24.)

10. *The Life of Constantine*

This tenth-century account of the life of Constantine (known later as Cyril) tells of a central dispute between the Eastern and Western churches over the appropriateness of translating the scripture into multiple languages, and by extension the formation of churches with both scriptures and liturgies in a variety of national languages. Constantine was depicted in earlier parts of this account as a supernaturally gifted linguist. The account reflects, of course, the point of view of the Eastern church.

When he was in Venice, bishops, priests, and monks gathered against him like ravens against a falcon. And they advanced the trilingual heresy, saying: "Tell us, O man, how is it that you now teach, having created letters for the Slavs, which none else have found before, neither the Apostle, nor the pope of Rome, nor Gregory the Theologian, nor Jerome, nor Augustine? We know of only three languages worthy of praising God in the Scriptures, Hebrew, Greek, and Latin."

And the Philosopher answered them: "Does not God's rain fall upon all equally? And does not the sun shine also upon all? And do we not all breathe air in the same way? Are you not ashamed to mention only three tongues, and to command all other nations and tribes to be blind and deaf? Tell me, do you render God powerless, that He is incapable of granting this? Or envious, that He does not desire this? We know of numerous peoples who possess writing and render glory unto God, each in its own language. Surely these are obvious: Armenians, Persians, Abkhazians, Iberians, Sogdians, Goths, Avars, Turks, Khazars, Arabs, Egyptians, and many others. If you do not wish to understand this, at least recognize the judgment of the Scriptures. For David cries out, saying: 'O sing unto the Lord, all the earth: sing unto the Lord a new song' (Ps. 96:1). And again: 'Make a joyful noise unto the Lord, all the earth: make a loud noise, and rejoice, and sing praise' (Ps. 98:4). And likewise: 'Let all the earth worship Thee, and sing unto Thee; let it sing to Thy name, God on High' (Ps. 66:4). And furthermore: 'O praise the Lord, all ye nations: praise Him, all ye people. Let everything that hath breath praise the Lord' (Ps. 117:1; 150:6). And in the Gospel according to John it says: 'But as many as received Him, to them gave He power to become the children of God' (John 1:12). And again in the same Gospel: 'Neither pray I for these alone, but for them also which shall believe in Me through their word, that they all may be one; as Thou, Father, art in Me, and I in Thee' (John 17:20, 21).

"And Matthew said: 'All power is given unto Me in heaven, and on earth. Go ye, therefore, and teach all nations, baptizing them in the name of the Father, and of the Son, and of the Holy Ghost; Teaching them to observe all things whatsoever I have commanded you: and, lo, I am with you always, even unto the end of time. Amen' (Matt. 28:18-20).

"And Mark says again: 'Go into all the world, and preach the Gospel to every creature. He that believeth and is baptized, shall be saved; but he that believeth not, shall be damned. And these signs shall follow them that believe; in my name shall they cast out devils; they shall speak with new tongues' (Mark 16:15-17).

"And unto you also is said, teachers of the law: 'Woe unto you, scribes and Pharisees, hypocrites! for ye shut up the kingdom of heaven against men: for ye neither go in yourselves, neither suffer ye them that are entering to go in' (Matt. 23:13).

"And furthermore: 'Woe unto you, lawyers! for ye have taken away the key of knowledge: ye entered not in yourselves, and them that were entering in, ye hindered' (Luke 11:52).

"And Paul said to the Corinthians: 'I would that ye all spake with tongues, but rather that ye prophesied: for greater is he that prophesieth, than he that speaketh with tongues, except he interpret, that the church may receive edifying . . .'" (1 Cor. 14:5-40).

[Constantine continues the long citation from 1 Corinthians 14.]

. . . And with these words and many more, he shamed them and went away, leaving them.

Upon learning of Constantine, the Pope of Rome sent for him. And when he came to Rome, the Apostolic Father himself, Hadrian and all the townspeople came out to meet him, carrying candles. For he was carrying the relics of St. Clement the Martyr and Pope of Rome. And at once God wrought glorious miracles for his sake: a paralytic was healed, and many others were cured of various maladies. And even captives were at once liberated from the hands of their captors when they invoked Christ and St. Clement.

Accepting the Slavic Scriptures, the Pope placed them in the Church of St. Mary called Phatne. And the holy liturgy was celebrated over them. Then the Pope commanded two bishops, Formosus and Gauderich, to consecrate the Slavic disciples. And when they were consecrated they at once celebrated the liturgy in the Slavic language in the Church of the Apostle Peter. And the next day they celebrated in the Church of St. Petronilla, and on the following day in the Church of St. Andrew. And then they celebrated the entire night, glorifying God in Slavic once again in the Church of the Apostle Paul, the great universal teacher. And in the morning they again celebrated the liturgy over his blessed grave with the help of Bishop Arsenius, one of the seven bishops, and of Anastasius the librarian . . .

And his many labors overtook him, and he fell ill. Enduring his illness for many days, he once had a divine revelation and began to chant the following: "When they said unto me, Let us go into the house of the Lord, my spirit rejoiced, and my heart was gladdened" (Ps. 122:1).

Having put on his venerable garments, he thus spent that entire day rejoicing and saying: Henceforth I am neither a servant of the Emperor nor of anyone else on earth, but only of God Almighty. I was not, and I came to be, and am forever. Amen.

On the following day he put on holy monastic dress and, receiving light to light, called himself Cyril. He spent fifty days in that dress. And when the hour to repose and remove to the eternal dwellings approached, he raised his arms to God and, in tears, prayed, saying thus: "O Lord, my God, who hast created all the ranks of angels and incorporeal powers, stretched out the heavens and founded the earth, and brought all things into being from non-being, who hast always heeded those that work Thy will, fear Thee and keep Thy commandments, heed my prayer and preserve Thy faithful flock which Thou appointed to me, Thy useless and unworthy servant. Deliver them from the godless and heathen malice of those speaking blasphemy against Thee, and destroy the trilingual heresy belief. Increase Thy church to a multitude, gather all together in unanimity, and make a chosen people of those who are of one mind in Thy true faith and just confession. And inspire in their hearts the Word of Thy Son, for it is Thy gift. If Thou hast accepted us, unworthy ones, to preach the Gospel of Thy Christ, then those who are striving for good deeds and doing what pleases Thee, whom Thou hast given to me, I return to Thee as Thine. Guide them with Thy firm right hand and shelter them with the cover of Thy wings, so that all might praise and glorify Thy name, the Father, Son and Holy Spirit. Amen."

He kissed everyone with a holy kiss and said: "Blessed be God, who hath not given us as prey into the teeth of our invisible enemies, but hath smashed their snare and saved us from their corruption." And thus he reposed in the Lord at 42 years of age, on the 14th day of the month of February, of the second indiction, the 6370th year from the creation of this world.

(Source: *Medieval Slavic Lives of Saints and Princes*, ed. and trans. Marvin Kantor [Ann Arbor: Michigan Slavic Publications, 1983], 25-31, 35-39, 41-49, 61-81 [parts 16-18].)

11. *The Russian Primary Chronicle*

This brief history of the conversion of Prince Vladimir of Kiev in the late tenth century, but written between one hundred and two hundred years later, shows how the Orthodox understood the witness of worship to God's reign, as well as the abiding influence of the miraculous as a sign of God's presence.

(987). Vladimir summoned together his boyars and the city-elders, and said to them, "Behold, the Bulgars came before me urging me to accept their religion. Then came the Germans and praised their own faith; and after them came the Jews. Finally the Greeks appeared, criticizing all other faiths but commending their own, and they spoke at length, telling the history of the whole world from its beginning. Their words were artful, and it was wondrous to listen and pleasant to hear them. They preach the existence of another world. 'Whoever adopts our religion and then dies shall arise and live forever. But whosoever embraces another faith, shall be consumed with fire in the next world.' What is your opinion on this subject, and what do you answer?" The boyars and the elders replied, "You know, oh Prince, that no man condemns his own possessions, but praises them instead. If you desire to make certain, you have servants at your disposal. Send them to inquire about the ritual of each and how he worships God."

Their counsel pleased the prince and all the people, so that they chose good and wise men to the number of ten, and directed them to go first among the Bulgars and inspect their faith. The emissaries went their way, and when they arrived at their destination they beheld the disgraceful actions of the Bulgars and their worship in the mosque; then they returned to their country. Vladimir then instructed them to go likewise among the Germans, and examine their faith, and finally to visit the Greeks. They thus went into Germany, and after viewing the German ceremonial, they proceeded to Tsar'grad, where they appeared before the Emperor. He inquired on what mission they had come, and they reported to him all that had occurred. When the Emperor heard their words, he rejoiced, and did them great honor on that very day.

On the morrow, the Emperor sent a message to the Patriarch to inform him that a Russian delegation had arrived to examine the Greek faith, and directed him to prepare the church and the clergy, and to array himself in his sacerdotal robes, so that the Russes might behold the glory of the God of the Greeks. When the Patriarch received these commands, he bade the clergy assemble, and they performed the customary rites. They burned incense, and the choirs sang hymns. The Emperor accompanied the Russes to the church, and placed them in a wide space, calling their attention to the beauty of the edifice, the chanting, and the pontifical services and the ministry of the deacons, while he explained to them the worship of his God.

The Russes were astonished, and in their wonder praised the Greek ceremonial. Then the Emperors Basil and Constantine invited the envoys to their presence, and said, "Go hence to your native country," and dismissed them with valuable presents and great honor.

Thus they returned to their own country, and the Prince called together his boyars and the elders. Vladimir then announced the return of the envoys who had been sent out, and suggested that their report be heard. He thus commanded them to speak out before his retinue. The envoys reported, "When we journeyed among the Bulgars, we beheld how they worship in their temple, called a mosque, while they stand ungirt. The Bulgar bows, sits down, looks hither and thither like one possessed, and there is no happiness among them, but instead only sorrow and a dreadful stench. Their religion is not good. Then we went among the Germans, and saw them performing many ceremonies in their temples; but we beheld no glory there. Then we went to Greece and the Greeks led us to the edifices where they worship their God, and we knew not whether we were in heaven or on earth. For on earth there is no such splendor or such beauty, and we are at a loss how to describe it. We only know that God dwells there among men, and their service is fairer than the ceremonies of other nations. For we cannot forget that beauty. Every man, after tasting something sweet, is afterward unwilling to accept that which is bitter, and therefore, we cannot dwell longer here." Then the boyars spoke and said, "If the Greek faith were evil, it would not have been adopted by your grandmother Olga who was wiser than all other men." Vladimir then inquired where they should all accept baptism, and they replied that the decision rested with him.

After a year had passed, in 6496 (980 C.E.), Vladimir proceeded with an armed force against Kherson, a Greek city, and the people of Kherson barricaded themselves therein. Vladimir halted at the farther side of the city beside the harbor, a bowshot from the town, and the inhabitants resisted energetically while Vladimir besieged the town. Eventually, however, they became exhausted, and Vladimir warned them that if they did not surrender, he would remain on the spot for three years. When they failed to heed this threat, Vladimir marshaled his troops and ordered the construction of an earthwork in the direction of the city. While this work was under construction, the inhabitants dug a tunnel under the city-wall, stole the heaped-up earth, and carried it into the city, where they piled it up in the center of the town. But the soldiers kept on building, and Vladimir persisted. Then a man of Kherson, Anastasius by name, shot into the Russ camp an arrow on which he had written, "There are springs behind you to the east, from which water flows in pipes. Dig down and cut them off." When Vladimir received this information, he raised his eyes to heaven and vowed that if this hope was realized, he would be baptized. He gave orders straightaway to dig down above the pipes, and the water supply was thus cut.

(Source: *The Russian Primary Chronicle: Laurentian Text*, ed. and trans. Samuel Hazzard Cross and Olgerd P. Sherbowitz-Wetzor [Cambridge, Mass.: Medieval Academy of America, 1953], 110-17.)

12. *The Heliand*

This ninth-century effort to tell the gospel story in terms comprehensible to peoples in a culture and situation far different from Israel in the time of Jesus may be considered a model of contextualization. Or it may be less a tool of evangelism than a product of contextualized Christianity in full expressive power. Given the initial and continued resistance of some Saxons to conversion, the Heliand may be seen as particularly artistic propaganda.

Song I

The Creator's spell, by which the whole world is held together, is taught to four heroes.

There were many whose hearts told them that they should begin to tell the secret runes, the word of God, the famous feats that the powerful Christ accomplished in words and in deeds among human beings. There were many of the wise who wanted to praise the teaching of Christ, the holy Word of God, and wanted to write a bright-shining book with their own hands, telling how the sons of men should carry out His commands. Among all these, however, there were only four who had the power of God, help from heaven, the Holy Spirit, the strength from Christ to do it. They were chosen. They alone were to write down the evangelium in a book, and to write down the commands of God, the holy heavenly word. No one else among the heroic sons of men was to attempt it, since these four had been picked by the power of God: Matthew and Mark, Luke and John were their names. They were dear to God, worthy of the work. The ruling God had placed the Holy Spirit firmly in those heroes' hearts, together with many a wise word, as well as a devout attitude and a powerful mind, so that they could lift up their holy voices to chant God's spell. There is nothing like it in words anywhere in this world! Nothing can ever glorify the Ruler, our dear Chieftain, more! Nor is there anything that can better fell every evil creature or work of wickedness, nor better withstand the hatred and aggression of enemies. This is so, because the one who taught them God's Spell, though generous and good, had a powerful mind: the noble, the almighty Creator Himself.

These four were to write it down with their own fingers; they were to compose, sing, and proclaim what they had seen and heard of Christ's powerful strength—all the many wonderful things, in word and deed, that the mighty Chieftain Himself said, taught, and accomplished among human beings—and also all the things which the Ruler spoke from the beginning, when He, by His own power, first made the world and formed the whole universe with one word. The heavens and the earth and all that is contained within them, both inorganic and organic, everything, was firmly held in place by the Divine words. He then determined which of the peoples was to rule the greatest territory, and at what times the ages of the world were to come to an end. One age still stood before the sons of men; five were past. The blessed sixth age was to come by the power of God the Holy Spirit and the birth of Christ. He is the Best of Healers, come here to the middle world to be a help to many, to give human beings an advantage against the hatred of the enemy and the hidden snare.

(Source: *The Heliand: The Saxon Gospel*, trans. G. Ronald Murphy, S.J. [New York: Oxford University Press, 1992], 3-4.)

13. *The Apology of the Patriarch, Timothy of Baghdad before the Caliph Madhi*

Engaging the nations with the gospel, particularly when the Christian community was a sometimes oppressed minority, meant stating publicly and Christianly how other religious faiths and leaders were understood by Christians. Such encounters entailed a more nuanced approach to witness than was found when Christians possessed overwhelming political and military power. In 781 C.E. the patriarch Timothy successfully negotiated this difficult task and thus both preserved his community and showed a way forward for a Christian understanding of Muhammad and Islam.

The Questions and Answers of the Second Day

The next day I had an audience of his Majesty. Such audiences had constantly taken place previously, sometimes for the affairs of the State, and some other times for the love of wisdom and learning which was burning in the soul of his Majesty. He is a lovable man, and loves also learning when he finds it in other people, and on this account he directed against me the weight of his objections, whenever necessary.

After I had paid to him my usual respects as King of Kings, he began to address me and converse with me not in a harsh and haughty tone, since harshness and haughtiness are remote from his soul, but in a sweet and benevolent way.

And our King of Kings said to me: "O Catholicos, did you bring a Gospel with you, as I had asked you?"—And I replied to his exalted Majesty: "I have brought one, O our victorious and God-loving King."—And our victorious Sovereign said to me: "Who gave you this Book?"—And I replied to him: "It is the Word of God that gave us the Gospel, O our God-loving King."—And our King said: "Was it not written by four Apostles?" And I replied to him: "It was written by four Apostles, as our King has said, but not out of their own heads, but out of what they heard and learned from the

Word-God. If then the Gospel was written by the Apostles, and if the Apostles simply wrote what they heard and learned from the Word-God, the Gospel has, therefore, been given in reality by the Word-God. Similarly, the Torah was written by Moses, but since Moses heard and learned it from an angel, and the angel heard and learned it from God, we assert that the Torah was given by God and not by Moses.

"In the same way also the Muslims say that they have received the Qur'an from Muhammad, but since Muhammad received knowledge and writing from an angel, they, therefore, affirm that the Book that was divulged through him was not Muhammad's or the angel's but God's. So also we Christians believe that although the gospel was given to us by the Apostles, it was not given as from them but as from God, His Word and His spirit.

(Source: *Woodbrooke Studies*, vol. 2, ed. and trans. A. Mingana [Cambridge: Heffer, 1928], 60-61.)

Documents of the Eastern Church in China

14. *The Xi'an Stele—* The Translation of the Inscription

The Nestorian monument gives a short account of the gospel intended to speak to eighth-century Chinese culture and explain the presence of Christian monks in China. Readers will note that it references scripture (Romans 1 and John 1, for example) but seeks to use terminology comprehensible to an audience of a very different cultural landscape.

A Monument Commemorating the Propagation of the Ta-ch'in Luminous Religion in the Middle Kingdom

Eulogy on a Monument commemorating the Propagation of the Luminous Religion in the Middle Kingdom, with a Preface to the same, composed by Ching-ching, a priest of the Ta-ch'in monastery (in Syriac), Adam, Priest and Chorepiscopus, and Papash' of Chinastan.

Behold! there is One who is true and firm, who, being Untreated, is the Origin of the Origins; who is ever Incomprehensible and Invisible, yet ever mysteriously existing to the last of the lasts; who, holding the Secret Source of Origin, created all things, and who, surpassing all the Holy ones, is the only unoriginated Lord of the Universe,—is not this our Aloha, the Triune, mysterious Person, the unbegotten and true Lord ?

Dividing the Cross, He determined the four cardinal points. Setting in motion the primordial spirit (wind), He produced the two principles of Nature. The dark void was changed, and Heaven and Earth appeared. The sun and moon revolved, and day and night began. Having designed and fashioned all things, He then created the first man and bestowed on him an excellent disposition, superior to all others, and gave him to have dominion over the Ocean of created things.

The original nature of Man was pure, and void of all selfishness, unstained and unostentatious, his mind was free from inordinate lust and passion. When, however, Satan employed his evil devices on him, Man's pure and stainless (nature) was deteriorated; what is just and noble was eliminated from that which is called right on the one hand (lit., in this place), and what is fundamentally identical (with wickedness) was abstracted from that which is named wrong on the other (lit., in that place).

In consequence of this, three hundred and sixty-five (spiritual beings) with different seeds (of error) arose in quick succession and left deep furrows behind. They strove to weave nets of the law's wherewith to ensnare the innocent. Some pointing to natural objects pretended that they were the right objects to worship; others got hold of (the idea that) non-existence (lit., Emptiness) and existence (are alike, after all). Some sought to call down blessings (happiness or success), by means of prayers and sacrifices; others again boasted of their own goodness, and held their fellows in contempt. (Thus) the intellect and the thoughts of Men fell into hopeless confusion; and their mind and affections began to toil incessantly; but all their travail was in vain. The heat of their distress became a scorching flame; and self-blinded, they increased the darkness still more; and losing their path for a long while they went astray and became unable to return home again.

Whereupon one Person of our Trinity, the Messiah, who is the Luminous Lord of the Universe, folding up Himself and concealing His true Majesty, appeared upon earth as a man. Angels proclaimed the Glad Tidings. A virgin gave birth to the Holy One in Ta-ch'in. A bright Star announced the blessed event. Persians saw the splendour and came forth with their tribute.

Fulfilling the old Law as it was declared by the twenty-four Sages [*names of books in the Old Testament—Ed.*], He (the Messiah) taught how to rule both families and kingdoms according to His own great Plan. Establishing His New Teaching of Non-assertion which operates silently through the Holy Spirit, another Person of the Trinity, He formed in man the capacity for well-doing through the Right Faith. Setting up the standard of the eight cardinal virtues, He purged away the dust from human nature and perfected a true character. Widely opening the Three Constant Gates, He brought Life to light and abolished Death. Hanging up the bright Sun, He swept away the abodes of darkness. All the evil devices of the devil were thereupon defeated and destroyed. He then took an oar in the Vessel of Mercy and ascended to the Palace of Light. Thereby all rational beings were conveyed across the Gulf. His mighty work being thus completed, He returned at noon to His original position (in Heaven). The twenty-seven standard works [*the books of the New Testament—Ed.*] of His Sûtras were preserved. The Great means of Conversion (or leavening, i.e., transformation) were widely extended, and the sealed Gate of the Blessed Life was unlocked. His Law is to bathe with water and with the Spirit, and thus to cleanse from all vain delusions and to purify men until they regain the whiteness of their nature.

(His ministers) carry the Cross with them as a Sign. They travel about wherever the sun shines, and try to re-unite those that are beyond the pale (i.e., those that are lost). Striking the wood, they proclaim the Glad Tidings (lit., joyful sounds) of Love and Charity. They turn ceremoniously to the East, and hasten in the Path of Life and Glory. They preserve the beard to show that they have outward works to do, whilst they shave the crown (tonsure) to remind themselves that they have no private selfish desires. They keep neither male nor female slaves. Putting all men on an equality, they make no distinction between the noble and the mean. They neither accumulate property nor wealth; but giving all they possess, they set a good example to others. They observe fasting in order that they may subdue "the knowledge" (which defiles the mind). They keep the vigil of silence and watchfulness so that they may observe "the Precepts." Seven times a day they meet for worship and praise, and earnestly they offer prayers for the living as well as for the dead. Once in seven days, they have "a sacrifice without the animal" (i.e., a bloodless sacrifice). Thus cleansing their hearts, they regain their purity. This ever True and Unchanging Way is mysterious, and is almost impossible to name. But its meritorious operations are so brilliantly manifested that we make an effort and call it by the name of "The Luminous Religion."

(Source: *The Nestorian Documents and Relics in China*, by P. Y. Saeki [Tokyo: Toho Bunkwa Gakuin: The Academy of Oriental Culture, Tokyo Institute, 1951], 53-56.)

15. *Hsü-T'ing Messiah Sûtra (or Jesus-Messiah Sûtra)*

This account of Jesus, in the form of a Buddhist Sutra, was translated into Chinese and used by the Nestorian mission. It is not purely a product of Christian engagement with China, but a more complex result of an engagement with Central Asian religions carried into China and reflecting a worldview formed by Buddhist teachings. The translation given here is more literal than the more recent translations prepared by Martin Palmer in his 2001 work The Jesus Sutras, *but may thus help the reader sense the awkwardness of such intercultural discourse, and the way that Christian concerns were expressed in relation to distinctly Chinese values. The reader should compare it with the* Heliand, *not only for the very different forms of presentation engendered by encounters with different cul-*

tures, but also for the way in which Jesus is presented in relation to imperial power.

(1)   At that time, preaching the laws of Hsü-po (i.e., Jehovah) who is the Lord of Heaven, the Messiah spoke thus:

(2)   There may be different Views more or less, but who can discourse upon "the remarkable nobleness" of the meaning of the sutras?

(3)   Who can discourse concerning the whereabouts of the Lord of Heaven previous to His revelation? What really was the place where He had dwelt till then?

(4)   All the Buddhas as well as Kinnaras and the Superintending-devas (?Yama) and Arhâns can see the Lord of Heaven.

(5)   No human being, however, has ever seen the Lord of Heaven abiding with people.

(6)   Who had ever the sublime dignity (of character) to see the Lord of Heaven?

(7)   And this is because the Lord of Heaven is like the wind in His countenance. And who could possibly see the wind?

(8)   The Lord of Heaven incessantly going around all over the world, is constantly present everywhere.

(9)   On account of this, every man existing in this world only obtains life and continues his existence by the strength of the Lord of Heaven.

(10)   Only then every man can peacefully remain in his own abode, and his mind and thought may be able to attain (a rest).

(11)   From sunrise to sunset, he remains in his home, and from what he sees there, he hopes in his mind to follow wherever he may be led to go to.

(12)   The Person (of the Lord of Heaven) is in brightness, joyous and peaceful, and dwells in Heaven in comfort.

(13)   All the Buddhas, "flow and flux" (i.e., wander here and there) by virtue of this very wind, while in this world, there is no place where the wind does not reach.

(14)   The Lord of the Heaven remains always in a place of comfortable joy and peace. But there is not a single consequence of (human) actions that will not be known to Him.

(15)   People in this world can know the movements of the wind. They only hear the sound thereof, but they cannot see the form thereof.

(16)   No one can tell what the countenance of the wind is, whether it is straight or upright. It is not yellow or white. Nor is it blue. Nor can anyone tell where the wind is constantly remaining.

(17)   The Lord of Heaven has the divine dignity of His own, and dwells at one place. But no one can apprehend the place where He dwells.

(18)   He knows, indeed/neither death nor separation (lit., separating from the world).

(19)   Ever since (the time) when heaven and earth were created in co-operation, the divine dignity of God has never been but manifested, and it has never been but the cause of immortality, enjoying everlasting happiness.

(20)   Man, therefore, in extremity, will always do honour to the name of Buddha.

(21)   There are, however, many people who are very ignorant to designate their gods, and try to compare some of them to a kind of the Lord of Heaven at their heart.

(22)   And they also compose their Sutras (and say) how noble and how sweet are those doctrines set forth therein.

(23)   Every man now talks in his vernacular speech, saying: we have each our own special Lord of Heaven. Each faith has its abiding (merit).

(24)   The Lord of Heaven, however, gives man mind and wisdom not a little.

(25)   Therefore, whoever wants to return for the charity-favour of Buddha should have, by reflection and self-examination, a clear comprehension of his own sins and wicked deeds.

(26)   If he does so, he will obtain Heaven even though he may not be well versed in the teaching.

(27)   And, it is the divine power that will nourish human bodies and make then grow big.

. . .

(54) All the sins themselves have come to this world, because our original ancestor committed the sin of disobedience in "the Garden of seed-and-fruit bearing (trees)."

(55) All the living beings then ought to consider "the consequences of actions in a previous state."

(56) But the Lord of Heaven Himself received the bitter suffering (in His own body) and then, for the first time, He managed to keep all the livings from falling.

(57) And consequently, all the livings and "the real Buddha" are made not to remain separated very far.

(58) He then exclusively devoted Himself to the work of keeping all people from falling.

(59) And thus He made the real blessings to accompany the good of people and the evil consequences to the wickedness.

(60) The foolish people, however, have come to make the images of camels, elephants, bulls, mules, horses, reindeer, deer, etc., with wood or clay.

(61) Though these people may make these images with their respective outward forms and appearances, and yet they cannot impart to them life by any means.

(62) If you have any wisdom, consider well and reflect on yourself and observe closely the concatenation of all the causes and effects, and know also that what is stated here is all true.

. . .

(148) All the living beings, however, have turned their face away from (God) and committed sins and finally rebelled against the Lord of Heaven.

(149) Seeing such was their manner of living, the Lord of Heaven took great pity on them and admonished them to do good deeds, and not to trust to (the old teaching).

(150) The Lord of Heaven, therefore, made "the Cool Wind" (i.e., Holy Spirit) to enter a virgin named Mo-yen (i.e., Mary).

(151) Hereupon, the "Cool Wind" entered the body of Mo-yen in accordance with the instruction of the Lord of Heaven.

(152) Suddenly Mo-yen became pregnant.

(153) This was done by the Lord of Heaven because He knew that the virgin had no man-husband yet, and because He wanted also to show the whole world that without a man-husband a virgin can be made pregnant.

(154) And thus He made the whole world to see and say that the Lord of Heaven had dignity and power.

(155) And thus He made all people to have a believing heart with purity and caused them to return to "good relation."

(156) After her conception, Mo-yen gave birth to a son named I-shu (i.e., Jesus), whose father was the above-mentioned "Cool Wind."

(157) There were, however, ignorant people who thereupon said that, if the above-mentioned "Cool Wind" had made the virgin to conceive a son and caused her to give birth to a son, then such son must be at the bottom of the world.

(158) Moreover, suppose a Sacred Superior (of the kingdom) should issue an Imperial Decree (about any matter), wherever that document should be sent, there all the living would make obeisance before it.

(159) Likewise, the Lord of Heaven dwells in Heaven above and completely controls the whole wide world.

(160) And when I-shu Mi-shih-ho (i.e., Jesus the Messiah) was born, all the people of the world saw bright signs in heaven and on earth.

(161) At last, a new Star appeared in heaven above, which the people saw from their dwelling places.

(162) The Star was as big as a cart-wheel shining bright and clear over the place where the Lord of Heaven was to be found.

(163) Just about that time, the One (Person) was born in the City of Wu-li-shih-lien (i.e., Jerusalem) in the country of Fu-lin (i.e., Ephraim).

(164) When He was born as the Mi-shih-ho (i.e., Messiah), after the elapse of "five times" of one year, He began to talk.

(165) And (afterward) He preached to the people admonishing them to do good deeds.

(166) When He was over twelve years old, He came to a purifying place named Shu-nan (i.e., the Jordan) and sought to be baptized (lit., to be named or to have a name given).

(167) And consequently, He went to Yao-ku-hun (i.e., John) and was immersed for washing.

(168) At first, the Messiah submitted to (Yao-ku-hun) as a disciple.

(169) (This) sacred (man) dwelt in a wild ravine. He neither ate meat nor drank wine from his birth. He only lived on raw vegetables and honey,—honey on the ground.

(170) At that time, there were many people who came to Yao-ku-hun. They all worshipped him, and from him they also "received the precepts."

(171) And now, Yao-ku-hun thought it proper to make the Messiah enter the To-nan (i.e., ? the Jordan).

(172) The Messiah, after finishing the washing, came out of the water, when the "Cool Wind" descended from the Heaven in appearance of a dove and sat upon the Messiah, whilst (a voice) sounded in empty-space, saying:

(173) The Messiah is my son; all the people in the world must do what is told by the Messiah, obeying His command to do good.

(174) The Messiah, then, showed to all the living beings that "the Way of Heaven" is no other than the decided will of the Lord of Heaven.

(175) His decided will is to make all the living beings give up serving false gods.

(176) Therefore, if any living being should hear these words, let him give up serving these false gods. Let him stop evil deeds, and forthwith do the good work in faith.

(177) The Messiah, (from) the twelfth year of His age until He was little over thirty-two years old, sought for all people of evil life and made them to return to the good life and the right way.

(178) When the Messiah got as many as the twelve direct disciples, He proceeded finally to endure suffering.

(179) The dead (lit., those that withdrew from this world) were restored to life. The blind received their sight, "the deformed and strangely coloured people" (i.e., ? lepers) got cured slowly, whilst the sick were healed and restored at once, and those who were possessed of devils got their devils cast out, and the lame were specially healed.

(180) Those who had all sorts of diseases came to the Messiah and wished to touch or get hold of His *Kachâya* and they all were cured.

. . .

(190) When He was over thirty-two years of age, those men, who excelled in wickedness, came in to the presence of the Great King P'i-lo-tu-ssŭ (i.e., Pilate) and managed to state out before P'i-lo-tu-ssŭ himself:

(191) The Messiah ought to be punished with death, O Great King! Do away with Him at once!

(192) "Those followers of the wicked cause of existence" (i.e., Inveterate adversaries) all bore (false) testimony (against) the Messiah in the presence of the Great King P'i-lo-tu-ssŭ, saying: The Messiah ought to be punished with death.

(193) Hereupon, the Great King desired to decide the case of that man, and said, a crime deserving the death-punishment I am not informed of yet, nor do I see it myself. This man ought not to be punished with death. Let this matter be decided by "these followers of the wicked cause of existence" as they like.

(194) And the Great King then added: I can not kill this (man).

(195) Then "these followers of the wicked cause of existence" said, if this man is not to be punished with death, what will become of us both men and women?

(196) The Great King P'i-lo-tu-ssŭ ordered water to be brought to him and washed his hands in front of "those followers of the wicked cause of existence" and came and stood before them and said, indeed, I discovered no cause to kill this man.

(197) Then "these followers of the wicked cause of existence" repeatedly implored the King to do what they wanted, and they so strongly pressed him that he could not help killing this man.

(198) The Messiah gave up His body to these "wicked men" to be sacrificed for the sake of all mankind and made the whole world know that a human life is so very precarious as a candle light.

(199) Thus, in charity He gave up His life for the sake of all mankind, suffering death for them.

(200) The Messiah at last gave His own body to charity accepting the death.

(201) These wicked men caught the Messiah and brought Him to "the separated place," and after they washed his hair there, they led Him to "the placard place" (i.e., the place of execution) named Chi-chü (i.e., Golgotha).

(202) Subsequently, they bound Him upon the tree between two highway men, one being on the right and the other on the left.

(203) That day on which they bound the Messiah upon the tree at the fifth hour was the sixth-day-fast.

(204) It was at dawn that they bound Him upon the tree, but by the time the sun came toward the west there was black darkness on every side, and the earth quaked and the mountains were rent, and all the gates of graves in the world were opened and the men got life.

(205) Seeing these things, how can anyone gainsay that he does not believe what is taught in the sûtras?

(206) Those who live or die only for the sake of the Messiah, are faithful believers, and consequently—[*Here the manuscript was apparently damaged and cut off—Ed.*]

(Source: *The Nestorian Documents and Relics in China*, by P. Y. Saeki [Tokyo: Toho Bunkwa Gakuin: The Academy of Oriental Culture, Tokyo Institute, 1951], 125-46.)

16. *A Protest against the Eastern Church in China*

The letter below gives us insight into how members of the Chinese imperial government responded to the actions of the Eastern Christian Church in China.

The Protest of Liu-Tse, Member of the Censorate, against the Activity of the Nestorian Bishop Chi-lieh

In the 2nd year of K'ai-yüan (714 A.D.) Liu-tse was appointed Censor of the Imperial Court and Supervising Censor over the provincial Circuit of the South of the (Plum) Range (i.e., the two provinces of Kuangtung and Kuangsi). Just at that time, Chou Ch'ing-li, who was the Director of the Board of Foreign Trade and the Lieut-General of the Right (wing) of the Imperial Guards, presented to the Emperor various articles, full of strange devises and wonderful cunnings, which he (i.e., Chou) had made by Chi-lieh a Persian priest.

Hereupon, Liu presented his official address to the Emperor admonishing the same in the following words: "May it please your Majesty to say that I, your most humble servant, have heard that one ought not to take a look of a thing which one may covet, in order that one should not allow one's heart to be disturbed by any means. But it is certain that if a man sees what he covets his heart cannot but be disturbed.

"Sire, I am informed that Ch'ing-li and his party got some artful things cut or cast, besides they had some curious and wonderful apparatus manufactured. Anything unsubstantially artful they admire as curious and rare things, while anything mysterious and tricky they call a treasure of wonderful and extraordinary value.

"Such being the case, he (and his party) must be pronounced a great grub in wood (i.e., the depredation of dishonest officials to prey upon the Emperor's country) from the view point of preservation of the national welfare, besides what he (and his party) is (are) doing is strictly prohibited by the Sacred superiors under the pain of severe punishment, since these things are apt to throw the Sacred plan into disorder and to derange the established laws and customs of the country.

"In old times, as your Majesty is well aware of, when the Emperor found that a balcony to be built for him was too expensive, not from the

Imperial opulence, but from the ordinary people's standard of wealth, the wise Emperor could not be persuaded by any means to have it built, while even that pair of ivory chop-sticks, which were not objectionable things in themselves, caused many faithful and loyal subjects to come forward to protest against it indignantly.

"It is written in the King's Regulations that 'Anyone who makes a strange dress or a curious apparatus shall be punished with death' while it is written in the Book of the Commands of the Month that 'It is prohibited that any one should make unsubstantially artful and licentious things and dissolute the superior man's mind.'

"Now, the word 'artfulness' here means anything unusual and strange which will excite curiosity, and the word 'dissolution' means anything to tempt anyone to passions and desires.

"If your Majesty condescend to believe in him (i.e., Chou Ch'ing-li) and suffer him to continue to do such a thing, then it would be altogether better for your Majesty to undertake to command the whole people under heaven to go to excessive lavishness and prodigality.

"If, however, Ch'ing-li did such a thing in opposition to the Imperial will, then he shall be forfeited of all the Imperial grace of pardon.

"Your Majesty has ascended to the throne recently, but the myriad regions have absolute confidence in your Majesty and it is very necessary that your Majesty should decree against mean and trifling manners to enforce frugality and thrift throughout the country. Then, all the myriad families will be happy and prosperous."

(Source: *The Nestorian Documents and Relics in China*, by P. Y. Saeki [Tokyo: Toho Bunkwa Gakuin: The Academy of Oriental Culture, Tokyo Institute, 1951], 460-62.)

Two Letters of Pope Gregory, from Bede's *History*

While Pope Gregory I ("the Great") is often remembered for a letter to Augustine of Canterbury in which he recommends that Augustine leave non-Christian shrines alone in favor of gradual persuasion, Bede's Ecclesiastical History *also contains a second, and rather different, letter from Gregory. It may be that the milder letter came later as a corrective, or that Gregory was not adverse to violent action against non-Christian shrines—provided that his missionaries had royal support. Both letters date from June of 601.*

17. *Bede's* Ecclesiastical History, Book 1, Chapter 30

A copy of the letter which he sent to the Abbot Mellitus, on his going to Britain.

Moreover, on the departure of the above-named deputies, the blessed father Gregory sent after them letters worthy of mention, in which he plainly shows how zealously he watched towards the salvation of our race, writing thus:—

"Gregory, the servant of the servants of God, to my most dearly beloved son, the Abbot Mellitus. After the departure of our congregation which is with you, we were rendered very anxious because it happened that we heard nothing concerning the success of your journey. When, therefore, the omnipotent God shall have brought you to that most reverend man, our brother Bishop Augustine, tell him what I have a long time thought over with myself, concerning the case of the English—to wit, that the temples of the idols in that nation ought not to be destroyed; but let the idols themselves that are in them be destroyed. Let water be consecrated, and sprinkled in the same temples; let altars be constructed, relics deposited: because if these temples are well built, they ought of necessity to be converted from the worship of devils to the service of the true God, that whilst this nation sees that its temples are not destroyed, it may put away error from its heart, and acknowledging and adoring the true God, may the more familiarly meet at its accustomed places. And because they are wont to kill many oxen in sacrifice to devils, some solemnity ought to be specially appointed for them on this account, as, that on the day of the dedication, or on the birthdays of holy martyrs whose relics are there deposited, they may make for themselves huts of the boughs of trees, around the same churches which have been altered from temples, and celebrate a solemnity with religious feasting, and no longer immolate animals to the devil, but kill them for their own eating, to the praise of God, and return thanks for their satiety to the Giver of all things; to the end that, whilst some outward joys are reserved for them, they may more easily be able to consent to inward joys. For, without doubt, it is impossible to cut off all things at once from their rough minds, because also he who endeavours to ascend to the highest place, is elevated by steps or paces and not by leaps. So, indeed, the Lord made Himself known to the Israelitish people, in Egypt, but reserved to them, in His own service, the use of the sacrifices which they were wont to offer to the devil, and charged them to immolate animals in His sacrifice, to the end that, changing their hearts, they might let go one thing with respect to the sacrifice and retain another; so that although they were the same animals as they were wont to offer, yet being immolated to God and not to idols, they were no longer the same sacrifices. These things therefore it is necessary that you, well-beloved, should yourself say to the aforesaid brother, that he at present being there placed, may consider how he ought to order all things."

18. *Bede's* Ecclesiastical History, *Chapter 32*

How he sent a letter and gifts to King Ethelbert.

The blessed Pope Gregory also, at the same time, sent a letter to King Ethelbert, and with it many gifts of divers kinds, being desirous to glorify the king with temporal honours, while he rejoiced that the knowledge of celestial glory had come to him by his own labour and zeal. This, moreover, is a copy of the said letter.

"Gregory, bishop, to the most glorious lord and his most excellent son Ethelbert, king of the Angles. Omnipotent God advances good men to the government of peoples in order that through them He may bestow the gifts of His goodness on all over whom they are set. This we understand to have taken place in the nation of the Angles, over which

your majesty was placed, to the intent that by the good things which are granted you, heavenly benefits might be bestowed on the nation that is subject to you. And therefore, most glorious son, keep with careful mind that grace which you have divinely received; hasten to extend the Christian faith among the peoples subject to you; multiply the zeal of your uprightness in their conversion; suppress the worship of their idols; overthrow the buildings of their temples; edify the manners of your subjects by great purity of life, by exhorting, terrifying, soothing, correcting, and by showing examples of good works; that you may find Him your rewarder in heaven, whose name and knowledge you shall have spread abroad upon earth. For He also will render the name of your majesty more glorious to posterity, whose honour you seek and preserve among the nations. And thus, indeed, Constantine formerly, the most pious emperor, recalling the Roman republic from the perverse worship of idols, subjected himself to omnipotent God, our Lord Jesus Christ, and turned himself with the peoples subject to him, with all his mind, to Him. Whence it came to pass, that this man surpassed in his praises the name of ancient princes, and excelled his predecessors as much in reputation as in good deeds. And now therefore let your majesty hasten to instil the knowledge of one God, the Father, the Son, and the Holy Ghost, into kings and peoples subject to them, that you may excel the ancient kings of your nation in praises and merits; and the more you wipe away the sins of others among your subjects, the more may you become secure concerning your own sins before the terrible judgment of omnipotent God. Hearken to, devoutly perform, carefully keep in memory, whatever our most reverend brother Bishop Augustine advises you, who is instructed in the monastic rule, filled with the knowledge of Holy Scripture, and, by the help of God, gifted with good works; because, if you hear him in that which he speaks for the omnipotent Lord, the same omnipotent Lord will more readily hear him when he prays for you. But if (which God forbid) you reject his words, how shall the omnipotent Lord hear him for you, whom you neglect to hear for God? With your whole mind, therefore, bend yourself to him with fervour of faith, and assist his efforts by the virtue which God has given you, that He may make you to be partakers of His kingdom, whose faith you make to be received and kept in your kingdom.

"Besides, we would have your majesty know that, as we find in Sacred Scripture from the words of the omnipotent Lord, the end of the present world is already at hand, and that the kingdom of the saints is about to come, which can never be terminated by any end. Moreover, on the approach of this same end of the world, many things impend which were not before—to wit, changes of the air, and terrors from heaven, and storms contrary to the order of the times, wars, famines, pestilences, earthquakes in divers places; which, however, are not all about to come in our days, but after our days all shall follow. If therefore you perceive any of these things hap-

pen in your land, in no wise trouble your mind, for these signs of the end of the world are sent before in order that we might be solicitous about our souls, in expectation of the hour of death, and be found by the Judge about to come to be prepared in good works. These things now, glorious son, I have said in few words, to the end that, when the Christian faith has increased in your kingdom, our speech also may increase more widely among you; and it may please us to say so much the more, according as the joys concerning the perfect conversion of your nation multiply themselves in our mind."

(Source: *Bede's Ecclesiastical History of the English Nation*, trans. L. Gidley [Oxford and London: James Parker and Co., 1870], 87-90, 91-94.)

Benedictine and Dominican Documents

19. *The Rule of Benedict*

The selections below contain two sections of the Rule of Benedict (sixth century C.E.) that indicate the daily discipline of a Benedictine Monastery, and how guests are to be received. The final section, although not a primary source, describes how these rules and those who kept them were part of Christian mission in Europe during the medieval period. Reading Newman's description of the Benedictines, however romanticized from his nineteenth-century standpoint, the reader may wish to consider how the varying ways the claim of Christianity to represent civilization engaged those who might be regarded as barbarians from a Roman standpoint, but who were also victims of violent and destructive acts of barbarism upon their settled lives.

Chapter XLVIII. On Manual Labor

As idleness is the enemy of the soul, the brethren are to be employed alternately in manual labour and pious reading. Hence, we think it well to regulate the time to be allotted to both these daily exercises, in the following manner. From the Feast of Easter till the 14th of September, exclusively,

the brethren going forth in the morning shall be employed at whatever is to be done, from the 1st till about the 4th hour; from the 4th until near the 6th hour, they will apply themselves to pious reading. Having dined after Sext, they will retire to the Dormitory to take some repose, observing in the mean time a profound silence.

Should any brother prefer to devote the time allotted to the mid-day repose to spiritual reading, he may do so, provided, however, he do not disturb his brethren. None shall be sung somewhat sooner than at other times of the year—about the middle of the 8th hour.

The brethren will, then, resume their work, at which they are to continue until evening.

Should the peculiar circumstances of the place, or the poverty of the Monastery require that the brethren be employed in reaping and gathering their own corn, let them not repine thereat; for, then, they shall be truly monks, in living by the labour of their hands, as did our fathers and the Apostles. Let moderation, however, be observed in all things, because of the weak.

From the 14th of September till the commencement of Lent, they are to be employed in reading from morning until the end of the second hour, after which Terce shall be sung. From Terce till None, all are to be employed at whatever work may be enjoined them. At the first signal for None the brethren will quit their work, in order to be ready for the Office, at the second signal.

After dinner the brethren will apply themselves to pious reading or the study of the psalms.

During Lent they will be employed in reading from morning until the end of the third hour; from that until the end of the 10th hour they are to be employed at the work enjoined them. At the beginning of Lent each brother is to get a book from the library, which he will read, in order, from the beginning to the end. Before distributing these books to the brethren, let one or two seniors be appointed by the Abbot to visit the different parts of the Monastery, during the time of lecture, in order to see if there be any brother whiling away his time, or chatting, instead of reading, and thereby inflicting an injury, not only on his own soul, but likewise on those of others. Should it happen (which God forbid) that any one be found so tepid, let him be reprimanded once or twice; and if he do not amend, let him be subjected to regular discipline, that others may be deterred from following his bad example, by the severity of the punishment inflicted upon him. Let no brother associate with another at undue hours. On Sundays, all will be engaged in pious reading, except those who have to discharge particular duties incompatible with that exercise. Should any one be so indolent, or tepid, that he either cannot or will not read, or meditate, let some employment be given him, that he may not be idle. To those of the brethren who are sick, or delicate, such employment shall be assigned, that they may not be altogether idle, nor, on the other hand, oppressed, and, consequently, tempted to quit the Monastery. The Abbot will take their weakness into consideration.

Chapter LIII. On the Reception of Guests

Let all guests arriving at the Monastery be received as Christ Himself, for He shall one day say, "*I was a stranger and ye took me in*" (Matt. 25:35). And let due honour be paid to all, especially to those who are of the household of the faith, and to strangers. Accordingly, as soon as a guest is announced, the Abbot and the brethren will go to receive him, with all charity. Let them first pray with him, and then give him the kiss of peace, which is never to be given, except after prayer, because of the illusions of the enemy. The guests shall be saluted with all humility; and, both on their arrival and departure, Jesus Christ, who has been received in them, shall be likewise worshipped in them, by an inclination of the head or a full prostration. After their reception, the guests shall be conducted to the Church to pray. Then the superior, or one authorised by him, shall sit with them, and read a portion of the Scriptures for their edification; and after that they shall be treated with all kindness. The Abbot will sit to table with them for the sake of hospitality, unless it be a fast-day of the Church. As to the brethren, they shall observe the regular fasts. The Abbot will give water to the guests to wash their hands, and shall, himself, assisted by all the brethren, wash their feet. After performing this duty of Charity, they will say the following verse: "We have received, O God, your mercy in the midst of your temple" (Ps. 47[48]:10). Above all, let the poor and strangers be attended to, with all care and solicitude, for in our reception and entertainment of these, we entertain Christ in a more special manner. As to the rich, their wealth and position preclude the necessity of our making any special provision for them, inasmuch as the fear one has of causing them any displeasure is, of itself, quite sufficient to obtain for them all due consideration. A kitchen shall be set apart for the Abbot and the guests, so that whenever they arrive at the monastery, which indeed is never without them, they may be entertained without any annoyance to the Community. To serve in this kitchen, there shall be appointed annually two brothers fully competent. They shall have assistants when necessary, that they may perform their duties without murmuring. Should their office not give them sufficient occupation, they will go out to whatever work they may be sent. The same rule is to hold with regard to all who have offices in the Monastery, that is to say, when they need assistants, they shall have them, whilst, if the duties of their respective offices be not sufficient to keep them wholly occupied, they shall be employed in some other work, by order of their Superior. Let the apartment destined for the guests be furnished with a sufficient number of beds for their accommodation; and let a brother, who fears God, be appointed to take charge of it, so that the house of God may be wisely governed by wise men.

Let no brother, except he be commanded to do so, either speak to, or associate with, the guests. Should a brother see them, or happen to come in their way, let him humbly salute them, as before directed, and having asked their prayers, let him pass on, saying that he is forbidden to speak to them.

(Source: *The Holy Rule of St. Benedict*, trans. a priest of Mount Melleray [London: Thomas Richardson and Son, 1865].)

20. *On Benedictine Monasticism, by Cardinal Newman*

(Introduction by David Bosch) *Precisely because of its profoundly spiritual yet at the same time eminently practical nature, the Benedictine Rule has been "one of the most effective linkages of justice, unity and renewal the church has ever known" (Henry 1987: 274). The Benedictine monastery indeed became "a school for the Lord's service." For upward of six centuries these monasteries were the model on which all others were designed and even to this day they exercise a profound influence. Seeking a life free from corruption and free from distraction in its daily worship, in which each day, each hour, would have its own completeness, Benedict introduced a tradition that had far-reaching and enduring consequences. Few scholars have captured the genius and lasting contribution of Benedictine monasticism the way the nineteenth-century Cardinal Newman had, as the following lengthy quotation illustrates:*

(St Benedict) found the world, physical and social, in ruins, and his mission was to restore it in the way, not of science, but of nature, not as if setting about to do it, not professing to do it by any set time or by any rare specific or by any series of strokes, but so quietly, patiently, gradually, that often, till the work was done, it was not known to be doing. It was a restoration, rather than a visitation, correction, or conversion. The new world he helped to create was a growth rather than a structure. Silent men were observed about the country, or discovered in the forest, digging, clearing, and building; and other silent men, not seen, were sitting in the cold cloister, tiring their eyes, and keeping their attention on the stretch, while they painfully deciphered and copied and re-copied the manuscripts which they had saved. There was no one that "contended, or cried out," or drew attention to what was going on; but by degrees the wooded swamp became a hermitage, a religious house, a farm, an abbey, a village, a seminary, a school of learning, and a city. Roads and bridges connected it with other abbeys and cities, which had similarly grown up; and what the haughty Alaric or the fierce Attila had broken to pieces, these patient meditative men had brought together and made to live again (Newman 1970: 410).

(Source: David J. Bosch, *Transforming Mission: Paradigm Shifts in Theology of Mission* [Maryknoll, N.Y.: Orbis Books, 1991], 234.)

21. *Dominican Documents*

Long before the Protestant Reformation, in the twelfth and thirteenth centuries, Roman Catholics were concerned about the incomplete conversion of Europe, and of the heresies found in various parts of Christendom. The Dominican Order was founded to combat these heresies through preaching. The first of these readings comes from an early history of the Dominicans, probably written in 1233, just before Dominic was canonized. The second is a letter from Dominic himself indicating the discipline necessary for a converted heretic.

Excerpts from: Blessed Jordan, the Libellus of Jordan of Saxony: The Advice He (Bishop Diego) Gave to Those Sent by the Pope

At the time the Lord Pope Innocent had directed twelve abbots of the Cistercian Order to take each a companion and preach the faith against the Albigensian heretics. Thereupon the abbots held a council with the archbishops, bishops, and other prelates of that region to discuss the most suitable means of fruitfully fulfilling the mission now entrusted to them.

20. During these discussions, the Bishop of

Osma happened to reach Montpelier, where the council was being held. He was received with honor and was invited to give his advice, since they knew that he was a saintly man, mature and just, and zealous for the faith. But, being circumspect and versed in God's ways, he began to inquire about the ceremonies and customs of the heretics. Then he commented that the methods these heretics were using to convert souls of their perfidy by persuasion, preaching, and the example of their false holiness were in striking contrast to the stylish and expensive carriages and furnishing displayed by those who had been sent. "This is not the way, my brethren, this is not the way for you to proceed. I do not think it possible, by words alone, to lead back to the faith such men as are better attracted by example. Look at the heretics! While they make a pretense at piety, while they give counterfeit examples of evangelical poverty and austerity, they win the simple people to their ways. Therefore, if you come with less poverty and austerity, you will give hardly any edification, you will cause much harm, and You will fail utterly of your objective. Match steel with steel, rout false holiness with the true religion, because the arrogance of these false apostles must be overthrown by genuine humility. Was this not the way whereby Paul became unwise, namely, by enumerating his true virtues and recounting his austerities and dangers, in order to burst the bubble of those who boasted about the merits of their holy lives?" So they asked him, "What is your advice, then, good Father?" and he answered, "Do what I am about to do." And the spirit of the Lord entering into him, he called the men he had with him and sent them and his carriages and furnishings back to Osma, and kept only a few clerics as his companions. After that he announced that his present intention was to spend some time in that region to spread the faith.

And this was the cause for instituting our Order. I heard this from the first brethren who were in that territory with Blessed Dominic.

21. Among those the Bishop kept with him was the subprior Dominic, whom he regarded highly and loved greatly. This was Brother Dominic, the founder of the Order of Preachers and its first friar, who, from that moment, began to be called, not subprior, but Brother Dominic. He was a true Dominic "man of the Lord," protected by the Lord, innocent of sin; a true man of the Lord, adorned with every virtue of the Lord.

22. After the abbots who had been sent heard this advice and saw the example set by the Bishop, they agreed with him and sent back each to his own monastery whatever seemed superfluous, keeping only the books they would need for the divine office, study, and disputations. Taking the Bishop as their superior and head of the whole affair, they began to go on foot without purse and, in voluntary poverty, to preach the faith. When the heretics saw this, they, too, began to preach more vigorously.

On his return journey from the Curia the Bishop of Osma reached Montpelier where he met the saintly Arnold, the abbot of Citeaux, as well as Brother Peter of Castelnau and Brother Ralph, Cistercian monks, all legates of the Apostolic See seeking to renounce the legacy enjoined upon them out of sheer discouragement, since they could attain nothing or hardly anything in preaching to the heretics. Whenever they began preaching to the heretics, the latter would taunt them with remarks about the scandalous lives of the clergy; so, if they wanted to correct the way of life among the clergy, they would have to give up their preaching.

The aforementioned bishop, however, offered them an effective solution to their dilemma by warning and counseling that, forgetting everything else, they should concentrate all their ardor on preaching. Moreover, to shut the mouths of their detractors, they should go forth humbly, doing and teaching according to the example of their Holy Master, go on foot without gold and silver, and thereby imitate the manner of the Apostles. However, since all this was something new, the above mentioned legates were not in favor of undertaking it by themselves. So they answered that if someone with due authority were willing to show them the way, they would gladly follow him. What else was there to do? The man of God offered himself, and soon, sending his carriages and his entire retinue to the city of Osma, he kept one companion and, with the two frequently mentioned legates, namely, the monks Peter and Ralph, he left Montpelier. The Cistercian abbot, however, returned to Citeaux, both because the general chapter of the Cistercians was to be held in the near future, and because, upon the completion of the chapter, he would return with some of the abbots of his Order who would help carry out the duties of preaching assigned to him (Cernai).

(Source: *Saint Dominic: Biographical Documents*, ed. with an introduction by Francis C. Lehner, O.P. [Washington, D.C.: Thomist Press, 1964]; available online at http://www.domcentral .org/trad/domdocs/default.htm.)

A Letter from Dominic

Brother Dominic, Canon of Osma, the Least Among Preachers, Sends Greetings in Christ to All of His Faithful to Whom This Letter Comes,

By the authority of the Lord Abbot of Citeaux, Legate of the Apostolic See, who enjoined this function on us, we reconcile the bearer of this letter, Pons Roger, who has, by God's mercy, been converted from the sect of the heretics.

In virtue of the Sacrament which has been administered, we command that, three Sundays or days of major feasts, a priest march him, stripped to the waist and under continuous flogging, from the entrance to the city to the church. Moreover, we command him to abstain at all times from meat, eggs, and cheeses, or all things which are conceived from the seed of flesh, except on Easter Sunday, Pentecost Sunday, and Christmas, when, for the rejection of his former error, we command him to eat these things. He should keep three Lents each year, fasting and abstaining from fish. Three days every week, perpetually, he should fast and abstain from fish, olive-oil, and wine, unless bodily infirmity or summer heat makes a dispensation necessary. He should wear clothes which are religious in both their style and color, with a small cross sewed on each side over the breast. If it is opportune, he should hear Mass daily and, on major feast days, he should go to church for Vespers. Wherever he may be, he should praise God at all [canonical] hours of night and day in the following way: seven times a day he should say the Our Father ten times, at midnight, twenty. He should observe total chastity and live at Treveille. He should show this letter to his chaplain every month. Moreover, we command the chaplain to supervise his life with diligent care, until the Lord Legate otherwise expresses his will on these matters. Should he refuse to observe these directives, we command that he be deemed a perjurer and a heretic excommunicated from association with the faithful.

(Source: *Saint Dominic: Biographical Documents*, ed. with an introduction by Francis C. Lehner, O.P. [Washington, D.C.: Thomist Press, 1964], chaps. 1 and 2; available online at http://www .domcentral.org/trad/domdocs/default.htm.)

7

Readings Related to Engaging New Peoples and Civilizations

22. *On the Peace of Faith* (Excerpts), by Nicholas of Cusa

Nicholas of Cusa (1401-1464) was a scholar, bishop, and eventually cardinal who was engaged at the end of his life in negotiations to reunify the Eastern and Western churches. In the selection below he imagines a heavenly conference in which the true unity of all different religions is revealed. It was not a view that gained immediate currency.

There was a certain man who, having formerly seen the sites in the regions of Constantinople, was inflamed with zeal for God as a result of those deeds that were reported to have been perpetrated at Constantinople most recently and most cruelly by the King of the Turks. Consequently, with many groanings he beseeched the Creator of all, because of His kindness, to restrain the persecution that was raging more fiercely than usual on account of the difference of rite between the [two] religions. It came to pass that after a number of days—perhaps because of his prolonged, incessant meditation—a vision was shown to this same zealous man. Therefrom he educed the following: the few wise men who are rich in the experiential knowledge of all such differences as are observed throughout the world in the [different] religions can find a single, readily available harmony; and through this harmony there can be constituted, by a suitable and true means, perpetual peace within [the domain of] religion. Hence, in order that this vision might one day become known to those who have a say in these especially important matters, he wrote down plainly, in what follows, as much of it as he recalled.

[An archangel addresses God:] "O Lord, King of the universe, what does any creature have that You did not give to it? It was fitting that the human body, formed from the clay of the earth, was inbreathed by You with a rational spirit, so that from within this body an image of Your ineffable power would shine forth. From one [man] there was multiplied the great number of people who inhabit the surface of dry land. . . .

"But You know, O Lord, that there cannot be a great multitude without much diversity. . . . You set over Your people different kings and different seers, called prophets—very many of whom, in their role as Your legates, instituted (in Your name) worship and laws and instructed an uneducated people. [Men] accepted these laws just as if You Yourself, the King of kings, had spoken to them face to face; they believed that they heard not kings and prophets but You Yourself in and through kings and prophets. Now, to various nations You sent various prophets and teachers—some at one time, others at another. But the earthly human condition has this characteristic: viz., that longstanding custom, which is regarded as having passed over into nature, is defended as the truth. In this way there arise great quarrels when each community prefers its own faith to another [faith].

"Aid [us], then, O You who alone are able to. For this strife occurs for the sake of You, whom alone all [men] worship in everything they are seen to adore. For no one, in whatever he is seen to desire, desires [anything] except the good, which You are. And in all intellectual inference no one seeks anything other than the truth, which You are. . . . You, then, who are the giver of life and of existence, are the one who is seen to be sought in different ways in different rites, and You are named in different names; for as You are [in Yourself] You remain unknown and ineffable to all. . . . [D]o not hide Yourself any longer, O Lord. Be propitious, and manifest Your face; and all peoples will be saved, who no longer will be able to desert the Source of life and its sweetness, once having foretasted even a little thereof. For no one departs from You except because He is ignorant of You.

"If You will deign to do the foregoing, the sword will cease, as will also the malice of hatred and all evils; and all [men] will know that there is only one religion in a variety of rites. But perchance this difference of rites cannot be eliminated; or perhaps it is not expedient [that it be eliminated], in order that the diversity may make for an increase of devotion, since each region will devote more careful attention to making its ceremonies more 'favorable,' as it were, to You, the King. If so, then at least let there be one religion—just as You are one—and one true worship of You as Sovereign. Therefore, be placable, O Lord, because Your wrath is Your graciousness and Your justice is Your mercy. . . .'"

After all the heavenly citizens alike bowed to the Supreme King, who was seated on the throne, He said in response to the supplication of the archangel that man was left to his own choice and that He had created man capable, through his choice, of fellowship with Himself. But man, who is animal and earthly, is kept in ignorance under the dominion of the Prince of darkness; and he walks in accordance with the conditions of the sensible life (which life comes only from the world of the Prince of darkness) and not in accordance with the intellectual, inner man (whose life comes from the region of man's origin). [The King] said that for this reason He had called upon wayward man to return—[calling] with much care and diligence through various prophets who (in contrast with others) were seers. At length, after not even all these prophets were sufficiently able to overcome the Prince of ignorance, He sent His own Word, through whom He made even the aeons. The Word

assumed a humanity in order that in this way, at least, He might enlighten man (who was teachable because of His most free choice) and [man] would see (in case he ever hoped to return to the sweetness of eternal life) that he must walk not in accordance with the outer man but in accordance with the inner man. . . .

[T]he Word that was made flesh and that held the preeminent position among all the heavenly inhabitants, answered on behalf of all: "Father of Mercies, Your works are most perfect, and there remains nothing to be added for their completion. Nevertheless, because You decreed from the beginning that man remain in possession of free choice, and since in the sensible world nothing remains stable, and since fluxible opinions and conjectures are changed from time to time, as are also tongues and interpretations, human nature needs frequent visitation in order that the false inferences which occur very often concerning Your Word may be eradicated and thereby truth may continually shine forth. Since truth is one and since it cannot fail to be grasped by every free intellect, all the diverse religions will be led unto one orthodox faith."

[This answer] was pleasing to the King. And upon summoning the angels who were in charge of all the nations and tongues, he commanded each [of them] to bring to the Word-made-flesh one very experientially knowledgeable [man]. And straightway there appeared in the presence of the Word the most judicious men of this world—as if caught up unto ecstasy. To them the Word of God spoke as follows: "The Lord, King of heaven and of earth, has heard the moaning of those who have been killed, those who have been imprisoned, and those who have been reduced unto servitude—[the moaning of those] who suffer on account of the diversity of the religions. All who either inflict or suffer this persecution are motivated only from their belief that such [action or passion] is expedient for salvation and is pleasing to their Creator. Therefore, the Lord has had mercy upon His people and is agreeable that henceforth all the diverse religions be harmoniously reduced, by the common consent of all men, unto one inviolable [religion]. To you select men He entrusts the burdensome responsibility of [this] commission, giving you from His own court assisting and ministering angelic spirits who will watch over you and guide you. And He designates Jerusalem as the most fitting place for this [work]."

. . . To the foregoing [words] a man who was older than the others and who was, as it appeared, a Greek [representing the Greek/Eastern Orthodox tradition], replied after expressing adoration: "We praise our God, whose mercy [is bestowed] upon all His works, who alone is able to cause such great diversity of religions to be brought into one harmonious peace, and whose bidding we His creation cannot fail to obey. But we ask to be now instructed as to how this oneness of religion can be instituted by us. For [each nation] will have difficulty accepting, through our persuading, a faith that is other than that [respective] faith which each nation has hitherto defended even with its blood."

The Word responded: "You will [all] find to be everywhere presupposed not a faith that is *other* but a faith that is one and the same. For among the countrymen of your own language-groups, you who are now present are called wise—or, at least, [are called] philosophers, or lovers of wisdom."

"So it is," said the Greek. . . .

The Word added: "There can be only one Wisdom. For if it were possible for there to be more than one Wisdom, these wisdoms would have to derive from a single [Wisdom]; for oneness is prior to all plurality."

Greek: None of us doubt that there is one Wisdom, which we all love and on account of which we are called philosophers. By participation in it many men are wise, though Wisdom itself remains, in itself, simple and undivided.

Word: You all agree, then, that there is one most simple Wisdom, whose power is ineffable. And in the unfolding of Wisdom's power, each [of you] experiences this ineffable and infinite power. For example, when sight is directed toward visible objects, and when it takes cognizance of the fact that whatever-it-sees was produced by the power of Wisdom (and similarly regarding hearing and each thing unto which the sense [of hearing] attains), it affirms that invisible Wisdom exceeds all things.

Greek: We who have taken up this profession of philosophy love the foretasted sweetness of Wisdom through no other means than through an appreciative desiring of the things that are subject to the senses. For who would not die in order to obtain such Wisdom, from which emanates all

beauty, all sweetness of life, and everything desirable? . . . Nonetheless, Absolute Wisdom, as it is [in itself], is never attainable in something other [than itself]. Consequently, eternal, inexhaustible Wisdom is, in this way, perpetual and unfailing intellectual food.

Word: You rightly come to the topic at which we are aiming. Accordingly, all of you, although you are said to be of different religions, presuppose, in all such diversity, one thing that you call Wisdom. But, tell me, does a single Wisdom encompass whatever can be spoken of?

. . . The Italian [representing Roman Catholicism, i.e., Western Christianity] replied: "Indeed, the Word is not present outside of Wisdom. For the Word of the Supremely Wise is present in Wisdom, and Wisdom [is present] in the Word; and not anything [is present] outside of Wisdom. For Infinite Wisdom encompasses all things."

Word: Then if someone were to say that all things were created in Wisdom and someone else [were to say] that all things were created in the Word, would they be saying the same thing or something different?

Italian: Although a difference appears in the verbal expressions, they are the same in meaning. For the Creator's Word, in which He created all things, cannot be [anything] except His Wisdom.

Word: What, then, seems to you to be the case? Is that Wisdom God or a creature?

Italian: Because God the Creator creates all things in Wisdom, He is, necessarily, the Wisdom of created wisdom. For prior to every creature there is Wisdom, through which every created thing is what it is.

Word: Thus, Wisdom is eternal, because it is prior to everything originated and created. . . .

Italian: No one can deny that that which is understood to be prior to everything originated is eternal. . . .

Word: Now, it is not possible that there be more than one eternity, because prior to all plurality there is oneness.

Italian: No one denies this, either.

Word: Therefore, Wisdom is the one, simple, eternal God, the Beginning of all things.

Italian: [This] is necessarily so.

Word: See how you philosophers of various sects agree on the religion of one God—whom you all presuppose, in that you profess to be lovers of Wisdom.

. . . At this point an Arab [representing Islam] spoke up: "Nothing can be said more clearly or more truly."

Word: Just as by virtue of your being lovers of Wisdom you declare that there is Absolute Wisdom, do you think that there are men of sound understanding who do not love Wisdom?

Arab: I think it altogether true that all men by nature desire Wisdom. For Wisdom is the life of the intellect, which cannot be sustained in its own vitality by any other food than by truth and by the Word of life (i.e., by the intellect's intellectual bread, viz., Wisdom). For just as every existing thing desires whatever it cannot exist without, so the intellectual life [desires] Wisdom.

Word: Therefore, all men declare together with you that there is one Absolute Wisdom, which they presuppose and which is the one God.

Arab: So it is. And no one who has understanding can affirm anything different.

Word: Therefore, for all those who are of sound understanding there is one religion and worship, which is presupposed in all the diversity of the rites.

Arab: You [Yourself] are Wisdom, because [You are] the Word of God. . . .

Word: All who have ever worshiped a plurality of gods have presupposed there to be deity. For in all the gods, they adore the deity as [one and] the same in [all] its participants. For just as there are no white things if whiteness does not exist, so if the deity does not exist, there are no gods. Therefore, the worshipping of [a plurality of] gods bespeaks the deity; and he who says that there is more than one god says [implicitly] that there is, antecedently, one Beginning of them all—just as he who maintains that there is more than one holy [man] admits that there is one Most Holy, by participation in whom all [these] others are holy. For no race was ever so obtuse that it believed there to be a plurality of gods each of whom was the universe's First Cause, Beginning, or Creator. . . .

Word: Therefore, if all those who worship a plurality of gods look unto that which they presuppose, viz., unto the deity, which is the cause of all [the gods], and if, as reason dictates, they accept this deity into their overt religious practices (even

as, implicitly, they worship it in all whom they call gods), then the dispute is dissolved.

Arab: Perhaps this [dissolution] might not be difficult [to effect]. But it will be hard to eliminate the worshipping of gods. For the people hold it to be certain that help is afforded to them from [such] worshipping; and, consequently, they are inclined to these gods for the sake of their own salvation.

Word: If the people were informed about salvation—[informed] in a manner comparable to the aforesaid one—then they would rather seek salvation in Him who has given being and who is Saviour and Infinite Salvation than [seek it] in those who of themselves have nothing unless it is conceded [to them] by the Saviour. . . .

. . . At this point a man from India [representing the Hindu and possibly the Buddhist traditions] [asked]: "What about statues and effigies?"

Word: Images that lead to a knowledge of the things which are admissible in the true worship of the one God are not condemned. But when they lead away from the true worshipping of the one God as Sovereign (as if in stones there were some portion of deity and as if [the deity] were bound to a statue), then, rightly, the images ought to be broken, because they deceive [men] and turn [them] away from the truth. . . .

(Source: Nicholas of Cusa, *Complete Philosophical and Theological Treatises of Nicholas of Cusa*, trans. Jasper Hopkins [Minneapolis: Banning Press, 2001], 1:633-42.)

23. *Papal Bull* Inter cetera, *of 1493* by Pope Alexander VI, the Missionary Charge to Ferdinand and Isabella of Spain

The following document lends insight into both Roman Catholic missionary understandings and motivations when the New Worlds were discovered.

Charge to Ferdinand and Isabella in relation to the New World

Among other works pleasing to the Divine Majesty and heartily desired by us is this: that the

Catholic Faith and the Christian Religion, especially in our time, should be exalted and everywhere increased and extended; the salvation of souls procured and barbarous nations put down and brought to the Faith. Wherefore, since by the divine favour we have been promoted, far beyond our deserts, to this sacred see of Peter, knowing that you, like true Catholic Kings and Princes . . . have devoted your whole mind and purpose to the recovery of the kingdom of Granada from the Saracens . . . do trust that you may be able to carry still further this your holy and laudable purpose, begun by the eternal God, with daily increasing zeal for the honour of God and the extension of the kingdom of Christ.

§ 1. We are aware that, for a long time, you have had it in mind to seek out and find certain islands and lands, remote, unknown, and hitherto undiscovered by others, in order that you might bring their inhabitants and the dwellers therein to the worship of our Redeemer and to belief in the Catholic Faith, but have been so much occupied hitherto by the conquest and recovery of the kingdom of Granada, that you have been unable to carry through, to its desired end, this holy and laudable purpose. At last, however, it has pleased God that you have recovered the kingdom aforesaid: and in your desire to fulfil your purpose, and have appointed our beloved son, Christopher Columbus, a man well worthy, well spoken of, and well fit for the said business, together with ships and crew well trained for it, and have done so not without great toil, danger, and expense, that he may diligently search for lands and islands, far distant and unknown beyond the seas, where hitherto no one has sailed.

§ 2. These, at last, have by divine aid discovered certain islands and lands, inhabited by several peoples who live peaceably there; go about naked, so it is said; and do not eat flesh . . . believe in one God the Creator; and seem disposed to embrace the Catholic Faith and to live moral lives; and there is good hope that, if they are taught, the name of our Lord and Saviour Jesus Christ will be confessed among them. Further, the aforesaid Christopher, in one of the principal islands aforesaid, has built a fort, and put certain of the Christians who went with him in charge thereof, that they might

discover other remote and unknown islands and lands.

§ 3. In the islands and lands already discovered, gold, spices, and all other sorts of things have been discovered.

§ 4. Whence, all things considered, and more especially the exaltation and extension of the Catholic Faith, you, as behoves Catholic Kings and Princes . . . propose to subject and reduce them to the Catholic Faith.

§ 5. We therefore . . . approving your holy and laudable purpose . . . exhort you . . . to bring these people to the Christian Religion, and to let no pains and labours deter you . . . being confident that God Almighty will prosper your efforts.

§ 6. And, in order that you, being endowed with the gift of apostolic grace, may the more freely and boldly enter upon the province of so vast an enterprise, we . . . by the authority of Almighty God bestowed upon us in blessed Peter, and of the Vicariate of Jesus Christ which we exercise upon earth, do by the tenor of these presents grant and assign to you all islands and lands, discovered or still to be discovered . . . towards the west and south, by the making and construction of a line to be drawn from the arctic or north pole to the antarctic or south pole (whether these lands or islands, discovered now or in the future look toward India or any other region): such line to be distant from the Azores and the Cape Verde Islands, as they are called, one hundred leagues towards the west and south, i.e., all such islands and lands west and south of the aforesaid line as are not actually in possession of any other Christian King or Prince before Christmas 1493. . . . These, with all their dominions, cities, camps, places, and villages, rights, jurisdictions and all things pertaining thereto, we do grant and assign to you, your heirs and successors aforesaid, in perpetuity; and we constitute you, your heirs and successors, lords thereof, with full, free, and entire power, authority and jurisdiction.

§ 7 . . . Further, we command you, in virtue of the holy obedience which you promised . . . to send to the said lands and islands good men who fear God and are learned, skilled, and expert, to instruct the inhabitants in the Catholic Faith and good morals, and to use all diligence therein.

§ 8. And we strictly prohibit any person of whatsoever dignity—be it even imperial or royal—

under pain of excommunication . . . from visiting these islands and lands for trade or any other cause, without the special licence of you and your heirs and successors aforesaid.—K.

(Source: *Documents Illustrative of the History of the Early Church,* vol. 1, ed. B. J. Kidd [London: SPCK, 1920]; and *Documents Illustrative of the History of the Early Church,* vol. 3, ed. B. J. Kidd [London: SPCK, 1928].)

24. *The Only Way,* by Bartolomé de Las Casas

In this work from the early sixteenth century, de Las Casas showed himself a pioneer both in observing the life of indigenous Americans and in addressing the question of the basis of responsible Christian witness.

Prologue: The Humanity of the Indians

It was due to the will and work of Christ, the head of the Church, that God's chosen should be called, should be culled from every race, every tribe, every language, every corner of the world. Thus, no race, no nation on this entire globe would be left totally untouched by the free gift of divine grace. Some among them, be they few or many, are to be taken into eternal life. We must hold this to be true also of our Indian nations. [They are as called as we.] . . .

The reason is, they are all human beings. Their minds are very quick, alive, capable, clear. This mind comes to them primarily from the will of God who wished to make them so. Then, secondarily, it comes from the fostering influence of the heavens, from the kind conditions of the places God gave them to live in, the fair and clement weather. For most of the Indies have land that is dry, land that is open, spacious, level, pleasant, fertile, and in fine locations. The hills, valleys, mountains, plains are uncluttered; they are free of stagnant pools; they are blanketed with aromatic plants, medicinal herbs of all kinds, and commonplace charmers spread everywhere so all the fields are smiling. Every morning they breathe a scent which lasts until noonday, a scent that delights and strengthens a traveler's soul. They

are a consolation. Both mountains and trees are lofty throughout the region, at least between the two tropics, the stretch of forty-five degrees to either side of the equator, to use nautical terms. They are huge, imposing. And it is a fact that often, for a man to be able to gauge their size, he has to throw his head back the way he must when he wants to look at the pitch of the sky. There is an experience which surely indicates the temperate nature of the region, its even, gentle, wholesome, delightful climate. When ships come from Spain and begin to raise the first islands or any of the coast of Tierra Firme, people aboard ship sense a marvelous fragrance, fresh smells coming offshore. It is as if rose flowers were right there present to them. . . .

Next, this condition of mind comes to them from the fine state of their bodies and sense organs, the inward, the outward, from sound and healthy nourishment, from the excellent sanitary conditions of the land, the habitations, the air of each place, from the people's temperance and moderation in food and drink, from the state of their sensual passions—calm, quiet, controlled—from the lack of upset and anxiety—their habitual state—about those worldly affairs which elicit the passions of the soul—pleasure, love, anger, grief—and even after being disturbed, for the things that passions do and the effects they cause. . . .

Then too there exist extraordinary kingdoms among our Indians who live in the regions west and south from us. There are large groupings of human beings who live according to a political and a social order. There are large cities, there are kings, judges, laws, all within civilizations where commerce occurs, buying and selling and lending and all the other dealings proper to the law of nations. That is to say, their republics are properly set up, they are seriously run according to a fine body of law, there is religion, there are institutions. And our Indians cultivate friendship and they live in lifegiving ways in large cities. They manage their affairs in them with goodness and equity, affairs of peace as well as war. They run their governments according to laws that are often superior to our own. . . .

The quality of their minds is seen finally in superb artifacts, finely, beautifully fashioned, fashioned by hand. They are so skilled in the practical arts that their reputation should place them well ahead of the rest of the known world, and rightly so.

The practical things these people make are striking for their art and elegance, utensils that are charmingly done, feather work, lace work. Mind does this. The practical arts result from a basic power of mind—a power we define as knowledge of how to do things the right way, a planning power that guides the various decisions the artisan makes so he acts in an ordered and economical fashion and does not err as he thinks his way along. . . .

And in the liberal and allied arts, to date, these people offer no less an indication of sound intelligence. They make objects that are high art and with a genius that awes everyone. The genius of an artist shows in the art work. It is as the poet says: "The work applauds its maker." Prosper remarks in one of his Epigrams: "It must be so, that an author shows in the fine things he has written. They sing praise to their maker."

The Indians are highly skilled also in the arts we educate ourselves to, the Indians we have taught thus far: grammar, logic. And they charm the ear of an audience with every kind of music, remarkable beauty. Their handwriting is skillful and lovely, such that one cannot tell often if the letters are handwritten or printed. . . . I have seen all this with my own eyes, touched it with my own hands, heard it with my own ears, over the long time I passed among those peoples. . . .

Due to all these influences—the broad/celestial, the narrow/terrestrial, the essential/accidental— the Indians come to be endowed, first by force of nature, next by force of personal achievement and experience, with the three kinds of self-rule required: (1) personal, by which one knows how to rule oneself, (2) domestic, by which one knows how to rule a household, and (3) political, knowledge of how to set up and rule a city.

Their political rule presupposes fully developed personal and domestic elements, i.e., farmers, artisans, soldiery, wealthy people; religion, temples, priests, sacrifices; judges and agents of justice; governors; customs; and throughout, everything touched by qualities of mind and will . . . their society is the equal of that of many nations in the world renowned for being politically astute. They surpass many another. They are inferior to none. Those they equal are the Greeks and Romans. And in a good many customs they outdo, they surpass the Greeks and Romans. They surpass the English, the French, and some groups in our native Spain. In the possession of good customs, in the lack of bad ones, they are superior to so many other peoples that these latter do not merit comparison to our Indians.

All of this stands clearly proven and explained. Our comparisons show that in the entire world, in the old days of paganism, there were countless peoples who were much less rational in their use of mind than our Indians, peoples who had customs far more horrible, vices far more depraved. That conclusion is enough to confound those who have so rashly, perhaps unforgivably, defamed our Indians, to make those defamers ashamed in and for themselves, to make them admit their error. . . . And all those who know of them should consider them false witnesses. The more so because, as we have seen through comparison and contrast, the Indians are and were ahead of others—many, many others—more ordered in their use of mind, more ordered in their use of will, with less of the taint of malice and malignancy.

Since all these Indian peoples, excepting none in the vast world of that hemisphere, universally have good and natural intelligence, have ready wills, they thus can be drawn to and taught a complete and sound morality, and more so to our Christian belief, even though some peoples in some places have not yet developed political maturity, an ordered body politic, the kind we said many possessed. And some have certain corrupt customs. But these are curable finally with human effort, and more so, better so, with the preaching of the gospel.

It is clear as clear can be that the nations of our Indies fall into [a special category of infidels]. They have and hold their realms, their lands, by natural law and by the law of nations. They owe allegiance to no one higher than themselves, outside themselves, neither de jure nor de facto. We find them in possession of their countries, with plenty of princes over plenty of principalities having great numbers of people, people who serve and obey their lords and masters, while the latter exercise full authority over their people without hindrance, exercise full power in large and in small, so no one would have the legitimate right to seize their power, or their realms, so distant from our own, so far from harming us or our Church or our Catholic faith or any member thereof. They are of the fourth kind of

71

infidels [faraway non-hostile pagans], no one can doubt it.

Cajetan spoke of this fourth kind of infidel more clearly and distinctly than of the other three when commenting on Thomas Aquinas, Summa Theologiae, Secunda Secundae, q. 66, art. 8, especially when he said as follows:

> There are some pagans who . . . have never been under Christian rule, who live in lands never reached by the name of Christ. Their rulers, though they are pagans, are legitimate authorities, whether they govern in a monarchy or a republic. They are not to be deprived of their authority because of their pagan belonging. Such authority is a matter of positive law. Divine law deals with pagan belief. Divine law does not invalidate positive law. I know of no law abrogating their temporal possessions. No king, no emperor, not the Roman Church itself, can make war on them for the purpose of occupying their territory or subjecting them to temporal rule. There is no just cause for such a war. The reason: Jesus Christ, the King of Kings (to whom all power is given in heaven and on earth) did not send armed soldiery to take possession of the earth but holy men, preachers, sent sheep among wolves.

Further on [Cajetan] says:

> So we would sin mortally if we sought to spread the faith of Christ by way of war. We would not be the legitimate rulers of the conquered, we would have committed a mighty theft, we would be held to restitution for being unjust aggressors in an unjust occupation. (*Doce dudas,* Second Principle, 3rd par.)

So let us turn now to explaining the way, the natural, overall, single, and settled way of calling God's chosen, God's elect, to the faith of Christ, of inviting them into the Christian way of life.

The Only Way: Winning the Mind and Soul

One way, one way only, of teaching a living faith, to everyone, everywhere, always, was set by Divine Providence: the way that wins the mind with reasons, that wins the will with gentleness, with invitation. It has to fit all people on earth, no distinction made for sect, for error, even for evil.

Many proofs support this thesis: proofs from reason, from the practice of the patriarchs, from the once-and-for-all way of preaching willed by Christ, from the practice of the apostles and the procedures they ordered, from the teachings of Church Doctors, the ancient Church customs, the long list of Church decrees.

First from reason, a crucial proof. One, only one way is characteristic of Divine Wisdom in its care for creatures, in its leading of them to fulfill their natural purposes—a gentle, coaxing, gracious way. Among creatures, the rational one is the higher, of more worth than the rest. The rest are not made in the image of God. Divine Providence cares for the rational creature in a special way, for itself. It cares for others for the sake of the rational creature. So Divine Wisdom leads the rational creature, the human, to fulfill its natural purpose in a gentle, coaxing, gracious way. But it is a teaching of the faith that people be called to, be led to a living faith under the universal command as it is stated in Matthew 28:19-20: "Go teach all nations, baptizing them in the name of the Father, and of the Son, and of the Holy Spirit, teaching them to obey all that I have commanded you." And Paul to the Romans (10:17): "Faith comes from hearing, hearing from the word of Christ." Therefore the way of teaching people has to be a gentle, coaxing, gracious way. It wins the mind with reasons, it wins the will with graciousness. So, one way, one way only, of teaching a living faith, to everyone, everywhere, always, was set by Divine Providence, a way that wins the mind with reasons, that wins the will with gentleness, with invitation.

The major premise is clear: Divine Wisdom cares for all its creatures, not just by leading them to fulfill their natural purposes, but also by endowing them with inner powers, with potentialities which are at the source of performance, so they would be able to act on their own initiative as well. Thus actions invited by God are actions native to creatures, consonant with them; they flow easily. Creatures possess the sources of response within themselves. For that reason their responses are natural and easy, the way gravity affects a stone, so it tends to fall naturally, easily.

In a certain sense, creatures are not just led to fulfill their purposes, they do so of themselves, as if the movement originates within. For this reason Wisdom 8:1 says that Divine Wisdom "reaches the whole of creation with its power." That is, it runs all things perfectly. As the gloss puts it: "It provides for everything smoothly."

So each creature moves toward what Divine Wisdom wants for it by means of a nature divinity gives it, according to the leaning built into nature. It is the goodness in God from which all natures

flow . . . so every creature has in it a power to want goodness due to the imprint of its Creator upon it. Goodness means fulfillment because each thing's activity is normed by its goal, the activity being one perfection, the fulfillment being a second. We call something good and virtuous when it acts harmoniously with itself, and thus with the goal set for it by God, in God's own way. And so, in creation, there is a certain circularity: goodness going out, goodness coming back.

(Source: Bartolomé de Las Casas, *The Only Way*, ed. Helen Rand Parish, trans. Francis Patrick Sullivan [Mahwah, N.J.: Paulist Press, 1992], 63-69.)

The Chinese Rites Controversy

25. *Decree of the Sacred Congregation for the Propagation of the Faith, September 12, 1645*

(Introduced by Ray R. Noll) *This document from the Congregation for the Propagation of the Faith, approved by Pope Innocent X, was the first judgment by Rome on the Rites Controversy. Seventeen propositions were presented to Propaganda by Juan Morales, O.P., against the mission practices of the Jesuits. These propositions were forwarded to the theologians of the Holy Office for judgment. Using only the information provided by Morales, who presuming the rites to be religious describes them in religious terminology, the Holy Office judges in favor of Morales and condemns the practices of the Jesuits. [CPF(1893)#1698]*

Questions of China missionaries. The following propositions, sent to the Holy Office by the Sacred Congregation for the Propagation of the Faith, were evaluated as follows by experts of the Holy Office:

6. Among the peoples and cities of China there is a custom of imposing certain collections, to which the people in each neighborhood are asked to contribute. These are spent in the celebration of the New Year, in sacrifices, in the worship of their

pagan deities, in extending invitations, in preparing banquets in their temples, likewise in festivities, and in other things, neither good nor bad, to express the people's joy. The question is, may Christians and their ministers, at least for now, contribute to things of this sort? They do ask these contributions from the missionaries, just as from people in the neighborhood. If Christians do not contribute, the pagans will cause trouble for the Christians.

They decided that Chinese Christians could contribute money, so long as through such contributions they do not intend to concur in idolatrous and superstitious acts. That is supposing the case is as described in the question. Especially may they contribute if they declare beforehand (supposing this can be done conveniently) that they are paying the imposed tax only so the people can have a good time, only for activities that are amoral, or at least are not incompatible with the practice of the Christian religion.

7. In all the cities and towns of China you can find temples built and dedicated to a certain idol named Chim Noam [*Cheng Huang*]. The Chinese believe it is the protector, ruler, and guardian of the city. An established law of China ordains that all the governors of cities and towns (they call them mandarins), when they take office, and twice a month throughout the year, must go to these temples, and there, kneeling before the altar of this idol, and,

bowing their head all the way to the ground, adore and venerate it. They are to offer it candles, incense, flowers, meats, and wine in sacrifice. When they take office, they are to take an oath before this idol about governing rightly. If they should do otherwise, they submit themselves to punishment to be inflicted by the idol. At the same time they ask it to show them how to govern well, and other things like this.

The question is: Whether, keeping in mind the ignorance of the Chinese, Christian governors could at present bring a crucifix which they would hide in the flowers around the idols, on the altar or hold in their hands. (Their intention would then be directed not to the idol, but to the crucifix). While making all those genuflections, reverences, and adorations before the altar, outwardly they would be just pretending, but inwardly, in their heart, they would be directing those acts of worship to the crucifix. If these governors are not allowed to do this, they will apostatize from our faith rather than relinquish their government office.

They decided that Christians may publicly pretend to worship and venerate the idol, with their intention directed to the crucifix which they either hold in their hand or hide in the flowers on the altar.

8. The Chinese have a teacher learned in moral philosophy. He died a long time ago. His name was Confucius. He is known all over China for his teaching, his rules, his writings. Kings and all others, whatever their condition or social level may be, regard him as someone to imitate and follow, at least as a philosopher. They venerate and praise him as a saint. In every city and town temples are built in his honor.

Twice a year governors are required to offer a solemn sacrifice in his temple. They themselves function as priests. Twice a month in the course of the year they are required to sacrifice without solemnity. Some scholars flock to him for help. Here are the things they offer in sacrifice: a whole slain pig, a whole she-goat, candles, wine, flowers, incense, etc. All scholars, when they receive their degree, have to enter the temple of Confucius, genuflect, and make an offering of candles and incense before his altar.

All that liturgy—the sacrifice, the reverence—is formally intended by the Chinese as thanksgiving

for the good teaching that he has left them in his writings. It is to ask of him through his merits the blessings of talent, wisdom, and intelligence.

The question is: Whether those who are or will be Christian governors and scholars, when they are summoned, may go into Confucius' temple, offer or assist at such a sacrifice, genuflect before the altar, partake of something from those idolatrous sacrifices and oblations. The pagans believe that whoever eats something from those sacrifices will make great progress in his studies and degrees.

Could they be allowed to do this, as was spelled out in the preceding question, carrying a crucifix in their hands? If they are forbidden to do this, the people will riot. Missionaries will be exiled. It will be hard to make converts. Conversions may stop altogether.

The decision: It cannot be allowed. As the case is presented, Christians may not pretend to participate.

9. The Chinese have a religiously observed custom, a teaching handed down by Confucius. Everywhere in China temples are built and dedicated to grandparents and ancestors. In every one of them members of the same family gather twice a year. With great display of ceremony they offer solemn sacrifices to their ancestors. They place a picture or statue of their deceased parents or grandparents on the altar beautifully adorned with candles, flowers, and incense. Present at this sacrifice is one who acts as priest, and his assistants. They offer meats, wine, candles, incense, goats' heads, etc.

What the Chinese intend by this sacrifice is to render thanks to their ancestors. It is to show reverence for the good things received from them, and for the good things they hope to receive from them. Prostrate before their altar they say many prayers, asking for health, a long life, abundant harvests, large families, economic success, and to be delivered from all evils. This sacrifice also takes place in their homes, and at the cemeteries, but with less solemnity.

The question is: Could Christians pretend outwardly, as was said above, to assist at such a sacrifice? Could they join with the pagans playing an active part in such sacrifice—in a temple, at home, at the cemetery, publicly, privately? How can Christians be permitted to do this? If they are absolutely forbidden to do this, they will lose the faith. Or, to put it more precisely, they will stop acting like Christians.

The decision: In no way may Chinese Christians pretend outwardly to assist at sacrifices honoring ancestors. They may not join in prayers, or in any superstitious heathen rites for them. Much less may they take any active part in such rites.

10. Chinese Christians maintain that in these oblations their only intention is to show their deceased ancestors the same reverence they would show if they were still alive. It is just a memorial service, showing reverence to those who have passed life on to their descendants. What is offered them is what would be given them if they were alive—food to eat and sustain them. They have no other intention in offering these things, no hope of retribution, since they know they are dead, and their souls are in the hereafter.

The question is: If these ceremonies were to take place among Christians alone—i.e., without the pressure of pagans—in temples, in homes, in cemeteries, putting a crucifix on the altar of the deceased, directing their intention to it in such a way that they offer nothing to the ancestors' image except the filial honor and reverence which, if they were alive, they would offer them to eat and to smell, and so satisfy their fellow citizens—could this be tolerated for the present, to avoid trouble?

The decision: In conformity with what was said above, the proposed way of acting cannot be justified either by use of the crucifix, or by absence of the pagans, or by an intention directing actions intrinsically illicit and superstitious to worship of the true God.

11. To preserve the memory of their ancestors the Chinese use tablets on which are written the names of their deceased. They call these the places where their souls dwell. They believe the souls of their dead come and are present in the tablets to receive the sacrifices and offerings. These tablets are placed on their own altars with roses, candles, lamps, and incense. Before these tablets they kneel down, pray, and expect help from those dead persons in their needs and labors.

The question is: If the Christians put aside all the pagan superstitions and errors, would it be permissible for them to use these tablets for the time being? Could they put them with images of the Lord's saints, on the same altar, or on another separate altar decorated as stated above—and so, satisfy the pagans? Could they pray and sacrifice with the intention explained earlier?

The decision: In no way are they allowed to keep those tablets on a true and proper altar dedicated to their ancestors. Much less may they offer them prayers and sacrifices, even with a hidden and feigned intention.

12. When someone dies in China, whether he is a Christian or a pagan, the religiously observed custom is to prepare an altar in the home of the deceased, and put on it an image of the deceased, or a tablet as described above, decorating it with incense, flowers, and candles, and laying the corpse behind it in a coffin. All who enter those homes to mourn genuflect three or four times before the decorated altar and the image of the deceased. They lie flat, their heads touching the floor. They carry candles and incense to burn on the decorated altar before the image of the deceased.

The question: Is it permissible for Christians, and especially for ministers of the holy Gospel, keeping in mind that this is a reciprocal sign of love and good will, to do these things, especially when the deceased are more prominent persons?

The decision: This can be tolerated as long as the table is an ordinary piece of furniture and not a true altar, and if the actions performed are within the bounds of civil and political compliance.

13. *The question:* Should we missionaries tell catechumens who are already prepared for baptism, should we teach them openly and in detail that the sacrifices, and all the things maintained above are illicit, even though troubles may follow from this: for example, withdrawing from the reception of Baptism, persecutions, death or exile for missionaries?

The decision: Missionaries are obliged to teach that all sacrifices except those that are offered to God are illicit. Worship of demons and idols must be abandoned. Every sort of worship which they all agree is false and incompatible with Christian faith will be given up. As for details, this depends on how ready the catechumens are. Circumstances, customs, and dangers must be kept in mind.

In the Chinese language the word *Xing* [*Sheng*] is the same as *holy*. In books of Christian doctrine that have been printed by some missionaries, that word *Xing* refers to the Holy Trinity, to Christ, to the Blessed Virgin, and to the saints.

The question: In books it is sometimes necessary to mention Confucius, who is called the Teacher of the Chinese, or a commandment of a Chinese ruler, or other rulers who in China are widely regarded as holy. These are unbelievers and idol worshippers. Is it permissible for us Christian missionaries to call them *Xing*?

The decision: Nothing can be stated about this word and its use until we know the idiom, and the true and proper meaning of the word. If the word has a broad meaning among the Chinese, missionaries can use it. But, if the word is restricted to meaning true and perfect holiness, missionaries cannot use it.

15. In many idols' temples in China a golden tablet is placed on a table or altar adorned with candles, roses, incense. On this tablet are written these words: "May the ruler of China live for many thousands of years." The idolaters are accustomed to offer sacrifice two or three times a year before this tablet, and to genuflect, honoring and reverencing it.

The question: Can we Christian missionaries put an altar of this kind in our churches, with the tablet, and other things mentioned above—and this in the presence of the altar where God's priests offer the holy Sacrifice?

The decision: As long as there are no sacrifices, and no altar strictly so called, the other things, which merely suggest civil honor, or can be reduced to it, are permissible.

His Eminence, Cardinal Ginetto, returned the questions as listed above along with the answers and decisions of the committee of theologians specially formed to examine these questions. The Cardinals of the Sacred Congregation for the Propagation of the Faith approved these answers and decisions. At the request of this Congregation, His Holiness strictly ordered each and every missionary to obey these answers and decisions diligently, to put them into practice, and to see to it that they are observed and practiced by others who are involved. He did this to keep our preaching and practice uniform. His precept is binding on missionaries of every order, religion, and institute, even the Society of Jesus, those now living in China, and those destined for China. This directive holds good until His Holiness or the Holy See will have ordained otherwise.

(Source: *100 Roman Documents Relating to the Chinese Rites Controversy [1645-1941],* trans. Donald F. St. Sure, S.J., ed. with introductions and summaries by Ray Noll [San Francisco: Ricci Institute for Chinese-Western Cultural History, University of San Francisco Center for the Pacific Rim, 1992].)

26. *Apostolic Constitution,* Ex illa die, *by Clement XI, March 19, 1715, as found in* Ex quo singulari *of Benedict XIV, July 11, 1742*

10. Precept of Pope Clement XI about complete, absolute, integral, and inviolable observance of what was elsewhere decreed by His Holiness in the case of the Chinese Rites or ceremonies. He rejects all alleged reasons or excuses for refusing to carry out these decrees. He prescribes an oath formula to be taken by those who how are or will be missionaries in those areas.

Pope Clement XI, lest we forget. In spite of our unworthiness, we, because God wanted it so, undertook the piloting of the Catholic Church. This is a burden very heavy because so far-reaching, and very challenging because of the evil times. In taking charge of the helm, what was the first thing we put our hand to? To end the bitter disagreements that had already started between the China missionaries. These disagreements were day by day always becoming more strident. They had to do with certain Chinese words used there to express the holy, inexpressible name of God. They also had to do with certain rites performed by the Chinese people. Some missionaries disapprove of these as being superstitions. Others, however, saying that they are merely civil, permit them. We hope that Our judgment will bring a happy halt to these disagreements. These disagreements are impeding the spread of the Christian religion and the Catholic faith. When they are ended, all can agree, saying the same thing. Thinking the same, and saying the same, they will glorify God. They have been sanctified in Christ Jesus.

With this in mind, we on November 20, 1704,

confirmed and approved those replies that were given to various questions raised about these matters. First there was a long investigation. That was a while ago, begun namely at the time of our Predecessor of happy memory, Pope Innocent XII. It was then continued for several years at Our command. Arguments of the opposing sides were heard. Also heard were the opinions of many theologians and experts. Also, heard was the Congregation of our Venerable Brothers, Cardinals of the Holy Roman Church, by Papal Authority appointed Inquisitors General against heresy throughout all of Christendom.

The following were decreed in these responses: The name of God cannot be suitably expressed among the Chinese by European words. The word *Tien Chu*, i.e., Lord of Heaven, should be allowed in referring to God. It is recognized by Chinese missionaries, and is established by long and approved use among the faithful. But the names *Tien* (Heaven) and *Xang Ti* (Supreme Emperor) are to be completely rejected.

Tables with the Chinese inscription *King Tien* (Caelum colito [Worship Heaven]) are not to be permitted in Christian churches. Where they have already been displayed they are not to be kept there in the future.

Christians should not be permitted to preside, to serve, or to be present at the solemn sacrifices or oblations which Chinese customarily make to Confucius and to deceased ancestors at the Spring and Autumnal Equinox every year. These ceremonies are tainted with superstition.

Likewise, Christians should not be permitted to perform the ceremonies, rites, and oblations which take place in shrines of Confucius which are called by the Chinese name *Miao*. These ceremonies, rites, and oblations are offered in honor of Confucius every month at the new moon and the full moon. They are offered by the mandarins, or chief magistrates, and other officials, and scholars. They are offered by the mandarins, or governors and magistrates before they take office, or at least after taking office. Finally, they are offered by students, who after receiving their degree, immediately betake themselves to a temple or shrine of Confucius.

Besides, Christians should not be permitted to offer the less solemn oblations to their ancestors in the temples or shrines dedicated to them. They should not be permitted to minister or to serve at them in any way, or perform other rites and ceremonies.

Likewise, Christians should not be permitted to perform oblations, rites, and ceremonies customarily enacted to honor ancestors before their tablets. They should not be permitted to serve or to be present at them. This prohibition holds both for private homes and for the tombs of ancestors. It holds before the deceased are handed over for burial. It holds whether these ceremonies are performed together with pagans or apart from them.

All these questions that were raised were pondered from every angle, discussed diligently and at length. It was found that they are carried out in such a way that they cannot be separated from superstition. That is why they cannot be permitted to Christians, not even if they openly or secretly make a prior avowal that they are not conferring any religious honor on the dead, but only civil and political, and that they are not asking or hoping for anything from them.

This is not meant to condemn merely material presence. While pagans perform superstitious actions, one could be a by-stander, giving no approval inwardly or outwardly of what is being done, taking no active part. It may sometimes be necessary for Christians to be present at superstitious actions in this way, otherwise hatreds and hostilities could not be avoided. However, if it can be done conveniently, they should first profess their faith, and be sure there is no danger of undermining it.

Finally, Christians must not be permitted to keep tablets of deceased ancestors in their own homes. The custom in that country is to keep them with a Chinese inscription indicating the throne or abode of the spirit or soul of so-and-so. The same prohibition holds even if the designation is made with a shorter inscription.

As regards tablets inscribed with only the name of the deceased, their use can be tolerated so long as in making them everything smacking of superstition is left out, and provided there is no scandal. This means, so long as non-Christians would not be able to think that these tablets are kept by Christians with the same understanding as they keep them. Also, there should be a statement at the side of these tablets explaining clearly what Christians believe about the dead, and what devotion children and grandchildren should have toward their ancestors.

Nevertheless, what has been said so far does not prevent performance of other rites in honor of the dead. That is supposing there are other rites customarily performed by the pagans which really are not superstitious, and do not look superstitious, but are within the limits of civil and political rites.

What these rites are, and with what precautions they can be tolerated, must be left to the judgment of whoever is Commissioner and Visitor General Apostolic, or whoever takes his place in China. Also to the judgment of the bishops and vicars apostolic in that part of the world. In the meantime, however, they should take care, with all the zeal and diligence they can, to do away with these pagan rites entirely. Gradually the rites, which the Catholic Church has devoutly prescribed for the dead, should become the practice of the Christians for Christians.

After about six years, namely on September 25, 1710, We decreed and declared that these replies should be observed exactly and scrupulously by each and every person concerned. We did this after again hearing the opinion of the Cardinals who discussed the matter lengthily and very diligently. We also decreed strict observance of the mandate or decree issued January 25, 1707, by Charles Thomas of happy memory. While he was alive, he was called Cardinal de Tournon of the Holy Roman Church. At that time he was Patriarch of Antioch, Commissioner and Visitor Apostolic General in China. His decree was completely in agreement with the replies of the other Cardinals. We wanted their replies and his decree to be obeyed under the censures and penalties spelled out in his mandate or decree. There was to be no excuse or pretext whatever. No appeal made to Us and to the Holy See was to stand in the way, no matter by whom made. We therefore decree that any such appeal was to be rejected forthwith, and in fact We rejected it, as can be read at greater length in the decree issued about this matter.

These decrees should have been enough to uproot from that field the weeds shown by the enemy. All the faithful would then be observing with due humility and obedience Our commands, and those of the Holy See. Especially since at the end of the aforesaid responses, confirmed and approved by Us, as is said above, it was stated clearly and unmistakably that the case was now closed.

We were sorry to hear from China that many for a long period of time are often evading or, at least, delaying too long the execution of these replies that We so earnestly prescribed. This is not without grave damage to Our pontifical authority, scandal to the faithful, and detriment to the salvation of souls. This is on the false and empty excuse that We suspended the decisions or that We did not properly promulgate them. It wrongly asserts that the conditions laid down in them, conditions that had to be verified before the decisions were carried out, and the facts on which the decisions were based were not verified. It is offered as an excuse that further declarations are to be made by Us in this regard. Fear is expressed that great danger would befall both the missionaries and the mission itself if the decrees were carried out. Finally, recourse is had to the decree issued a long time ago, namely on March 23, 1656, concerning these Chinese rites or ceremonies. It was issued by a Congregation of Cardinals, as stated above, and approved by Pope Alexander VII and also by Our Predecessor.

In fulfillment of the duty of apostolic service God has entrusted to Us, We want to wipe out completely and end these difficulties, delays, evasions, and excuses. As far as God lets Us, We want to provide peace for the faithful and salvation for souls. Therefore, with the advice of the Cardinals, as also on Our own initiative, and with sure knowledge and mature deliberation on our part and with the fullness of Our apostolic power, we intend by this present Constitution, and in virtue of holy obedience We command that each and every one of the previously spelled out responses and every thing contained in them be observed exactly, totally, absolutely, inviolably, and firmly. This obligation is enjoined on each and every archbishop and bishop in China and adjoining countries and provinces.

It is enjoined on those who are there now and on those who will be there at some future time. It is enjoined under suspension from exercise of the episcopacy and interdict from entering a church. It is enjoined on their officials and vicars general in spiritual matters, and other ordinaries in those places. It is also enjoined on vicars apostolic who are not bishops and on their provicars. It is enjoined on missionaries, both secular and religious of any order, congregation, institute, and society—even the Society of Jesus. It is enjoined under automatic excommunication. No one, except at the point of death, can be absolved from this excommunication by anyone except by Us, or whomever is Roman Pontiff at the time.

As regards religious, they are also to be deprived of active and passive voice. Transgressors are to incur these penalties automatically, without any further declaration. Their superiors are to do everything they can to see that these directives are carried out. They must not in any way dare or presume to act contrary to these directives. Nothing that was said above can justify such conduct. There can be no other reason, motive, exigency, excuse, or pretext for not conforming.

Moreover, We by this Constitution decree and ordain that each and every ecclesiastic now living or destined to live in China, or other aforesaid kingdoms and provinces, should and is obliged to swear that he will observe this precept and mandate of Ours faithfully, integrally, and inviolably. We are doing this of our own volition, with equal knowledge, deliberation, and fullness of power. This is under pain of reserved excommunication, and privation of active and passive voice. It applies both to secular and to religious of the aforesaid orders, congregations, institutes and societies—even the Society of Jesus. It includes those who have been sent, and those who at some future time will be sent, either by this Holy See, or by their own superiors. It includes those who are now living there, or who will live there in the future, no matter what title or faculty they may have. Those who have been sent are obligated as soon as this present Constitution becomes known to them. Those who are going to be sent must take the oath before they begin to perform any missionary activity there. The formula for the oath may be found at the end of this present Constitution.

After taking and signing the oath, they are to hand it to whoever is at the time commissioner and Apostolic Visitor in China, or to his delegate, or, if he is not available, to the bishop or vicar apostolic in whose jurisdiction they are living, or will be living, or to others delegated by them. Religious, however, are to hand it to the superiors of their order, or to their delegates living in the same area.

Each one who takes this oath is to sign it with his own signature. Before doing so no one is to undertake or continue any missionary activity.

This holds for those appointed by bishops or local ordinaries. It holds for simple religious order priests. It holds no matter what other title, cause, or privilege they may have, calling for explicit and special mention. They may not in any way hear confessions of the faithful, preach, or administer sacraments. They may not use any faculties, whether granted to them personally, or granted in general by the Holy See to their respective orders, congregations, institutions, and societies—even the Society of Jesus. But over and beyond, the penalties mentioned above, each and every aforesaid faculty ceases completely. They are utterly worthless, and are to be so reckoned.

Religious superiors of every order, congregation, institute, and society—even the Society of Jesus—the ones who are there now, and those who will be there at some future time—are obliged to take the same oath. They are then obliged to deliver its signed formula, as was said above, either to whoever is commissioner and apostolic visitor at the time, or to the bishops, or vicars apostolic. They must also see to it that their subjects do the same. They must then as soon as possible send authentic records of this transaction to their respective superiors general. These must immediately turn over to the Congregation of Cardinals spoken of above. Decreeing etc. . . . Notwithstanding etc. . . .

The formula for the oath to be taken, as is stated above, is as follows, namely: *I (Name), missionary to China, or to the Kingdom of (Name), or to the Province of (Name), sent or destined by the Holy See, or by my superiors, according to faculties granted them by the Holy See, will fully and faithfully obey the precept and apostolic mandate about the Chinese rites and ceremonies contained in the Constitution issued about this matter by His Holiness, Clement XI, by Divine Providence Pope. This Constitution prescribed the formula for this oath. I will observe the papal decree exactly, absolutely, and inviolably. I will fulfill it without any hesitation. It is well known to me; I have carefully read Clement XI's Constitution.*

But if (God forbid!) I should in any way transgress, as often as that happens, I acknowledge and declare that I am subject to the penalties imposed by the aforesaid Constitution. With my hand on the holy Gospels, I so promise, now, and swear. So help me God, and these Holy Gospels of God.

Moreover, it is Our wish and We expressly command that this Constitution, or copies of it, even printed copies, be brought to the attention of each and every member of the above-mentioned orders, congregations, Institutes, and societies—even the Society of Jesus. We want it brought to the attention of the superiors general, and the procurators general. We want them to promise in their own name and in the name of their respective subjects to faithfully carry out and obey the Constitution. We want them to send back a written record that such a promise has been made.

In all sorts of ways they should, as quickly as possible, send to their subjects living in China and in other kingdoms and provinces copies of this Constitution. They should command them very sternly to carry out and obey this Constitution, and everything in it, fully and integrally, and truly, really, and executing it in and through its every detail.

It would be difficult for the original of a written document like this to be displayed everywhere before the public. Therefore, it is Our wish and decree that transcripts of it, or copies, even printed ones be given the same credibility as would be accorded the present document if it were brought out for inspection. Such copies should bear the signature of some notary public, and the seal of a person holding an ecclesiastical office. They should then be honored both in and out of court.

Given at Rome in the Church of St. Mary Major under the sign of the Fisherman, March 19, 1715—the fourteenth year of Our Pontificate.

(Source: *100 Roman Documents Concerning the Chinese Rites Controversy [1645-1941]*, trans. Donald F. St. Sure, S.J., ed. with introductions and summaries by Ray Noll [San Francisco: Ricci Institute for Chinese-Western Cultural History, University of San Francisco Center for the Pacific Rim, 1992].)

27. Plane compertum est, December 8, 1939, approved by Pope Pius XII

(Introduction by Ray R. Noll) *An instruction of Propaganda Fide,* Plane compertum est, *was approved by Pius XII, bringing to an official end the Chinese Rites Controversy in four brief articles. The Instruction states that*

the honors paid to Confucius are not religious acts taken in themselves, but rather civil honors and therefore Christians may honor Confucius in this way; that it is lawful and upright to observe toward deceased ancestors the traditional civil observances, and that all clergy are dispensed from the obligation to take the Ex quo singulari *oath. [AAS, Vol. 32 (1940), pp. 24-26]*

The Sacred Congregation for the Propagation of the Faith, Instruction concerning Certain Ceremonies and the Oath about the Chinese Rites

Everyone knows that some ceremonies in Oriental countries, although in earlier times they were tied in with pagan rites, now that customs and minds have changed with the flow of the centuries, merely preserve civil expression of devotion toward ancestors, or of patriotism, or of respect for fellow countrymen.

That is why this Congregation for Propagating the Christian Name, with the approval of Pope Pius XI, issued new norms about this matter in 1935 and 1936. The norms were addressed to the ordinaries of Manchuria and Japan, according to canon 22. These norms are more in tune with present-day circumstances.

Recently, the Cardinals, who head this Sacred Congregation for Propagating the Christian Name, in a general assembly, held on the 4th of this December, considered whether in other places too, where the passage of time has evidently brought about similar change of circumstances, a similar way of acting should be countenanced.

Therefore, after listening attentively to arguments pro and con, and after asking prudent and experienced men what they thought, these Cardinals decided that the following declaration should be made:

1. The Chinese government has said repeatedly and openly that all are free to profess whatever religion they prefer. It is not the government's intention to issue laws or commands about religious matters. Therefore, the ceremonies which the public authorities either stage or prescribe in honor of

Confucius are not carried out with the intention of rendering religious worship, but only for this purpose: to cultivate and display suitable honor for a very illustrious man, and the respect due the traditions of ancestors. Therefore, Catholics are allowed to be present at testimonials honoring Confucius, held before an image or tablet of Confucius, or in buildings dedicated to him or in schools.

2. Therefore, it is not forbidden, especially if the authorities require it, for Catholic schools to set up an image of Confucius, or even a tablet inscribed with his name, or to honor it by bowing the head. If ever there is fear of scandal, the correct Catholic intention should be made clear.

3. If Catholic teachers and students are ordered to be present at public ceremonies that present the appearance of superstition, it is all right for them to attend, as long as they remain passive, according to the directive of canon 1258, and make only signs of that respect which could rightly be thought of as merely civil. If at times it should be clearly necessary to avoid misinterpretation of their actions, they should, as stated above, make their intention known.

4. Bowing the head and other tokens of civil honor before the deceased or images of the deceased, and even before a tablet of a deceased person, inscribed with nothing but the person's name, should be regarded as permissible and proper.

Besides, these Cardinals see that the oath about the Chinese Rites, that through the Constitution, *Ex quo singulari* of July 11, 1742, was imposed on all priests in the Empire of China and in kingdoms and provinces bordering it or near to it, is not entirely compatible with recent norms given by this Sacred Congregation. They see that at the present time this oath is not needed as a disciplinary instrument. Everyone knows that the former controversies about the Chinese Rites have been settled. Moreover, missionaries and other priests do not have to be forced by an oath to render prompt and filial obedience to the Holy See. Therefore, they have decided to dispense with the obligation of that oath, wherever, either in China or elsewhere, it was still being enforced. Insofar as they have not been changed by more recent Instructions, the other directives of Pope Benedict XIV are still binding, especially the prohibition against arguing about the Chinese Rites.

In an audience granted December 7, the undersigned Cardinal, Prefect of this Sacred Congregation for Propagating the Faith, presented this decision of the Cardinals to His Holiness, Pope Pius XII. His Holiness deigned to approve and ratify it in its entirety.

Given at Rome, from the Halls of the Sacred Congregation for the Propagation of the Faith, December 8, 1939, on the feast of the Immaculate Conception of the Blessed Virgin Mary.

Pietro Cardinal Fumasoni-Biondi, Prefect. Archbishop Celso Constantini, Secretary

(Source: *100 Roman Documents Relating to the Chinese Rites Controversy [1645-1941]*, trans. Donald F. St. Sure, S.J., ed. with introductions and summaries by Ray Noll [San Francisco: Ricci Institute for Chinese-Western Cultural History, University of San Francisco Center for the Pacific Rim, 1992].)

Early Protestant Documents on Cross-Cultural Mission

28. *The History of Missions; or, of the Propagation of Christianity among the Heathen,* by William Brown

William Brown's 1816 history of Christian missions is both a key source of information and a window into missiological thinking among Protestants in the late eighteenth and early nineteenth centuries. Brown clearly *knows something of non-Christian religions outside Europe. His analysis of their flaws, and thus the need for evangelism, is indicative of his self-understanding as a Protestant.*

Excerpt from the Introductory Preface

The missionary cause is a distinguishing characteristic of the gospel system of religion. No other system in the world has ever made it the indispensable duty of its votaries to disseminate its principles throughout the world, in order to ameliorate the moral condition of the human family, from a principle of pure good-will to man. Innumerable have been the machinations of worldly policy, and sordid ambition to extend territorial jurisdiction, and even in many instances under the mask of Christianity; but, it has always been done by compulsory measures—by fire and sword; such as the Gospel system disapproves and scorns. The language of the Gospel is, "do violence to no man, neither accuse any falsely."—Luke 3, xiv. And the apostle of the Gentiles, breathing the spirit of the Gospel, says, "though we walk in the flesh, we do not war after the flesh; for the weapons of our warfare are not carnal, but mighty, through God, to the pulling down of strong holds." All the Gospel needs, is a *free course*, and it will run and be glorified. St. John saw it in the emblem of "a pure river, as clear as crystal, proceeding out of the throne of God and of the Lamb, on either side of which was the tree of life, whose leaves were for the healing of the nations." The Gospel is an expression of the free, unmerited, sovereign love of God, to perishing fallen man; and it has found its way only through the channel of *Missions*. . . .

The necessity of divine agency, and, the reasonableness of human instrumentality in this august work are obvious, when we realize the inveterate nature of human depravity, and the constitution of things. . . .

Ignorance of the *nature* of God is the corrupt fountain of all the absurdities of the Heathen worship. No worship can be acceptable to God, but that which is rendered in obedience to his will, and proceeds from a heart rightly affected towards his government, and towards all the natural and moral attributes of the Divine nature. Nothing is more rational, and nothing is more necessary, according to the nature and fitness of things, than these words of Divine revelation, "God is a Spirit, and they who worship him, *must* worship him in spirit and in truth." The Heathen, by the light of nature, know there *is* a God, but being ignorant of his peculiar nature, "they glorify him not as God." Being vain in their imaginations, and their foolish heart darkened, they have ever been "changing the glory of the incorruptible God into images made like to corruptible man, to birds, to four footed beasts, and to creeping things." Hence it is, that they can have no proper conception of the infinite demerit of sin, as committed against an infinitely just and holy God. Through the lapse of near 6000 years, we observe the Heathen, with all the combined resources of mere human wisdom and strength, have not been able to *set forth* an altar and a sacrifice, sufficiently meritorious, to obliterate the *hand writing* of *ordinances* that stands against sinful man, and thereby open a communication from Heaven to earth, that God might be just in dispensing pardon and all spiritual blessings. Where then, amidst this tempestuous sea of human miseries, shall we find solid rock, on which we may rationally cast the anchor of our hope, and look for deliverance? From what source draw refreshing draughts of strong consolation? And upon what justifiable grounds may men unite all their energies to ameliorate the moral condition of the Heathen, and confide in the patronage of Heaven, and an all pervading Providence? These are questions that demand the most serious attention of the evangelized world. He who can remain indifferent to them, while he professes himself a Christian, betrays not only inconsistency of character, but a sottish stupidity, foreign from that temper which the Gospel inspires; because, on their answer depend, as it respects all human determinations, the temporal and eternal prospects of millions of the human family. Whereas, he who is alive to their just importance, will act, not only consistent with the rational dignity of human nature, but will shew a *proof* of that love to God, and of that true philanthropy which have ever been recognized as the distinguishing characteristics of "pure and undented Religion." . . .

But *faith*, that is connected with salvation comes by hearing the Gospel preached, and a preached Gospel comes by the means of Missions; for, how shall men preach except they be sent. (Rom. x. 12-17) Thus "the *tree* is known by his *fruit*," and thus it becomes evident, that, after the world by wisdom knew not God, it hath pleased God in the wise economy of redemption, by, what many esteem, the foolishness of preaching to save them that believe. . . .

The *righteousness* of Christ, comprising his

obedient life and death, is, therefore, a distinguishing trait and cardinal point of the Gospel. "Herein," says the apostle, "the *righteousness of God* is revealed from faith to faith." Indeed, he speaks of it as the very essence of the Gospel; and calls the opposite to it *Gentilism*, the *works* of the Law, and *another Gospel*. It is a golden thread, running through the whole tissue of Divine revelation. By this doctrine, the reformers of the fourteenth and fifteenth centuries cut the very sinews of Popery, those antichristian tenets of penance and purgatory, pardons and indulgencies, of the merit of works, &c. hence we may, with Luther, justly call it, "*articulus stantit vel cadentis ecclesia*," the article on which the Church stands or falls. Before this doctrine, all the Pagan and Papal superstitions fall, like Dagon before the ark of the Lord. Where this righteousness goes forth as brightness, the salvation of the Lord also goes forth as a lamp that burneth. . . . .

(Source: William Brown, M.D., *The History of Missions; or, of the Propagation of Christianity among the Heathen, since the Reformation* [Philadelphia: B. Coles, 1816].)

29. *An Enquiry into the Obligation of Christians to Use Means for the Conversion of the Heathens,* by William Carey

From 1792, William Carey's famous call to mission is a classic Protestant apology for Christian mission, answering objections to the enterprise, but, as important, seeking to place it in the context of colonialism as understood in Carey's own time.

Mark 16:15—"Go ye into all the world, and preach the gospel to every creature."

. . . In order that the subject may be taken into more serious consideration, I shall: enquire whether the Commission given by our Lord to His disciples be not still binding on us; consider the practicability of doing something more than is done; and discuss the duty of Christians in general in this matter.

An Enquiry whether the Commission Given by Our Lord to His Disciples Be Not Still Binding on Us

Our Lord Jesus Christ, a little before his departure, commissioned his apostles to "Go, and teach all nations"; or, as another evangelist expresses it, "Go into all the world, and preach the gospel to every creature." This commission was as extensive as possible, and laid them under obligation to disperse themselves into every country of the habitable globe, and preach to all the inhabitants, without exception or limitation. They accordingly went forth in obedience to the command, and the power of God evidently wrought with them. Many attempts of the same kind have been made since their day, and which have been attended with various success; but the work has not been taken up, or prosecuted of late years (except by a few individuals) with that zeal and perseverance with which the primitive Christians went about it. It seems as if many thought the commission was sufficiently put in execution by what the apostles and others have done; that we have enough to do to attend to the salvation of our own countrymen; and that, if God intends the salvation of the heathen, he will some way or other bring them to the gospel, or the gospel to them. It is thus that multitudes sit at ease, and give themselves no concern about the far greater part of their fellow-sinners, who to this day, are lost in ignorance and idolatry. There seems also to be an opinion existing in the minds of some, that because the apostles were extraordinary officers and have no proper successors, and because many things which were right for them to do would be utterly unwarrantable for us, therefore it may not be immediately binding on us to execute the commission, though it was so upon them. To the consideration of such persons I would offer the following observations.

First. If the command of Christ to teach all nations be restricted to the apostles, or those under the immediate inspiration of the Holy Ghost, then that of baptizing should be so too; and every denomination of Christians, except the Quakers, do wrong in baptizing with water at all.

Secondly. If the command of Christ to teach all nations be confined to the apostles, then all such ordinary ministers who have endeavoured to carry the gospel to the heathens, have acted without a warrant, and run before they were sent. Yea, and though God has promised the most glorious things to the heathen world by sending his gospel to them, yet whoever goes first, or indeed at all, with that message, unless he have a new and special commission from heaven, must go without any authority for so doing.

Thirdly. If the command of Christ to teach all nations extend only to the apostles, then, doubtless, the promise of the divine presence in this work must be so limited; but this is worded in such a manner as expressly precludes such an idea "Lo, I am with you always, to the end of the world." . . .

It has been said that some learned divines have proved from scripture that the time is not yet come that the heathen should be converted; and that first the witnesses must be slain, and many other prophecies fulfilled. But admitting this to be the case (which I much doubt [footnote: See Edwards on Prayer, on this subject, lately re-printed by Mr Sutcliffe.]) yet if any objection is made from this against preaching to them immediately, it must be founded on one of these things; either that the secret purpose of God is the rule of our duty, and then it must be as bad to pray for them, as to preach to them; or else that none shall be converted in the heathen world till the universal down-pouring of the Spirit in the last days. But this objection comes too late; for the success of the gospel has been very considerable in many places already.

It has been objected that there are multitudes in our own nation, and within our immediate spheres of action, who are as ignorant as the South-Sea savages, and that therefore we have work enough at home, without going into other countries. That there are thousands in our own land as far from God as possible, I readily grant, and that this ought to excite us to ten-fold diligence in our work, and in attempts to spread divine knowledge amongst them is a certain fact; but that it ought to supersede all attempts to spread the gospel in foreign parts seems to want proof. Our own countrymen have the means of grace, and may attend on the word preached if they choose it. They have the means of knowing the truth, and faithful ministers are placed in almost every part of the land, whose spheres of action might be much extended if their congrega-

tions were but more hearty and active in the cause: but with them the case is widely different, who have no Bible, no written language (which many of them have not), no ministers, no good civil government, nor any of those advantages which we have. Pity therefore, humanity, and much more Christianity, call loudly for every possible exertion to introduce the gospel amongst them.

The Practicability of Something Being Done, More Than What Is Done, for the Conversion of the Heathen

The impediments in the way of carrying the gospel among the heathen must arise, I think, from one or other of the following things;—either their distance from us, their barbarious and savage manner of living, the danger of being killed by them, the difficulty of procuring the necessaries of life, or the unintelligibleness of their languages.

First. As to their distance from us, whatever objections might have been made on that account before the invention of the mariner's compass, nothing can be alleged for it, with any colour of plausibility in the present age. Men can now sail with as much certainty through the Great South Sea, as they can through the Mediterranean, or any lesser Sea. Yea, and providence seems in a manner to invite us to the trial, as there are to our knowledge trading companies, whose commerce lies in many of the places where these barbarians dwell. At one time or other ships are sent to visit places of more recent discovery, and to explore parts the most unknown; and every fresh account of their ignorance, or cruelty, should call forth our pity, and excite us to concur with providence in seeking their eternal good. Scripture likewise seems to point out this method—"Surely the Isles shall wait for me; the ships of Tarshish first, to bring my sons from far, their silver, and their gold with them, unto the name of the Lord, thy God" (Isa. 60:9). This seems to imply that in the time of the glorious increase of the church, in the latter days (of which the whole chapter is undoubtedly a prophecy), commerce shall subserve the spread of the gospel. The ships of Tarshish were trading vessels, which made voyages for traffic to various parts; thus much therefore must be meant by it, that navigation, especially that which is commercial, shall be one great mean of carrying on the work of God; and perhaps it may imply that there shall be a very considerable appropriation of wealth to that purpose.

Secondly. As to their uncivilized, and barbarous way of living, this can be no objection to any, except those whose love of ease renders them unwilling to expose themselves to inconveniences for the good of others.

It was no objection to the apostles and their successors, who went among the barbarous Germans and Gauls, and still more barbarous Britons! They did not wait for the ancient inhabitants of these countries, to be civilized, before they could be christianized, but went simply with the doctrine of the cross; and Tertullian could boast that "those parts of Britain which were proof against the Roman armies, were conquered by the gospel of Christ." . . .

After all, the uncivilized state of the heathen, instead of affording an objection against preaching the gospel to them, ought to furnish an argument for it. Can we as men, or as Christians, hear that a great part of our fellow creatures, whose souls are as immortal as ours, and who are as capable as ourselves, of adorning the gospel and contributing by their preaching, writings, or practices to the glory of our Redeemer's name, and the good of his church, are enveloped in ignorance and barbarism? Can we hear that they are without the gospel, without government, without laws, and without arts, and sciences; and not exert ourselves to introduce amongst them the sentiments of men, and of Christians? Would not the spread of the gospel be the most effectual mean of their civilization? Would not that make them useful members of society? . . .

Thirdly. In respect to the danger of being killed by them, it is true that whoever does go must put his life in his hand, and not consult with flesh and blood; but do not the goodness of the cause, the duties incumbent on us as the creatures of God, and Christians, and the perishing state of our fellow men, loudly call upon us to venture all and use every warrantable exertion for their benefit? Paul and Barnabas, who hazarded their lives for the name of our Lord Jesus Christ, were not blamed as being rash, but commended for so doing, while John Mark, who through timidity of mind deserted them in their perilous undertaking, was branded with censure.

Fourthly. As to the difficulty of procuring the necessaries of life, this would not be so great as may appear at first sight; for though we could not procure European food, yet we might procure such as the natives of those countries which we visit, subsist upon themselves. And this would only be passing through what we have virtually engaged in by entering on the ministerial office. A Christian minister is a person who in a peculiar sense is not his own; he is the servant of God, and therefore ought to be wholly devoted to him. By entering on that sacred office he solemnly undertakes to be always engaged, as much as possible, in the Lord's work, and not to choose his own pleasure, or employment, or pursue the ministry as a something that is to subserve his own ends, or interests, or as a kind of by-work. He engages to go where God pleases, and to do, or endure what he sees fit to command, or call him to, in the exercise of his function. He virtually bids farewell to friends, pleasures, and comforts, and stands in readiness to endure the greatest sufferings in the work of his Lord, and Master. It is inconsistent for ministers to please themselves with thoughts of a numerous auditory, cordial friends, a civilized country, legal protection, affluence, splendour, or even a competency. . . .

It might be necessary, however, for two, at least, to go together, and in general I should think it best that they should be married men; and to prevent their time from being employed in procuring necessaries, two, or more, other persons, with their wives and families, might also accompany them, who should be wholly employed in providing for them. In most countries it would be necessary for them to cultivate a little spot of ground just for their support, which would be a resource to them, whenever their supplies failed. Not to mention the advantages they would reap from each other's company, it would take off the enormous expense which has always attended undertakings of this kind, the first expense being the whole; for though a large colony needs support for a considerable time, yet so small a number would, upon receiving the first crop, maintain themselves. They would have the advantage of choosing their situation, their wants would be few; the women, and even the children, would be necessary for domestic purposes; and a few articles of stock, as a cow or two, and a bull, and a few other cattle of both sexes, a very few utensils of husbandry, and some corn to sow their land, would be sufficient. Those who attend the missionaries should understand husbandry, fishing, fowling, etc., and be provided with the necessary implements for these purposes. Indeed a variety of methods may be thought of, and when once the work is undertaken, many things will suggest themselves to us, of which we at present can form no idea.

Fifthly. As to learning their languages, the same means would be found necessary here as in trade between different nations. In some cases interpreters might be obtained, who might be employed for a time; and where these were not to be found, the missionaries must have patience, and mingle with the people, till they have learned so much of their language as to be able to communicate their ideas to them in it. It is well known to require no very extraordinary talents to learn, in the space of a year, or two at most, the language of any people upon earth, so much of it at least, as to be able to convey any sentiments we wish to their understandings.

The missionaries must be of great piety, prudence, courage, and forbearance; of undoubted orthodoxy in their sentiments, and must enter with all their hearts into the spirit of their mission; they must be willing to leave all the comforts of life behind them, And to encounter all the hardships of a torrid, or a frigid climate, an uncomfortable manner of living, and every other inconvenience that can attend this undertaking. Clothing, a few knives, powder and shot, fishing-tackle, and the articles of husbandry above-mentioned, must be provided for them; and when arrived at the place of their destination, their first business must be to gain some acquaintance with the language of the natives (for which purpose two would be better than one), and by all lawful means to endeavour to cultivate a friendship with them, and as soon as possible let them know the errand for which they were sent. They must endeavour to convince them that it was their good alone which induced them to forsake their friends, and all the comforts of their native country. They must be very careful not to resent injuries which may be offered to them, nor

to think highly of themselves, so as to despise the poor heathens, and by those means lay a foundation for their resentment, or rejection of the gospel. They must take every opportunity of doing them good, and labouring, and travelling, night and day, they must instruct, exhort, and rebuke, with all long suffering, and anxious desire for them, and, above all, must be instant in prayer for the effusion of the Holy Spirit upon the people of their charge. Let but missionaries of the above description engage in the work, and we shall see that it is not impracticable.

It might likewise be of importance, if God should bless their labours, for them to encourage any appearances of gifts among the people of their charge; if such should be raised up many advantages would be derived from their knowledge of the language, and customs of their countrymen; and their change of conduct would give great weight to their ministrations.

(Source: *The Highway of Mission Thought*, ed. T. B. Ray [Nashville, Tn.: Sunday School Board of the Southern Baptist Convention, 1907].)

30. *Christianity and Commerce, a Speech by David Livingstone*

David Livingstone (1813-1873) was a pioneer missionary to Africa. His understanding of the relationship between Christianity, commerce, and civilization was not universally embraced by missionaries of his generation, but aptly characterized the chief rationale of colonial missions. The reading below contains excerpts from a speech in Cambridge in 1857.

My object in going into the country south of the desert was to instruct the natives in a knowledge of Christianity, but many circumstances prevented my living amongst them more than seven years, amongst which were considerations arising out of the slave system carried on by the Dutch Boers. I resolved to go into the country beyond, and soon found that, for the purposes of commerce, it was necessary to have a path to the sea. I might have gone on instructing the natives in religion, but as civilization and Christianity must go on together, I was obliged to find a path to the sea, in order that I should not sink to the level of the natives. The chief was overjoyed at the suggestion, and furnished me with twenty-seven men, and canoes, and provisions, and presents for the tribes through whose country we had to pass. . . .

My desire is to open a path to this district, that civilization, commerce, and Christianity might find their way there. I consider that we made a great mistake, when we carried commerce into India, in being ashamed of our Christianity; as a matter of common sense and good policy, it is always best to appear in one's true character. In travelling through Africa, I might have imitated certain Portuguese, and have passed for a chief; but I never attempted anything of the sort, although endeavouring always to keep to the lessons of cleanliness rigidly instilled by my mother long ago; the consequence was that the natives respected me for that quality, though remaining dirty themselves. . . .

A prospect is now before us of opening Africa for commerce and the Gospel. Providence has been preparing the way, for even before I proceeded to the Central basin it had been conquered and rendered safe by a chief named Sebituane, and the language of the Bechuanas made the fashionable tongue, and that was one of the languages into which Mr Moffat had translated the Scriptures. Sebituane also discovered Lake Ngami some time previous to my explorations in that part. In going back to that country my object is to open up traffic along the banks of the Zambesi, and also to preach the Gospel. The natives of Central Africa are very desirous of trading, but their only traffic is at present in slaves, of which the poorer people have an unmitigated horror: it is therefore most desirable to encourage the former principle, and thus open a way for the consumption of free productions, and the introduction of Christianity and commerce. By encouraging the native propensity for trade, the advantages that might be derived in a commercial point of view are incalculable; nor should we lose sight of the inestimable blessings it is in our power to bestow upon the unenlightened African, by giving him the light of Christianity. Those two pioneers of civilization—Christianity and commerce—should ever be inseparable; and Englishmen should be warned by the fruits of neglecting that principle as exemplified in the result of the

management of Indian affairs. By trading with Africa, also, we should at length be independent of slave-labour, and thus discountenance practices so obnoxious to every Englishman.

Though the natives are not absolutely anxious to receive the Gospel, they are open to Christian influences. Among the Bechuanas the Gospel was well received. These people think it a crime to shed a tear, but I have seen some of them weep at the recollection of their sins when God had opened their hearts to Christianity and repentance. It is true that missionaries have difficulties to encounter; but what great enterprise was ever accomplished without difficulty? It is deplorable to think that one of the noblest of our missionary societies, the Church Missionary Society, is compelled to send to Germany for missionaries, whilst other societies are amply supplied. Let this stain be wiped off.— The sort of men who are wanted for missionaries are such as I see before me;—men of education, standing, enterprise, zeal, and piety. It is a mistake to suppose that *any one*, as long as he is pious, will do for this office. Pioneers in every thing should be the ablest and best qualified men, not those of small ability and education. This remark especially applies to the first teachers of Christian truth in regions which may never have before been blest with the name and Gospel of Jesus Christ. In the early ages the monasteries were the schools of Europe, and the monks were not ashamed to hold the plough, The missionaries now take the place of those noble men, and we should not hesitate to give up the small luxuries of life in order to carry knowledge and truth to them that are in darkness. I hope that many of those whom I now address will embrace that honourable career. Education has been given us from above for the purpose of bringing to the benighted the knowledge of a Saviour. If you knew the satisfaction of performing such a duty, as well as the gratitude to God which the missionary must always feel, in being chosen for so noble, so sacred a calling, you would have no hesitation in embracing it.

For my own part, I have never ceased to rejoice that God has appointed me to such an office. People talk of the sacrifice I have made in spending so much of my life in Africa. Can that be called a sacrifice which is simply paid back as a small part of a great debt owing to our God, which we can never repay?—Is that a sacrifice which brings its own blest reward in healthful activity, the consciousness of doing good, peace of mind, and a bright hope of a glorious destiny hereafter?—Away with the word in such a view, and with such a thought! It is emphatically no sacrifice. Say rather it is a privilege. Anxiety, sickness, suffering, or danger, now and then, with a foregoing of the common conveniences and charities of this life, may make us pause, and cause the spirit to waver, and the soul to sink, but let this only be for a moment. All these are nothing when compared with the glory which shall hereafter be revealed in, and for, us. I never made a sacrifice. Of this we ought not to talk, when we remember the great sacrifice which He made who left His Father's throne on high to give Himself for us.

(Source: *Dr. Livingston's Cambridge Lectures,* ed. Rev. William Monk [Cambridge: Deighton, Bell and Co., 1858], 19-21.)

31. *The Responsibility of Young People for the Evangelization of the World,* by John R. Mott

John Mott (1865-1955) was the leader of the YMCA and the World Student Christian Federation. He presided over the 1910 Missionary Conference in Edinburgh. His speeches and essays, like the one below, played an important role in continuing the missionary enthusiasm of the nineteenth century into the twentieth. His reference to Rome may provide insight into his thinking. This speech was given in 1901.

The need of the non-Christian world is an extensive need. South of this country we have not less than fifty millions of people in Mexico, the West Indies, Central America, and the South American republics. In the Levant there are tens of millions of others. In the Dark Continent, at the most conservative estimate, there are over one hundred and fifty millions; in the East Indies and the other islands of the Southern seas, fifty millions more; in India, Burma, Ceylon, and Siam, not less than three hundred millions; in the Sunrise Kingdom

of Japan, over forty millions; and not less than four hundred millions in China and the states that fringe upon her, Korea, Manchuria, Mongolia, and Tibet.

Over one thousand millions! Can we grasp the number? No, indeed! It is indeed an extensive need. It is not only an extensive need, but it is an intensive one; and the intensive need of the non-Christian world is indescribably great. The Scriptures maintain this much. They show us most vividly the condition of men apart from Jesus Christ. They present today, as every world traveler will tell you, an unexaggerated picture of the moral and spiritual condition of over two-thirds of the human race. Not only the Scriptures but scientific observation proves to be a demonstration that those peoples without Christ have a need which is very deep. Think of them tonight, living in darkness and ignorance, steeped in superstition and idolatry, in degradation and corruption; see them, under what a load of shame and sorrow and sin and pain and suffering, as they live and move on in silence to the tomb; notice the fearful inroads and onslaughts of the forces of evil. And remind yourselves that they do not have those powers of resistance which we have as the result of Christian heredity, Christian environment, and the domination of Christian ideas and ideals. They fight a losing battle. If I could take every one of you on a long journey of nearly two years, through those great sections of the non-Christian world, that you might see what I have seen, that you might hear what I have heard, that you might feel what I have felt, the last iota of skepticism which may linger in the mind of any one here as to the need of these people of knowing Christ would vanish. Truly their need is indescribably great. It comes back to haunt me in the watches of the night; and if God spares my life and my plans can be properly shaped, I want in a few months hence to put my life once more alongside those young men who are fighting their losing fight.

We need not to be world travelers; we need not to be missionaries; no, we need not to be profound students of the Bible—to be convinced that men need Christ. Look only into your own heart. If you and I know that we need Jesus Christ, that he has been and is essential to us, is it not presumptuous to suppose that people living in less favored lands, without the ennobling and inspiring forces and associations with which we are familiar, can get along without him? Moreover, it should be emphasized that the non-Christian religions are inadequate to meet this need. Over fifteen thousand four hundred Protestant missionaries, scattered throughout the world, present a united front on this question. There is no division of opinion among them. Standing face to face with the need itself, and, therefore, in a position to make a thorough study of the problem, they say with one voice that, unless Christ is borne to these regions, these people are without hope. I used to doubt that Mr. Chairman, when I was studying comparative religion, and when I went as a delegate to the Parliament of Religions in Chicago several years ago. But when I had opportunity to make a scientific study of the problem (and a scientific study takes account of all the facts, and not simply of theories) all my skepticism vanished. As I went up and down densely populated provinces and presidencies and native states, as I conversed with over thirteen hundred missionaries, representing some eighty missionary societies (and I know of no university education that means more to a man than to sit at the feet of missionaries), as I talked with hundreds of civilians and native students and priests, as I visited countless shrines and temples and holy places,

as I witnessed the superstitions, the abominations, the cruelties, the injustices, within the immediate confines of these sacred places, so called, the conviction became ever deeper and stronger that these nations without Christ are without hope. Yes, I believe to the core of my being that Christ someday must have sway over this whole world. He is not going to divide the world with Buddhism and Confucianism and Hinduism and Mohammedanism; he is going to have complete sway. It takes no prophet in our time to see that that Church which conquered the Roman Empire, which cast the spell of the matchless Christ over the nations of Western and Northern Europe, which, has moved with giant strides among the nations and is shaking them today—that that Church will prevail. He shall reign from sea to sea. When He girds on his conquering sword all the ends of the earth shall see the salvation of our God.

(Source: *Missionary Issues of the Twentieth Century: Papers and Addresses of the General Missionary Conference of the Methodist Episcopal Church, South, Held in New Orleans, April 24-30, 1901; With a Number of Maps and Charts in Illustration of the Work of Missions, the Latest Statistical Tables and a Select Bibliography* [Nashville, Tn.: Executive Committee of the Methodist Episcopal Church South].)

8

Readings Related to the Long End of Empire and Colonialism

Documents concerning the Orthodox Mission to Alaska

32. *Letter from Archimandrite Ioasaph to Gregory Shelikov, May 18, 1795*

The Orthodox Mission to Alaska reached a turning point when a mission of the Russian empire found itself in the midst of what was effectively an American colony. The letters that follow indicate the intensity with which Russian Orthodox missionaries tried to understand and respond to the culture of the native Alaskans and their tension with the economic interests of the Russian-American company that was exploiting the resources of this "new" land. They also illustrate Orthodox frustration as Alaska passes from Russian to American hands, and their conflicts with American Protestant missionaries who follow. In their efforts to be observant of and sensitive to culture, their conflicts with the interests of those seeking to economically exploit indigenous peoples, their ongoing ties to empire, and their irritation when supplanted by a different empire and its Christian mission are themes found around the world in nineteenth- and twentieth-century missions.

Benevolent Sir, Gregory Ivanovich [Shelikov]

Dear Friend and Patron! The love, respect and affection I have for you I can feel better than I can express the same on paper. I do not think that it is even necessary to do so, as it is not flattery and therefore does not require much proof. Thus leaving aside empty compliments, I shall talk to you about the following:

Having departed from Okhotsk August 13, we arrived in Kodiak safely on the 24th of September [1794]. Throughout the winter there were many visitors who came voluntarily—inhabitants of Kodiak and also Alaskans [from the Alaska Peninsula], Kenai people, and Chugach. We did baptize many.

We as yet have no church. We asked for a tent of the manager, Alexander Andreevich [Baranov], but so far without result. Though Alexander Andreevich himself arranged for the construction of a small church—the cornerstone was laid the 21st of November [for a 4 sazhen church, with a 1½ trapeza]—the building stands to this day unfinished. I decided not to report about the field church to the Metropolitan. Since my arrival at the harbor, I find nothing whatsoever that should have been done in accordance with your good intentions accomplished. My only delight is in the [indigenous]Americans who are coming from everywhere to be baptized. The Russians not only do not aid them in this but on the contrary employ all possible means to scare them off. The reason for this is their dissolute life which is put to shame by the good conduct of the Americans. I was barely able to convince some of the promishlenniki to get married. The rest do not want to hear of it, but openly keep women, even more than one each, which constitutes a great insult to the Americans. You know how Baranov likes women, and he will chase them in the face of any kind of danger! I am unable to ascertain what enraged Mr. Baranov more—our arrival here itself or our impassioned reprimands of him. All signs indicate he agitates the promishlenniki and sets them against us. Besides constant intrigues, he tries to persuade everyone to agree in writing that everything is company property, not the property of the company investors. He tells them that settlers are harmful to the interests of the company and all these state interests [matters of state] he presents to them in a perverted way. He tells them that it is a burden on the company, and has ordered that no less than 30 people would be assigned to become settlers; that from this the resources decrease because of taking the settlers along the coast for 500 versts; that the promishlenniki who arrive newly hired are incompetent and useless, that only a few investors will get rich and not the entire company, that the dead [illegible] and also the economic profits do not belong to members of the company in any way, etc., etc. You can learn more of this from those who have returned to Okhotsk, including those who left against their will, and also from company records here.

In terms of economics, nothing good can be noted. Since our arrival, there was hunger all winter. We ate rotten three-year-old dried fish, to the last bit, although when we arrived here, fish were still running but not harvested. The herring run was also there later, but the catch was conducted only two or three times. The Aleuts were not ordered to take halibut and it was said that since the settlers do not work, in putting up food supplies, it is not needed. The seines lay on the shore all winter long. The cows which were brought by the ships are only skins now, and most died. Two calves (besides those few born here) were eaten by dogs. Many mountain sheep have also been attacked. Only two goats remain, and recently the dogs feasted on one for their good health. Phillip will elaborate on this.

Under our parkas, we are always half naked, and those parkas get very dirty. In the daytime, we feed the people. At night we [the clergy] collect wood and bring it out of the forest ourselves. It is laugh-able that a household may not put up one single stick of wood, but whenever Baranov wants his tea pot heated, he sends men out for wood. They break corners off of buildings, or rob the coal from the metalsmith. I have never seen these things done in an economically sensible way. He spends his days inventing various schemes. He did not make any attempts to grow any vegetables. Phillip planted potatoes and turnips, but he was alone in this, but the crop was good. Sokozhnikov says that he experimented with barley at his bay. He sowed one pound and harvested one and a half. I have advised that in spring we should plant something here in Kodiak, but I do not know if it will happen. I would like to see some potatoes, cabbages, and some other vegetables planted here. But here is an obstacle: I have asked for a few hoes or adzes and a few spades, but I do not know if I will be able to get them. Right now, we are working the ground with sharpened wooden sticks we have fashioned ourselves.

We have only five students whom we are teaching. The older students are living in their settlements without any supervisions [the students of Shelikov's earlier school]. They do not show any difference from any other Aleuts. One of them, for the sake of Baranov's woman, has been forced to run the gauntlet. His head and his eyebrows were shaved, the front of his parka was cut off, and he was banished to Yedrishnikov settlement where he is under guard. I do not know how to teach the five I have. Our room is always filled with people. Some are being baptized, some married, some visit. Besides we do not have a church, so that the services can not be conducted.

Of all the books which you sent for us, I received only a few, not more than twenty. Ten of these are sluzhebniki [service books] and they all have rotted and can not be used. The rest I have not seen yet. I baptized the Americans, creating no difficulties for the company. An indentured servant remains indentured, a hostage remains a hostage. And a hunter remains at his post—it should not interfere, that he is now baptized. But every time obstacles are created for me, I was able to baptize people in the settlements, or to marry Aleuts with the partner with whom they were living, but this resulted in such situations that as soon as they were married, the women were taken away from their spouses and given to others or became indentured servants or hostages, and I am sure only to disturb me. I am being patient, awaiting a resolution from you of this situation.

In one settlement I married an Aleut to his girlfriend. She was sent to me with an interpreter, and I was told that this woman had been kidnapped some time ago, when they used to attack one settlement against another. She was taken prisoner first by one chief then another and finally by a Russian. When the Russian abandoned her, she returned to the chief with whom I married her. I was asked for what reason I baptized and married a prisoner who at one time was the wife of a chief. I excused myself as ignorant of the past situation. Then they found another reason: they say that the chief who had first taken her prisoner is indebted to the company for one bird parka and a metal container, so he should pay by means of this woman. If not, the debt should be settled by the Aleut who married her. Otherwise he must return her to the first chief. I agreed to pay the company, although it should not be done. But Alexander Andreevich said that if I am permitted to do so we will suffer terrible losses. Do you see what small matters are inflated and contrary to common sense?

I would like to cite another example and write you about it. There are even sillier instances. I would suffer it in silence myself but there are outsiders to our brotherhood who will speak instead of myself bringing testimony of their immoral deeds. They are exploiting in every possible way and one must testify about their barbarous treatment of the Americans. Recently I do not marry a single Aleut without reporting to him. But one can not satisfy him. He always tries to agitate the promishlenniki. He started rumors that there are no reasons to be shamed by me and that the promishlenniki have nothing to fear. Baranov claims he has orders from you to keep the clergy firmly under his control.

We are told we must use local food, local boats, etc. Without any orders from you, our need will indeed teach us to be used to the local food! There is no chance that we will use too much of the provisions. We regularly go to the beaches to collect sea snails and mussels and we have only some leftover bread which will not last long. Mr. Baranov and his colleagues do not experience hunger. For him they

hunt sea lions and seals. From the Alaska Peninsula they bring caribou meat, and he always has milk. During the winter we were kept well by Phillip. There were two cows then. At the very least we had milk for the tea, but now the cows are gone and we get for the ten of us no more than a tea cup each day, excluding the fast days. With great difficulties we obtain whale oil. We have neither the time nor the means to produce handicrafts for sale. As the day dawns we think about food. We walk five versts to get snails and mussels, as near the harbor they are not available. Actually there are some mussels at the harbor, but they are food for the workers and therefore not enough. We must haul fire wood and do our sewing and laundry. There are over 100 women laborers here, but not one is assigned to assist us.

The windows of our quarters were not sealed and were very poor; we barely survived the winter. It is true initially he honored me. He reserved a pretty good room for me, but the brethren were placed in the barracks, where the men lived with their prostitutes. I did not want to live apart from the brothers, and moved with them to other quarters. Besides the prostitutes, they used the barracks for games and dances that lasted all night, so that even major [religious] feast days were not observed. Sometimes they stage these parties even on ordinary days. He would come to me and say that they are having a party because of bad weather. His only pleasures are women and dancing. That is the kind of men he and his closest advisors are.

He is not ashamed to use profanity publicly, nor to argue with me about morality. He says that we are hypocrites who do not want to understand anything, that all those moral rules are for the ignorant. He and Yakov Igorovich [Sheilds] have taught many French free-thinking which he himself accepts. He has ordered the baidarshi to keep their women without fear, and not only the old voyagers can do so. Nowadays, the one who keeps women is honored. It has happened that the day the woman is baptized, she would be taken from her settlement to promishlenniki by force. They kept changing them very often very young, ten-year-old girls. Some may be convinced to marry, but Mr. Baranov says that anyone who marries becomes a poor promishlennik. Another will get married but loses his credit, and is forced to leave for Russia.

I observe that the men do not travel from one settlement to another without their women, so that if they would have wives, they would be more reliable for the company. Those who are married would buy more goods from the company store and the others who follow their example would take provisions for their lovers. Prior to our arrival, not a single woman had anything but a parka. Nowadays each has a shirt and blouse. When they have children they will not want to return to Russia. (Regular family life will bring social and economic stability to the colony.)

If I were to describe all his actions to you in detail, I would have to write an entire book, and not a letter. About his loose life, even so, I should according to the instructions His Eminence gave me, I should report to him and to the Holy Synod, but my affection and respect for you convinced me to refrain from this for the time being. I am hoping that you in your wisdom will take measures to alleviate the situation. But wisdom does not find home in an evil soul. Wisdom does not take abode there where sin is active either. So that if you want to write to Mr. Baranov, I am convinced that nothing will come of it except more evil, especially if he finds I have written you. If he remains as manager here, evil will not cure evil. Even so, he is entering in his books 1500 roubles for the church and the clergy, but it would be better for me if he had taken as *much from* me but acted here with greater decency. I am mentioning all this because I fear there will be worse consequences if he learns that I am writing. According to his custom, he would be forced to denigrate me further, and I might lose my patience and raise my voice to him and express my own dissatisfaction. I did not express my opinion about Baranov until I learned that he told his friends that he is against me. I would like to counsel you to send here Ivan Losipovich, or someone as good as he is. I could at least take counsel in private with a trusted man, and bring some order to some matters where it might be possible. I am not one who demands that everything be repaired immediately, but I do trust that in the long run God will set things right. It is not possible to take counsel with Baranov—he has his own. I am too timid to.

He sells his tobacco at exorbitant prices while there is in the storehouse twenty pud of company tobacco. When there are murmurs against his price, he blames you. You can look into this matter better than I, and I will attend to others.

Children born to Russian fathers with the permission of the manager are taken from their mothers—one or two years old—and try to take them to Russia. I do not like this at all. This kind of transport will be seen as cruelty and evidence of our dishonor. For the children it will be catastrophic. It would be better to bring them up here in the Russian manner. They should be taught to read, and then according to their abilities educated in other liberal arts. Then we could have people here as good promishlenniki instead of importing them from Russia. The state interest would also be served better. I see that there is an opportunity to raise them here if there were a good manager. In the meantime, they should leave the children here, and not allow them to take them to Russia. In all of this, I would like instructions from His Eminence, the Metropolitan, but in the meantime I want to know what you think about it and if we are in agreement.

The French free-thinking which is popular here gives me reason to think a lot. Here in the harbor there are robbers disturbing the peace, but also many good people, but the others are vulgar. When one passes a group of them they loudly curse me as an agent of the distant members of the company, while they openly swear at married companions and their wives in the market place. The prekrasniks are also persecuted. Hoping for Baranov's protection, I don't see how I can go to Yakutat. Baranov always makes difficulties for me and Ivan Gregorievich. He keeps apart from him and refuses to speak to him. He says let them go and settle with Archimandrite. In the fall he promises to give some planks, but now he says he remembers nothing about them. He has used all the lumber himself, and he told me that he would send me beyond the company possessions before Sheilds goes, while he will proceed along the coast with a party.

(Source: *Alaskan Missionary Spirituality*, ed. Michael Oleksa [New York: Paulist Press, 1987], 58-62.)

33. *Description of Traditional Kodiak Religious Beliefs Comparing Them with Scripture,* by Bishop Petr, Compiled from the Valaam Archives, 1894

This description of the peoples of Alaska represents the growing awareness of the importance of understanding indigenous beliefs for missionaries and missions, and the ways in which that understanding was frequently built on firsthand observation by missionaries acting as ethnologists and anthropologists.

We have only very sparse information about the religious beliefs and ideas of the Kodiaks. They, like the Aleuts, believed in the immortality of the human soul and in life after death. This belief of theirs is indicated by two lines from a song noted down by Hieromonk Gedeon.

Enough of weeping! This world is not immortal: Aknak [the name of the deceased] has died as a person and will come to life again.

And so, according to the Kodiaks, this world is not immortal: the dead will be reborn, but where and how man will live when he is reborn, as the Kodiaks understand it, about this we know nothing.

The Kodiak people also believed in a Creator of the Universe: but this belief of theirs was extremely ill-defined, vague, and in part naive. About the creation of the world they have the following idea or, to put it more precisely, opinion. There was a certain Kashshakhiliuk [wise man or clever man]. At that time there was neither day nor night. He began to blow on a straw. This caused the earth gradually to grow out of the water and imperceptibly to spread. Then, while he was still blowing, the heavens opened and the sun appeared: and after dusk the stars came out, and the moon rose. Finally men and beasts appeared. This is all that we know about the religion of the Aleuts and the Kodiaks. We should add that both the former and the latter have all possible kinds of superstitions, but amongst them there is none which is persistent

or especially harmful, with the exception of the savage custom, mentioned above, of killing kalgas [slaves] over the graves of their masters. Neither the Aleut shamans, nor those of the Kodiaks, had the status of a powerful caste of priests and any powerful religious or moral influence; their role was more that of witch-doctors, or magicians, who had dealings with spirits.

Let us allow ourselves to direct the reader's special attention to some of the religious concepts and moral rules of the Aleuts and the Kodiaks. These concepts and laws have sometimes a very distant and sometimes a very close similarity to the message preached in the Holy Scriptures:

(a) "The place where the first people came from was warm; there were no winters or storms, but always gentle healthy breezes. To begin with people lived in peace and knew no want. The first people were gifted with long life," and so forth [the Aleut belief about man's origins and subsequent development which we quoted above in full]. What do we find in these ideas? In the distant past people led a peaceful life in a beautiful place where eternal Spring reigns—a life without enmity or want. This is the biblical paradise, the innocent and blessed condition of the first men, reflected, of course, not with literal exactness, but in a certain, very similar way. The longevity of the first people is the longevity of the patriarchs of the Bible. Later, so the Aleut belief goes, need and enmity arise—this is the story of man, from its natural side and development, after the Fall, and it does not contradict the Biblical account. The essential difference is that in the Aleut account the causes also are shown to be only natural, and not the darkening of man's nature through his transgression against God's teaching through the Fall, as happened in fact.

(b) According to the Kodiak account of the Creation there was a certain Kashshakhiliuk [wise man], i.e. [to put it into more readily intelligible terms], there was a certain all-knowing and at the same time personalized principle, a Creator. This is not to say even then that there actually was anyone, or anything; in other words, apart from the all-knowing Creator, there was nothing and no one. But can this unenlightened idea of the human condition, distorted by many centuries, be an idea of the eternal, ever-present God? At that time, according to Kodiak belief, there was neither day nor night; and the Bible says the same. He [Kash-shakhiliuk, the wise man] began to blow on a straw; and this is how the land gradually rose out of the waters and grew. The Bible also relates a similar gradual process, with the land appearing from the depths of primeval chaos. And so, the wise man, the all-knowing Creator, created the Earth simply by the blowing of his breath. In the 32nd psalm [*sic.* Ps. 19:1] the King and Prophet David says: "The heavens declare the Glory of God; and the firmament sheweth his handiwork"; in other words, "By the word of the Lord were the heavens made; and all the host of them by the breath of his mouth" [Ps. 33:6]. Are the heavens not higher than the land? "And all the majesty of the heavens is created by the Voice of God": such is the limitless force, the boundless might of Him who is without beginning and without end. Does not the naive *straw* of the legend point to the Glory of the Creator and the pettiness of the Earth by comparison with Him? He, the Creator of the world, is so immeasurably great and powerful by comparison with his creation, that for him the act of breathing alone is sufficient to create the Earth, for there was nothing there before. Then, while he [the wise man] was still blowing (in other words while the creation was still taking place), the sky opened, the sun appeared, and after dusk the stars appeared and the moon rose. This, according to the Bible, was on the fourth day of the Creation. Finally, animals and people came. If by "animals" we understand all species without distinction, then this is the fifth and sixth days of the Creation according to the Bible story. There are omissions, there are distortions by comparison with the Bible, but the actual sequence of the Creation has not been lost at all. The wise man went on blowing throughout the whole process of creation. This blowing, this breathing of the breath of life, however naively it is expressed in the beliefs of these savage people of Kodiak, becomes for us an intelligible [although doubtless distorted] reflection of the Holy Truth—when we compare it with the words of the psalmist. In the Bible we read: "And the Lord God formed Man of the dust of the ground, and breathed into his nostrils the breath of life" (Gen. 2:7). Here again we find—breathing, breath of life. In the half-savage Aleuts or Kodiaks we can see only too clearly a half-understanding of God; and for us, Christians, enlightened by the

Son of God to the fullness necessary for a man of Holy Revelation [for the Lord has revealed to us only that which we are capable of understanding], God is an unreachable Being—"God is not a name, but an idea, deep-seated in the nature of man, about something which cannot be explained," said the holy martyr Justin, the philosopher (Apologia 2:6).

(c) The detailed moral laws about respect for one's parents and for older people in general, with the promise in return of a long life and other earthly reward (. . . in *Notes on the Island of the Unalashka District,* part II, pp. 136-137), are they not the same moral injunctions which are present in the fifth commandment of the laws of Moses: "Honor thy father and thy mother: that thy days may be long upon the land . . ." (Ex 20:12)?

(d) "We are all born from one father and mother, and are all brothers one of another" (*Notes,* chap. 22, p. 142). Here are expressed both the moral concept of the brotherhood of all peoples one of another, and the conviction about the origin of all peoples from one pair, which is what the Holy Scriptures tell us.

In general the pure and elevated moral ideas of the Aleuts and Kodiaks and their religious views are in essence similar to the Bible stories, although they are fragmented and obscured by the continuing moral condition of these peoples, and they lead us to the very instructive conclusion quoted below. The legends of these peoples confirm the origins of all people, of all the human race from one pair of progenitors. Otherwise how would we be able, in the case of the Aleuts and Kodiaks, living at an enormous distance from the places and people amongst whom the Bible came into being, and several thousand years later, to come across conceptions of the creation of the world and the beginnings of the life of man similar to the Bible stories? The incomplete and fragmentary nature of the religious views of the Aleuts and Kodiaks can simply be explained by the fact that they have been too long, like many other peoples, removed from the direct influence of God's Revelations, which alone can communicate to people in all its fullness the knowledge they need to have about God and the World, whereas originally God's Revelation was limited in all its purity to the European peoples alone. It must be noted that in accordance with

God's Holy Revelations the Aleuts and the Kodi-aks were not completely bereft of God's Grace, as a result of which there remained with them a sense of morality which prevented them from falling into ultimate sin.

The unity of man's nature, for us, is not a matter for question; it is a firm conviction. But let us also note that anthropology, from that time [on], since more attention has been directed to studying various peoples from a psychological point of view, cannot now but recognize that "the basic traits of human psychology appear to be similar in people with different colored skins." True science only confirms the Holy Scriptures. And although mistakes are unavoidable in every human endeavor, we must, however, be careful not to accept frivolously as science that which only calls itself by that great name.

Moral laws can only be firm, effective, can only have a binding force when they are based upon religion, when they flow out of a religion which is sacred to the people, not only in words but in deeds, or—when the very moral laws themselves are as sacred as religion. This latter we can observe in the case of the Aleuts and the Kodiaks. They had no strict system of concepts about the true God, the Creator and the Founder of the world. The moral laws, which they respected as religion, replaced this latter for them, up until that time when merciful God was so good as to send them the light of His true knowledge.

(Source: *Alaskan Missionary Spirituality*, ed. Michael Oleksa [New York: Paulist Press, 1987], 68-72; the preceding text and the letter from Bishop Petr are originally taken from *The Russian-Orthodox Mission 1794-1837* [Kingston, Ontario: Limestone Press, 1978].)

34. *Secret Letter from Hieromonk Makarii*

In the following selection we find the Ortho-dox missionaries using Imperial interests as leverage against the Russian American Com-pany and its manager through a secret letter to his Metropolitan by Hieromonk Makarii.

1805 1st June, Kodiak
Secret
Benevolent Metropolitan

Since the receipt of reliable information about the unfortunate wreck of the company vessel *Phoe-nix,* on which the Very Reverend Bishop of Kodiak, Ioasaf, had set out from Okhotsk, the following has happened to the clergy remaining here. In addition to encouraging the Aleuts to commit many stupid acts, which could have only been thought up on the company's part to besmirch the honor of the clergy, out of envy for the great love which this childlike people has for its enlighteners, the manager Baranov, thinking this to be the reason for a diminution of his authority over the Americans, worn out by their various duties and the company taxes, on 14th July 1800, in a letter to the steward of the Religious Mission, the Monk Herman, forbade the clergy to have any contact with the Americans and ordered all those who were on close terms with the preachers to be driven off.

In accordance with the Imperial Manifesto published in the year 1796, the Kodiak people should have been brought to swear an oath of allegiance to the Russian Throne. As a result of being sent great distances by the company and lack of time this had not been done. Therefore, on 1st January 1801, Hieromonk Afanasii sought Baranov's permission to do this. In return the Hieromonk himself was shouted out and driven off with a warning not to come back. Then some twenty men from various villages gathered with their *taions* to ask Baranov to release them from the obligation of any further distant hunting trips by the Sitkha party, promising in return to hunt near their villages, but they were chased away and threatened with dire consequences. Then all were ordered to prepare for another spring expedition. They were then very bitter and desperate and dared inform the missionaries that they did not want to go on this expedition because many of their relatives had died [on previous ones to Sitkha] and some of their villages were deserted. And if Baranov were to have them killed as a result they had each brought a new parka along and they asked the missionaries to bury them afterwards in their new clothes, and bear witness to this killing of innocents. On hearing this the clergy and the officers who were present—navigator Talin and the Religious Mission's interpreter Prianishnikov—were horrified and tried to talk them into forbearance, assuring them that His Imperial Majesty would be favorably disposed. When the *taions* had calmed down a little the matter of the oath of allegiance to the Sovereign was raised. They readily agreed to this and promised to obey in all things. Thus they set off for the church, accompanied by the same two officers and the swearing of the oath was conducted by Hieromonk Afanasii. As they left the church and were only just getting into their *baidarkas*, Baranov's deputy, Kuskov, with his hunters, seized one of the leading *taions* and took him off to the company barracks. Here he was put in irons and flung into a dark cell where not only the windows but every crack had been boarded up. The hunters then set out after the others in a *baidara*, with their rifles, but they caught no one.

After this incident Baranov wanted to seize and imprison another *taion*, a godson of the Bishop, who had come to see the priests on a friendly visit. When they learned of this the priests decided to accompany him that night on his return journey. As a precaution the Hieromonk Afanasii I ordered his own *baidarka* to be made ready first, then he walked to it and was about to enter it to travel for a short distance when suddenly some hunters, acting on Baranov's orders, stopped the *baidarka* and seized the Hieromonk. Then Baranov himself, in a towering rage, began to curse, calling Afanasii a runaway state serf and all the priests and the two above-mentioned officers rebels.

Faced with such an unpleasant series of events, the monk Herman asked Baranov to declare in decent language the reason for his displeasure. The manager shouted: "Now you've found some kind of oath and used it to turn the Americans against us!"

The humble elder replied: "The Imperial Manifesto was made public to all; if indeed the Religious Mission has acted at all illegally then the matter should be reported to the government where everything can be examined in accordance with the law."

But Baranov paid no heed to this and continued shouting: "What manifesto? What court?" And at the height of his rage he made many threats. First he said he would have them put in irons and taken to Unalashka, then that the mission's quarters would be locked and boarded up so that no one could get to them and they could not go out. This made everyone greatly afraid and they all expected

at any moment to be seized by the hunters on Baranov's orders and dragged off or beaten. They hardly dared leave the shore to return to their house, around which they could see a crowd of armed hunters. For the same reason they did not even dare go freely to the church, and consequently for more than a year they conducted all their services in the house, and they also doubted their loyalty, because the oath of allegiance had been forbidden.

When the time came round to form the otter hunting party, Kuskov armed a *baidara* not only with rifles but also with a cannon and set out for the village inhabited by the natives who had sworn the oath. In order to achieve a greater effect, *partovshchik* Kondakov was ordered to travel ahead. Arriving at the village he cursed foully, made sneering remarks about the priests, and then shouted loudly: "Come out to meet us—the priests are coming, and Osip (the interpreter) is here to get you to swear the oath!" And when the rudder was carried ashore from the *baidara* they all shouted: "Here's your cross! Get down and worship it!" And they went on to commit angry, violent, and shameless acts against the islanders, too shameful to mention.

Baranov explained this evildoing by alleging that the Americans, at the instigation of the priests and the two above-mentioned officers, had rebelled and would have killed all the Russians, and this was why Kuskov took hostages on this expedition. After this Baranov began in every conceivable way to oppress the priests, in the preparation of winter food stocks and in other vital matters.

In 1802 in Holy Week the hunter Chernov arrived drunk and said with great coarseness that he came from Baranov with orders that Hierodeacon Nektarii should unlock the belfry. The Hierodeacon was unwilling to give him the key because the church was only secured with one lock, and the large bell was broken. The hunter then flew into a rage and brazenly threatened either to drag him there by force or to smash the windows in the bell tower. Meanwhile the interpreter Prianishnikov, who was ill, had sent a note to the Hieromonk and the Hierodeacon asking them to sanctify his house with the Holy Cross. No sooner had they gone there when Baranov came running up together with his hunters, beside himself with rage, shouting, cursing and threatening to put the Hieromonk in a *baidarka* and set him adrift. He grabbed the

Hierodeacon violently by the chest and wanted to hang him from the bell tower. This caused the latter such fright that he was forced to yield the key to the church. During all these brazen acts the hunters would say with reference to their manager, "God is high and the Tsar is far away—all is fine as long as our boss is alive and well!"

For reasons described above, as well as the fact that the Americans no longer dared to visit the priests openly, and the priests for their part were afraid to have the relations with them that their calling demanded—when they would have been able to instill Christian teachings into them—the success of the Religious Mission did not come up to expectations. For those of our compatriots who were obliged to work for the company were of the lowest and most immoral kind, as the local manager himself testifies constantly when he calls them people from the Kama and the Volga. The Americans, on the other hand, are so burdened by endless labors and so harassed that wherever the Russians set up settlements they attract hatred. Even distant peoples on the fringes of our territories found the word "Russian" an object of hatred. The women kill their babies in the womb and sometimes later, rather than let them be tortured by the company. In this current year in the settlements on the island of Shalitok mothers deliberately stopped feeding children aged between eight and ten, and killed five by starving them in this way so that they should not become workers for the Russians.

The Manager, growing fearful lest the oath should be confirmed and that reports of oppression of the clergy should become known to officers on visiting company ships tried to smooth over what he had done; and for this reason he found himself forced to forward the Manifesto and letters belonging to the Religious Mission which had up to then been held back, and let it be known that all should be made to swear the oath—thus the priests, no longer in doubt about loyalty, began, as from 15th September 1802 to conduct services in the church once more. Baranov became more favorably disposed towards them: first he sent two pounds of tea and four pounds of sugar, then a barrel of whale fat, a cask of whale meat, and a barrel of *shiksha* berries mixed with fat, which is known in the northern area of Russia as *voronitsa*, but the people there do not eat it. A short while later he sent a

paper which, in return for the conducting of the service for those killed at Sitkha, gave the bearer the right to draw any goods from the stores to the value of 500 rubles. Subsequently another note arrived from the same office, in which as a result of a collection among some hunters and the manager during their operations there was forwarded to be used as befitted more than three thousand rubles, the greater part to go to the church and a lesser portion for the brothers. Against such a sum they took what they needed from the company stores at the very highest prices as, for example, a *pud* of tobacco at 75 rubles, a pound of sugar at 3 rubles 60 kopeks, a pound of tea at 8 and 6 rubles, a *pud* of wheat biscuits at 20 rubles, a measure of vodka at 25 rubles and for domestic use hempen rope of the lowest quality at one ruble a pound.

The clergy all live in one house allotted them by the company, in a cramped position between the manager's house and the communal company baths. They feed themselves, by and large, on the fruits of their own labors. Apart from their vegetable crops they gather various berries and mushrooms, catch fish, and receive supplementary supplies from the company. All of these tasks are carried out with the help of Americans, whom the company tries in every way to drive away.

The priests wear clothing and shoes from the stock remaining since the time of Bishop Ioasaf; they also have grain—which was originally brought here by Shelekhov—namely, 250 *puds* of rye, 20 *puds* of wheat for holy wafers and 20 *puds* of assorted groats. Before the departure of the Bishop, the Bishop's house on Kadiak was credited with 150 *puds* of rye.

Hierodeacon Nektarii is 36 and the monk Ioasaf is 32, and both wish greatly to return to Russia and with heavy hearts they beg and beseech You, Most Holy and Most Merciful Father, for your Archpastoral blessing: Let their prayers be fulfilled before you, in Christ, like holy incense. For their hearts are full of sorrow. Comfort them, blessed comforter of the Church of Russia!

The Hieromonk is 50, and the Monk Herman 48. Both are lovers of solitude and wish to remain in America. But because of the fact that the house allotted to them is right next to secular ones, making it impossible for them to escape the noise and temptations, the boundless acts of crude inhuman-ity committed by the Russians on each other, but mostly on the Americans under them, as well as the fact that they have far to go to fetch firewood and other things needed in the house and because of the general unsuitability and cramped conditions of the place, they are very frustrated. Their intention is to put some distance between themselves and these noisy places, to have a calm life in particular somewhere near the church, and if there is no source (i.e., either official or private) from which they can get food and the necessary supplies, then at least they can place their hopes on the fruits of their own labors. They can choose a spot which has ready supplies of wood for building, is near a stream for fishing and has suitable ground for tilling.

Most Holy Archpastor! Hear my cry! Do not turn Thy face away, most Merciful Father, from this single, humble son of Thy Holy House, for I suffer. Quickly, quickly, hear me! Lead my soul out of the darkness to confess in Thy name.

Your Holiness's etc. . . .

(Source: *Alaskan Missionary Spirituality*, ed. Michael Oleksa [New York: Paulist Press, 1987], 58-64.)

35. *A Petition from the Tlingit Orthodox Chiefs to the President of the United States, 1897*

Sir:

From the very time that the United States raised her flag here and in the whole Territory, our people represented by their chief's prominent members, have not ceased to address themselves direct to the Government at Washington, while knowing the fact that the Government is represented here by the Governor and other officials. The reason of this is following; because here we cannot get any satisfaction to our just and lawful demands. We know that the Russian Government at the time of the transfer of Alaska to the U.S. did not sell us as slaves to America, but left us some rights and privileges which were later made lawful and firm by the U.S. Congress. The Organic act, providing a civil Government for Alaska in section 8 provides that the Indians or other persons in said district shall not be disturbed in the possession of any lands actually in their use or occupation or now claimed by them. On the strength of this law we always understood that every Indian has a right to dispose of his own life and liberty and his own property whether it consists in personal possessions or real estate, for instance: lands, forests, lagoons, some small bay and rivers in which we could procure for ourselves the necessary food and other things for existence.

We always thought and surmised that the civil Government sent out from Washington would punish criminals equally whether white or native, if a white man spills the blood of an Indian or an Indian spills the blood of a white man, the justice would mete out equal punishment. But in reality this equality was never practised. It is true that the first four years of the protection of the American Eagle remain in our minds clear and unsullied cloud of the misunderstanding between a white man and an Indian. It is true that, from the time of Governor Kinkaid until Governor Swineford, when the scales of justice were held by the hands of Haskett, we could sometimes receive satisfaction, but during the remaining time there never was justice and is none now, it has perished.

More so from the time the Presbyterian Mission with such workers as Mr. J. J. Brady & Co. came to Sitka, our condition became unbearable.

In our mind's eye there rise 28 souls of our friends and relatives that innocently perished from the hand of white men. Of course we always made complaints to the U.S. Courts, and in Courts everywhere received from the Authorities only promises and never satisfaction. Not a single white murderer ending with the last Mills, by name, who killed Donald Austin, a native, ever received retaliation and now enjoys full liberty. With all this we never lost faith in the Government at Washington. This sorrowful reality only made us lose faith in persons sent out here by the Government.

From the Government we always expected and do expect to receive satisfaction to our lawful demands. We believe that the promises of the Vice President who recently visited Sitka were not empty words. And at the present moment bearing the proposition of Government Official Commissioner Geo. R. Tingle to try once more with his help, we believe that our petition will reach the desired end. We leave out the old petitions offered to the Government in former years we offer our petition which is as follow:

1) Not to allow Mr. Brady a right of way through the centre of village along the narrow beach which is situated between the water and our houses, where we keep our boats, canoes, and other things. To forbid him to destroy buildings and other property while building this road. We do not offer pretensions to the land that he now possesses, which was from time immemorial the property of our ancestors, and served us as cemetery. It is enough for him that he unlawfully took possession of this land, and with the bones of some he banked his ground and some he threw into the water. We do not wish to have such work going on, and do not wish other white men to follow Mr. Brady's example.

2) We beg to have Mr. Smith, the superintendent of the Baranoff Packing Co., forbidden to take away from us our bays, streams, and lagoons where we fished long before white man came. We want him to do such fishing as necessary for him with our consent. We demand that he stop throwing bars and traps across the streams, where by the fish can not enter the lakes for the purpose of spawning. His method of fishing in the last 8 years in Redout, Cross Sound, Hoonah, Whale Bay, Nika Bay, Red Fish Bay, compels us to see very plainly that the places mentioned are becoming empty.

Now the Thlingits are compelled to put up their fish in distant places, which with the canoe is reached only with great deal of hard ship.

3) We do not want American saloons. We beg the Government to close them. We understand now that whiskey is poison for us. Tramps and Idle people like soldiers and sailors bring whiskey into our midst from those saloons. They give it our wives and daughters make them drunk and often seduce them in that state. We have brought such cases to the local authorities here and the result is that the white man goes free and unpunished, but the native suffers fines, imprisonment, and punishment. Saloons and other places of amusement of such caliber are not necessary for the welfare of our daughters. We do not want the civilization that only does not stop saloons but encourages them. We do not want the education by which our daughters are torn from their homes and alienated, taught the English language only to give them an easier scope and advantage to practice prostitution. Drunkenness brought

adultery with our families, adultery destroyed all ties by which our family relation existed. We do not want to look upon these horrible existing evils with ease and light minds and we wish that the crimes committed would be punished not by light fines, but in some way which they could do most good. We do not imagine for one moment that the dance halls and dives of Juneau and Sitka must necessarily be filled with our educated daughters.

We could go on without end to our petitions. We have shown facts and beg the Government to allow us some recognition. The answer to former petitions was never received by the Indians perhaps through the fault of the mediator, in the petition, and we beg the Government to the answer to this to Khlantich, head chief of Sitka tribe.

We have the honor to subscribe ourselves your Most Obedient Servants.

John Khlantich, Tom Katzekoni, Sergay Anlizhe, Alexander Natzlen, Paul Kattan, Oushkinakk, Nowaya, Saha, Vattaan, Quitka.

(Source: *Alaska Missionary Spirituality*, ed. Michael Oleksa [New York: Paulist Press, 1987], 323-26.)

36. *A Letter to the Jesse Lee Methodist Home from an Orthodox Priest, Unalashka, October 16, 1900*

This brief exchange between a representative of the long-established Orthodox mission in Alaska and the much newer Protestant mission offers insight into both the difficulties faced when imperial oversight of a mission field changed and the attitudes of two religious groups that scarcely had contact toward one another. Relationships between Protestant missionaries and established Orthodox churches has frequently been difficult, as each tried (or failed to try) and understand the consequences of living in a Christianly plural world.

To the Manager of Jesse Lee Home

Dear Manager

Lately with sorrow I found out about the assumption, without necessary Christian viaticum (i.e., confession and holy communion of mysteries of the Body and Blood of Our Lord Jesus Christ), to life beyond the tomb of my spiritual daughter Irene Titoff, a resident of your home.

Your inimical action surprises me as much in respect to deceased! Admitting to your home for culture this Irene Titoff, you pledged yourself to leave her religious sentiment inviolable in regard to confession of creed which she had before entering your establishment. And this your obligation to your honor, need be noted, you fulfilled nearly to the end of her earthly life, namely: You let her come to our house of God for church services on Sundays, and she yearly (and even this ensuing year 1900) was to confession and communion of holy mysteries in our temple of God. Why did you deprive her of the latter before her end? If you fulfilled this, by inviting me—her spiritual father, you would afford her a great spiritual consolation in her last days of earthly life, once she was by this comforted her whole life! I am certain that deprivation by you of this distressed her, and she with grief in her youthful heart passed from you to life beyond the tomb! It signifies, the fulfilment of your obligation above noted in regard to now deceased Irene Titoff, was from your side purely external, and for evasion as the saying is from our eyes! Is it possible, such course of your proceedings in given case can be called by you Christian actions, and is it possible, that you think they are agreeable to our Lord Jesus Christ!

If you have no possibility through some cause to notify me of such, especially ailing condition of my spiritual children found in your house, whom follows their end; then allow me, if not daily, then, at least, weekly to visit your house myself personally for this purpose. I will for granting of this my request, be very grateful to you. I think that this permission of yours from your side, concerning me and my spiritual children, will be fully judicious and Christian. I want to ask you on certain foundation the following: If there is a "Russian" or American religion I know no such religions. I only know that there is a Christian religion, to our misfortune divided in two: one orthodox; and the other unorthodox.

Therefore, if you happen sometime to address some one with a question about Christian religion, them guided by the above said, it is necessary to ask by the way, this: "Do you want to be an *orthodox Christian or unorthodox*," and not thus, "Do

you want to have a Russian religion or American," so as *to lead into fatal temptation*. . . .

But, it is hardly possible that such question about religion can be intelligible to children found with you, especially at their earthly end?! If even the child did answer as you wish it to, you must know that such answer will be extorted and not given voluntarily, for the sick child, seeing your attention to it for the relief of its suffering, will not want to affront you by an undesirable to you answer to your question.

Above all in given case,—besides wishing not to affront you, there is a child's fear, for an answer which may fail to satisfy you! Judge then for yourself, if this is an example of Christian actions? It seems to me, that yourself will admit unseemliness of your actions as given concerning me.

That, I observe by the way, partly from this, that you as if secretly from us, at the time of our church service, buried the deceased.

I write this to you without the ill intention to mortify or to insult you and, what more, not with—1-st that you would strengthen still more your unfounded inimical action toward me, and 2-d that between us might be animosity,—mother of every dissent and whose father is the first murderer; But this firstly to express to you my bitterness and my view of your action concerning the deceased and myself, and secondly to give feasibility to think of this and to be impressed!

May there be God's peace between us.

Yours respectfully

Rev. Father Alexander Kedrofsky

P.S. At the time of my absence this summer, my spiritual children living with you, for a cause unknown to me, very seldom visited the God's house for prayer on Sundays, to this also I would wish to call your benevolent attention.

Rev. A. K.

(Source: *Alaska Missionary Spirituality*, ed. Michael Oleksa [New York: Paulist Press, 1987], 329-31.)

37. *A Reply from the Methodist Matron, 1900*

Unalashka, Alaska, Nov. 12, 1900.
Rev. A. Kedrofsky
Dear Sir.

In reply to your letter of Oct, 16-th, will write as follows:—

The Jesse Lee Home is an institution under the Woman's Home Missionary Society of the Methodist Episcopal church.

Its objects—the advancement of Christ's Kingdom and the uplifting of fallen humanity. Its special interest and work lies in the children of Alaska. The children placed in our care are clothed, fed, cared for, educated and their moral and spiritual welfare carefully guarded. We assume complete charge of the children while under our care. As the religious instruction is wholly under the direction of the Home management, and according to Protestant faith, your request to visit the Home for religious instruction cannot be granted. For this reason, no children are admitted to the Home with the privilege of attending the Greco-Russian Church. To be sure, four Seal Islands girls and two others are allowed to attend said church when, according to *our* judgment, the weather and their condition of health will permit.

In case of death, services and burial are conducted by the Home management except in such cases as *we* shall decide otherwise. Interference in these respects will not be tolerated. It is our aim and prayer that these children may be led to become true Christians. Is it enough to take the name of Christ upon our lips, to witness the forms and ceremonies of worship week after week, and still go on in sin and wickedness? We think not.

Is not the moral condition of the greater part of the natives in this village deplorable? Very religious as outward forms go, but intensely sinful in life. Most of their homes veritable brothels of sin.

Is not dishonesty, profanity, adultery, fornication, lasciviousness, strife, and drunkenness rife? Is it not an insult to God and the cross of Christ for such workers of iniquity to call themselves Christian? We think so.

I know you realize these things and are pained by them. I know you desire to see these people true followers of God. Oh that God's Spirit may work upon their hearts! that there might be a godly sorrow for sin, a turning from their evil ways to paths of righteousness! Our hearts are made sad to think of our children going out to lead such lives. What else can be expected with such environments? Only the Power of God through the atoning and cleansing power of Jesus' Blood can change the heart and transform the life. Irene Tetoff died in this Home and by her own request you were not called. Services were conducted according to her own wishes. She was given the privilege of calling you, if she so desired. This was not a hasty decision on her part.

For more than a year Irene had been striving to lead a Christian life. As a matter of choice she attended the Greco-Russian Church, but occasionally, during that time. Irene did not attend church Easter week nor go to confession (1900). Nevertheless Irene did not depart this life without holy confession, for she made an honest confession to God, which in our faith, is more than confession to man, and realized pardon and peace from above. Hers was a triumphant death such as the children had never witnessed and can never forget. In religion we must agree to disagree and in the Spirit of Christ pursue our way. Personally, we have great respect for you and recognize the fact that *your character and daily life are an example,* such as the people *have not often had before them during the past.*

May God's blessing be with you and make you a blessing in this place,

Yours Respectfully
Agnes L. Newhall
(Matron Jesse Lee Home)
(Source: *Alaska Missionary Spirituality*, ed. Michael Oleska [New York: Paulist Press, 1987], 331-32.)

Timothy Richard on Chinese Religions

Timothy Richard (1845-1919) was a Baptist missionary to China who became deeply engaged in understanding how Buddhism shaped Chinese thought and culture, and how an appreciation of Buddhism and Chinese culture could shape Christian missionary efforts. Appreciated by Chinese reformers, and often in conflict with more conservative missionaries, he was a pioneer in developing an understanding of how God manifested God's nature in non-Christian cultures. The first reading is an appendix to Richard's translation of the work of Ta Ching Ki Shin Lun, or The Awakening of Faith, *or* The Mahayana Faith. *The second is his introduction to the same work.*

38. *To Sin King*

This Creed deserves to rank among the sublimest literary productions of the human mind, from Job to Kant, together with those of the best thinkers of India and China.

Many devout people of the Confucian and Taoist schools, as well as Buddhists, recite it daily just as Christians sing a choice hymn.

It states the solid fundamental principles of religion which commend themselves, not merely to the majority of Asiatics, but also to the majority of men universally. It includes the need of Divine Power to save men, the great At-One-ment, Divine Inspiration, Divinest Miracles, past, present, and to come, and Immortality.

When this best Eastern thought is united to the best Western thought, whatever may be deficient in definition in either singly, may meet the approval of that conscience which God has given to mankind collectively.

The Creed is as follows:—

Hail self-existent Illuminator, Who in exercising deepest Wisdom seest the unreality of all that is reached by the five senses, and canst save from all troubles and dangers.

O Sariputra (the Divine Seed?), the Manifested is not different from the Eternal, and the Eternal is not different from the Manifested. Thought and Action are also thus mutually related.

The Divine Seed (?) is the Eternal in all laws of the Universe. He was never born, nor will ever die.

He is neither clean nor unclean, is neither added to nor subtracted from. He is without sorrow, and will not perish. He is without acquired Wisdom, because he has received none.

The Illuminators depending on this Eternal Wisdom are without anxiety. Having no anxiety, they have no fear and are far from impossible dreams and thoughts. They are eventually immortals.

All the Illuminated past, present, and to come, depending on this Divine Wisdom, obtain the Highest Wisdom.

Therefore know that this Divine Wisdom is a great Divine Magic, a great brilliant magic, the greatest magic, and a magic without a peer.

It can deliver you from all kinds of troubles. This is a real truth without any falsehood.

Therefore in repeating this magic incantation, sum up and say—

> Praise, Praise,
> Praise God.
> Praise His eternal wisdom (Law)
> Praise the students of this Law,
>   The Illumined!

(Source: Translated from the Buddhist Tripitaka, Nanjio's Catalogue, no. 20, in Timothy Richard, *The New Testament of Higher Buddhism* [Edinburgh: T&T Clark, 1910].)

39. *The Religion of the Future*

We Christians believe that the kingdoms of this world shall become the kingdom of our Lord, and that then there will be but One Faith. Meanwhile, we look out on the religious world as it exists today, and note that among all the habits of men none are more permanent than the religious. It is the habit of caste in India carried on for millenniums that makes it second nature to the Hindu, as if caste were as fixed as the stars in the heavens or as immovable as the earth beneath them.

The same is true of Chinese religions—Confucianism, Buddhism, and Taoism; and is equally true of Christianity, Islam, and the minor reformed branches of Sikhs and Bahaists. The children of all lands follow their parents from age to age, not so much from knowledge as from habit.

The Buddhists believe that Sakyamuni was all-wise, therefore taught the highest truths for mankind.

Confucianists vaguely believe that the Emperor of China is the only son of Heaven, and therefore nations should obey him.

The Shintoists believe that the Emperor is different in kind from ordinary mortals descendant of the gods, therefore superior to all beings of earth.

The Pope believes that he represents God on earth, and that all rulers should obey him.

The Mohammedans believe that Mohammed is the last prophet of God to men, and that all men should obey him.

The Sikhs and the Bahaists believe the same of the founders of their religions.

It is only once in five hundred or a thousand

years that a man arrives with strength enough to change the religious custom of many generations as a result of study and knowledge of the need of the times. So long as national intercourse was partial, these religious founders stereotyped the habit of their respective religions in local districts or nations, until now we have about seven men in all the world who claim obedience from all the rest.

The time of universal intercourse dawned upon mankind with the advent of steam and electricity within the last century. With this there has arisen the feeling that the next step in religious evolution is not a monopoly of any one of these competitive religions but a federation of all, on a basis that acknowledges with gratitude all that is best in the past in different parts of the earth as Divine, and then finally following the one which surpasses all the rest in authority and in usefulness to the human race.

There would be no difficulty in getting the most intelligent to recognise Moses and the prophets of Israel, Confucius and Mencius, the Sages of China, Mohammed, God's ambassador to the Arabs, as all sent of God. And the final step in religion is foreshadowed by the firm belief of Hindus, Buddhists, and Christians, that the supreme Saviour of men must be God Incarnate. Latently, if not expressed, Confucianism, Taoism, and Shintoism base their claim to obedience on the belief that their teaching is derived from Heaven, where alone Power, Wisdom, Justice, and Mercy are to be found in perfection.

The Religion of the future which will satisfy all nations and all races will not be born of any party cry, but will be born from the habit of looking at the highest and permanent elements in all religions and gladly recognizing all that helps to save man, body, soul, and spirit, individually or collectively, as Divine.

The whole intelligent world is getting tired of the struggle concerning the different doctrines and practices of the various religions and their subdivisions into many hundreds of sects, but all are eager to know what light any or all of them can throw on—

How to deliver one-tenth of the world from poverty and oppression.

How to deliver one-half of the world from violent men, who produce strikes, riots, rebellions, and wars.

How to deliver more than half of the world from ignorance and superstition, so that the fruits of the best knowledge God has given us may be reaped.

How to deliver all human hearts from the disease of selfishness and sin, that they may be made right with God and man.

To answer these questions aright is to begin the establishment of the kingdom of God on earth, which Jesus Christ commanded His disciples to preach, and this is the one Great Religion of the future.

(Source: Timothy Richard, *The New Testament of Higher Buddhism* [Edinburgh: T&T Clark, 1910], 267-69.)

A Western Encounter with World Christianity

40. *The World Mission of Christianity: Messages and Recommendations of the Enlarged Meeting of the International Missionary Council,* Jerusalem, 1928

The Jerusalem meeting of the International Missionary Council in 1928 breathed a very different spirit from that of earlier councils. In particular the excerpt below illustrates the chastened attitude of a European Christianity only beginning to emerge from the horrors of the First World War both listening to Christian leaders from outside the West and recognizing the limits and possibilities of recognizing the value of non-Christian religions.

The Call to the World

Filled with conviction that Jesus Christ is indeed the Saviour of the world, and conscious of a desperate need in ourselves and in all the world for what He only can supply, we call upon our fellow Christians and all our fellow men to turn again to Him for pardon and for power.

To all the Churches of Christ we call: that they stand firmly upon the rock of Christian conviction and whole-heartedly accept its missionary obligations; that they go forward in full loyalty to Christ to discover and to express, in the power and freedom of the Holy Spirit, the treasures in His unsearchable riches which it is the privilege and duty of each to win for the Universal Church; that they strive to deliver the name of Christ and of Christianity from complicity in any evil or injustice.

Those who proclaim Christ's message must give evidence for it in their own lives and in the social institutions which they uphold. It is by living Christ among men that we may most effectively lift Him up before them. The spirit that returns love for hate, and overcomes evil with good, must be evidently present in those who would be witnesses for Christ. They are also bound to exert all their influence to secure that the social, international, and inter-racial relationships in the midst of which their work is done, are subordinate to and expressive of His spirit. Especially must it be a serious obstacle to missionary effort if a non-Christian country feels that the relation of the so-called Christian countries to itself is morally unsound or is alien from the principles of Christ, and the Church must be ready for labor and sacrifice to remove whatever is justly so condemned.

The task before us is beyond our powers. It can only be accomplished by the Holy Spirit, whose power we receive in its completeness only in the fellowship of Christ's disciples. We call all followers of Christ to take their full share as members of His Body, which is the Church; no discontent with its organization or tradition or failings should be allowed to keep us outside its fold; the isolated Christian is impoverished in his spiritual life and impotent in his activities; our strength, both inward and outward, is in the living fellowship. But in these hurried and feverish days there is also more need than ever for the deepening of our spiritual life through periodical detachment from the world and its need in lonely communion with God. We desire also to call for a greater volume of intercessory prayer. The whole Church should be earnest and instant in prayer, each part for every other, and all together for the Church's unity and for the hallowing of God's Name throughout the world.

Further, we call on Christians in all lands who are trained in science, art, or philosophy to devote their talents to the working out of that Christian view of life and the world which we sorely need to secure us against instability, bewilderment, and extravagance.

Lastly, we urge that every possible step be taken to make real the fellowship of the Gospel. The churches of the West send missions and missions-of-help to the churches of Africa and Asia. We believe that the time is come when all would gain if the younger churches were invited to send missions-of-help to the churches of Europe and America, that they may minister of their treasure to the spiritual life of those to whom they come.

To non-Christians also we make our call. We rejoice to think that just because in Jesus Christ the light that lighteneth every man shone forth in its full splendor, we find rays of that same light where He is unknown or even is rejected. We welcome every noble quality in non-Christian persons or systems as further proof that the Father, who sent His Son into the world, has nowhere left Himself without witness.

Thus, merely to give illustration, and making no attempt to estimate the spiritual value of other religions to their adherents, we recognize as part of the one Truth that sense of the Majesty of God and the consequent reverence in worship, which are conspicuous in Islam; the deep sympathy for the world's sorrow and unselfish search for the way of escape, which are at the heart of Buddhism; the desire for contact with Ultimate Reality conceived as spiritual, which is prominent in Hinduism; the belief in a moral order of the universe and consequent insistence on moral conduct, which are inculcated by Confucianism; the disinterested pursuit of truth and of human welfare which are often found in those who stand for secular civilization but do not accept Christ as their Lord and Saviour.

Especially we make our call to the Jewish people, whose Scriptures have become our own, and "of whom is Christ as concerning the flesh," that with open heart they turn to that Lord in whom is fulfilled the hope of their nation, its prophetic message, and its zeal for holiness. And we call upon our fellow Christians in all lands to show to Jews that loving-kindness that has too seldom been shown towards them.

We call on the followers of non-Christian religions to join with us in the study of Jesus Christ as He stands before us in the Scriptures, His place in the life of the world, and His power to satisfy the human heart; to hold fast to faith in the unseen and eternal in face of the growing materialism of the world; to cooperate with us against all the evils of secularism; to respect freedom of conscience so that men may confess Christ without separation from home and friends; and to discern that all the good of which men have conceived is fulfilled and secured in Christ.

Christianity is not a Western religion, nor is it yet effectively accepted by the Western world as a whole. Christ belongs to the peoples of Africa and Asia as much as to the European or American. We call all men to equal fellowship in Him. But to come to Him is always self-surrender.

We must not come in the pride of national heritage or religious tradition; he who would enter the Kingdom of God must become as a little child, though in that Kingdom are all the treasures of man's aspirations, consecrated and harmonized. Just because Christ is the self-disclosure of the One God, all human aspirations are towards Him, and yet of no human tradition is He merely the continuation. He is the desire of all nations; but He is always more, and other, than they had desired before they learnt of Him.

But we would insist that when the Gospel of the Love of God comes home with power to the human heart, it speaks to each man, not as Moslem or as Buddhist, or as an adherent of any system, but just as man. And while we rightly study other religions in order to approach men wisely, yet at the last we speak as men to men, inviting them to share with us the pardon and the life that we have found in Christ.

To all who inherit the benefits of secular civilization and contribute to its advancement we make our call. We claim for Christ the labors of scientists and artists. We recognize their service to His cause in dispersing the darkness of ignorance, superstition, and vulgarity. We appreciate also the noble elements that are found in nationalist movements and in patriotism, the loyalty, the self-devotion, the idealism, which love of country can inspire. But even these may lead to strife and bitterness and narrowness of outlook if they are not dedicated to Christ; in His universal Kingdom of Love all nations by right are provinces, and fulfil their own true destiny only in His service. When patriotism and science are not consecrated they are often debased into self-assertion, exploitation, and the service of greed. Indeed, throughout all nations the great peril of our time arises from that immense development of man's power over the resources of nature which has been the great characteristic of our epoch. This power gives opportunity for wealth of interest, and, through facilities of communication, for freedom of intercourse such as has never been known. But it has outgrown our spiritual and moral control.

Amid the clashes of industrial strife the Gospel summons men to work together as brothers in providing for the human family the economic basis of the good life. In the presence of social antipathies and exclusiveness the Gospel insists that we are members of one family, and that our Father desires for each a full and equal opportunity to attain to His own complete development, and to make his special contribution to the richness

(Source: *The World Mission of Christianity: Messages and Recommendations of the Enlarged Meeting of the International Missionary Council Held at Jerusalem, March 24-April 8, 1928* [New York: International Missionary Council, 1928].)

Pre-Vatican II Roman Catholic Documents

The following documents are pioneering papal letters and encyclicals reforming the practice of Roman Catholic mission in the first part of the twentieth century. In their emphasis on indigenous clergy, the importance

of social missions, the need for modern education, and mission establishments of befitting humility, they mark the beginning of a new era in Roman Catholic mission fully catalyzed in the documents of the Second Vatican Council found in the next section. In their concern for the problem of emerging nationalism, the rise of communism and other ideologies, they anticipate the struggle of Roman Catholicism to Christianly comprehend all the challenges of modernity found in late-twentieth-century documents like Dominus Iesus. *Not coincidentally they track similar concerns by Protestants, such as those found in the document* Lands of Witness and Decision *below.*

41. *Maximum illud*—Apostolic Letter of Benedict XV, 1919

Introduction

1. Before He returned to His Father, Our Lord Jesus Christ addressed to His disciples the words: "Go into the whole world and preach the gospel to all creation" (Mark 16:15). With these words He committed to them a duty, a momentous and a holy charge, that was not to lapse with the death of the Apostles but would bind their successors, one after another, until the end of the world—as long, that is, as there remained on this earth men whom the truth might set free. Entrusted with this mandate, "they went forth and preached everywhere" (Mark 16:20) the word of God, so that "through all the earth their voice resounds, and to the ends of the world, their message" (Psalm 18:5). From that time on, as the centuries have passed, the Church has never forgotten that command God gave her, and never yet has she ceased to dispatch to every corner of the world her couriers of the doctrine He entrusted to her, and her ministers of the eternal salvation that was delivered through Christ to the race of men.

Great Apostles of the Gospel

2. Even in the first three centuries, when persecution after persecution, inspired by Hell, fell upon the infant Church in a raging attempt to crush her, even then when the whole of civilization was deluged with Christian blood, out on the far frontiers of the Empire the heralds of the gospel journeyed, announcing their tidings. Then, after peace and religious freedom had been officially granted to the Church, her apostolate to the world made far greater progress. In this achievement a num-ber of men of striking sanctity played outstanding roles. One of them was Gregory the Illuminator, who brought the Faith to Armenia. Another was Victorinus, the apostle of Styria. Frumentius, who evangelized Ethiopia, was a third. Later on Patrick brought forth the Irish in Christ; Augustine introduced the Faith among the English; and Columba and Palladius preached the gospel to the Scots. Later still Clement Willibrord, the first Bishop of Utrecht, brought the radiance of the gospel to Holland; Boniface and Anagar carried the Faith to the Germans; and Cyril and Methodius won Slavonia for the Church. . . .

6. Anyone who studies the facts of this great saga cannot help being profoundly impressed by them: by all the stupendous hardships our missionaries have undergone in extending the Faith, the magnificent devotion they have shown, and the overwhelming examples of intrepid endurance they have afforded us. And to anyone who weighs these facts the realization must come as a shock that right now, there still remain in the world immense multitudes of people who dwell in darkness and in the shadow of death. According to a recent estimate, the number of non-believers in the world approximates one billion souls.

Purpose of This Letter

7. The pitiable lot of this stupendous number of souls is for Us a source of great sorrow. From the days when We first took up the responsibilities of this apostolic office We have yearned to share with these unfortunates the divine blessings of the Redemption. So We are delighted to see that, under the inspiration of the Spirit of God, efforts to promote and develop the foreign missions have in many quarters of the world increased and intensified. It is Our duty to foster these enterprises and do all We can to encourage them; and this duty

coincides perfectly with Our own most profound desires. Before writing this letter, venerable Brethren, We begged the Lord for His light and His aid. While writing it, We had two purposes in mind: to encourage you, your clergy, and your people in these efforts, and secondly, to point out methods you can adopt to further the fulfillment of this momentous undertaking.

To Those In Charge of the Missions

11. . . . the superior of a mission should make it one of his primary concerns to expand and fully develop his mission. The entire region within the boundaries of his mission has been committed to his care. Consequently, he must work for the eternal salvation of every person living there. If, out of an immense populace, he has converted a few thousand people, he has no reason to lapse into complacency. He must become a guide and a protector for these children he has brought forth in Jesus Christ; he must see to their spiritual nourishment and he must not let a single one of them slip away and perish. But he must do more than this. He must not consider that he is properly discharging the duties of his office unless he is working constantly and with all the vigor he can muster to bring the other, far more numerous, inhabitants of the area to partake of the Christian truth and the Christian life.

An Effective Means

In this connection, the preaching of the gospel can be brought more immediately and more effectively to everyone in an area if more mission stations and posts are established as soon as it is practible to do so. Then, when the time comes to divide the mission, these will be ready to serve as centers for new Vicariates and Prefectures. While We are on this subject, We wish to single out for commendation some Vicars Apostolic who have richly earned it: those who have kept this future development steadily in mind and are constantly engaged in the work of readying new provinces for the kingdom of God. If they find that their own order or congregation is not supplying enough manpower for the task, they are perfectly willing to call in helpers from other religious groups.

. . . The man entrusted with a Catholic mission, if he is working single-mindedly for the glory of God and the salvation of souls, goes out whenever it is necessary and searches, searches everywhere, for helpers in his holy ministry. He does not care who they are; he does not care whether they belong to his order or to another, or whether or not they are of his nationality, "provided only that, in every way . . . Christ is being proclaimed" (Philippians 1:18). And he does not limit his welcome to men, either. He will bring in sisters to open schools, orphanages, and hospitals, to found their hostels and establish other charitable institutions. He is happy and eager to do this, because he realizes how remarkably works of this kind, with God's help, contribute to the spread of the Faith.

Local Clergy

14. There is one final, and very important, point for anyone who has charge of a mission. He must make it his special concern to secure and train local candidates for the sacred ministry. In this policy lies the greatest hope of the new churches. For the local priest, one with his people by birth, by nature, by his sympathies and his aspirations, is remarkably effective in appealing to their mentality and thus attracting them to the Faith. Far better than anyone else he knows the kind of argument they will listen to, and as a result, he often has easy access to places where a foreign priest would not be tolerated.

15. If, however, the indigenous clergy is to achieve the results We hope for, it is absolutely necessary that they be well trained and well prepared. We do not mean a rudimentary and slipshod preparation, the bare minimum for ordination. No, their education should be complete and finished, excellent in all its phases, the same kind of education for the priesthood that a European would receive. For the local clergy is not to be trained merely to perform the humbler duties of the ministry, acting as the assistants of foreign priests. On the contrary, they must take up God's work as equals, so that some day they will be able to enter upon the spiritual leadership of their people.

Church Not Alien

16. The Catholic Church is not an intruder in any country; nor is she alien to any people. It

is only right, then, that those who exercise her sacred ministry should come from every nation, so that their countrymen can look to them for instruction in the law of God and leadership on the way to salvation. Wherever the local clergy exist in sufficient numbers, and are suitably trained and worthy of their holy vocation, there you can justly assume that the work of the missionary has been successful and that the Church has laid her foundations well. And if, after these foundations have been laid and these roots sunk, a persecution should be raised to dislodge her, there need be no reason to fear that she could not withstand the blow.

Concern for Training of Local Clergy

17. The Apostolic See has always urged the directors of missions to realize that this is a very serious obligation of their office and vigorously to put it into action. Here in Rome the colleges—both the old colleges and the newer ones—that train clerics for the foreign missions, have already shown their earnestness in the matter. This is particularly true of those training men for the Oriental rites. And yet it is a deplorable fact that, even after the Popes have insisted upon it, there still remain sections of the world that have heard the Faith preached for several centuries, and still have a local clergy that is of inferior quality. If is also true that there are countries that have been deeply penetrated by the light of the Faith, and have, besides, reached such a level of civilization that they produce eminent men in all the fields of secular life—and yet, though they have lived under the strengthening influence of the Church and the gospel for hundreds of years, they still cannot produce Bishops for their spiritual government or priests for their spiritual guidance. From these facts it is obvious that in some places the system ordinarily used in training future missionaries has up to now been feeble and faulty. To correct this difficulty, We are ordering the Sacred Congregation for the Propagation of the Faith to apply remedies adapted to the various regions of the world, and to see to the founding of seminaries for both individual regions and group of dioceses. Where seminaries already exist, this Congregation will see to it that they are adequately administered.

However, the task to which the Congregation is to devote itself with particular care is the supervision of the growth and development of the local clergy in our Vicariates and other missions.

To the Missionaries

A Spiritual Goal

19. It would be tragic indeed if any of our missionaries forgot the dignity of their office so completely as to busy themselves with the interests of their terrestrial homeland instead of with those of their homeland in heaven. It would be a tragedy indeed if an apostolic man were to spend himself in attempts to increase and exalt the prestige of the native land he once left behind him. Such behavior would infect his apostolate like a plague. It would destroy in him, the representative of the Gospel, the sinews of his love for souls and it would destroy his reputation with the populace. For no matter how wild and barbarous a people may be, they are well aware of what the missionary is doing in their country and of what he wants for them. They will subject him in their own way to a very searching investigation, and if he has any object in view other than their spiritual good, they will find out about it. Suppose it becomes clear that he is involved in worldly schemes of some kind, and that, instead of devoting himself exclusively to the work of the apostolate, he is serving the interests of his homeland as well. The people immediately suspect everything he does. And in addition, such a situation could easily give rise to the conviction that the Christian religion is the national religion of some foreign people and that anyone converted to it is abandoning his loyalty to his own people and submitting to the pretensions and domination of a foreign power.

20. We have been deeply saddened by some recent accounts of missionary life, accounts that displayed more zeal for the profit of some particular nation than for the growth of the kingdom of God. We have been astonished at the indifference of their authors to the amount of hostility these works stir up in the minds of unbelievers. This is not the way of the Catholic missionary, not if he is worthy of the name. No, the true missionary is always aware that he is not working as an agent

of his country, but as an ambassador of Christ. And his conduct is such that it is perfectly obvious to anyone watching him that he represents a Faith that is alien to no nation on earth, since it embraces all men who worship God in spirit and in truth, a Faith in which "there is no Gentile, no Jew, no circumcised, no uncircumcised, no barbarian, no Scythian, no slave, no free man, but Christ is everything in each of us" (Colossians 3:12).

Training

22. Before he enters upon his apostolate the missionary should have a very careful training. This is true despite the possible objection that a man destined to preach Christ in places far removed from civilization has no need of a broad education. It is beyond dispute, of course, that for the work of converting the minds of men the refinements of virtue are more valuable than a knowledge of the fine points of literature. If, however, a man has not been supplied with a creditable provision of learning, it is going to be brought home to him quite frequently that he lacks what could have been an important asset in the fruitful fulfillment of his ministry. It is not a rare occurrence for a missionary to find himself without books and with no opportunity to consult someone more learned than himself. Yet he has to reply to any arguments against the Faith that are brought to him and he is often required to provide answers to very difficult questions. The more learned he proves himself in circumstances like these the greater will be his reputation and his authority, especially if he is dealing with people who hold scholarship and learning in high regard. In such a situation it would be a shocking anomaly to see those entrusted with the message of truth bested by teachers of error.

Knowledge of Language

24. Among the attainments necessary for the life of a missionary, a place of paramount importance must obviously be granted to the language of the people to whose salvation he will devote himself. He should not be content with a smattering of the language, but should be able to speak

it readily and competently. For in this respect he is under an obligation to all those he deals with, the learned and the ignorant alike, and he will soon realize the advantage a command of their language gives him in the task of winning the confidence of the populace. If he is earnest about his work, he will be particularly reluctant to delegate the explanation of Christian doctrine to his catechists. He will insist upon reserving this duty to himself. Since he has been sent to the missions for no other purpose, after all, than to preach the gospel, he will even come to look on these instruction periods as the most important part of his work. There will also be occasions when, in his position as representative and interpreter of our holy Faith, he will have to associate with the dignitaries of the district. Or he may be invited to appear at scholarly gatherings. How will he maintain his dignity under these circumstances if he cannot make himself understood because he does not know the language?

Praise of Nuns

30. We must not go further without saying something about the work that is being done by women, for since the very earliest days of the Church they have always been remarkable for their diligence and zeal in assisting the preachers of the gospel. We want to single out here, and single out for Our highest praise, those many women who have vowed their virginity to God and have gone to pursue their vocation on the missions. There they have devoted themselves to the education of children and to a great many other works of charity and devotion. This recognition of their achievements will, We hope, encourage the sisters and inspire them to further efforts on behalf of the Church. We hope too that they will hold fast to the conviction that the usefulness of their work will increase in proportion to the care they give to their own spiritual perfection.

To All Catholics

Three Ways to Help

32. There are three general ways in which a Catholic can assist the missionary effort, and missionaries themselves constantly remind us of them.

The first is within everyone's capacity. This first means is prayer, prayer that God may grant the missions His merciful aid. We have already insisted that the toil of our missionaries would be futile and barren unless divine grace rendered it vital and fruitful. St. Paul referred to this fact when he said, "It was I who planted the seed; it is Apollo who waters it; but it is God Who makes it grow "(1 Corinthians 3:6). We must remember, however, that we have a way of obtaining this grace—the way of humble and persevering prayer. As Our Lord said, ". . . regarding anything they ask for, their prayer shall be granted by My Father in heaven" (Matthew 18:19). This kind of prayer cannot fail, especially in this cause. For no cause is dearer or more pleasing to God than this one. While the Israelites fought their battle with Amalech, Moses took his stand on a great hill and, lifting up his hands, implored God's aid for his people. The teachers of the gospel are manfully at work in the Lord's vineyard, and it is the duty of all the faithful to follow the example of Moses and grant them the support of their prayers.

Fostering Vocations

34. Secondly, something must be done about the scarcity of missionaries. Their number was small enough a few years ago; but now, since the war, it has been so reduced that many areas of the Lord's vineyard are without laborers. We appeal to you, venerable Brethren, for a particularly vigorous approach to this problem. You will be performing a service eminently worthy of your love of the Faith if you take pains to foster any signs of a missionary vocation that appear among your priests and seminarians. Do not be deceived by the claims of a false prudence; do not let human reasoning deter you with the plea that what you send to the foreign missions you will be subtracting from the resources of your diocese. To fill the place of each priest you send to the missions, God will give you many priests, and very able priests, for your work at home.

Economic Help

36. Finally, the missions need economic help, and a substantial amount of it. The war has enor-mously increased their difficulties. It has wiped out a great number of schools, hospitals, and hostels, has destroyed organized charities and put an end to many other types of foundation they once operated. In this crisis We appeal to all good Christians for whatever liberality they can afford. "How can the love of God abide in him who possesses worldly goods, and, seeing his brother in need, closes his heart to him?" (1 John 3:17). When he said this the Apostle John was referring to people who suffer physical need. But does not the law of charity bind even more strictly when there is even more at stake than the rescue of enormous numbers of people from hunger and destitution and the other forms of physical suffering? Does not this law bind us more stringently when the issue is also, and primarily, the rescue of this stupendous multitude of souls from the arrogant domination of Satan, and their entrance into the freedom of the children of God?

Conclusion

41. We have now said, venerable Brethren, what We wanted to say to you about the work of propagating the Catholic Faith through the world. If all Catholics, both the missionaries in the field and the faithful at home, meet the obligations of this task as they should, then We have good reason to hope that our missions will quickly recover from the severe wounds and losses inflicted by the war, and that they will in a short time again show their old strength and vigor. As We look into the future, We seem to hear the Lord's voice, urging Us to "Launch out into the deep water" (Luke 5:4), as He urged Peter long ago. Our paternal charity spurs Us to the work of leading into His welcoming arms the multitudes now living with Us in this world. For the Church is sustained by the Spirit of God, and under the influence of this Spirit she remains always strong and vigorous. Then too, the work of the thousands of apostolic men who have labored in the past and are laboring now to promote her growth cannot fail to have its effect. And their example will attract numerous others to imitate them, and to go out, supported by the generosity and devotion of the good Christian people, to reap for Christ a rich harvest of souls.

42. May the great Mother of God, the Queen of Apostles, hear our united prayers and call down upon the heralds of the gospel the graces of the Holy Spirit. As a token of these graces, venerable Brethren, and as a proof of Our cordial good will, We very affectionately impart to you, and to the clergy and people in your charge, Our apostolic benediction.

Given in Rome at St. Peter's, on the 30th of November, 1919, the sixth year of Our Pontificate.
—Benedict XV

(Source: Pope Benedict XV, Apostolic Letter on the Propagation of the Faith throughout the World [*Maximum Illud*], November 30, 1919, trans. Thomas J. M. Burke, S.J. [Washington, D.C.: National Catholic Welfare Office]; online at http://www.svdcuria.org/public/mission/docs/encycl/mi-en.htm.)

42. *Rerum ecclesiae*— Encyclical Letter of Pope Pius XI, 1925—Sections 1, 18-34

1. In reviewing attentively the history of the Church, one cannot fail to notice how, from the first ages of Christianity, the especial care and solicitude of the Roman Pontiffs have been directed to the end that they, undeterred by difficulties and obstacles, might spread the light of the Gospel and the benefits of Christian culture and civilization to the peoples who "sat in darkness and in the shadow of death." The Church has no other reason for existence than, by developing the Kingdom of Christ on earth, to make mankind participate in the effects of His saving Redemption. Whoever, by Divine Commission, takes the place on earth of Jesus Christ, becomes thereby the Chief Shepherd who, far from being able to rest content with simply guiding and protecting the Lord's Flock which has been confided to him to rule, fails in his special duty and obligations if he does not strive by might and main to win over and to join to Christ all who are still without the Fold.

18. It is now time, Venerable Brothers and Beloved Sons, that We speak to you who, because of your long labors and wise service as missionaries among the heathen, have been found worthy to be promoted by Apostolic authority to the office of Vicars and Prefects. First of all, We speak of the general progress which the missions have made in the last few years due to your charity and zeal, for which progress We offer congratulations both to you and to the missionaries under your charge. What your principal duties are and what you especially have to guard against in the discharge of these duties, has already been set forth with such wisdom and eloquence by Our immediate Predecessor that nothing along that line needs be added to his words. However, over and above that, We deem it well, Venerable Brothers and Beloved Sons, to make known Our own mind on certain matters.

19. Before everything else, We call your attention to the importance of building up a native clergy. If you do not work with all your might to attain this purpose, We assert that not only will your apostolate be crippled, but it will become an obstacle and an impediment to the establishment and organization of the Church in those countries. We gladly recognize and acknowledge the fact that in some places steps have already been taken to provide for these needs by the erection of seminaries in which native youths of promise are well educated and prepared to receive the dignity of the priesthood, and are trained to instruct in the Christian Faith members of their own race. But in spite of all this work, we are still a great distance from the goal which we have set for ourselves.

20. You certainly have not forgotten how Our Predecessor, Benedict XV of happy memory, was saddened by this fact. He wrote: "It is a matter of genuine sorrow that there still exist countries to which the Catholic Faith was brought centuries ago but where, in spite of that fact, one does not find even now native priests except possibly those occupying minor posts; also, that there are races who were converted long ago and who have risen from a state of barbarism to such a high degree of civilization that they have produced men of standing in every profession and walk of civil life; yet these very people, despite the fact that they have lived under the saving influence of the Gospel and of the Church for centuries, have not been able to produce a bishop to rule them or priests whose teaching authority is respected as it should be by their fellow citizens" (apostolic letter, *Maximum Illud*).

21. Perhaps it may be said that sufficient atten-

tion has never been paid to the method whereby the Gospel began to be preached and the Church of God established all over the world. We touched on this subject briefly at the closing of the Missionary Exhibition and recalled the fact that from a study of the earliest monuments of Christian antiquity it is clearly evident that the clergy placed in charge of the faithful in each new community by the Apostles were not men brought in from the outside but were chosen from the natives of that locality. From the fact that the Roman Pontiff has entrusted to you and to your assistants the task of preaching the Christian religion to pagan nations, you ought not to conclude that the role of the native clergy is merely one of assisting the missionaries in minor matters, of merely following up and completing their work. What, We ask, is the true object of these holy missions if it be not this, that the Church of Christ be founded and established in these boundless regions? How can the Church among the heathens be developed today unless it be built of those very elements out of which our own churches were built; that is to say, unless it be made up of people, clergy, and religious orders of men and women recruited from the native populations of the several regions? Why should the native clergy be forbidden to cultivate their own portion of the Lord's vineyard, be forbidden to govern their own people? In order to enable you to progress in winning from heathenism new converts to Christ, would it not be of great assistance if you would entrust to the native clergy the people already converted so that they could minister to them and preserve their faith? As a matter of fact, the native clergy will prove to be most useful (more useful than some people imagine in extending the Kingdom of Christ "for since the native priest," to quote Our Predecessor, "by birth, temper, sentiment, and interests is in close touch with his own people, it is beyond all controversy how valuable he can be in instilling the Faith into the minds of his people. The native priest understands better than any outsider how to proceed with his own people. Such being the case, he can often gain access to places where a foreign priest would not be permitted to enter" (apostolic letter, *Maximum Illud*).

22. Moreover, the foreign missionary, because of his imperfect knowledge of the language often finds himself embarrassed when he attempts to express his thoughts with the result that the force and efficacy of his preaching are thereby greatly weakened. In addition to the aforementioned difficulties there are others which must always be taken into account, notwithstanding the fact that these difficulties are of rare occurrence and can oftentimes be overcome easily. Let us suppose, for example, that either because of the fortunes of war, or because of certain political happenings in a mission field, the ruling government is changed in that territory and that the new government decrees or requests that the missionaries of a certain nationality be expelled; or let us suppose—something which rarely, if ever, occurs—that the inhabitants of a particular territory, having reached a fairly high degree of civilization and at the same time a corresponding development in civic and social life, and desiring to become free and independent, should drive away from their country the governor, the soldiers, the missionaries of the foreign nation to whose rule they are subject. All this, of course, cannot be done without violence. Everyone can see what great harm would accrue to the Church in that land in the circumstances, unless a native clergy had been spread beforehand throughout the country like a network and were, by consequence, in a position to provide adequately for the population which had been converted to Christ.

23. Moreover, since the words of Christ "the harvest indeed is great, but the laborers are few" (Matt. 9:35; Luke 10:2) are true, even in the present condition of affairs, Europe from whence most of the missionaries have come is itself in need of priests, and this at a time when, with the help of God, it is most important that our separated brethren be led back to the unity of the Church and that non-Catholics be convinced of and delivered from their errors. It is a well-known fact that today the number of young men called to the priestly and religious life is not less than in former times, still the number of those who obey the call of God is certainly much smaller.

24. From what We have written, Venerable Brothers and Beloved Sons, it follows that it is all-important to supply your different fields of labor with as many native priests as shall be sufficient, by their individual efforts, to extend the conquests of Christianity and to rule the faithful of each nation without the necessity of depending

upon the help of a foreign clergy. In some places, as We have already pointed out, seminaries for the native clergy have been opened. These seminaries are being erected in points central to the nearby missions and entrusted, as a rule, to the same religious order or congregation which has charge of the missions. At these central institutions the Vicars and Prefects send their chosen men and pay for them while they are being trained, to receive them back one day ordained priests ready for the sacred ministry. This policy, which has been followed in some places, We sincerely wish, nay, We command, shall be followed likewise by the Superiors of all missions, so that it cannot be said that any native youth has ever been kept out of the priesthood and the apostolate, provided, of course, he exhibits the mark of a true vocation and is a young man of genuine promise.

25. It need scarcely be added that the greater the number of students you select for this training (there is need of greater numbers) the greater will be the expense. Do not lose heart because of this fact, but have confidence in the most loving Savior of men to Whose Providence We must look to find ways and means whereby the generosity of Catholics shall be stimulated so that there may come to the Holy See the increased funds required to aid more adequately such worthy enterprises. If each of you must do all he can to obtain as large a number as possible of native ecclesiastical students, you must also strive to mold and form them in that sanctity which is becoming to the priestly life and in the true spirit of the apostolate. Filled with these virtues and with zeal for the conversion of their brothers, they should be ready even to lay down their lives for the salvation of the people of their own tribe or nation. It is also important that simultaneously with this priestly formation these seminarians receive a scientific education both in the sacred and profane sciences. This education should follow the most approved methods. The course of study should not be unduly shortened or curtailed in any of its important features. The students as a matter of fact should follow the general accepted course of studies. Have no fear that if in the seminary you educate subjects conspicuous for the integrity and purity of their lives, men well prepared for the work of the sacred ministry and skilled teachers of the law of God, that you will not

have turned out men who will not only attract the attention of the leading and learned men of their own country but also priests who will be destined one day to govern parishes and dioceses which shall be erected when it pleases God, and all this with the prospect of lasting gain for the Church.

26. Anyone who looks upon these natives as members of an inferior race or as men of low mentality makes a grievous mistake. Experience over a long period of time has proven that the inhabitants of those remote regions of the East and of the South frequently are not inferior to us at all, and are capable of holding their own with us, even in mental ability. If one discovers an extreme lack of the ability to understand among those who live in the very heart of certain barbarous countries, this is largely due to the conditions under which they exist, for since their daily needs are so limited, they are not often called upon to make use of their intellects. You, Venerable Brothers and Beloved Sons, can bear testimony to the truth of what We write, and we Ourselves can testify to these facts since We have here under Our very eyes the example of certain native students attending the colleges of Rome who not only are equal to the other students in ability and in the results they obtain in their studies, but frequently even surpass them. Certainly you should not allow the native clergy to be looked upon as if they were a lower grade of priests, to be employed only in the most humble offices of the ministry. These priests have been admitted to the same priesthood that the missionaries possess, they are members of the selfsame apostolate. On the contrary, you should prefer the native priests to all others, for it is they who will one day govern the churches and Catholic communities founded by your sweat and labor. Therefore, there should exist no discrimination of any kind between priests, be they European missionaries or natives, there must be no line of demarcation marking one off from the other. Let all priests, missionaries and natives be united with one another in the bonds of mutual respect and love.

27. Since it is necessary in order to organize the Church in these regions, as We have already remarked, that you make use of the very elements out of which under Divine Providence they have been composed, you ought as a consequence to consider the founding of religious Congregations of men and women made up of natives to be one

of the principal duties of your holy office. Is it not meant that these newly born followers of Christ be able to follow a life of evangelical perfection if they feel themselves called to take the vows of religion? With reference to this point, the missionaries and nuns who labor in your dioceses should not permit themselves to become prejudiced out of sheer love each for his own religious Congregation, a love which in itself is undoubtedly sound and legitimate. They should learn to view this matter broadly and to act accordingly. Therefore, if there are natives who desire to join one or other of the older Congregations, it assuredly would not be right to dissuade them or to prevent their joining, provided, of course, they give signs of being able to acquire the spirit of these Congregations and of establishing in their own countries houses of the Order which shall not be unworthy of the Congregation of which they are members. Perhaps it would be well if you would consider seriously and without admixture of self-interest, if it would not be more advantageous all around to establish entirely new Congregations, which would correspond better with the genius and character of the natives and which would be more in keeping with the needs and the spirit of the different countries.

We cannot pass over in silence another point most important for the spread of the gospel, namely, the necessity of increasing the number of catechists. Catechists may be Europeans, or preferably natives, who help the missionaries in their work especially by instructing and preparing catechumens for baptism. It is quite unnecessary to write of the qualities which these catechists should possess in order to be able to draw to Christ those who do not believe in Him; this they can do more by the example of their lives than by word of mouth. You, Venerable Brothers and Beloved Sons, make a firm resolution to train them with all possible care in order that they may acquire a profound knowledge of Christian doctrine, and that in teaching the Faith they may be able to adapt themselves both to the natural abilities and the level of intelligence of their catechism classes. In this catechetical work their success will be in exact proportion to the intimate knowledge which they possess of the mental ability and habits of the natives.

28. Up to this point We have written of the selecting and recruiting of those who are to share with you your labors. There still remains for Us in this context to commend to your zeal a plan which, if it should be put into operation, We believe would greatly help in the wider diffusion of the Faith. In what high esteem We hold the contemplative life is made abundantly clear in the Apostolic Constitution of two years ago, whereby We most gladly confirmed by Our Apostolic authority the rule of the Carthusians which had been revised to conform with the new Code of Canon Law, a rule which had been approved by Pontifical authority from the time of the origin of the Carthusian Order. Now, as We exhort from Our heart the Major Superiors of similar contemplative orders, so you too in like manner give them repeated evidences of the fact that they, by founding such houses in the mission field, can spread and promote the more austere types of contemplative life. These contemplatives, too, will obtain from heaven for you and for the work to which you are devoted an abundance of graces. Nor is there any danger that such monks will not find conditions for their mode of life satisfactory. The inhabitants, particularly in certain places, although pagan in large majority have a natural inclination towards solitude, prayer, and contemplation. In this special connection may We call to your notice that great monastery which the Reformed Cistercians of La Trappe founded in the Vicariate Apostolic of Peking. In this monastery there are nearly one hundred monks, the major portion of whom are Chinese. As they, by the exercise of the most perfect virtue, by constant prayer, by the austerity of their lives, by manual labor placate the Divine Majesty and bring down the mercies of God both upon themselves and their pagan neighbors, so also by the force of their example they win these very pagans to Jesus Christ. It is, therefore, not to be questioned that these hermits, while they guard intact the spirit of their holy Founder and therefore do not engage in an active life, nevertheless they prove themselves of great assistance in the successful work of the missions. If, perchance, the Superiors of any of these Orders should heed your requests and establish houses for their subjects in places judged best by common agreement between you, they shall do something which will be, in the first place, very beneficial to the great multitudes of pagans and which will be, secondly, more pleasing to Us personally than any words can express.

29. We may now pass, Venerable Brothers and Beloved Sons, to the consideration of a matter which has to do with the better management of the missions. Although on this subject Our immediate Predecessor has already given his advice and instructions, We desire to repeat them here because We rightly think them to be of the utmost importance in the fruitful exercise of the apostolate. Because in great part the success of Catholic missions among the heathen depends upon you, We desire you to have a better organization of your mission work than formerly, an organization which may serve to make easier for you in the future the work of propagation of Christian beliefs and the increase of converts to the Faith. Therefore, you must see to it that the missionaries are so distributed about that no part of the territory assigned you shall be neglected and that no part shall be left to be evangelized at some future and remote date. To accomplish this purpose, found many new stations (allowing the missionary to live in some central place) in the vicinity of which you may establish smaller houses, which can be left in charge of at least a catechist, each of which should have a chapel so that the missionary may from time to time come on certain fixed days to visit the people and exercise his ministry.

30. Missionaries should remember that in preaching to the natives they must follow the same methods which the Divine Teacher used while He was on earth. Before He began to preach to the crowds, He first healed the sick: "and all that were sick he healed; and many followed him, and he healed them all: he had compassion on them, and healed their sick" (Matt. 8:16; 12:15; 14:14). He commanded the Apostles to do likewise and bestowed upon them the power of healing: "And into what city so ever you enter . . . heal the sick that are therein, and say to them: The Kingdom of God is come nigh unto you" (Luke 10:8, 9), and "going out they went about through the towns, preaching the gospel, and healing everywhere" (Luke 9:6). Neither should the missionary ever forget how kind and loving Jesus always showed Himself to babes and little children, or how when the apostles remonstrated with them, He bade them to "suffer little children to come unto Him" (Matt. 19:13, 14). Apropos of this, let Us recall what We said on another occasion, namely, that the mis-

sionaries who preach to the heathen know only too well how much good-will and real affection is gained for the Church by those who look after the health of the natives and care for their sick or who show a true love for their infants and children. All of which only goes to prove how readily the human heart responds to charity and to kindness.

31. To return to a subject which We discussed above. If it is necessary, Venerable Brothers and Beloved Sons, in the cities where you have your residences and in other more important centers, to erect large churches and other mission buildings, you must, however, avoid building churches or edifices that are too sumptuous and costly as if you were erecting cathedrals and episcopal palaces for future dioceses. This type of structure will come in due time and when the need really exists. Assuredly, you are aware of the fact that there exist dioceses which have been canonically erected, and that a long time ago, and yet only now are they constructing or have just finished the construction of churches and buildings of this kind. Moreover, it would be neither right nor advisable to bring together, really to crowd together, in one of the principal cities or in the town where you reside the various institutions erected for the welfare of both the souls and bodies of the people. If such institutions are really large and important they will need on the spot both your presence and that of the missionaries, and thus your visits in the interests of the propagation of the faith to the remainder of the territory committed to your charge will necessarily cease. Since mention has been made of such good works, over and above hospitals and institutions for the care of the sick and for the distribution of medicines, and elementary schools which you ought to open in every town, it is important that you found other types of schools for the young people who do not intend to take up agriculture, and thus by these schools open the way to them to acquiring a higher education, particularly in the arts and sciences and in the professions. We also exhort you not to neglect in this work of education the better classes, especially the rulers of the locality and their children. It is beyond question that the word of God and its ministers are received more readily by the poor and humble than by the proud and rich. It is also true that Jesus Christ said to Himself, "the spirit of the Lord hath sent me to

preach the Gospel to the poor" (Luke 4:18). Yet, at the same time, We must not forget what St. Paul writes: "to the wise and unwise, I am a debtor" (Romans 1:14). Both history and experience teach that when once the rulers of a people have been converted to Christianity, the common people follow closely in the footsteps of their leaders.

32. Finally, Venerable Brothers and Beloved Sons, receive, in the well-known spirit of zeal for religion and the salvation of souls which consumes you, with docile minds and with the will to obey promptly, this, Our last but most important recommendation of all. The districts confided by the Holy See to your care and labors in order that they too may be added to the Kingdom of Christ the Lord, are for the most part vast in extent. It may thus happen that the number of missionaries belonging to your particular Institute is much smaller than your actual needs require. In this case, just as in well-established dioceses members of different religious families, priests, laymen, and nuns of many different Congregations, are accustomed to come to the aid of the bishop, so you also, where there is question of spreading the Faith, of educating the native youth or other similar undertakings, ought not to hesitate to invite and to receive as companions of your labors religious missionaries, even though they be of a different Institute than your own, and also priests or others though they are members of lay Institutes. The Orders and Religious Congregations may well be proud of the missions given them among the heathen and of the conquests made up to the present hour for the Kingdom of Christ. Let them remember, however, that they do not possess the mission fields by a peculiar and perpetual right, but that they hold them solely at the discretion and pleasure of the Holy See which has both the duty and the right to see to it that these missions are well and adequately taken care of. The Roman Pontiff would not be doing his full Apostolic duty if he limited his interest solely to the distribution of missions of greater or lesser extent to one or other Institute. What is of much more importance is that he must always, and with great care, see to it that these different Institutes are sending into the regions confided to them as many qualified missionaries as are needed to carry on in a thorough manner the task of diffusing the light of the truth over the whole extent of these countries.

33. Therefore, since the Divine Pastor shall demand of Us an accounting of His Flock, We, without hesitation and whenever it shall appear to be either necessary, more opportune, or useful for the larger growth of the Catholic Church, shall transfer the mission territory of one Institute to another Institute; We shall also divide and subdivide a mission territory and shall confide it to the care of native priests or shall assign new Vicariates and new Apostolic Prefectures of other religious Congregations than those occupying the original territory.

34. It but remains for Us now to exhort you again, Venerable Brothers, all the bishops of the Catholic world, to share with Us the cares and consolations of Our pastoral office and to come to the aid of the missions in the enthusiastic manner and with the methods We have suggested in order that the missions themselves, quickened as it were by this renewed strength, may bring forth a more abundant harvest in the future. May Mary, the Most Holy Queen of Apostles, graciously look down with favor upon this our common undertaking; that selfsame Mary who, since she keeps within her motherly heart all men committed to her protection on Calvary, cherishes and loves not only those whose fortune it is to enjoy the fruits of the Redemption, but all those others likewise who do not yet know that they have been redeemed by Jesus Christ. In the meantime, Venerable Brothers, as a pledge of heavenly favors to come and a mark of Our fatherly love for you, We most lovingly bestow upon you, your clergy, and your people the Apostolic Blessing.

Given at Rome, at St. Peter's, the twenty-eighth of February, in the year 1926, the fifth of Our Pontificate.

—PIUS XI

(Source: Pope Pius XI, *Rerum Ecclesiae*, Encyclical Letter of Pope Pius XI, 1925; online at http://www.svdcuria.org/public/mission/docs/encycl/re-en.htm.)

43. *Evangelii praecones—* Encyclical Letter of Pius XII, 1951

Venerable Brethren,
Greetings and Apostolic Benediction.

1. Catholic missionaries toiling in a vast field of labor "that the word of the Lord may run its course

117

triumphantly" are in Our thoughts in a special way on the occasion of the 25th anniversary of the Encyclical Letter *Rerum Ecclesiae* of Our Predecessor of immortal memory Pius XI, wherein he laid down wise norms for the greater development of Catholic missions. The consideration of the progress this holy cause has made in the intervening years has brought Us no small consolation. As We remarked in an audience on June 24, 1944, to the directors of the Pontifical Missionary Work: "The Catholic missionary movement both in Christian and pagan lands has gained such force and momentum and is of such proportions as perhaps was never witnessed before in the annals of Catholic missions."

2. In view of the upheavals and dangers of the present time, when not a few peoples are divided by conflicting interests, We consider it very opportune on the present occasion to reiterate Our approval of this work. For missionaries preach to all men the practice of natural and Christian virtues and that brotherly and common fellowship which transcends racial conflicts and national frontiers.

3. On that occasion when We addressed the directors of the above mentioned Work, We made the following observations among others: ". . . It is in keeping with your apostolate not to be hampered by any national frontiers; for your work which unites you in fraternal cooperation, clearly manifests to all that note of the Catholic Church which rejects discord, flees division, and abhors all disputes which agitate nations and sometimes bring them to utter ruin. We refer to that Christian faith and universal Christian charity which transcend all opposing camps and national boundaries and reach out to the ends of the earth. They are the motives that spur each one of you on to reach your goal, which is the establishment of the Kingdom of God throughout the whole world."

15. News very frequently reaches Us of their invincible and virile faith, which fills Our heart with great consolation. Though some have tried to separate the children of the Catholic Church from Rome and from this Apostolic See, as though patriotism and loyalty so required, yet Catholics have been and are able to make the fully justified rejoinder that, while they are second to none in the matter of patriotism, they genuinely desire to enjoy a rightful liberty.

16. Now what We have touched upon above must be particularly borne in mind, namely, that what still remains to be accomplished in this field calls for an enormous effort and innumerable laborers. Let us remember that our brethren "who sat in darkness and shadow" form an immense multitude that can be reckoned at about 1,000,000,000. Hence it appears that the ineffable sigh of the most loving Heart of Christ is echoing still: "And other sheep I have that are not of this fold: them also I must bring. And they shall hear my voice: and there shall be one fold and one shepherd."

17. There are some shepherds, as you know, Venerable Brethren, who strive to lead away the sheep from this one fold and haven of salvation; you likewise know that this danger is daily growing greater. When We consider before God the immense number of men without the truth of the Gospel, and duly reckon the grave danger that faces many from the prevalence of atheistic materialism or from a certain so-called Christian creed which is infected by the tenets and errors of communism, We feel the deepest concern and solicitude that nothing be left undone to promote the work of the apostolate throughout the world. We make Our own the exhortation of the Prophet saying: "Cry, cease not, lift up thy voice like a trumpet."

18. We pray God especially for those missionaries who labor in the interior of Latin America, since We are aware of the dangerous pitfalls to which they are exposed from the open and covert attacks of heretical teaching.

19. With a view to promoting still more effectively the work of evangelization by our missionaries and to prevent one drop of their sweat and blood from being shed in vain, We should like here to explain briefly the principles and norms that must guide the zeal and activity of Catholic missionaries.

20. First of all it is to be observed that the person who had been called by God to evangelize distant non-Christian lands, has received a very great and sublime vocation. He consecrates his life to God in order to spread His Kingdom to the farthest ends of the earth. He does not seek what is his, but what is Christ's. He can apply to himself in a special way those beautiful sayings of St. Paul: "For Christ . . . we are ambassadors." "Though we walk in the flesh, we do not war according to the flesh." "To the

weak I became weak that I might gain the weak." He must, therefore, consider the country he is going to evangelize as a second fatherland and love it with due charity. Furthermore let him not seek any earthly advantage for his own country or religious Institute, but rather what may help towards the salvation of souls. Certainly he should dearly love his fatherland and his Order, but the Church should be loved with a still more ardent devotion. And let him remember that nothing will be to the advantage of his own Order that is detrimental to the good of the Church.

21. Moreover it is necessary that those who are called to this kind of apostolate should not only get the spiritual and intellectual training that befits ecclesiastical students, before going out on the mission field, but should learn in addition those subjects which will be most useful to them when they come to preach the Gospel in foreign lands. Hence they should be given a sound knowledge of languages, especially of those which they will require at some future date. Besides, they should be sufficiently instructed in the sciences of medicine, agriculture, ethnography, history, geography, etc.

22. The object of missionary activity, as all know, is to bring the light of the Gospel to new races and to form new Christians. However, the ultimate goal of missionary endeavor, which should never be lost sight of, is to establish the Church on sound foundations among non-Christian peoples, and place it under its own native Hierarchy.

27. We are profoundly grieved as We behold these conditions which Our immediate Predecessor described with almost prophetic vision verified in many parts of the Far East. There what were most flourishing missions ripe for the harvest, are now, alas, reduced to the direst straits. Would that it were permitted Us to hope that the peoples of Korea and China, who are naturally cultured and honorable and have been renowned from early times for their high standard of civilization, may as soon as possible be freed not only from turbulent factions and wars, but from the inimical doctrine which seeks only the things of earth and scorns the things of heaven; and, moreover that they may appraise rightly the Christian charity and virtue of foreign missionaries and native priests who strive only to promote the genuine good of the people by their labors and if necessary, by the sacrifice of their lives.

28. We return heartfelt thanks to God that in both countries a numerous clergy chosen from among the people has grown up as the future hope of the Church, and that not a few dioceses have been entrusted to the care of native Bishops. That this stage of development should have been reached redounds to the credit of the foreign missionaries.

29. In this respect We think fit to point out something which should be carefully borne in mind when mission territory that has been under the care of foreign missionaries is entrusted to a native Bishop and clergy. It is not necessary that the religious institute whose members tilled the mission field with their sweat, should leave it altogether when by decree of the S. Congregation of Propaganda Fide the vineyard, which was cultivated by them and is not flourishing, is handed over to other husbandmen. It will be advantageous and becoming that such a religious institute remain on to cooperate with the newly appointed native Bishop. As in the rest of the Catholic dioceses of the world Religious usually assist the local Ordinary, so in mission countries let them not cease, though foreigners, to labor for the Church in an auxiliary capacity. Thus what the Divine Master proclaimed at the well of Sichar will be happily fulfilled: "And he that reapeth, receiveth wages and gathereth fruit unto life everlasting: that both he that soweth and he that reapeth may rejoice together."

30. We desire to address and exhort in this Encyclical Letter not only missionary priests but also those laymen who "with a great heart and a willing mind" collaborate with the missionaries in the ranks of Catholic Action.

36. Thus in every age, thanks to the tireless labors of the clergy and also to the cooperation of the laity, the Catholic Church has not only advanced its spiritual kingdom, but has also led nations to increased social prosperity. Everybody knows the social reforms of St. Elizabeth in Hungary, of St. Ferdinand in Castile, and of St. Louis IX in France. By their holy lives and zealous labors they brought about salutary improvement in the different classes of society by instituting reforms, by spreading the true faith everywhere, by valiantly defending the Church and above all by their personal example. Nor are We unaware of the excel-

lent merits of the guilds during the Middle Ages. In these guilds artisans and skilled workers of both sexes were enrolled, who, notwithstanding the fact that they lived in the world, kept their eyes fixed upon the sublime ideal of evangelical perfection. Not only did they eagerly pursue this ideal, but together with the clergy they exerted every effort to bring all others to do the same.

37. The same conditions which prevailed in the early days of the Church are still to be found in many areas which have been evangelized by missionaries; or at least their peoples suffer disadvantages which had to be left to a future generation to face and remedy. For that reason it is imperative that the laity should in great numbers enter the serried ranks of Catholic action, and thus cooperate generously, earnestly, and diligently with the Hierarchy in promoting the apostolate. The work of catechists is assuredly necessary and we wish to give them due praise; yet no less necessary is the industry and skill of those who out of pure charity are ready to help gratuitously the ministers of God in the performance of their duties.

38. We therefore desire that there be everywhere erected, as far as is possible, associations of men and women, and also of students, of workers, of artists, of athletes, and other clubs and sodalities, which can be considered the auxiliaries of the missionaries. In the erection and constitution of these organizations, let character, virtue, and zeal be preferred to numbers.

39. It is to be borne in mind that nothing is more efficacious in winning for missionaries the confidence of fathers and mothers than devoted care bestowed upon their children. If the minds of the young are moulded to Christian truth and their characters fashioned according to Christian virtue, they will enrich and bring distinction to not only their families but also their communities. It not rarely happens that if the life of a Christian community be in any way remiss or lax, they succeed in restoring it to its pristine vigor.

40. Although it is clear that Catholic Action should exercise its influence primarily in promoting the works of the apostolate, its members are not prevented from joining other organizations whose purpose is to reform social and political life according to the principles and teaching of the Gospel; in fact, their participation not only as citizens, but as

Catholics also, is a right which they possess and a duty to which they are bound.

41. Since young men, and those especially who have had the advantage of a classical and liberal education, will direct the course of the future, no one can be blind to the supreme importance of devoting the best of care to elementary schools, high schools, and colleges. Therefore, with paternal solicitude We exhort superiors of missions to spare neither labor nor expense in proportion to their means in vigorously promoting this phase of missionary activity.

42. The utility of schools for the young lies especially in this that they establish advantageous relationships between the missionaries and pagans of every class, and above all, they more easily influence the docile minds of the young to understand, appreciate and embrace Catholic doctrine. As we all know, the educated youth of today will form the governments of tomorrow and the masses will follow their leadership and guidance. The Apostle of the Gentiles propounded the sublime wisdom of the Gospel before a learned audience when in the Areopagus of Athens he proclaimed the unknown God. Even though this method does not make many converts outright to the teaching of our Divine Redeemer, still there will be many who, as they contemplate the supernatural beauty of this religion and the charity of its disciples, will feel its benign influence.

43. Schools and colleges are moreover especially helpful in refuting the errors which now especially are daily infecting more and more non-Catholic and communist activities and which are being openly and overtly instilled into the minds especially of youth.

44. An equally useful service is the dissemination of timely publications. It is scarcely necessary for Us to dwell at length on this point, for everyone knows how effectively newspapers, magazines, and reviews can be employed either to present truth and virtue in their proper light and inculcate them deeply upon men, or to expose fallacies masquerading under the guise of truth, or to refute certain false opinions which are hostile to religion, or which do great spiritual harm by distorted presentation of vexed social questions. Hence We warmly commend those Bishops who interest themselves in the widest possible distribution of printed works of

this sort which have been carefully edited. Though much has already been done in this regard, much remains to be done.

45. We also wish at this point to pay the highest tribute of praise to the care taken of the sick, the infirm and afflicted of every kind; We mean hospitals, leprosaria, dispensaries, and homes for the aged and for maternity cases, and orphanages. These are to Our eyes the fairest flowers of missionary endeavor; they give us as it were a vision of the Divine Redeemer Himself, who "went about doing good, and healing all that were oppressed."

46. Such outstanding works of charity are undoubtedly of the highest efficacy in preparing the souls of non-Christians and in drawing them to the Faith and to the practice of Christianity; besides, Our Lord said to His Apostles: "Into what city soever you enter, and they receive you, . . . heal the sick that are therein, and say to them: the Kingdom of God is come nigh unto you."

47. However, the Brothers and nuns who feel that they are called to undertake such work must, before leaving their own country, acquire the professional training and knowledge which are today required in these matters. We know that there are nuns with full professional qualifications who have earned well merited recognition by the special study of loathsome diseases, such as leprosy, and by discovering remedies for them. These and all other missionaries who are giving their service so generously in leper hospitals have Our paternal blessing, and their exalted charity compels Our admiration and praise.

48. With regard to medicine and surgery, however, it will certainly be advisable to enlist the services also of laymen, provided not only that they have taken the necessary degrees for this work, and are willing to leave their homeland in order to help the missionaries, but also that in the matter of faith and morals they leave nothing to be desired.

49. Passing now to another aspect of the subject which is of no less importance, We wish to speak of social reforms demanded by justice and charity. Whilst the propaganda of communism, today so widespread, is readily deceiving the minds of the simple and untutored, We seem to hear an echo of those words of the Divine Saviour: "I have compassion on the multitude." It is imperative to put into practice with zeal and diligence the right

principles taught by the Church in this matter. It is imperative to keep all nations free from those pernicious errors, or, in case they are already tainted with them, to set them free from these inimical doctrines which represent the enjoyment of this world as the unique goal to be attained by men in this mortal life. At the same time, by subjecting everything to state ownership and control, they reduce the dignity of the human person almost to zero. It is imperative to proclaim in private and in public that we are all exiles making our way to our immortal home; and are destined to eternal happiness, to which truth and virtue must lead us. Christ is the only real defender of human justice, the only true consoler of the human misery that in this life is unavoidable. He alone points out to us that haven of peace, justice, and everlasting happiness which all of us, redeemed by His blood, are to gain after our earthly pilgrimage is finished.

50. However, it is the duty of all, as far as possible, to mitigate the distress, sweeten the sorrow and relieve the anguish of their brethren during this life.

51. Charity indeed can remedy to a certain extent many unjust social conditions. But that is not enough. For in the first place there must be justice which should prevail and be put into practice.

52. Apropos of this, We might cite Our words to the College of Cardinals and the Bishops at Christmas time, 1942: "The Church has condemned the various forms of Marxist Socialism; and she condemns them again today, because it is her permanent right and duty to safeguard men from fallacious arguments and subversive influence that jeopardize their eternal salvation. But the Church cannot ignore or overlook the fact that the worker, in his efforts to better his lot, is opposed by a machinery which is not only not in accordance with nature, but is at variance with God's plan and with the purpose He had in creating the goods of the earth. In spite of the fact that the ways they followed are false and to be condemned, what Christian, and especially what priest, could remain deaf to the heartfelt cries that call for justice and a spirit of brotherly collaboration in a world made by a just God? Such silence would be culpable and unjustifiable before God, and contrary to the inspired teaching of the Apostle, who, while he inculcates the need of resolution in the fight against error,

also knows that we must be full of sympathy for those who err, and give due consideration to their arguments, encourage and help them. . . . The dignity of the human person then, speaking generally, requires as a natural foundation of life the right to the use of the goods of the earth. To this right corresponds the fundamental obligation to grant private ownership of property, if possible, to all. Positive legislation, regulating private ownership may change and more or less restrict its use. But if legislation is to play its part in the pacification of the community, it must see to it that the worker, who is or will be the father of a family, is not condemned to an economic dependence and servitude which is irreconcilable with his rights as a person.

53. "Whether this servitude arises from the exploitation of private capital or from state absolutism, the result is the same. Indeed, under the pressure of a State which dominates all and controls the whole field of public and private life, even going into the realm of personal opinions, projects and beliefs, the loss of liberty is so great that still more serious consequences can follow, as experience proves" [1942 Christmas Address, 39].

56. Another end remains to be achieved; and We desire that all should fully understand it. The Church from the beginning down to our own time has always followed this wise practice: let not the Gospel on being introduced into any new land destroy or extinguish whatever its people possess that is naturally good, just, or beautiful. For the Church, when she calls people to a higher culture and a better way of life, under the inspiration of the Christian religion, does not act like one who recklessly cuts down and uproots a thriving forest. No, she grafts a good scion upon the wild stock that it may bear a crop of more delicious fruit.

57. Although owing to Adam's fall, human nature is tainted with original sin, yet it has in itself something that is naturally Christian; and this, if illumined by divine delight and nourished by God's grace, can eventually be changed into true and supernatural virtue.

58. This is the reason why the Catholic Church has neither scorned nor rejected the pagan philosophies. Instead, after freeing them from error and all contamination she has perfected and completed them by Christian revelation. So likewise the Church has graciously made her own the native art

and culture which in some countries is so highly developed. She has carefully encouraged them and has brought them to a point of aesthetic perfection that of themselves they probably would never have attained. By no means has she repressed native customs and traditions but has given them a certain religious significance; she has even transformed their feast days and made them serve to commemorate the martyrs and to celebrate mysteries of the faith. In this connection, St. Basil says very well: "Just as dyers prepare the material to be dyed by certain processes beforehand and only when this has been done do they color it with purple or some other color: likewise if the unfading glory of the just is to be ours for all time we shall first be prepared by these external rites and then we shall master the teachings and mysteries of Faith. When we become accustomed to looking at the reflection of the sun in the water, we shall turn to gaze upon the sun itself. . . . Certainly the essential function of a tree is to produce fruit in season; still the foliage that its branches also bear serves to adorn it. In the same way the primary fruit of the soul is truth itself; but the garb of natural culture is a welcome addition, just as leaves provide shade for the fruit and add to its beauty. Thus Moses, a man of the greatest renown for his wisdom, is said to have come to the contemplation of Him, Who is, only after being trained in Egyptian lore. So later the wise Daniel is said to have been first schooled in Babylon in the wisdom of the Chaldeans, and only then to have come to know Divine Revelation."

59. We ourselves made the following statement in the first Encyclical Letter We wrote, *Summi Pontificatus*: "Persevering research carried out with laborious study, on the part of her missionaries of every age, has been undertaken in order to facilitate the deeper appreciative insight into the various civilizations and to utilize their good qualities to facilitate and render more fruitful the preaching of the Gospel of Christ. Whatever there is in the native customs that is not inseparably bound up with superstition and error will always receive kindly consideration and, when possible, will be preserved intact."

60. And in the discourse which We gave in 1944 to the directors of the Pontifical Missionary Society, We said: "The herald of the Gospel and messenger of Christ is an apostle. His office does not

demand that he transplant European civilization and culture, and no other, to foreign soil, there to take root and propagate itself. His task in dealing with these peoples, who sometimes boast of a very old and highly developed culture of their own, is to teach and form them so that they are ready to accept willingly and in a practical manner the principles of Christian life and morality; principles, I might add, that fit into any culture, provided it be good and sound, and which give that culture greater force in safeguarding human dignity and in gaining human happiness. Catholic inhabitants of missionary countries, although they are first of all citizens of the Kingdom of God and members of His great family, do not for all that cease to be citizens of their earthly fatherland."

61. Our Predecessor of happy memory, Pius XI, in the Jubilee Year 1925, ordered a great missionary exhibition to be held; he described its striking success in the following words: "It seems almost a miracle, which gives us a new experimental proof of the vital unity and harmony of the Church of God among all nations. . . . Indeed the Exhibition was and still is like a mission encyclopedia."

From a desire to make known as widely as possible the outstanding merits of missionary endeavor, more especially in the field of culture, We also ordered that during the past Holy Year a large number of exhibits be collected, and We appointed, as you know, that they be shown publicly near the Vatican, in order to demonstrate clearly how missionaries have introduced Christian civilization into nations of advanced and less advanced culture.

(Source: *Evangelii Praecones*, encyclical of Pope Pius XII on Promotion of Catholic Missions; online at http://www.svdcuria.org/public/mission/docs/encycl/ep-en.htm.)

44. *Fidei donum*— Encyclical Letter of Pius XII, 1957

On the Present Condition of the Catholic Missions, Especially in Africa

To the Venerable Brethren, the Patriarchs, Primates, Archbishops, Bishops, and other Local Ordinanes in Peace and Communion with the Apostolic See.

Venerable Brethren, Greetings and Apostolic Benediction.

1. The gift of faith, which through the goodness of God, is accompanied by an incomparable abundance of blessings in the soul of the Christian believer, clearly requires the unceasing homage of a grateful heart to the divine Author of this gift.

2. Indeed, it is faith that allows us to draw near to the hidden mysteries of the divine life; it is faith that encourages us to hope for everlasting happiness; it is faith that strengthens and consolidates the unity of the Christian society in this transitory life, according to the Apostle: "One Lord, one faith, one Baptism." It is chiefly by reason of this divine gift that our grateful hearts of their own accord pour forth this testimony: "What shall I render to the Lord for all that he hath rendered unto me?"

5. This sort of consideration, a very serious one indeed, has been advanced more than once by Our Predecessors, and We Ourselves, as you well know, have been most earnest in touching upon it. It should inspire all Catholics with apostolic zeal, as their awareness of having received the faith demands. Let them direct this zeal toward those regions of Europe in which the Christian religion has been cast off, or to the boundless spaces of South America; in both of these continents there are great difficulties to be overcome, as We know well. Let them give financial assistance to the Catholics of Oceania and to the missions in Asia; such assistance is of the utmost importance, especially in those countries where the battles of the Lord are being fought so fiercely. Let them likewise perform the duties of fraternal charity on behalf of those countless Christians who are very dear to Us and are the glory of the Church, since they have earned the evangelical beatitude proper to those "who suffer persecution for justice' sake." Let them grieve for the lamentable state of innumerable souls, especially of those young people who because of the atheistic propaganda of our times are growing up in the wretched condition of complete ignorance of religion and, in some cases, of active hatred of God.

17. Yet We are aware that seeds of trouble are being sown in various parts of Africa by the proponents of atheistic materialism, who are stirring up the emotions of the natives by encouraging mutual envy among them and by distorting their unhappy

material condition in an attempt to deceive them with an empty show of advantages to be won, or to incite them to seditious acts.

18. Such is Our anxiety that the peoples of Africa should attain to an ever increasing and genuine prosperity, both civic and Christian, that We are desirous of applying to them the grave admonitions that We have on other occasions solemnly directed to the Catholics of the whole world; and We take great pleasure in extending Our paternal congratulations to those Bishops who have, more than once, firmly protected from the dangers of false leaders the sheep entrusted to them.

19. Now that those who hate God are zealously bringing their insidious attacks to bear upon this great continent, other serious difficulties have arisen to hinder the spread of the Gospel in certain districts of Africa. Of course, you know the religious tenets of those people who, although they are quick to profess that they worship God, nevertheless are easily attracting and enticing the minds of many into another path which is not that of Jesus Christ, the Savior of all nations. Our heart, which is that of the common Father of all, is open to every man of good will; but We, who are the representative on earth of Him, Who is the Way, the Truth, and the Life, cannot contemplate such a situation without great sorrow.

20. This situation has come about from a number of causes, which are in general the outcome of rather recent historical events, and it has further been influenced to some extent by the conduct of certain nations that glory in the fact that the light of Christianity illuminates their annals. There is every reason, therefore, why We should be subject to no small anxiety with regard to the fortunes of Catholicism in Africa. There is every reason too why all the Church's children should clearly realize their serious obligation to give more effective assistance to the missionaries. This they must do at the opportune moment in order that the message of saving truth may be brought to what is called "darkest" Africa, where some 85,000,000 people still sit in the darkness of idolatry.

21. The gravity of these statements is further increased by the too precipitate course of events—this can be observed everywhere—which has by no means escaped the notice of the Catholic bishops and the leading Catholics. While the peoples of

this continent are striving to adopt new ways and new methods (and some of them appear to be only too eager to lend an ear to the fallacies of that species of civilization known as technological), it is the solemn duty of the Church to impart to these same peoples, so far as possible, the outstanding blessings of her life and her teaching, from which a new social order should be derived, based on Christian principles.

22. Any delay or hesitation is full of danger. For the people of Africa have made as much progress toward civilization during the past few decades as required many centuries among the nations of Western Europe. Thus they are more easily unsettled and confused by the introduction of theoretical and applied scientific methods, with the result that they tend to be unduly inclined to a materialistic outlook on life. Hence a condition of affairs is sometimes brought about that is difficult to correct and in the course of time may prove to be a great obstacle to the growth of faith, whether in individuals or in society at large. For this reason it is imperative that help should be given now to the shepherds of the Lord's flock in order that their apostolic labors may correspond to the ever-growing needs of the times.

23. At the same time, the various forms of aid supplied at present to the sacred missions are everywhere short of the amount required for a satisfactory prosecution of missionary effort. This insufficiency of means, which, unfortunately, is not confined to Africa, seems to affect this continent more seriously than other missionary fields on account of Africa's peculiar situation at the present moment. For this reason, We deem it opportune, Venerable Brethren, to go into some detail with regard to the problems that are met in Africa.

24. For example, mission stations recently founded (i.e., within the last ten or twenty years) will have to wait a long time before they can enjoy the effective assistance of a native clergy. To this problem is added the small number of missionary workers, who are scattered widely throughout an immense population where not infrequently non-Catholic ministers are also active; they therefore cannot possibly perform all the tasks they are called upon to undertake. In one district some forty priests are working very hard among a million natives of whom only 25,000 profess the Catholic

faith. In another locality fifty priests are stationed in the midst of a population of 2,000,000 persons, where the care of 60,000 Catholics in the area alone requires almost full-time service.

25. No true Catholic can fail to be concerned by these statistics. If twenty apostolic men were sent to the assistance of the local clergy in these regions, the standard of the Cross could be moved forward today, where tomorrow perhaps, after the activities of others who are not the followers of Christ have already cultivated the field, there will no longer be any opening for the true faith.

26. Moreover, it is not enough merely to preach the Gospel as if this were the whole of the missionary's task. The present situation in Africa, both social and political, requires that a carefully trained Catholic elite be formed at once from the multitudes already converted. How urgent it is then to increase the number of missionaries able to give a more adequate training to these native leaders!

27. The drawbacks experienced by the few apostolic workers in the field are increased by their want of material means, which often approaches real poverty. Who will furnish these recently established missions with the generous financial backing they so urgently need? For they are situated, for the most part, in poverty-stricken districts which are, nevertheless, promising fields for the spread of the Gospel. The apostolic laborer is deeply grieved by his lack of so many things while the performance of so many tasks rests upon him. He does not need our admiration aiding the missions, if they are fully informed of the situation.

35. This state of the African apostolate, which We have summarily set before you, Venerable Brethren, makes it manifest that in Africa it is not a question of merely local problems that can eventually be solved without any reference to those that touch upon the entire Christian community.

36. Although formerly "the life of the Church in its visible aspects showed its vigor chiefly in the older parts of Europe from which it began to spread out to the shores that may be called the periphery of the world, now however there is a kind of mutual exchange of life and strength among all the members of the Mystical Body of Christ."

37. What befalls the Church in Africa is not confined to that continent, but also affects those who dwell far beyond its borders. It follows then that, in accordance with the admonitions of the Apostolic See, fraternal assistance must be extended by all parts of the Church to meet the needs of Catholics anywhere.

48. From the beginning holy Church by her very nature has been compelled to spread the Word of God everywhere, and in fulfilling this obligation to which she knows not how to be unfaithful she has never ceased to ask for a threefold assistance from her children: namely, prayers, material aid, and, in some cases, the gift of themselves. At the present day, too, her missionary activities, especially in Africa, demand this threefold assistance from the Catholic world.

49. First of all, therefore, Venerable Brethren, We trust that more continuous and fervent prayers will be raised to God for this cause.

52. Of course, the most excellent prayer of all is the one offered daily at the altar by Christ Jesus, the High Priest, to God the Father when the holy sacrifice of Redemption is renewed. Accordingly, let many Masses be offered for the sacred missions, especially in this our time on which the future growth of the Church in many areas is perhaps dependent. This is in accordance with the prayers of our Lord Who loves His Church and wishes her to flourish and enlarge her borders throughout the whole world.

53. Although the private prayers of Christians are to be considered entirely appropriate, it is nevertheless advantageous to recall to their minds the chief and essential purpose of the celebration of the Sacrifice of the Altar, as it is stated in the Canon of the Latin Mass: "in the first place . . . for Thy holy Catholic Church, that it may please Thee to grant her peace, to protect, unite, and govern her throughout the world." These profound intentions of the Church will be more readily grasped by the faithful, if they will meditate on the doctrine laid down by Us in the Encyclical Mediator Dei, in which We taught that every Eucharistic sacrifice must be considered an action performed in the Church's name, because "the celebrant at the Altar takes the part of Christ as our Head offering in the name of all His members."

54. This being the case, the whole Church offers her holy oblation through Christ to the Eternal Father "for the salvation of the whole world." Surely then, the prayers of the faithful offered dur-

ing this same sacrifice, in union with the Sovereign Pontiff, the bishops, and the entire Church, will be very fervently offered to Almighty God to implore a fresh outpouring of the graces of the Holy Spirit, because of which "the whole world rejoices with exceeding great joy."

57. We might ask, further, whether our prayers come from a sincere heart if we pray for the success of the missions without accompanying our prayers with charitable offerings in accordance with our means. We are well acquainted—in fact, better than anyone else—with the profuse liberality of Our sons, as many wonderful examples constantly testify. To these generous souls is due, beyond a doubt, the marvelous growth of our missions since the beginning of this century. In consequence We desire to express Our profound gratitude to those beloved sons and daughters of Ours who contribute their zealous efforts and charitable support to many missionary enterprises.

61. We are aware of the difficulties of our times, and of the dire straits to which the ancient dioceses of Europe and America are reduced. But if we reason correctly, we can easily see that the poverty of some dioceses will appear to be abundant by comparison with the extreme need that prevails in others. Such a comparison, however, is without any point, since it is of less importance to balance statistics than to urge all the faithful, as We have done on another auspicious occasion, "to range themselves voluntarily beneath the Christian standards of abstinence and self-denial, beyond the requirements of the moral law, in accordance with each one's ability, as the grace of God inspires them and as their station in life permits." We also added, "let people devote to charity what they withdraw from vanities, and mercifully meet the needs of the Church and of her poor."

62. How many good works some missionary, now hindered in his apostolic labors by poverty, might not accomplish with the money not infrequently squandered on fleeting enjoyment by some thoughtless Christian! It behooves every child of the Church, every family, every group of Christians to examine themselves diligently on this point. Let them reflect on these words: "You know the graciousness of our Lord Jesus Christ—how, being rich, he became poor for your sakes, that by his poverty you might become rich." Then let them set aside

some of their superfluities, nay, at times, something of what they need. Remember that in your charity are found the means whereby the boundaries of religion may be broadened; and the face of the earth will be renewed if charity prevails.

63. The Church in Africa, as well as in other parts of the mission field, needs missionaries. Hence We appeal once again to you, Venerable Brethren, beseeching you that with every resource at your command you show your zeal in supporting all those who have been divinely called to undertake the burdens of the missionary apostolate, whether they be priests or religious men and women.

64. It is especially your task, as We have already pointed out, to encourage the faithful and arouse in them such zeal in this cause that they will share the solicitudes of the entire Church and will readily lend an ear to the Lord's word, commanding, as of old, so in every age: "Go forth from thy land and thy kindred, and from the house of thy father, and come into a land which I shall show thee."

65. Now if the people are trained in this truly Catholic attitude in the domestic circle, in the schools, in the parishes, in Catholic Action groups, and in other pious societies, there can be no doubt that they will give the Church those ministers she needs in preaching the divine message to all nations. Nor should this point be overlooked: if an enthusiastic interest in the missions is aroused in your particular dioceses, it will be a pledge of the renewal of religion and devotion in the minds and hearts of your people. It is impossible for a Christian community to perish that gives its sons and daughters to the Church. Consequently, if the supernatural life is the fruit of charity and is increased by the spirit of self dedication, one may rightly assert that the Catholic life of any nation is measured by its generosity in supporting and maintaining the missionary activity of the Church.

66. It is not enough, however, to make your people more zealous in supporting this work; much more is required. Not a few dioceses are so well supplied with clergy, thanks be to God, that no loss would be felt if some of their priests should enter the mission field. To such dioceses We would apply, with fatherly solicitude, the Gospel saying: what you have that is over and above your needs, give that to the poor. Our heart goes out to Our brother bishops who are filled with distress and

fear as they see the number of candidates for the priesthood and the religious life growing fewer, and are thus unable to provide properly for the spiritual needs of their own flocks. We share their anxiety and say to them as St. Paul did to the Corinthians: "Not that the relief of others should become your burden, but that there should be equality."

67. Nonetheless, dioceses that are suffering from such a shortage of clergy should not therefore close their ears to Our supplications for help in the foreign missions. The widow's mite is proposed by our Lord for our imitation. If a poor diocese helps another poor diocese, it cannot possibly grow poorer in so doing; God does not allow Himself to be outdone in generosity.

83. Meanwhile, confident that the active will of all Catholics will respond to these Our exhortations to such a degree that, with the help of divine grace, these missionary endeavors will be able to carry to the very ends of the earth the light of Christian faith and virtue together with advances in material civilization, We lovingly impart to all of you, Venerable Brethren, to your flocks, and specifically to all the preachers of the Gospel, who are so near to Our heart, the Apostolic Blessing as a testimony of Our good will and a pledge of heavenly gifts.

84. Issued at St. Peter's in Rome, on the twenty-first day of April, the Feast of the Resurrection of our Lord Jesus Christ, in the year 1957, the nineteenth of Our Pontificate.

(Source: Pope Pius XII, *Fidei Donum*, 1957; online at http://www.svdcuria.org/public/mission/docs/encycl/fd-en.htm.)

Protestant Reassessments of the Role of Mission in the Twentieth Century

45. *Re-thinking Missions,* by William Ernest Hocking

The section entitled "Attitudes toward Other Faiths" in the report Re-Thinking Missions *by William Ernest Hocking represented an alternative voice to that of the International Missionary Council. It was self-consciously a layman's enterprise and was based on extensive visits to missionary enterprises around the world. Its conclusion, found in this excerpt from a digest of the report, foreshadowed in many ways the mission philosophy that emerged full-blown among liberal Protestants after World War II.*

At the beginning of the Protestant missionary movement, the Christian message was delivered to men of other faiths. Its primary object was to wean them from those faiths. But the day of that struggle of religion against religion is, or ought to be, past. It ought to be past, not because one religion is no longer superior to another, but because other more important issues confront religion than the establishment of that superiority.

Today the battle lines are drawn, not between Hinduism, Mohammedanism, and Christianity, but between religion and materialism, secularism, naturalism. In all mission lands thoughtful individuals are, increasingly, concerned not to weigh one religion with another, but to consider the advantages of any religion against no religion at all. All beliefs, in short, are faced with a rising tide of unbelief. To refuse to face this fact, or to belittle the sincerity of those who are responsible for its significance, is to show neither good sense nor honesty. Nevertheless, to stem this tide of unbelief should be the common task of all believing men and women, Christian and non-Christian.

"What becomes of the issues between the merits of one sacred text and another when the sacredness of all texts is being denied? Why compare Mohammed and Buddha, when all the utterances of religious intuition are threatened with discard in the light of practical reason? It is no longer, Which prophet? or Which book? It is whether any prophet, book, revelation, rite, church, is to be trusted. . . . The case that must now be stated is the case for any religion at all."

To meet this new challenge should be the first business of religion. It should, in particular, be the first business of Christianity. Henceforth, unless our faith and all faiths are to be driven back by the new force arrayed against them, those engaged in the missionary enterprise should make an effort to know and understand, more sympathetically, the religions that surround it. That ground of understanding having been established, the mission should openly recognize and associate itself with whatever kindred elements and common purposes those religions contain. Out of such a relationship, the Christian in the mission field will come to regard himself, not as an altogether special order of creation but, rather, as "a co-worker with the forces which are making for righteousness within every religious system."

Such a realignment of all religions against irreligion will be difficult, perhaps, but it is by no means impossible. It is made easier by the fact that non-Christian faiths, themselves, have lately undergone vast changes. To a marked degree they have been aroused from their age-old lethargies. This awakening has been due, in considerable part, to the stimulus of Christianity in their midst. As a result, great movements of reform and revitalizing are under way. The theological message of Christianity has not been accepted. But the personal and social implications of the Christian way of life are being, increasingly, appropriated. There is, therefore, far more of a common ground on which to meet them than ever existed before.

Uniqueness of Christianity

This means no compromise of the uniqueness of the Christian message. It means, rather, a deeper expression of it. Christianity declares that the most real of all realities is God; that God is not far off but in all our actions; that, though He is everywhere, He is also one. It insists that though this is a world of law, the supreme law is not physical but moral. Moreover, this world is ruled by a God who is loving, not capricious, nor vengeful and who, as a loving God, can be made real in one's personal experience.

Christianity refers its conception of God, of man and of religion to the life and teachings of Jesus. Religion, to many Christians thus becomes a life of actual fellowship with Jesus conceived as a living spirit. These various conceptions constitute, for the Christian, not a way of life for himself alone, but

for all men and for the world. On the mission field, this faith reveals itself in an effort "to seek with people of other lands a true knowledge and love of God, expressing in life and word what we have learned through Jesus Christ, and endeavoring to give effect to his spirit in the life of the world."

Wherever, therefore, that spirit is revealed, the Christian should feel at home. Every individual who shows forth that spirit should be the Christian's compatriot. Every movement that has as its purpose the establishment of that spirit in the lives of men and the relations of society should be hailed and strengthened as a force for advancing Christianity's most fundamental purposes for the world.

The Larger Purpose of Missions

The acceptance of those principles affects not only the objectives, but the scope of the foreign mission. The first missionaries were evangelists, and the saving of individual souls was their objective. But they were much more than evangelists. And they did more than to lead men into a spiritual experience. They ministered, also, to the minds and the bodies of those among whom they worked. Through the last century this ministry has expanded. It has expanded until, today, "salvation" has been given a new meaning; men are to be saved, not for the next world alone, but for this world; not out of human life but within human life. Not all missionaries have accepted this broader interpretation of their enterprise. Nevertheless, the conviction has steadily gained headway, that the foreign mission—at its best—should aim to develop individuals who—physically and mentally as well as spiritually—are fit to be accepted as citizens in a social order founded upon the ideals that Jesus preached.

Christian Philanthropy Valid on Its Own Account

To put this conviction into more effective practice calls for a new type of evangelism. This does not mean that ministry to the bodies and the minds of men should be divorced from direct evangelistic effort. It means, rather, that such ministry should not be looked upon as a means to evangelism but regarded, rather, as important in itself. That is, hospitals and schools and agricultural stations need to be regarded less as work with which to tempt non-Christians to expose themselves to Christian preaching and more as Christian ends in themselves. Evangelism—through such enterprises—will be, of course, more indirect; it will be by example rather than by preaching; the results will be less tangible; actual Christian converts probably fewer. But the consequences are likely to be more significant. For through such indirect evangelism, the social life of the East will be more deeply permeated with the spirit of Jesus Christ. The choice involved is, of course, fundamental. It is a choice between foreign missions as an expression of the spirit of Jesus Christ or as an agency for the extension of Western ecclesiasticism and theology.

On such a platform like-minded men of many faiths will be able to stand, increasingly, together. In it there is involved "beside the full development of individuals and the maturing social groups, also the spiritual unity of all men and races. This means something more than agreement in the essentials of religious faith. It means that the moral sense of mankind comes to accord on the deeper principles of right and wrong. . . . If the future way of the mission is to be, as it can be, the exacting way of the best, its welcome abroad will be secure, its position permanent, and its command reestablished over the hearts of those to whom the difficulties of great tasks are an added incentive."

(Source: *A Digest of Re-Thinking Missions, A Layman's Inquiry after One Hundred Years*, by Stanly High, National Committee for the Presentation of the Layman's Foreign Missions Inquiry [Chicago. no date], 20-22.)

46. *Wake Up or Blow Up,* Postscript, by Frank C. Laubach

The Cold War, and the atomic age, influenced missionary thinking as the post-colonial world emerged. For some the dangers of the age only intensified the need for the kind of evangelism John Mott had called for at the opening of the century. For others a new missionary attitude and approach was demanded. Frank Laubach, a pioneer missionary promoter of literacy, believed that mission was urgent, the mission demanded by the judgment parable of Matthew 25 he saw as paramount.

We are in a race against time. Perhaps not enough people will be willing to join you and me in applying the Christian program of helping people up soon enough. It may prove to be too little and too late. We may lose the world and be blown up. But if we believe Christ we do not lose ourselves.

If we believe our religion it is far better to face our Maker having done what we could than to go before Him whimpering that we did not try because we thought it was useless or because we hoped that fifty billion dollars a year invested in hell's weapons would be enough.

Jesus said that every dollar we invest in helping need becomes a treasure (today we would call it "bank account") in heaven. Listen to His words: "Lay not up treasures for yourselves upon earth, where moth and rust doth corrupt, and where thieves break through and steal: but lay up for yourselves treasures in heaven, where neither moth nor rust doth corrupt, and where thieves do not break through nor steal: for where your treasure is, there will your heart be also."

Then He tells exactly how to lay up those treasures in heaven. A rich young ruler asked Him, "Good master, what shall I do to inherit eternal life?" Jesus told him to keep the commandments. He replied, "I have kept them since my youth." Then Jesus said, "Give all you have to help the poor, and you will have treasure in heaven, and come, follow me." But when he heard this he became very sad, for he was very rich. Jesus, looking at him, said, "How hard it is for those who have riches to enter the kingdom of God!" Their money will keep them out if they refuse to help need.

Jesus said this in the story of the rich man and Lazarus. He told it in the story of the rich man whose land brought forth plentifully, and who said, "I will pull down my barns and build larger ones, and there I will store all my grain and my goods. And I will say to my soul, Soul, you have ample goods laid up for many years; take your ease, eat, drink, and be merry." But God said to him, "Fool, this night your soul is required of you, and the things you have prepared, whose will they be?" Then Jesus gives the meaning: "So is he who lays up treasure for himself, and is not rich toward God."

In Luke 12:33 He tells us: Help meet need, and in this way provide yourselves with "a treasure in the heavens that faileth not."

Everything, everything Jesus said agrees with His words: "Make to yourselves friends of the mammon of unrighteousness; so that when ye fail, they may receive you into everlasting habitations." Those we have helped, Jesus says, have gone to heaven to testify for us and to welcome us when we arrive.

So—what we keep we lose at last, and that may not be far off! What we give to help need becomes an everlasting treasure in heaven. This is driven in with rather terrible insistence in Matthew 25:31-46. Not one minister in ten dares to read that passage to his congregation—they don't like it because they don't want to hear it or believe it or obey it.

But to you and me it is really a wonderful promise, if we have helped those who are hungry, or thirsty, or naked, or a stranger, or sick, or in prison, for Christ tells us what He will say:

"Come, you blessed of my Father, inherit the kingdom prepared for you from the foundation of the world; for I was hungry and you gave me food; I was thirsty and you gave me drink; I was a stranger and you welcomed me; I was sick and you visited me; I was in prison and you came to me. . . . Truly I say to you, As you did it to one of the least of these my brethren, you did it to me."

It is terrible only to those who refused to help need.

"I was hungry and you gave me no food; I was thirsty and you gave me no drink; I was a stranger and you did not welcome me; naked, and you did not clothe me; sick and in prison, and you did not visit me. . . . Depart from me, you cursed, into the eternal fire prepared for the devil and his angels."

That "eternal fire" sounds uncomfortably like the terrible blast of the atom bomb or the hydrogen bomb. And the words "you cursed" sound too much, altogether too much, like the voice of that innumerable multitude of hungry people who plead with America to help them, and who, if we refuse their plea, will hate us and finally blast us with the bomb which we invented. It is real enough and close enough to give us goose flesh.

The Christian promise is infinitely comforting

if we have obeyed it, but hell if we have said no. Yet, who can complain? For nothing, nothing, could be more just than His promise: "Inasmuch as ye have done it unto the least of these my brethren, ye have done it unto me." "With what judgment ye judge, ye shall be judged." "Whatever you give is given, full measure, shaken down, running over. . . ."

Well, then, this book is a lesson in applied Christianity—or that part of Christianity we neglect—practicing what we preach, not stingily, or gingerly, but all-out, total, magnificent, amazing love in action. It is the kind of religion that makes sense, the kind of religion that gets results, its head in the clouds, but its feet on the ground.

(Source: Frank C. Laubach, *Wake Up or Blow Up* [New York: Revell Publishing, 1951], chap. 17.)

47. *Lands of Witness and Decision, "The Valley of Decision," by Eugene L. Smith*

Eugene Smith, writing for the Methodist Mission Board in 1957, gave a concise view of the decisions that post-colonial societies would be making in the future, and of the challenges these posed for mission. The historical periods to which he compares those days give a glimpse at how he understands the changes taking place around him.

Mankind has marched into the valley of decision. The valley we now occupy is more perilous and more promising than any before in history.

We are in the valley of decision politically. Half of the world's human beings have changed their political status in the last twelve years. Hundreds of millions have won political freedom. Hundreds of millions have lost their freedom to Communist tyranny. Enormous power vacuums exist in Southeast Asia and the Near East. Such vacuums always cause vast and violent struggle. The history of our children hinges on the methods and men who fill these vacuums.

We are in the valley of decision in the use of our technical skills. This day a handful of men could obliterate mankind by use of bombs now ready for explosion. Meanwhile, the same skills that produced those bombs have made it technically possible to conquer starvation and most of mankind's worst diseases.

Mankind is in the valley of decision spiritually. In every country people caught in cyclonic uncertainties are seeking religious rootage. Spiritual vacuums are found in every city, every countryside. Ancient religions, dormant for centuries, are seeking to fill these empty hearts. Nationalistic passions fan into flame ancient religious loyalties. Never have the massive religious ideologies been caught in such swirling conflict. In fifty years Islam has grown from 175 million to 300 million followers. Buddhism has again become missionary. Even Hinduism is moving outside its national lines with missions in Africa, Europe, and America. All three consider the United States a primary mission field. We were born into a world where Christianity moved out to challenge rival faiths. Today they are moving into the heartlands of Christianity. Asia is determined to win not only political but also religious initiative away from the West. The major ideological conflicts in our country in the decade ahead are not going to be between different sets of Western ideas, as before, but between the fundamental presuppositions of East and West.

Never before have so many adults faced the conscious choice of the gods they shall serve. On miniature scale this situation existed in the last days of the Roman Empire, and the early days of the Protestant Reformation. We are forced to decide, where most of our ancestors could only accept. Herein lies the enormity of mankind's anxiety and the magnitude of the church's opportunity.

(Source: The Methodist Church (U.S.) Joint Section of Education and Cultivation, *Lands of Witness and Decision* [New York: Board of Missions, 1957].)

48. *Missions Learn from the Communist Triumph in China*

The following chapter from the book Missions in Crisis *illustrates the deeply troubled state of missions after the Second World War, particularly with the rise of Communist China. The expulsion of missionaries from China, while*

dramatic, appeared at the time a harbinger of things to come as newly independent nations flexed their muscles with regard to Western influences and minority Christian communities were forced to rely on themselves.*

Chapter 4: Missions Learn from the Communist Triumph in China

The universal mission of the Church of Christ is caught up in the crisis of our time. In the midst of the world's current turbulence and upheaval, the Almighty is unfolding His undeviating purpose. Even before the creation of man, God anticipated a day such as this in which power and change would be worshiped as deities. He anticipated and will defeat every device of Satan, for the Lord God is sovereign. Here is the strength and comfort of His people. Yet it is possible to recognize the sovereignty of God without being fully aware of the extent of God's activity both within and without the Church.

For instance, do we recognize the enormous advances being made in the physical sciences as being part of God's plan? Or are we able to trace His sovereign operation among those nations where the testimony to His Son is seemingly so insignificant? To be specific, is God manifestly at work in Moscow and Peking? If we believe that a sovereign God is ruling, we are obliged to accept as fact that the most seemingly chaotic events of our time have their spiritual significance.

For example, consider the communist expulsion of missionaries from China in 1950-51, and the subsequent termination of all foreign missionary activity in that vast and populous land. In the entire scope of the worldwide witness of the Church today, the China disaster was so colossal and complete that we must inevitably assume that God was seeking to speak through such a calamity to His people throughout the earth. If Christians desire to prepare themselves to serve their own generation in the will of God, they can do no better than ponder the lessons of that painful period. It is difficult not to conclude from them that Protestant missionary activity in China was under the judgment of God. David M. Paton in his severe book *Christian Missions and the Judgment of God* says that "the best of us [missionaries] left China sadly, with many happy memories, but with a sense that . . . we were wrong . . . that God found us wanting" (David M. Paton, *Christian Missions and the Judgment of God* [London: SCM Press, 1953], 54). One dare not be indifferent to or seek to withdraw from the painful lessons to be learned. God has spoken; His people must pause and listen.

When it comes to evaluating the China exodus in terms of God's specific lessons to His Church, its missionary force and strategy, one is pressed to assume a posture and spirit of deep humility. Man's sinfulness and ignorance increase the possibility of being in error about these lessons. Rarely is our information completely adequate; seldom is our judgment both balanced and wise. There is a large measure of agreement, however, as to the lessons God was seeking to teach His people during the final decade of missionary opportunity in China. We therefore should regard these lessons with all seriousness. They have come from the Head of the Church to His people.

Lessons about Theology

Prominent in the postexilic writings of former China missionaries is their profound realization that the deepest lessons learned from God concerned faith and not service. Several reasons contributed to this conclusion. In earlier decades, when most societies were in basic doctrinal agreement, there had been a rather general movement of interdenominational societies into rural and tribal areas. Comity arrangements with denominational societies had resulted in the cities (embracing the educated and industrial classes) being turned over to the denominational societies. This was a tidy and workable arrangement as long as all societies remained true to historic biblical Christianity. Recent decades, however, saw the rise of heterodox, liberal theology, especially in America. This overflowed into China. Mission schools, colleges, and most theological seminaries came under the domination of a theology that was little more than a superficial humanism. A great deal of Western money was poured into these institutions, which attracted a host of able students. But the tragedy was that the instruction confined itself

to acquainting the Chinese with the industrial and cultural achievements of the West while leaving them largely in ignorance of the Christian faith. The result was disastrous.

Bishop Stephen Neill, noted for his contribution as the Associate General Secretary of the World Council of Churches, described the situation in the following words:

> Christianity was presented [in China] much more as a program of social and political reform than as a religion of redemption. But the concepts of liberal Christianity proved in the end, less dynamic than those of Marxist Communism. . . . The liberal interpretation of the Bible, from which both the prophetic and eschatological dimensions were almost wholly absent . . . produced a widespread lack of interest in theology, an almost total lack of the sense of worship, and an almost total lack of understanding of the nature of the church. (Stephen Neill, *The Unfinished Task* [London: Lutterworth Press, 1957], 127)

Leonard M. Outerbridge, a prominent missionary of the United Church of Canada, appraised the theological failure thus:

> Christianity [in China] neglected to give priority to the teaching of the first and great commandment. We sought popularity and prestige by stressing the material benefits the church had to offer. Christianity was the success religion. Too large a proportion of all Protestant missionary energies was thus expended. China willingly received every social service expression of Christianity in schools, colleges, hospitals, humanitarian aid, famine relief, and famine prevention projects. Through these agencies Christianity became popularly conceived in China as the social reform religion. But too little emphasis was placed upon the actual teaching of the message of Jesus. Our social Gospel was our only Gospel. . . . Confronted with the rising tide of Communism, the Christian churches merely offered the Chinese a more attractive materialism than could be given by the Communists. It was in this hour that the churches were lost. The popularity of Christian-

ity in modern China often constituted its peril. It had become soft, pleasant, and social in its application. Storm warnings should have been read in the fact that for many years the majority of the graduates of Christian schools were leaving these institutions not only without having become Christians but without any religion at all. Christian missions produced a talented but lost generation. Communism appealed to these trained young people by demanding of them greater sacrifices than Christianity, in its day of soft ease, dared demand. Students found in Communism a realism which they missed in Christianity. (Leonard M. Outerbridge, *The Lost Churches of China* [Philadelphia: Westminster Press, 1952], 159-60, 166-67)

Charles C. West, of the Ecumenical Institute, Bossey, Switzerland, writing under the pen name "Barnabas," summarized this theological failure with the damning indictment:

Christian Liberalism turned itself easily, too easily, into Christian-Communist Liberalism in China. Christian Liberalism failed to recognize the depth of sin, and hence the need of personal salvation, humility and curbs on all social power. . . . The most vigorous Christian life in Peking today lies not in the churches but in Inter-Varsity organized student groups and sects. (Barnabas, *Christian Witness in Communist China* [London: SCM Press, 1951], 63)

These admissions of theological failure need to be pondered. For in spite of Protestantism's postwar repudiation of the liberalism of the 'thirties, many church leaders in the 'sixties are still unwilling to embrace the faith "once delivered to the saints." Their preoccupation with Bultmann's demythologizing, Tillich's depersonalized theism, or Neibuhr's Christian socialism, coupled with their continued revolt against the authority and message of Scripture, indicate they have not yet discerned the hard theological lessons that came to their fellow-liberals in China.

In contrast, those missionaries who preached the biblical message of Jesus Christ and Him crucified have no such regrets. Their theology was not of man, but of God. As a result, they witnessed in

China His marvellous activity by means of this message. The lives of thousands were supernaturally transformed by His grace and His Church was planted widely throughout the length and breadth of that dark land.

And yet, even evangelical missionaries have felt the judgment of God. For many, their last impressions of Chinese brethren were of a people tragically ill-prepared to cope with the intellectual and sociological ferment generated by the communist revolution. God had not failed; but even His most faithful servants had failed to realize, and thus fulfill, the full import of the gospel. The question then arises, did they not teach the whole counsel of God contained in Scripture? It is now apparent that much of the instruction given erected a false antithesis between the spiritual and the material world. It failed abysmally to transmit to the Chinese Church the deep-rooted social concern so dynamically evidenced by the Holy Spirit through the Old Testament prophets and the New Testament apostles. It produced a form of discipleship that reflected a painfully limited viewpoint—indifference to China's social, economic, and political needs, devoid of a sense of civil responsibility. Whereas the social gospel was inadequate because of its omission of the theistic dimension, the gospel as evangelicals presented it largely ignored the biblically obvious: the gospel *has* social implications.

Today we are faced with urgent questions: Was the whole of God's purpose confined to that which took place within the walls of local churches or in evangelistic efforts among the unsaved? Did He really endorse the terrible passivity of Christians toward social problems? Was their withdrawal from the harsh realities of the suffering world outside the church walls His good, acceptable, and perfect will? Did not their negativism reinforce the Marxist thesis that the bourgeois church drugs its devotees with an all-absorbing concern for personal salvation, rendering them indifferent to the injustice and bad government of the society in which they live? Did this unreality, moving toward soporific abstractions, make for a healthy church life? Was it biblical? Did not Christ come to fill the lives of His people with vital concern and useful service on behalf of their fellow-men?

Many an evangelical missionary left China heavy with regret and burdened in heart over the incompleteness of the gospel he had preached in that needy, unhappy land. Not a few can recall instances when Chinese Christians were challenged by the Communists to work with them in righting wrongs and in remaking China. Their rapid reaction was unmistakable. Almost immediately they demonstrated their capacity to respond to the stimulus of vigorous leadership. Undoubtedly their very Christian training had given them an instinctive desire to serve others. Almost unmitigated tragedy lay in the unpalatable fact that their devotion and strength were being enlisted by a dynamically down-to-earth but ultimately Utopian philosophy.

Nevertheless, to the Christian who looks for the underlying purpose of God in history there is much to be learned from the foregoing, whatever shade of theological interpretation he may favor.

Lessons about Method

1. *Living in simplicity.* Soon after his arrival in China, J. Hudson Taylor, founder of the China Inland Mission, adopted Chinese dress, lived in a Chinese-style house, and sought by every means to live close to the people to whom God had sent him. Thus the pattern was established to adopt, as far as possible, the standard of living of the local high-school teacher. "Minimize the differences between yourselves and the people to whom God sends you; eliminate all that is unnecessary." Key phrases such as these became watchwords. Many a missionary embraced them heartily and sacrificially. And yet did we live simply enough? Were we really close to the people, mentally as well as materially? Were we really friendly enough, accessible enough, and sufficiently fluent in language and culture to bridge the gulf between East and West? True, the problem isn't one of location as much as spirit, and yet many an ex-China missionary now wishes he had lived more like his Chinese or tribal colleagues in the work of the Lord. The call to Western missionaries to live in simplicity overseas has never been so loudly sounded as it is today.

2. *Recovering mobility.* The apostolic pattern of missionary service relied heavily on an essential mobility. The Apostle Paul's peripatetic pastoral and evangelistic ministry is the classic example. Districts were opened by itinerant gospel preaching. Converts were carefully established in the faith. Congregations were organized. Then the apostles moved on into new areas. Their method was to concentrate on districts by planting churches in key cities and towns. Their follow-up programs did not necessitate prolonged residence in any one locale. They came and went, and by their absence created situations that forced converts to cling the closer to the Lord himself. They produced sturdy disciples and vigorous churches.

Unfortunately this pattern is quite contrary to even the best in human nature. It was a very real problem for missionaries in China to maintain sufficient foresight to retain mobility as a biblical *sine qua non.* So many pressures were on them constantly to settle down, and, however unintentionally, to develop the work with themselves at the center. This led quite naturally to paternalism and its attendant weaknesses. When the exodus from China took place, many an uprooted missionary thanked God for the disruption. Many prayed that if He re-commissioned them, they would vow never to lose either mobility or action or loyalty to the apostolic pattern of a district-wide ministry.

3. *Conducting church finance.* There is no authority in Scripture, no precept or apostolic example, for the practice of employing converts as preachers of the gospel. And this was the pattern widely followed by all missionary societies for many years in China. Since the Chinese have a propensity for fixed routines and precedents, this pattern only began to be challenged by nationals and missionaries after a series of chaotic upheavals—wars, internments, evacuations, and inflation—demonstrated beyond question its glaring weaknesses. Slowly Christian leaders became aware of the folly of such a procedure. They began to recognize that converts just emerging from spiritual darkness, still surrounded by heathen influences, and imperfectly emancipated from non-Christian habits should not be recruited for service in the church on a monetary basis.

When the Communists' takeover was complete, all true Christians came under severe testing. A costly price was to be paid by all who persisted in identifying themselves publicly with the cause of Jesus Christ. Nominal or weak church members melted away. Even staunch Christians felt the pressure and began to waver. It soon became evident that those paid workers who had been subsidized with foreign funds were exposed to a withering blast of communist scorn. They were singled out as "running dogs of the imperialists." Under the scorching scrutiny of public inquisition loyalty to the People's Republic was mercilessly probed. Fearfully and sometimes frantically they vehemently disowned their past associations with the foreign missionaries! Such a sudden, violent aversion, evinced by some against those who a few months earlier had been their closest associates, presented an indelibly pathetic picture. The most godly of men were not spared the infamy of shamelessly false abuse. No further evidence was necessary to sound the death knell of paternalism, at least in China!

(As early as 1928, the China Inland Mission, in full consultation with the national church began to cut back its earlier commitments and adopted the policy that no new work was to be opened on this basis. Stimulus for this sweeping decision also came from the spiritual momentum generated by two notable exceptions in the C.I.M. to the subsidized program: the "people movement" led by Pastor Hsi in South Shansi [from 1880 onward] and the widespread work among the tribes of Southwest China [from 1910 onward] associated with James O. Fraser.)

As a result of this harsh China experience, new principles, though as old as the apostles, were adopted for the conduct of church finance. "Do not go beyond the life of the local church. If a congregation is unable to support a pastor, it would be both premature and stultifying to spiritual growth to appoint a foreign-subsidized man to care for them. Make the sole motivation for Christian service the constraint of the love of Christ. Do not deny the emerging church the privilege and blessing of looking to God himself to deepen its stewardship and supply its need." No lessons have come more clearly from China's fiery furnace than those relating to money, its use and abuse.

4. *Utilizing mass media.* This is the day of communication through mass media. The printed page, the public address system, the motion picture film, radio and TV—all can be used effectively to proclaim Jesus Christ.

"Literature molds minds," the communist slo-

gan bragged truthfully for once. And those of us who were in China under communist occupation would add, "Slogans too, painted on every wall; posters, hanging in every window; pictures, displayed in every shop or hall; inexpensive books, for sale in every post office; radios, blaring into every street a continuous torrent of music and words; loud speakers, filling every car on every train with the blandishments of the New Order." The pressure is ceaseless and irresistible.

Christians should utilize these means, not because the Communists employ them so effectively, but because God himself has made them available as vehicles of the message of redemption.

How rebuked we were by the profound respect the Communists paid to the human mind. They tackled the enormous task of indoctrinating the peasant classes with an astonishingly accurate conviction that untrained minds can master complicated thoughts, given teachers and time. They utilized every available means to disseminate their message.

By contrast missionary efforts were tragically slender. Limited thought-content in their tracts and books; timid attempts to use the newspapers (advangelism!) and radio: all contributed and led inexorably to a failure to reach the masses. No reflective missionary who went through the 1949-1951 "turn over" emerged unburdened by the need to capitalize on all contemporary media to convey ideas, that the despairing millions of this generation might be reached with the gospel.

Lessons about Priorities

It is the responsibility of mission leaders to define strategic priorities that the strength and skills of their missionary force might be put to the best possible use. It is always easy to waste time and dissipate strength in peripheral matters. Nowhere is it easier to play at busyness (much ado about nothing) than on the mission field. Priorities must be prayerfully fixed and workers must be carefully allotted to strategic tasks most consonant with their gifts and training. The China experience caused many a mission leader to have "second thoughts" after the door to further missionary service in that land was irrevocably closed.

What is top priority? "The unreached: the gospel must be preached to every creature." Yes, but which segment of the unreached is the responsibility of the foreign missionary force? What is the over-all strategic concept of a missionary society? "The planting of a national church that will accept and discharge the responsibility for evangelizing the rest of its countrymen." Yes, but where should this church be established in strength? "In the cities, among the educated classes, the two per cent that will produce the future leaders of the nation." But does this not overlook rural and tribal peoples? "By no means. Follow the sovereign leading of the Spirit and you will discover that He does not follow a rigid, undeviating pattern. He may guide unmistakably that a certain rural area or despised tribe become the object of His electing grace." Then all talk of strategy and priorities is irrelevant? "No. The Apostle Paul worked the cosmopolitan cities, the university and commercial centers, but did not resist the unusual leading of the Lord that occasionally took him to rural areas."

Some might argue that theoretical discussions of mission strategy are pointless. The allegation is that in actual practice personal and circumstantial factors often largely dictate policy. There is no little truth to this melancholy charge. Non-strategic factors often tend to blur and distort strategic planning. Unless field leadership is able to keep ultimate goals rigidly in view, planning tends to degenerate, permitting every man to do what appears right in his own eyes.

This undoubtedly occurred in China. Great cities had weak churches. The student classes, so productive in communist leadership, were largely neglected until it was a case of "too little, too late." Whereas the more aggressive and able Chinese were drawn from their villages to urban centers, mission societies sent many of their best men to work in rural areas. Tribal and Tibetan work tended to be glamorized out of all proportion to the numbers of souls actually involved. All in all, strategic considerations seemed to play little part in the over-all development of the work. As a result, when the evacuation took place, it was sadly realized that insufficient emphasis had been placed on training a vigorous and able leadership

for the national churches. The few small evangelical training schools that existed were of poor academic quality. With a few notable exceptions, such as the Kiangwan Bible Seminary, missionary vision had not been widely imparted. Why were there so few churches and men willing to evangelize areas within China and beyond its borders in the Far East? At the time of the evacuation in 1951, missionary work in the Orient was almost solely a Western activity. The Apostle Paul planted some churches that became notably missionary-minded. Many an ex-China missionary now wishes that decades earlier Protestant missions had been more priority-minded, more desirous of producing a responsible leadership that would have taken the lead in church extension in the Far East. With the coming of the Communists this opportunity to produce key men and impart missionary vision has been ended—by the Lord of the harvest. May God forgive the Western missionary, who by his limited vision provided the Communists with some of their most effective propaganda thrusts: "Only white men are missionaries. Christianity is the religion of the white imperialists. When imperialism is destroyed, Christianity will wither and die. The Asian who becomes a Christian turns his back on his home, his people, and his country."

Conclusion—The Spiritual Lesson

The most serious communist charge leveled against missionaries was that they were the agents of imperialism. This was an oblique attack intended to discredit and undercut all the positive social and spiritual good the missionary movement had brought to China. But when this propaganda assault was supported by selective and subtle appeals to some of the more sordid events in the previous hundred years of Western machinations in the Orient— the Opium Wars, the "incidents" that led to various uprisings, and other international disturbances— missionaries became uneasy. Some tended to lose sight of the fact that they had come to China at the call of God. Not a few bowed to the force of these distorted charges. They began to fear they had been the unconscious pawns of a studied Western cultural and political penetration of China. Although previously largely disinterested in politics, they now came to fear they had been political symbols, who by their very presence had influenced the Chinese against China's best interests. The more they pondered these implications the more distressed they became. "The day of the foreign missionary is over—perhaps throughout the Far East"—this now became their mournful dirge.

In contrast, other missionaries reacted against this communist propaganda assault with much indignation and wild generalizations. "Our motives have been pure. God's blessing has been on our work. What we have said and done has been at His bidding. What wrong have we done?" They unfortunately erred on the side of losing a sense of historic perspective. Thinking that to confess failure would reflect on Christ, they lost the grace of self-criticism. Their self-justifying refutations appeared almost to confirm communist propaganda. They revealed their inability to appreciate the revolutionary situation that had engulfed China including themselves. Their pride was pricked. This was apparent to the Chinese. As a result their righteous indignation only served to isolate them from the Chinese church. All in all, the Communists executed a diabolically clever stroke when they pinned the imperialist label on Western missionaries.

All this points up the final lesson, the spiritual lesson we must learn from the mass exodus of missionaries from China. This great crisis demonstrated that the Western missionary today is a marked man. He is handicapped by history. He represents a segment of the world which is nervously on the defensive. He is the symbol of racial and color conflict. He is the target of jealous nationalist resentment. He must forever face the strain of discrimination and the possibility of expulsion. He must be prepared to bear the reproach of Christ in a singular fashion common to none else.

But he can continue to rejoice! Regardless of how despised he may be by this generation, he nevertheless believes in God's sovereignty. God is in control of history, including the harrowing present. God has ordained that His witnesses evangelize this generation, despite its materialism and revolutionary climate. The very pilgrim nature of His witnesses is one of the wonderful assets He has bestowed on the missionary movement today. True, His witnesses have no standing, no prestige, no power-of-themselves. But they are symbols of the universality of the gospel. They represent the Lord Jesus Christ whose kingdom is "not of this world." Therefore they can rejoice in their high calling, while putting their entire heart and will into the task of proclaiming Christ to men.

(Source: Eric S. Fife and Arthur F. Glasser, *Missions in Crisis: Rethinking Missionary Strategy* [Chicago: InterVarsity Press, 1961].)

The Critical Voice from Outside the Western Church

49. *Black Consciousness and the Black Church in America,* by C. Eric Lincoln

If there had been no racism in America, there would be no racial churches. As it is, we have white churches and Black churches; white denominations and Black denominations; American Christianity and Black religion. From the very beginning, American Christianity was in a quandary about what to do with Black Christians once their numbers began to grow. It seems that they were a problem inside the white church, and out of it. The Presbyterian Synod of South Carolina and Georgia addressed the subject in 1834 in this way:

The gospel, as things are now, can never be preached to the two classes successfully in conjunction. The galleries or the back seats on the lower floors of white churches are generally appropriated to the Negroes, when it can be done without inconvenience to the whites. When it cannot be done conveniently, the Negroes must catch the gospel as it escapes through the doors and windows. (A.U.P., 1968: 27)

Professor Kelly Miller (1968: 193), whose forebears knew from first-hand experience the inner torture of trying to worship God in a gallery, explains that "When the Negro worshipper gained conscious self-respect he grew tired of the back pews and upper galleries of the white churches, and sought places of worship more compatible with his sense of freedom and dignity." The problem was that finding more compatible places of worship was not always a simple matter. The only place a Black Christian was likely to find where he could worship in an atmosphere compatible with his sense of freedom and dignity was, in the nature of circumstances, in a Black church. But Black churches were considered dangerous, and in every Southern state they were forbidden, suppressed or regulated by law until the Civil War settled the Black Christian's right to independent worship as one of the incidentals to the termination of slavery. As early as 1715 a North Carolina law provided a heavy fine:

> If any master or owner of Negroes, or slaves . . . shall permit or suffer any Negro or Negroes to build . . . on their lands . . . any house under pretense of meeting-house upon account of worship . . . and shall not suppress or hinder them (A.U.P., 1968: 11)

> In 1800, a law in South Carolina made it unlawful for: Any number of slaves, free Negroes, mulattoes or mestizoes, even in the company with white persons to . . . assemble for the purpose of . . . religious worship, either before the rising of the sun, or after the going down of the same. (ibid.: 22)

In North Carolina no slave or free Black could legally preach or exhort "in any prayer meeting or other association for worship where slaves of different families were collected together" (ibid.: 25). Other laws required the presence of whites—from five or six to "a majority" at any meeting or worship service Blacks could attend. Some of the harsher laws were in response to the slave insurrections of L'Ouverture in Haiti, and Nat Turner and Denmark Vesey in Virginia. But a far-reaching deliberate intention to control the Black man's religion seems discernible even underneath the cover of a practical response to the always-present danger of insurrection.

Because of the disparity of their respective interests, and because of their differences in the ordering of priorities, some spiritual and some profane, the Black-church-within-the-white-church

arrangement was never a completely satisfying experience for either Blacks or whites. As a matter of fact, the peculiar arrangements for Black worshippers to attend white churches was nothing less than the calculated subversion of the sacred to the crassest interests of the profane. The Blacks recognized and resented so obvious an abuse of the faith. They were never reconciled to their status in the white church, and when the occasion presented itself they made their own arrangements. The benevolent arms of white Christendom were found to be quite cold. Black Christians had their own thoughts about their bodies and their souls and their destinies, but it was politic to humor the white man's Christian judgment because the white man represented the sum total of temporal power within the universe of the Black experience. So in the white man's church they sat wherever his pleasure indicated they should. They stifled the urge to scream and to shout and to raise their arms to heaven; and they strangled the sobs and the moans that welled up inside and made their bodies shake and tremble like leaves in a storm. Only their tears could not be stayed—tears of sorrow and distress—so often mistaken for tears of joy for having the privilege of confronting God in the presence of the slavemaster.

But it was when the white man's worship service was over that the Black man's might begin. For neither his heart nor his private membership was in the white man's church—a church that scorned him and demeaned him.

There was that *other* church, that invisible institution of Black religion which met in the swamps and the bayous, and which joined all Black believers in a common experience at one level of human recognition. Deep in the woods where nature's own artifices could hold and disperse the sound, away from the critical disapproving eyes of the master and the overseer, the shouts rolled up—and out. The agony so long suppressed burdened the air with sobs and screams and rhythmic moans. God's praises were sung, his mercy enjoined, his justice invoked. This was the invisible church, where the Black man met God on his own time and in his own way without the white intermediary.

One of the most critical interests of the contemporary Blackamerican is the search for the definition of the Black heritage—a search which begins inevitably with the Black church, for the Black church is the mother of the Black experience in America. When I say "Black church," obviously I do not refer to the Blacks gathered in white churches, nor to those Black gatherings monitored by white overseers, for the inherent limitations such instances imposed upon the Black psyche made for the negation rather than for the flowering of an authentic religious experience. Today's Blackamericans are very earnestly involved in the struggle to determine who they *were* in order that they may better know who they *are* and who they may become. The process of rediscovery is complex and difficult. The official version of the history of this nation and its people is laid down with intended finality in our official literature of instruction. But much of that literature is often consciously, and sometimes inadvertently committed to perpetuating the Great American Myth of white supremacy and Black debasement. The Myth is protected by an intricate system of taboo, and it is buttressed with a clever folklore which functions to lend credence to what is patently incredible. Fortunately, the "finality" of American history is of course not final at all. This is an age of skeptics, an age in which "men want dug up again." A new breed of scholars more interested in recovering the truth than in merely covering up the past are at work re-examining the evidence of the American experience, for the prevailing interpretation of that experience as it is laid down in the textbooks, romanticized in the supportive literature, and sanctified by racial fervor was designed for a society which is past. Most Blackamericans and an increasing number of white Americans have grown weary of The Myth. They want to know the facts behind The Myth. And this is as true of our true religious heritage as for any other.

Any understanding of the significance of the Black experience in America, and any successful attempt to put that experience in perspective must begin with the Black church, for this is the key institution which spans most of the history of the Black experience, and offers the most readily accessible doorway to understanding the complexity and the genius of the sub-culture that is Blackamerica. The part that the Christian religion played in shaping the identity of the Blackamerican has been interpreted variously, depending upon the perspectives brought to the situation. But while the consequences of the Christianization of the slave have been the subject of debate, no one has ever denied that there *are* consequences, and that they are of the highest order of significance.

Perhaps for more than any other people since the Israelites were enslaved in Egypt, the Blackamerican's religion has been characterized by the absolutely unique place it occupied in his personal life and in his understanding of his existence. For much of Black history, religion was all he had to give meaning to that existence. There were no other institutions upon which to fall back for strength to confront the exigencies of his uniquely distressed condition. It was he and his God, God and his people in the intimate intercommunion shaped by that very "peculiar institution" called human slavery. The Christianity the Black man received at the hands of the slavemasters was not calculated to make him, the Black man, free either in his mind, his body or his spirit. Freedom was not a possibility for which he was considered worthy this side of the grave. That version of the faith given the slaves was administered as a spiritual narcotic intended to protect the economic interests of the slavemaster by so confusing the mind of the slave as to make his dehumanization seem to him reasonable, right and consistent with the will of God. Was he not the accursed son of Ham? (Albeit he was not a Hebrew!) Was not his blackness a sign of his degradation? And did not Paul admonish the slave who wanted to join his fellowship of Christians that he must return to his master? "Double-double, toil and trouble," was the proper lot of the Black slave, and this by divine decree. He must labor in the fields for his earthly master "from can-to-can't," from "can see to can't see," i.e., from daylight until dark, the traditional work day for slaves. And he must not complain. It was God's will. He must not run away, because to do so would be to steal his master's property, viz., himself. Above all, he must not commit suicide, because to do so would be to destroy property not his own, to the extreme and final disadvantage of those God had set over him and given stewardship of his body. A slave who committed suicide could receive no rites of the church and must burn in hell forever for his crime against his master. But if he bore his lot with love and patience, being at all times loyal and obedient to the masters set over him in this world, would not God see him properly rewarded in the world to come? Such were the teachings of the Christian church as they were offered to the African, who because of the white Christians' alleged concern for the purification of his black and heathen soul, found himself involuntarily resident in America.

But that was not Black religion and that was not the Black church.

Those who laid claim to the Black man's body, his labor, his children, born and unborn, were Christians, and the strange claims these white Christians made upon their fellow Black Christians were validated by a system of law anxious to accommodate the claims of property, but peculiarly insensitive to the claims of persons—Black persons in particular. In the context of the American priority of interests it could have been reasonably expected, and it did in fact develop that when the question arose as to whether the saving of the Black man's soul ought to make his retention in slavery no longer defensible, the accepted answer was that the Black man had no soul and could therefore not be a proper subject of salvation in heaven, or freedom on earth; or that God only required that he be free from sin, not free from men. The point is that with his body already in eternal bondage, the religion given the Black man was calculated to put his soul in perpetual escrow. And there it undoubtedly would have remained save for the development of the invisible institution, the Black church.

If the matter had ended with the fulfillment of the white man's intentions, the development of Black religion would have been quite different from what did in fact occur. Unquestionably, three centuries or so of the American Protestant Ethic— well augmented by and indistinguishable from a counterpart American Catholic Ethic—have left their mark. The Black Christian who still yearns to have his Blackness washed away at that magic fountain believed to flow beyond the veil of mysteries deep in the inner sanctum of the American church, has not fully recovered from the spiritual narcolepsy engendered by his uncritical acceptance of that version of the faith he received as a slave in his spiritual infancy. In contrast, the liberated, self-confident Black Christian is fully aware of himself as a Christian among Christians, possibly for the first time since the declamations on the status

of his soul were the popular sport of the learned divines who perceived it their duty to account for his Blackness as an act of God, and his bondage as an act of man.

Whenever the Black man accepted uncritically the American version of the Christian faith, he was stifled by it, for from the beginning the American version was designed to reduce the inherent hazards of slave-keeping to manageable proportions by interposing God's will between master and slave. Christianity was the critical link in a malevolent strategy by means of which the involuntary diaspora of West Africa were to be the uncompensated human instruments by means of which white Christians intended to enrich themselves, and Christianity came to be a prime agency of control in an interlocking system of physical intimidation, legal manipulation, and religious divarication. Contemporary history does not rule out the possibility that such a strategy so combining the law, religion, and force, in whatever guise, may still function with sinister effectiveness in controlling, or augmenting the control of the aspirations and the possibilities of Black people in America. Certainly, the dehumanization of Christians by Christians is not unheard of in our day. Yet so bald a strategy, even in the days of slavery, was seen for what it was, and rejected. The remarks of Lunsford Lane, an ex-slave, are illustrative:

> I was permitted to attend church, and this I esteem a great blessing. It was there that I received much instruction, which I trust was a great benefit to . . . [But] there was one hard doctrine to which we . . . were compelled to listen, which I found difficult to receive. We were often told by the ministers how much we owed to God for bringing us over from the benighted shores of Africa and permitting us to listen to the sound of the Gospel. In ignorance of any special revelation that God had made to [the white man] or to his ancestors, that my ancestors should be stolen and enslaved on the soil of America to accomplish their salvation, I was slow to believe all my teachers enjoined on this subject. Many of us left [the church], considering like the doubting disciple of old: this is a hard saying; who can hear it? (A.U.P., 1968: 29-30)

Despite this aspect of the Christianization of the Black contingent of the faith, the *Black* church as an institution soon took on important ramifications for the unfolding of the Black experience in America. Religion implies a cultus, a church, and the church became the organizing principle for the social development of the Blackamerican. The story of the Black slaves' disjunction from their African heritage and the ancient cultures to which they had belonged previously is well noted, and frequently employed as a kind of "missing link" explanation for all that is not known or understood about the Black experience in the West. Whether the disjunction was as summary or as conclusive as some scholars assume it to be, remains, I think, a question not satisfactorily resolved. Some vestiges of social and cultural traditions which could not possibly be "American" do persist in the Black sub-culture. Nevertheless, the fact is that the most important structural and unitizing institutions through which the individual African in America might have hoped to retain some sense of social identity—the tribe, the council, the tribal societies, etc.—could not be replicated under the circumstances of American slavery. The oral literature recounting the ancient cultures could, and did survive for a time, but generally speaking, the African's cultural institutions could not hope to survive for long under the all-encompassing suppression that was the American slavocracy. The dispersal of slaves owning a common language or tribal tradition was a routine precaution against revolt. The suppression of the African languages was accomplished through threat and ridicule. The fine art of oral history of the Africans was reduced to the harmless tales told by the plantation's Uncle Remus; and the African religions were relegated to the realm of paganistic superstition. In the void left by the fragmentation and the distortion of the African heritage, the Christian religion eventually caught fire and flourished; and the church became the inevitable central institution around which the social development of the Blackamerican could take place. The Black church became the chief organizing principle around which, and through which the slave and his successors would find meaning and identity in the land of the western pharaohs.

The genius of the Christian religion is that it has always managed to survive its distortions. For two thousand years the faith has been compromised by countless schisms and 'isms' without succumbing completely to any of them. Popes, priests, preachers and parishioners, governments and private interests have sought to convert the authority and prestige of the faith to private ends. None has enjoyed lasting success. Hence, the strategy of the slavocracy to use religion as the clinch pin for the perpetuation of slavery and caste in America was ultimately doomed to failure although the failure of that strategy is hardly due to its renouncement, early or late. To be sure, there have always been prophetic voices in the American church, but they have never been of sufficient power or amplitude to effectively dampen the racism which still structures that church and determines the behavior of its constituency. The strategy of white Christianity failed in its intent to make Black Christians its spiritual subordinates because in accepting Christianity in America, the Blacks were not accepting American Christianity. Rather, when it was offered them, they availed themselves of the opportunity to re-identify with a God and a faith which transcended the parochial interests of the American Christians.

Probably the first church intended specifically for Blacks was established between 1773 and 1775 "on the South Carolina side of the Savannah River . . . twelve miles from Augusta, Georgia," at Silver Bluff, South Carolina, and later moved to Savannah (Brawley, 1970: 66). In 1791, a group of Blacks in Philadelphia, having first formed a benevolent society, erected a building and voted to become an Episcopal Church, subject to certain conditions named in their petition to the Bishop. The conditions stipulated that they be received as a body; that they retain local autonomy; and that their lay reader be ordained as minister. These conditions were acceptable to the Bishop, and in 1794 St. Thomas Church became the first Black Episcopal Church in America. Absalom Jones was ordained deacon, and shortly afterwards, the first Black Episcopal priest (Wesley, 1969: 72-73). There were to be thirteen others by the end of the War in 1865.

The first Black denomination grew out of the humiliation of Black Christians attending the St. George Methodist Episcopal Church in Philadelphia in the late 18th century. Richard Allen, a lay minister who had preached frequently at St.

George since 1786, Absalom Jones and other Black worshippers, were on an occasion removed bodily from the gallery of the church as they knelt in prayer. Stung by the behavior of the white brethren, Allen subsequently organized Bethel African Methodist Episcopal Church (1794) (ibid.: 78) [Separated from the (white) Methodist Episcopal Church, South, and formally incorporated at Jackson, Tennessee, in 1870. See H. Shelton Smith, 1972, p. 231.], and was ordained by Bishop Asbury in 1799. Blacks in other middle Atlantic communities soon began withdrawing from white churches and organizing their own "African Methodist Episcopal" churches. In 1816 these independent churches met in Philadelphia to establish the African Methodist Episcopal Church as a denomination, and Allen was elected first bishop. Thus was the Black Church formally established as a separate entity of the Protestant Church in America.

Today the AME denomination has over a million members. The African Methodist Episcopal Church Zion (which was organized in 1796 when Black members withdrew from the white John Street Methodist Episcopal Church in New York) (Brawley, 1970: 69-70) has a membership close to a million. There are more than eight million Black Baptists in three "conventions," and a half million Black Methodists in the Christian (previously "Colored") Methodist Episcopal Church (ibid.: 78) [Historian Charles Wesley points out that only twelve days separated the dedication of St. Thomas Protestant Episcopal Church and Bethel African Methodist Episcopal Church, founded by Absolom Jones and Richard Allen respectively, who had shared racial humiliations at St. George Methodist.]. Perhaps two million other Blacks are scattered among various sects and cults including "store front" communions and Black Muslims. What is left belong to the "white" denominations, principally Roman Catholics, United Methodists, and Presbyterians, with smaller numbers of Episcopalians and Congregationalists.

One of the peculiar attractions Christianity could offer Blacks was that it provided a ready-made culture and a ready-made tradition for a people who had been brutally separated from their own. The Christian God was active in history. He involved himself in human affairs. He delivered Israel from bondage. Were the Black slaves themselves not in the hands of pharaoh, and would not God deliver them? If God was just and if God was merciful, if God was on the side of the oppressed, then must not they be the chosen people of God? Who else could better qualify! But the Blacks were not looking for a tradition to adopt; they had their own. While the bondage of Israel was a useful illustration of the power and justice of God, except for an occasional sect with severely limited membership, the Blacks in America never confused themselves with Israel. They knew themselves to be God's *Black* people—an affirmation of the illimitability of divine love and concern. If God could choose once, God could choose again. He could choose *Black* people. Although they have been wasted in the drainage of the white man's culture, to the surprise and consternation of well-meaning social scientists, theologians, and government planners, Blackamericans have resisted all efforts to deny them a sub-culture of their own. Out of the body of their unique experiences in America, there gradually emerged a new ethnic profile that is neither African nor American, but distinctly *Afro-American*. The Black experience looks back to its long pilgrimage from slavery to freedom and remembers all the techniques of survival; and it looks forward to, and addresses itself to a strategy of complete liberation. The Black experience is inevitably modified and constricted by the white overculture which surrounds it, but it has deep roots in the Black church and Black religion, and these have always been beyond the effective reach of white America.

The Black Christians identified themselves as the people of God, but they did not attempt to substitute the history and the traditions of the Jews for their own. Like the Jews, they chose God and conceived themselves as chosen by God because of their understanding of the nature of the love of God and the character of his justice. While there have been some minor cults which found the appropriation of a synthetic Jewish culture less anxiety-producing than the search for and the development of their own cultural identity, Black Christians have generally avoided the fantasies of such cults without submission to the even more demeaning presumptions of American Christianity. Black religion is assuredly not the religion the Blacks received from the American practitioners, for that religion was compromised by racism and human slavery. By contrast, Black religion sees itself as the religion of liberation, bringing good news to the poor in spirit and freedom to the oppressed. It is a faith born of the Black experience, a unique encounter with God in the concept of a developing American civilization.

The Black church, the *cultus* of Black religion, was affected with a crucial social interest from its inception. It was for much of its history an invisible system of relationships, a nexus of ungathered power. It was not a place, and often it *had* no place except the bayous and the swamps where the search for a more suitable truth than a segregated church provided, gathered the Black faithful in furtive, clandestine assemblage. It was the Black church that organized the energies and systematized the beliefs and practices of the slaves and their descendants in such a way as to transcend the cultural deficit caused by their estrangement from Africa. But more than that, the Black church was the unitizing agent which more than any other factor, made of a scattered confusion of African peoples *one* people, a self-conscious ethnicity with a common religious reference.

The Black church has always been more than a religious society. It has been the Black man's government, his social club, his secret order, his espionage system, his political party and his vanguard to revolution. It became the counterpart of the important social institutions he had known and participated in the African culture from which he was separated so precipitously. Under its aegis were the rites of passage from puberty to adulthood, from singleness to marriage, from life to death. The church sponsored the communal meal, the ritual of community togetherness. When freedom came and the invisible church could be made manifest in wood and glass and stone, wherever Black people gathered, and by whatever exigencies of fortune, there they built a church, a symbol of their faith in God's continuing deliverance, and of their common bond in the Black experience. The church house was funded and raised as a community effort. The church building was the community forum, the public school, the conservatory of music, the place where the elocutionary arts, the graphic arts, the literary arts, and the domestic arts were put on prideful display. It was *lyceum*

and *gymnasium* as well as *sanctum sanctorum*. It was the prime developer of Black leadership, a fact that is still critical to the Black struggle for full participation in the American spectrum of values. The Black church produced Nat Turner and it produced Martin Luther King; and ranging between their respective conceptualizations of the most effective means to accomplish Black liberation, the Black church has been womb and mother to an extraordinary phalanx of Black leaders for every generation of its existence.

The Black church has been the one institution the Black man could call his own. During the slave era it was monitored by the white overseers, or by white clergymen, but there was little proclivity on the part of the white man to take it over or to identify with it except to neutralize it as a potential focus of rebellion. So long as he could be satisfied that the Black church was not a threat to his economic and political interests, the white man was willing to let it alone. There were exceptions, but for the most part, white people were careful to ignore what went on in Black religion except insofar as they were amused by its style or made patrons to its indigence. In consequence, the way in which the Black church has contributed to the shaping of the developing cultural ethos is essentially a reflection of the character of Black involvement. The Black church has been the definition and determination of the Black experience which in turn produced the Black church.

The Black church is the Blackamerican's most focal institution, but times change and institutions change. Institutions do not change precipitously, and not always perceptibly, but they do change. It is the nature of an institution to resist impulsive change, lest the appearance of stability be compromised or destroyed, for an institution is a social device by means of which the salient values of a community are preserved from generation to generation with a high degree of integrity. Yet if the institution is to remain viable and relevant it must not confuse integrity with intactness. Integrity demands the responsible transmission of the spirit or the essence of the values institutionalized. Intactness demands that the institutionalized values be transmitted as received, without change or modification. The Black church is now confronted with the necessity of re-defining its role in the contemporary scheme of things. How it shall finally conceive itself will determine whether it shall continue to be a key factor in the liberation and dignification of Black people, or whether it will yield its place to some of the rapidly proliferating secular institutions which are bidding for its traditional position of pre-eminence; or whether it will opt to lose itself in the larger communion of American Christianity. Religion is a basal, vital aspect of the Black man's identity, and of his concept of who he is in a world where his humanity is still questioned by many he must confront at various levels of human intercourse. At the same time, the contemporary world is a kaleidoscope of changing patterns in social relations. The religious presuppositions upon which we used to rely for interpreting the world and its meaning are no longer a sufficient index to that end. What is the future of Black religion and of the Black church in times like these? First of all, it is to be true to its institutional heritage, Black religion (or any religion) must not limit its perspective to the short-term interests and to the problems of immediacy which demand instantaneous solution or response. That may be the role of magic, or of politics, or of social welfare. It is not and cannot be the responsibility of religion. On the other hand, religion cannot remain totally static in a world of change and still command the world's interest or respect. The relevance of religion derives from its ability to relate change and the consequences of change to itself, and to interpret the world at any given moment in terms of the internal truths which are not the subject of change. If the Black church is to retain its viability and its credibility as a factor important to the Black experience, it must withstand transition while at once anticipating and evaluating new patterns of human existence, and interpreting them in terms of the values of Black religion and what transcends Black religion. In short, a viable religion must change, but it must persist through change; always remaining what it was, always becoming what it must be as it unfolds itself to meet the needs of its people wherever they are in the flux of human history. And since the Black church is the cultus of Black religion, its credibility and its viability cannot be separated from the aspirations and the hopes of the Black people it represents. A church which does not lead where the people should be going is a dead church;

and a church that goes where the people are leading is superfluous. The Black church will remain alive and necessary so long as it has credibility, and it will retain its credibility only so long as its fundamental values, i.e., its basic appeals, transcend the parochialism which called it into being.

Revolution is the characteristic phenomenon of these times. The Black revolution is the corporate expression of thirty million people of African descent against the ancient regime which has used religion as an instrument of dehumanization and exploitation. The critical, evaluative faculties which inform human behavior in ordinary times are often muted or short-circuited in the fervor of social change. The validity of all religion in general and certainly the relevance of Black religion in particular is, and will be called into question again and again.

If the Black revolution intends to transform this society into the democratic entity it has so long claimed itself to be, if in the process of democratizing America the revolution intends to legitimize and dignify the Black experience for all time to come, and if it expects to be relevant tomorrow, the Black church may not rest on the accomplishments of yesterday. The revolution I am talking about is a revolution of ideas and of attitudes. It is a revolution of perspective and of response to perspective. It is designed to insure the emergence of the Black-american as a full man with full responsibility and full power to make responsibility real. It intends to help America move back from the edge of the abyss. It is redemptive rather than retaliatory, but it must not close its mind to the realities which scandalized the traditional faith, aborted the noble intentions of the founding fathers, and brought us to our present predicament in religion and social relations. To do so would be to deny the relevance of history, and history is the experience by which we learn.

References Cited

A.U.P. 1968. *Atlanta University Publications*. New York: Arno Press.

Brawley, Benjamin. 1970. *A Social History of the American Negro*. New York: Collier Books.

Miller, Kelly. 1968. *Radicals and Conservatives and*

Other Essays on the Negro for America. New York: Shocken Books.

Smith, H. Shelton. 1972. *In His Image, But . . .* Durham, NC: Duke University Press.

Wesley, Charles. 1969. *Richard Allen: Apostle of Freedom*. Washington: Associated Publishers, Inc.

(Source: This article is C. Eric Lincoln's 1973 Fondren Lecture for Christian Workers, delivered at Scarett College, Nashville, Tennessee. The text appeared as "Black Consciousness and the Black Church in America," in *Missiology: An International Review*, April 1973.)

50. *Six Theses: Theological Problems in the South African Context,* by Dr. Manas Buthelezi

Dr. Manas Buthelezi was a Lutheran theologian and church leader of South Africa. His criticism of the apartheid regime and the churches that supported it, as demonstrated in this work from 1974, led to a banning of all public distribution of his writing.

1. The future of the Christian faith in this country will largely depend on how the Gospel proves itself relevant to the existential problems of the black man. This is so not only because the blacks form the majority in the South African population, but also because Christendom in this country is predominantly black. Almost all the churches have more blacks than whites in national membership. This means that the whites currently wield ecclesiastical power out of proportion with their numerical strength.

2. The whites in as far as they incarnated their spiritual genius in the South African economic and political institutions have sabotaged and eroded the power of Christian love. While professing to be traditional custodians and last bulwarks in Africa of all that goes under the name of Christian values, the whites have unilaterally and systematically rejected the black man as some one to whom they can relate with any degree of personal intimacy in daily life and normal ecclesiastical situation. They have virtually rejected the black man as a brother. Love can never be said to exist where normal fel-

lowship is banned. Christian love is one of the most misunderstood Christian concepts in South Africa. This has created credibility problems not only for white men as messengers of the Gospel, but also for the Gospel itself. The days for the white man to tell the black man about the love of God are rapidly decreasing as the flood of daily events increase the credibility gap.

3. For the sake of the survival of the Christian faith it is urgently necessary that the black man must step in to save the situation. He should now cease playing the passive role of the white man's victim. It is now time for the black man to evangelise and humanise the white man. The realisation of this will not depend on the white man's approval, but solely on the black man's love for the white man. From the black man's side this will mean the retrieval of Christian love from the limitations of the white man's economic and political institutions.

4. For this to be a reality it is imperative for the black man to reflect upon the Gospel out of his experience as a black man in order to discover its power as a liberating factor for him as well as for the white man. The black man needs to be liberated from the white man's rejection so that the white man's rejection may cease to be a decisive factor in the process of the black man's discovery of his human worth and potential. He needs to see his own blackness as a gift of God instead of the biological scourge which the white man's institutions have made it to be. The white man will be liberated from the urge to reject the black man in that his rejection will be rendered irrelevant and inconsequential.

5. The black theologian must therefore discover a theological framework within which he can understand the will and love of God in Jesus Christ outside the limitations of the white man's institutions. He is the only one best equipped to interpret the Gospel out of the depths of the groanings and aspirations of his fellow black people.

6. The future of evangelism in South Africa is therefore tied to the quest for a theology that grows out of the black man's experience. It will be from this theological vantage point that the black man will contribute his own understanding of Christian love and its implications in evangelism.

(Source: "Six Theses: Theological Problems in

the South African Context," *Journal of Theology for Southern Africa* [June 1973].)

51. *From Israel to Asia: A Theological Leap, by Choan-Seng Song*

This paper was presented at the consultation on "European theology challenged by the worldwide church," held by the Conference of European Churches in Geneva, April 1976.

Disruption of History

The premise on which history is normally predicated is continuity. To speak of history is to speak of continuity. This applies to almost any kind of history, from the geological history of the planet earth to the history of ideas. This is no less true with personal history—the history of a person from the cradle to the grave. Every object including a pebble or a tree, every idea such as logos or matter, every race from the bushman in Australia to the Finns in Scandinavia, has its own history to tell as to how it came into existence, how it happens to be where it is and not somewhere else, what function it has played and still plays in the whole complex of changes which have occurred in the entire physical world and in the world dominated by the human race. History, if it is to have meaning, must be inherently related. It must be directed by a certain inner logic, for if history is disjointed, if it has no coherent picture to present, the message it hopes to communicate and the information it tries to give become less intelligible. Faced with a badly constructed history, one is forced to guess how the history in question might be continued. The sequence, which is essential to the making of a history, is broken. One is left in suspense until the thread of continuity is picked up again and joined together.

History, to use plain language, is story. The historian is a story-teller. In order to make his story intelligible and meaningful to his audience, he is obliged to arrange into a more or less coherent and continuous whole things and events which at first sight seem fragmented and lack relatedness.

His task is therefore to read continuity out of discontinuity, to discern relatedness in the midst of unrelatedness. He must make every effort to fill the lacunae whenever and wherever they are. In short, it is his primary responsibility to weave meaning out of episodes, parables, symbols, events, or objects, of many and varied kinds thrown together with no apparent connection at all. In a sense, history can be compared to painting. There are objects which the artist seeks to capture on his canvas. There are ideas and visions in his mind which he wants to express and communicate. And of course there are different colours on the palette. Until these things become related to each other in a coherent and creative way, the picture on the canvas will not take shape, convey meaning, and inspire human sympathy and wonder.

If history can be compared to an art such as painting, then there must be something more than continuity in it, however important continuity might be for constructing and understanding history. That is to say, history does not consist solely in chronological data, objective facts, or statistical accuracy. These are of course important, for without these skeletons the building called history cannot be constructed. But as skeletons they are not ends in themselves. They serve a purpose higher and beyond themselves, namely, the meaning of life and death latent in everything that exists in the whole creation. Ultimately, our historical activity is directed to the search for the meaning of life and death. It is a human determination not to let absurdity have the final word about life. It is a fight against the power of oblivion and death which constantly threatens to consign all that exists into the realm of lifelessness and meaninglessness. But the role of historical activity is not merely negative. It does not exhaust its effort by just struggling against the force of absurdity. More importantly, it tries to discern traces of hope in the desert of despair. It attempts to inspire the manifestation of human creativity. It seeks to liberate the human mind from bondage to the past and to fulfill the meaning of the present with the vision of the future. In this sense, a historian is not merely a story-teller, or an artist. He is also a believer. It is as story-teller, as artist, and above all as believer that men and women in the Bible confront history with the meaning of salvation.

146

But a strange thing happens. The meaning which is expected to give continuity to history often disrupts precisely that continuity. It stops the flow of history, diverts its course, and introduces new elements into it. The dynamics of history does not therefore seem to be derived primarily from continuity. In fact, what makes history an exciting experience is the interruptions which are out of human control and calculation. History that can be predicted, although it is still in the future, belongs already to the past. History then becomes an experience of death in advance. It is a history without a hope and a future. The word for the negative meaning of such history is fate—fate pre-arranged for the humans by the Olympian gods, fate in the endless migration of the soul, or fate predetermined by the law of salvation. Religious effort is closely related to the confrontation with history as fate. Types of religious faith and behaviour can be regarded largely as types risen out of such confrontation.

In socio-political life dictatorship gives rise exactly to the kind of history bound tightly with fate. The power seized and consolidated by a dictator steers the history of a people along a carefully marked course towards a predetermined destiny. Continuity is ensured by the institution of dictatorial power. Life under dictatorship becomes internalized. Conformity to the dictates of the ruling power becomes a supreme virtue. The historical continuity of a nation under dictatorship is therefore a bondage rather than a blessing. It must be broken to liberate people for human freedom and integrity. Often it is revolution which becomes instrumental in breaking the continuity imposed by the power of dictatorship. Revolution assumes the role of introducing a new meaning into the life of the people. It creates a new beginning for the nation. Thus, revolution interrupts the on-going life of the people and the history of the nation, sometimes peacefully but more often violently. History then gains a new lease on life and resumes its uncertain course towards the future.

Redemption as God's Revolution

Reading the Bible on the basis of the reflection made above yields interesting, and in fact exciting,

insights into the nature of God's work in the world. History in the Bible derives its meaning chiefly from God's redemptive acts. Redemption is the key to unlocking the mystery of life and interpreting the meaning of history, be it personal, national, or transnational; and the principle of interpretation with redemption as its key consists in interruption. Those events and experiences seen in the perspective of redemption do appear to interrupt the normal course of life and history. They become the bearers of meaning which brings something qualitatively new into the realm of history. Redemption is thus the power which enables us to tread the path unknown to us before. It is the power which takes us into the future and frees us from slavery to the sinful past and to absurd fate.

God's redemption can therefore be compared to revolution. To put it differently, redemption is God's revolution within his own creation. It brings about radical interruptions and qualitative changes in the life and history of humankind. Through redemptive events God wages revolution with the world in order to fulfill the purpose of his creation. On account of its revolutionary nature, God's redemption cannot always be a peaceful affair. In fact, it could shake history violently. How violent God's redemptive acts could be is illustrated by many an example in the Bible. But the event of the exodus was experienced by the people of Israel as God's revolution in history par excellence. It began in an atmosphere filled with ominous signs of violence. It was to cost the Egyptian families all their first-born sons. It threw the pursuing soldiers sent by the Pharaoh into the Red Sea. When the people of Israel touched the shore of freedom, they must have felt staggered by the enormous human price which had to be paid for their salvation from the house of bondage. But God's revolution continued with them. It pursued them relentlessly. Time and again the violence of God broke in to change the course of their life in the desert. In "the wrath of God" they experienced the violent character of God's redemption often almost to the point where they could not bear it any longer. At first some of them tried to seek escape back to the flesh pots of Egypt. Later, when they were able to organize themselves into a more or less coherent political and racial entity in the land of promise, they sought escape in the institutions of religion and monarchy.

They attempted to institutionalize God's revolution within the framework and structures of their political and religious institutions. But they had to pay dearly for all their attempts. Prophets issued the warning that God's redemption could not be contained in a human institution. Israel simply could not institutionalize itself into a history of salvation, assuming that salvation was something which had come to be at its disposal. The warning was not well heeded, however. The prophets often found themselves engaged in a war of attrition with their own people. Despite all this, the dream of a national messiah never ceased to haunt the people of Israel as a nation. Ironically, Jesus the Christ was born into this nation and interrupted the continuity of its life and history built on the dream of a national messiah.

Jesus Christ is therefore the most revolutionary act of God. In him the violent nature of God's redemption becomes most manifest. It shakes the structures of human society. It transforms drastically moral and religious values. It re-establishes human relations on the basis of what a person is worth, not in the sight of society but in the sight of God. Jesus Christ has initiated and carried out a painful revolution which goes deep into the very foundation of human existence. In him an interruption of a most fundamental kind has taken place in the life of people and in the history of the world. This revolution of God in Jesus Christ culminated on the cross. There on the cross God's revolution and human resistance to that revolution confronted each other. Jesus' execution was carried out by a political institution which had yielded to the pressures of a religious institution. This latter clung tenaciously to a historical and ideological continuity which made its nation quite distinct from other nations. They sought to arrest God's revolution in Christ in order to maintain their historical continuity. By crucifying Christ, they responded to that divine revolution with human violence. For a time they seemed to have succeeded. Jesus' cry on the cross seemed to have sealed their victory over God's revolution: "My God, my God, why hast thou forsaken me?" But there was a fatal miscalculation on the part of the religious leaders of his time. The historical continuity they deemed sacred was nevertheless disrupted. God's revolution of redemption was carried forward, beginning "in Jerusalem and in all Judea and Samaria and to the end of the earth" (Acts 1:8). God's mission of redemption began with a disruption of the history of the nation which had organized itself into a history of salvation.

A Theological Leap

If what has been said is true, then we must call into question the claim of the Christian Church to represent the so-called history of salvation, the claim which is deep-rooted in the mind of western Christianity. In the course of its development the Christian Church has tended to regard itself as an institutional heir to the messianic hope for the Kingdom of God. This tendency is strongly reflected in the formation of ecclesiastical structures, crystallization of creeds and confessions of faith, and in theological formulations of the contents of faith. Above all, the history which the Christian Church has carved out for itself from world history has come to be identified with God's redemption in history. The classical example of this is the famous dictum of Cyprian who said that outside the Church there was no salvation. The Church thus comes to regard itself as the custodian of God's redemption. It holds the key to the Kingdom of God. The fact that the Christian Church has played an enormously important role in the formation of western civilization reinforces the identification of the Church with the so-called history of salvation. The Church in its historical existence becomes the *fons et origo* of God's truth and salvation. When the Church constitutes itself into a history of salvation, holding the ultimate truth related to God's purpose in the world, God's redemption becomes a powerful ideological force undergirding the mind and action of the Church. To a large extent western Christian mission has been motivated by such an ideological force. People in the histories and cultures outside western Christendom are regarded as redeemable insofar as they are salvaged for the salvation history represented by and embodied in the history of Christianity.

Such an understanding of history and salvation cannot but impoverish the richness of God's creation and do injustice to the histories and cultures which express in varied degrees God's saving relationship with the world. True, the horizon of some western theologians has broadened in this so-called post-Christian era, and the Church is forced to see its faith and hope not only in the light of its self-understanding but also in the light of the challenges from outside the Church. But there is still an obstinate resistance in the western theological mind to treat Asian or African cultures and histories from a vantage point other than that of the historical continuity of a messianic hope believed to be lodged in the history of the Christian Church. From this kind of theological perspective, the relation between God's redemption and these cultures and histories becomes an intermediate one. This, it seems to me, is a basic hindrance for Christians to see others as they are, as children of God and not just as objects of their evangelical zeal. More seriously, this results in God's redemption losing its intrinsic meaning within the cultures and histories outside the context of Christianity. The universal nature of God's dealing with his creation forfeits its particular and direct application except within the cultures and histories affected and fostered by Christianity. I cannot but believe that this is a distortion of the message of the Bible. How is this distortion to be corrected? How is the impact of God's saving acts to be seen and interpreted within the cultures and histories outside the immediate influence of the Christian Church? How are we Christians to understand the complex relations in which God's impulse of love and the human need for God's love are inter-related? To put it differently, what are the biblical and theological grounds whereby Asian Christian thinkers can and must engage in theological reflection on the basis of a direct relation of God's redemption to Asia? And why should Asian Christians avoid a theological detour through the norms, concepts and, above all, cultural idiosyncrasies of the churches in the West in order to gain insights into what God is doing in Asia today?

God's Saving Love Must Not Be Taken for Granted

To answer these questions, I want to stress that the community of faith we find in both the Old and the New Testaments has a symbolic function derived from its immediate relation to God's purpose of salvation. I have said earlier that the great merit of the prophetic tradition in the Old Testament consists in its refusal to recognize the history of Israel as such as identifiable with the totality of God's redeeming acts in the creation. True, God works within the history of the people of Israel. This is how they read the meaning of the exodus and the tumultuous vicissitudes they had to go through. They experienced God's redemption in personal and national crises. But they must not take God's saving love for granted. The prophets did their best to drive home to them this very point. God is no guarantee against national disintegration when the nation becomes infested with moral decay and social injustice. Amos, for example, is most explicit about this when he says:

These are the words of the Lord:

For crime after crime of Israel
I will grant them no reprieve,
because they sell the innocent for silver
and the destitute for a pair of shoes.
They grind the heads of the poor into the earth
and thrust the humble out of their way.
Father and Son resort to the same girl,
to the profanation of my holy name.
(Amos 2:6-7)

Furthermore, the prophets realize that the hand of God is also at work outside their national boundaries. There is a curious passage in the Book of Isaiah (19:21-25) which, although in all probability is neither from the prophet Isaiah nor from his time, envisions the time when the blessings of God will be conferred on Israel's traditional enemies such as Egypt and Assyria. The passage runs as follows:

The Lord will make himself known to the Egyptians; on that day they shall acknowledge the Lord and do him service with sacrifice and grain-offering, make vows to him and pay them. The Lord will strike down Egypt, healing as he strikes; then they will turn back to him and he will hear their prayers and heal them.

When that day comes there shall be a highway between Egypt and Assyria; Assyrians shall come to Egypt and Egyptians to Assyria; then Egyptians shall worship with Assyrians.

When that day comes Israel shall rank with Egypt and Assyria, those three, and shall be a blessing in the centre of the world. So the Lord of Hosts will bless them: A blessing be upon Egypt my people, upon Assyria the work of my hands, and upon Israel my possession.

There is no thought in this passage of Israel standing out as a unique blessing to the world. Israel is seen rather in the company of Egypt and Assyria receiving blessings from Yahweh. What an exciting and thought-provoking insight into the work of God among the nations!

Israel Is But a Symbol

A passage such as this which appears in the Bible like a flash of new revelation gives us a rare glimpse of how God also deals with other nations. I must repeat that Israel is chosen not to present herself to the rest of the world as a nation through which God's redeeming love will be mediated, but to be a symbol, or an example, of how God is also at work among the nations in a redemptive way. In the light of the experiences unique to Israel, other nations should learn how their histories too are endowed with redemptive significance. The history of Israel experienced and interpreted redemptively provides a pattern or a framework by which other nations may scrutinize their history for its redemptive quality and meaning. That is to say, an Asian nation such as Japan, China, Indonesia, and so on, should have its own experiences of exodus, captivity, nation-building, rebellion against heaven or dance around the golden calf. It should have its own long trek in the desert of poverty, slavery, and dehumanization. It should also have its vision of future hope which can only be given by God when he brings history to a fulfillment. A nation will thus find itself placed under the redemptive acts of God in the company of Israel and other nations. In this way, Israel is symbolically transported out of its original context to a foreign context. This is a theological leap which must be taken by Asian theologians. For them Asia is a theatre of God's direct redemptive operation.

Perhaps it is difficult for the theologians steeped in the tradition of the so-called salvation history to be convinced that this theological leap, or leap of faith, from Israel to Asia is justifiable. What to me is an existential necessity may prove to be a theological blunder to them. But I am more and more inclined to think that a theological blunder of the first magnitude has been committed by those theologians who have confined God's redemption to a particular nation and to the Christian Church. The essential question is not how God's redemption can be channeled into a historical entity which in turn provides a continuity for the fulfillment of a messianic hope. What is of the utmost importance is to discern how people in different cultural and historical situations can see and experience the hope of salvation in the sufferings which descend on them with cruel consistency. The people in Asia, for example, want to know how the chains of suffering can be broken. They eagerly want to experience salvation for the present as well for the future. It is to these people that Asian Christians must address themselves. Asian Christians are the integral part of the Asian humanity longing for liberation from physical and spiritual sufferings. Surely there must be a direct relation between their sufferings and God's suffering in Jesus Christ. There must be an immediate link connecting their hope with God's saving love manifested in the people of Israel and especially in Jesus Christ.

Blessings in Reverse-Flow

To better understand the nature of the theological leap from Israel to Asia, let us see how it calls forth a theological leap, a leap of faith, from Asia back to Israel. It should be pointed out that this is not such a novel idea as it may seem. In fact there are in the Bible some important cases of this leap from the nations back to Israel, resulting in a substantial rethinking of the role and place of Israel in world history. There is, in the first place, this rather strange story of Abraham being blessed by Melchizedek, king of Salem after his victory over Lot's looters (Genesis 14:17-20). Supposedly Melchizedek was a priest of *el-elyon* (God Most High). Abraham paid homage to *el-elyon* who was "the creator of heaven and earth," and who "delivered his enemies into his hand." It is a well-known fact that *el* of *el-elyon* became part of one of Old Testament nomenclatures for God, namely, *elohim*, and *elyon* (Most High) came to be associated with God Yahweh as one of his titles. This is one of the rare incidents recorded in the Old Testament in the pre-classical period indicating that blessings could flow from other nations and peoples towards the people of Israel.

The inevitable impact of the nations upon the people of Israel became almost part of their religious thought from the time of the classical prophets onward. In the Book of Ezekiel one reads how the invasion of Egypt undertaken by the Babylonian king Nebuchadrezzar was interpreted as God's payment to him for his campaign against Tyre.

> Therefore thus says the Lord God: Behold I will give the land of Egypt to Nebuchadrezzar of Babylon; and he shall carry off its wealth and despoil it and plunder it; and it shall be the wages for his army. I have given him the land of Egypt as his recompense for which he laboured because they worked for me, says the Lord God. (Ezek. 29:19-20)

Tyre was a proud city of commerce and wealth. Besides her many sins, which included the sin of considering herself as wise as a god (Ezek. 28:1-3), shrewdly she was going to turn the fall of Jerusalem into her commercial gain. This seems to be the implication of what Tyre has said about Jerusalem:

> Aha! she that was the gateway of the nations is broken,
> her gates swing open to me;
> I grow rich, she lies in ruins. (Ezek. 26:2)

But Tyre's exaltation is short-lived. Yahweh turns king Nebuchadrezzar, who sacked and put Jerusalem to ruins, against Tyre. Nebuchadrezzar is now Yahweh's agent against the impious Tyre, and for his service to Yahweh the land of Egypt will be given to him. It must be admitted that the interpretation of the chain of historical events here is not entirely free from Jewish centrism. However, the prophet sees the future restoration of his nation dependent on a foreign agent whose mighty sword will remove the obstacles such as Tyre and Sidon.

In this way, the prophet begins to be aware of the possibility of positive interplay between Israel and foreign nations. Interpretation of history based on Jewish centrism will, in the prophetic tradition, find a corrective in what may be called international interdependence.

What is implicit in the passage from the Book of Ezekiel referred to above becomes explicit in the Second Isaiah. The most famous example is of course the "messianic role" accorded to Cyrus, king of Persia. He, the anointed of God, is to make it possible for the people of Israel to carry out the task of national reconstruction. In the beautiful language of the unknown prophet, the Lord says to Cyrus,

> You shall be my shepherd
> to carry out all my purpose
> so that Jerusalem may be rebuilt
> and the foundations of the temple may be laid.
> (Isa. 44:28)

This is indeed revolutionary thinking. A foreign king, a Gentile who has no knowledge of the God of Israel, will carry out God's purpose and rebuild the holy city and the holy temple! What a daring leap of faith! It would not have been surprising if he had been treated as a heretic by his own people. It would amount to an almost similar situation today if someone were to affirm that a communist government would play a constructive role in the advancement of a Christian cause. A communist regime has proved itself to be antagonistic to religious faith and taken steps to render it inactive. It is only natural that Christians tend to see in it nothing but negative signs of God for humanity.

Without the Leap Not Prophetic

A faith that is not able to take such a leap and sees nations and peoples outside the immediate sphere of the Christian Church play a constructive role in God's purpose for the entire world, is less than a prophetic faith. The tradition of western Christianity has tended to foster this kind of faith in the non-western world. Direct links established between the churches in the West and their offshoots in other parts of the world have not helped to broaden the scope of faith of the latter.

Moreover, western theology, with its West-centred norms and concepts, has done much to strengthen and ensure the one-way traffic of faith from the West to the rest of the world. In contrast, the prophet in Second Isaiah is a bold visionary who seems to surmise differently the thoughts and ways of God. After identifying Cyrus as God's shepherd, he goes on to say:

> Thus says the Lord to Cyrus his anointed,
> Cyrus whom he has taken by the hand
> to subdue nations before him
> and undo the might of kings;
> . . .
> For the sake of Jacob my servant and Israel my
>   chosen
> I have called you by name
> and given you your title, though you have not
>   known me. (Isa. 45:1-4)

In this vein the prophet goes on and on to stress the direct relation that exists between God of Israel and the alien king, affirming the latter's "saviour role" for the "chosen" people of Israel. The theme here runs parallel to the passage quoted before: Cyrus as the anointed of God is parallel to Cyrus the shepherd of God; Cyrus the liberator for the sake of Jacob is parallel to Cyrus the builder of the temple in Jerusalem. What implication can we draw from this? Surely it is this: Unless we Christians, like the prophet here, are led to see those alien to the Christian faith and to the culture built on it making a positive impact on the construction of human community as agents of God, our reading of history is one-sided, poor, and inaccurate. And here is an important corollary: Christian interpretation of history is not complete until it is tested and corrected by non-Christian, or even anti-Christian, interpretation. Furthermore, a Christian theology which does not come to grips with the depth of agony and hope with which people of other faiths, ideologies, and cultures seek to grapple, is not more than a half-truth. If such theology excludes from its formulation of Christian faith the concerns and issues which those outside the Christian religion have to face in their daily struggle for meaning and life, it is less Christian. It is from perspectives such as these that western theologies must be re-evaluated and Asian theologies should begin to take shape.

What Makes a Leap Possible?

The question which we must ask ourselves in this connection is this: What makes such a leap of faith possible? What makes the leap of faith in relation to God's redemption mandatory? What enables us to look at events and happenings within history from the perspective other than that of the historical continuity represented by the Christian Church? The answer must be found in the classical expression "the Word become flesh," the Johannine formulation of God's redeeming love in history. If the Word had remained transcendent, if it had not embodied itself in the flesh of human history, an interruption of a radical kind would not have taken place in the history of Jewish religion. The Word become flesh was a stumbling block to the preservation of the continuity of history. It had to be ignored. Since it could not be ignored, it had to be removed. And the continuity of the Jewish nation, of Jewish religiosity, could be maintained, in the shrewd calculation of Caiaphas, the high priest, by having Christ executed to placate the Romans who constituted a political threat to that cherished continuity.

The conversation between the members of the Sanhedrin and Caiaphas thus stands out as an ominous human conspiracy against the divine intervention in human history. "What are we to do? For this man performs many signs." This was the expression of consternation followed immediately by the feeling of a political dilemma. "If we let him go on thus, everyone will believe in him and the Romans will come and destroy both our holy place and our nation." In response to this, Caiaphas made a most cunning political counsel: "You know nothing at all; you do not understand that it is expedient for you that one man should die for the people, and that the whole nation should not perish" (John 11:46-50). The stage was thus set for the cross on Golgotha. But lo and behold, the first to acknowledge Jesus as the Son of God was the Roman soldier at the foot of the cross!

The flesh which the Word had assumed was broken so that the Roman soldier was enabled to recognize in the crucified Jesus the Son of God.

It was broken so that Paul himself was freed from the historical continuity of his own nation and its institutional pietism to carry the Gospel of the resurrected Christ to the Gentiles. In his letter to the Philippians he conveyed most vividly and forcefully his break with his own religious tradition: I was "circumcised on the eighth day, of the people of Israel, of the tribe of Benjamin, a Hebrew born of Hebrews; as to the law a Pharisee . . ." He could have been proud of all this and perhaps more. Then came the radical break from it all. He continued: "But whatever gain I had, I counted as loss for the sake of Christ" (Phil. 3:5-7). It is significant that it is this Paul who seemed to have a firm grasp of dialectic relationships between Israel and other nations. He was called to bring the blessings of the Gospel to the Gentiles. He counted it as his joy and privilege to be the herald of good news to those outside his own race. But he did not consider his ministry to stop there. He also sought to bring the blessings of God's salvation back to Israel from the Gentiles. In Romans he belaboured this dialectic of God's redemption which he called mystery (Rom. 11:25) and expressed it in what we may call today a highly emotive kind of language:

> Now I am speaking to you Gentiles: inasmuch then as I am an apostle to the Gentiles, I magnify my ministry, in order to make my fellow Jews jealous, and thus save some of them. (Rom. 11:13)

His own response to this mystery of God's salvation is doxology—who can help but be doxological when given a glimpse into the mystery of God's salvation? "O the depth of the riches and wisdom and the knowledge of God! . . . For from him and through him and to him are all things. To him be glory for ever. Amen" (Rom. 11:33-36).

It is this mystery of God's salvation which holds history together and gives continuity to the meaning and value in our lives as individuals and as human community. History is not a linear movement carried forward by the history of Israel and the Christian Church as the sole agents of God's salvation. The disarray of the churches in the West and also elsewhere in this post-Christian era alone makes nonsense of such a simplistic design on the thoughts and ways of God.

Theology of Existence

Present-day Asia poses a fascinating challenge to Christian theology, especially in light of the above discussion. Several factors have contributed to the change of attitude in Asia towards Christianity. There is first of all the tide of secularization which engulfed the West in the post-war decades. The spiritual role of the churches in western society has greatly weakened. Western Christians' response to the new cult of secularism has been in general panic and confusion. This state of affairs of the churches in the West cannot but have negative repercussions in Asia where, as in Africa, Christianity has been thought to be closely associated with western colonialism. Related to this are various attempts in the West to find in Asian spirituality answers to the spiritual vacuum created by secular culture in western consumer society. Of course not all the attempts in this direction can be considered as serious in intent and conductive to the recovery of western spirituality. However, this new phenomenon of seeking in Asian faiths and ideologies a rejuvenation of western spirituality should urge Christian theologians both in the West and in the East to take seriously faiths and ideologies which have developed independently of Christianity. A Christian understanding of revelation and salvation, for example, is seriously inadequate when it fails to give account of how God has been positively at work in Asia through indigenous religions and ideologies.

Another major factor which has made an irreversible change in people's orientation towards western Christianity comes from the resolute rejection of it by China turned into a communist state. The colossal efforts on the part of western churches for more than a century to incorporate the masses of humanity in that Asian continent into "salvation history" faltered and consequently were shaken to the foundations. The fact that more than a quarter of humanity has rejected, at least officially, the Christian faith from the West should remain a serious subject of endless reflection, soul-searching and discussion. A Christian theology which conducts its business as if the ideological challenge of China matters little is bound to be defective and useless. The understanding of Christian mission as evangelizing, converting the pagans and bringing them into the fold of the Church has little relevance in the context of modern China. Even the concept of the Church as a spiritual force making prophetic witness in society does not apply to that country. We are faced with an agonizing question: What does it mean to speak of God's acts in China today?

It is a question such as this that makes me realize one thing: the norms and concepts which have a time-honoured place in the traditions of western theology have very limited use in Asia today. Doing theology today in multi-religious contexts and in the context of a political ideology offering an alternative way of salvation cannot assume the Church to be its base as western theology has done. This alone forces theologians in Asia to do theology in a very different way. The question is not what God is doing through the Church but what He is doing in the world where the Church as we normally understand it is non-existent or too weak to make significant impacts. This question takes on an urgent note when we are forced to witness the continuous expansion of communist regimes beyond their national frontiers in Asia and pose as liberators for the masses submitted to the fate of poverty, starvation, social injustice, and human indignity.

One thing is clear: the historical continuity of God's salvation which the churches in the West and their offshoots in Asia have sought to represent is interrupted and broken. It was a violent break with great human sacrifices and costs. But as I said earlier, the God experienced by the people of Israel was often a violent God. And the cross on which Jesus was crucified is a violent symbol. We also have to remember that the vision of a new heaven and a new earth in the Bible is preceded by violence of cosmic magnitude. Theology has to be done in the midst of violence—both human violence and divine violence. It is true there is this important difference, namely, God's violence leads to life and hope, whereas human violence tends to lead to despair and death. Be that as it may, theology is born out of violence. Its task is to discern the seed of divine violence in the midst of human violence. Its mission is to enable Christians to turn human violence of despair and death into divine violence of hope and life. From such a new point of departure Asian theologians must reflect on the mission of God in Asia today, what He is to Asian masses, and what He is doing with the poverty and suffering which constantly keeps Asia in its grip.

What God Does, Not What He Is

Thus a conceptual and propositional theology, which has been characteristic of western theology, can hardly touch the heart of Asian humanity. Western theologians must first address themselves to their own situations. They too must wrestle with the question of how Israel can be existentially related to suffering and hope in the West today. Israel must become their existential experience. The danger of propositional theology lies in its hidden claim to universal validity. Black theology in the United States has forcefully rejected such a claim. The God of a white theologian who has no experience of what it means to be black in a society captivated by white supremacy is not the God of black people. God for black people must be black. Jesus too must be black. In other words, they look for a black messiah. Let us face the fact that one cannot do theology for those who live, suffer, and die in a society with different cultural, socio-political demands and responsibilities. At most what one can hope for is mutual support and encouragement through sharing theological experiences and interpretations of human suffering and hope in given situations. Theology of essence, which western theology has tended to be, must be replaced by theology of existence. Theology cannot deal with the question: What is God? Its task is to come into grips with what God does. If this is true, how can we know what God does apart from events and realities in which we are involved existentially?

Black theology is such a theology of existence. The theology of liberation in Latin America is another powerful example of theology of existence. Black theology in the United States cannot be transferred to Europe. It cannot even be exported to Africa. Black theologians in the United States cannot do theology for their black brothers and sisters in Africa, for what the latter have to face is qualitatively different from the former. Likewise, the liberation theology of Latin America cannot be imported by others who live in different socio-political situations. The theology in which Asian

Christians are engaged in the face of aggressive communist ideology, desperate poverty, suffering and continuing religious search for the ultimate destiny of man, should not seek relevance beyond Asia. It is freedom from external theological interference, conscious effort to become true to a particular situation and liberation from claim to universal validity, that make theology alive, useful, dynamic, and above all authentic. An ecumenical theological community must be built on the foundation of situational authenticity. Thus, the great missionary principle propounded and practised by Paul applies equally to the doing of theology. He says:

I am a free man and own no master; but I have made myself every man's servant, to win over as many as possible. To Jews I became like a Jew, to win Jews; as they are subject to the Law of Moses, I put myself subject to it. To win Gentiles, who are outside the Law, I made myself like one of them, although I am not in truth outside God's law, being under the law of Christ. To the weak I became weak, to win the weak. Indeed, I have become everything in turn to men of every sort, so that in one way or another I may save some. (1 Cor. 9:19-22)

If this great Pauline principle had been taken more seriously by theologians as well as missionaries, the impact of the saving love of God in Jesus Christ on Asian peoples and their long and rich cultures would have definitely been more profound and decisive.

In the final analysis, the Word has to assume the Asian flesh and plunge itself into the agony and conflict of salvation. This flesh will be broken as it was broken on the cross. When this Asian flesh assumed by the Word is broken, the saving and healing power of God will be released into the struggle of men and women for meaning, hope and life. And Christians outside Asia, especially those under the long history of the Church in the West, will be enriched by it. This is the mystery of God's salvation which works both ways between Israel and the nations. We must be open to this divine mystery and make it the alpha and the omega of our Christian commitment and theological reflection. (Source: "From Israel to Asia: A Theological

Leap," *Theology* [March 1976] [London: SPCK]. This version was corrected by Choan-Seng Song and reprinted in *Mission Trends 3,* edited by Gerald Anderson and Thomas Stransky [New York: Paulist Press, 1976], 211-22.)

52. *"Pilgrim or Tourist?"* by Kosuke Koyama

(Introduction by Gerald Anderson and Thomas Stransky.) The massive impact of technology on traditional Asian societies "is shaking our basic self-identity because it is disturbing our spiritual relationship with the holy," says Kosuke Koyama, a Japanese theologian on the faculty of Otago University in New Zealand. Koyama illustrates this with his experience of riding in an elevator barefooted, holding his shoes in his hand, on a visit to the Pagoda of the Sacred Eight Hairs in Rangoon. The "elevator" approach to a "slow" God, says Koyama, symbolizes the problem of relating technology to the holy—it causes a "temporary loss of self-identity," and makes one "neither pilgrim nor tourist." He offers no solutions, only a question—"Can technology be made a creative servant of the person who lives by the grace of the searching God?" Koyama is a former missionary in Thailand and executive director of the Association of Theological Schools in Southeast Asia. This piece is taken from his book Pilgrim or Tourist?—*a collection of fifty short theological meditations, published in 1974 in Singapore by the Christian Conference of Asia.*

In Rangoon, Burma, the famous Shwe Dagon Pagoda stands on Singuttara Hill. It is an impressive monument. Its perimeter at the base is 1476 feet. Its height is 344 feet. The octagonal base of the Pagoda is surrounded by 64 small pagodas. I have been there a few times. It was built, tradition says, to enshrine the Eight Sacred Hairs of the Buddha which the Buddha himself personally gave to faithful visitors from Rangoon. The gold gilded Pagoda is a marvel to view from nearby as well as from a distance. Visitors are required to remove their shoes and socks at the foot of the hill (". . . put off your shoes from your feet, for the place on which you are standing is holy ground" [Exodus 3:5]). The approach itself is already in the sacred territory of the Sacred Eight Hairs. Every barefoot step prepares one to come into the presence of the holy.

This becoming barefoot is not for getting ready to run. It shows respect and humility to the holy object which the devotee is approaching. There is an interesting story in the Hindu tradition. Krishna, an incarnation of Vishnu, stole the clothing of the shepherdesses while they were bathing. The maidens, realizing what happened and where their clothes were, cried for their clothes. Krishna told them that they must come and get them. The maidens, seeing no other way possible, came to Krishna wholly naked to retrieve their clothes. In this seemingly erotic story is hidden the rather impressive religious insight that one must not come to god "covered up." He must come to god "naked."

When I took off my shoes I felt that I was exposed. My modernized and well-protected feet found it hard to walk bare over gravel, stones, and heated pavement. The acceptance of all this inconvenience, and in particular of the feeling of being exposed, forms the religious sense of humility and respect. Under the hot Rangoon sun I began to trudge up to the hill where the Pagoda stands. It was a slow climb. Every step was a ceremonially slow step. The sweat on my forehead was, as it were, religious sweat. The time I spent walking up to the Pagoda was a holy time. When I arrived at the foot of the Pagoda itself, my mind was prepared to see it right in front of me. I recalled how in Japan the Meiji Emperor Shrine in Tokyo, Ise Imperial Grand Shrine in Mie Prefecture, and a host of others have long approaches to the main shrine, some as long as a mile or more. No bicycles and no automobiles are allowed. Even the emperor himself must walk from a certain point. The holy must be approached slowly and carefully with respect and humility. The holy must not be approached by motorcycle or helicopter. It must be approached by walking.

Walking is the proper speed and the proper posture that can prepare a person to meditate. Thus the universal use of the automobile is, I am afraid, producing a less-meditative mankind! The unholy (everyday things) may be approached by running

or on motorcycle (even if the muffler is broken). But that which is holy must be approached slowly. Such thoughts came to me as I walked up to the Pagoda.

The God that the Bible proclaims reveals himself to be the holy God. He revealed himself to be holy by becoming *slow* for us. The central affirmation of the Bible is that God does not forsake man.

> Can a woman forget her sucking child,
> that she should have no compassion on the
> son of her womb?
> Even these may forget,
> yet I will not forget you. (Isaiah 49:15)

> For a brief moment I forsook you,
> but with great compassion I will gather you.
> In overflowing wrath for a moment
> I hid my face from you,
> but with everlasting love I will have
> compassion on you. (Isaiah 54:7, 8)

The whole Bible is a commentary on that one passage in the Book of Genesis: "Where are you?" (3:9)—*God in search of man!*

What man of you, having a hundred sheep, if he has lost one of them, does not leave the ninety-nine in the wilderness, and go after the one which is lost, until he finds it? (Luke 15:3, 4)

This search is the *holy* search. In his holy search the holy God did not go "on a motorcycle" or by "supersonic" jet. He became *slow,* very slow. The crucifixion of Jesus Christ, the son of God, means that God went so slow that he became "nailed down" in his search of man. What speed can be slower than the dead stop of being "nailed down"? If God revealed in such a way his holy character, people must approach him in the same manner.

On my second trip to Rangoon I found that meantime they had built an elevator to the top of the hill where the Pagoda stands! Invasion of technology and speed! No longer a slow approach is necessary. Electric energy will put you instantly in front of the Pagoda of the Sacred Eight Hairs in a matter of 15 seconds or so. No steps. No sweat.

At the entrance of the elevator on the ground level, however, there is a sign which says that shoes must be removed before entering the elevator. For the first time in my life I rode an elevator barefooted. My shoes in my hands shouted at me that they must be worn on my feet. While I was feeling the strange sensation of suspension between becoming a pilgrim and becoming a tourist I reached the top. If I had walked up the hill barefoot, I would have been a pilgrim, and if I had kept my shoes on in the elevator I would have been a tourist. But now I was neither pilgrim nor tourist! A strange sensation of temporary loss of self-identity swept over me.

The traditional way of *slow* approach has been disturbed by the massive impact of technology. The whole of Asia is disturbed and disrupted in this way today and perhaps so is the whole world. Technology is shaking our basic self-identity because it is disturbing our spiritual relationship with the holy. Today all kinds of "elevators" are being built in front of the "holy pagodas." Singapore hotel elevators do not give me this problem. A Hong Kong shopping center elevator does not give me this problem. But the Shwe Dagon Pagoda elevator does! The number of "Shwe Dagon Pagoda elevator" situations is increasing today all over the world.

Should we prepare to come into the presence of the holy "on a motorcycle"? Should we train ourselves in a new style of relating ourselves with the holy? Am I old fashioned in speaking of "the *slow* God"? What should be the relationship between technology and our relationship with the holy? Can technology be made a creative servant of the person who lives by the grace of the searching God?

(Source: Kosuke Koyama, *Pilgrim or Tourist?* Christian Conference of Asia, 1974. Reprinted in *Mission Trends No. 3*, ed. Gerald H. Anderson and Thomas F. Stransky [New York: Paulist Press, 1976], 223-26.)

53. *Theological Declaration by the Ministers of Korea, 1973*

(Introduction by Gerald H. Anderson and Thomas F. Stransky.) Since the declaration of martial law in South Korea on October 17, 1972, Christians—clergy, laity, missionaries— have taken a leading role in the protest against the "absolutization of dictatorship and ruthless political oppression" by President Park Chung Hee. As a result of their prophetic witness, missionaries have been deported, clergy and laity have been arrested, tortured, and imprisoned, and students and professors have been dismissed from their universities (any criticism of the government is illegal). To set forth the faith that undergirds their struggle for democracy, and to chart the course of that struggle, a group of Christian ministers in South Korea issued this underground declaration on May 20, 1973. The call for solidarity with their struggle to the churches throughout the world should have particular significance for churches in the U.S.A. since the South Korean government of President Park is supported substantially by United States financial and military aid. The declaration was brought out of Korea secretly and has been circulated widely through various religious news services. It is reprinted here from Documentation on the Struggle for Democracy in Korea, *edited by the Emergency Christian Conference on Korean Problems, and published through the National Christian Council of Japan in 1975.*

We make this declaration in the name of the Christian community in South Korea. However, under the present circumstances, in which one man controls all the powers of the three branches of government and uses military arms and the intelligence network to oppress the people, we hesitate to reveal those who signed this document. We must fight and struggle in the underground until our victory is achieved.

The historical situation of the Korean people has been very grave since last October. President Park's consolidation of power has had certain demonic consequences for the life of the Korean nation and people.

The Christian community, as an integral part of the Korean people, now stands up and speaks out on the present situation, compelled by the divine mandates of the Messianic Kingdom.

Since World War II, our people have gone through trials and sufferings, of social chaos, economic deprivation, and especially the tragic Korean War and the resulting political dictatorships. It has been an ardent aspiration of our people that a new and humane community might be restored to their lives. However, the hopes of the people for such a restoration of humane community have been cruelly crushed by President Park in his absolutization of dictatorship and ruthless political repression. This is done in the name of the so-called October Revitalization, a set of false promises which is only the sinister plan of some evil men.

We Christians are compelled to speak out and take accompanying actions on the following grounds:

1) We are under God's command that we should be faithful to his Word in concrete historical situations. It is not a sense of triumphant victory that moves us today; rather it is a sense of confession of our sins before God; and yet we are commanded by God to speak the truth and act in the present situation in Korea.

2) The people in Korea are looking up to Christians and urging us to take action in the present grim situation. It is not because we deserve to represent them. We have often fallen short of their deeper expectations, and yet we are urged and encouraged to move on this course of action, not because we envision ourselves as the representatives of our people, but because we are moved by their agony to call upon God for their deliverance from evil days.

3) We stand in a historical tradition of such struggles for liberation as the independence movement by Christians against Japanese colonialism. We realize that our Christian community has often lacked the courage to take a decisive stand, and that the theological outlook of the official bodies of our Christian churches has been too pietistic to take up revolutionary roles. However, we do not feel disheartened by the weakness of some of our brothers; rather we are determined to seek our theological convictions from the historical traditions of our church.

The firm foundation of our words and deeds is our faith in God the Lord of history, in Jesus the proclaimer of the Messianic Kingdom, and in the Spirit who moves vigorously among the people. We believe that God is the ultimate vindicator of the oppressed, the weak, and the poor; he judges the evil forces in history. We believe that Jesus the Messiah proclaimed the coming of the Messianic Kingdom, to be subversive to the evil powers, and that his Messianic Kingdom will be the haven of

the dispossessed, the rejected, and the downtrodden. We also believe that the Spirit is working for the new creation of history and cosmos, as well as for the regeneration and sanctification of individual man.

In this grave historical situation, we as a Christian community believe:

1) that we are commanded by God to be representatives before God the Judge and Lord of History, to pray that the suffering and oppressed people may be set free.

2) that we are commanded by our Lord Jesus Christ to live among the oppressed, the poor, and the despised as he did in Judea; and that we are summoned to stand up and speak the truth to the powers that be, as he did before Pontius Pilate of the Roman Empire.

3) that we are compelled by the Spirit to participate in his transforming power and movement for the creation of a new society and history, as well as for the transformation of our character; and that this Spirit is the Spirit of Messianic Kingdom who commands us to struggle for sociopolitical transformation in this world.

Therefore, we express our theological convictions on the following issues:

1) The present dictatorship in Korea is destroying rule by law and persuasion; it now rules by force and threat alone. Community is being turned into jungle. Our position is that no one is above the law except God; worldly power is entrusted by God to civil authority to keep justice and order in human society. If anyone poses himself above the law and betrays the divine mandate for justice, he is in rebellion against God. Oriental tradition, too, understands that good rule is carried out through the moral persuasion and virtue of the ruler. One may conquer people by the sword; but they cannot be ruled by the sword.

2) The present regime in the Republic of Korea is destroying freedom of conscience and freedom of religious belief. There is freedom neither of expression nor of silence. There is interference by the regime in Christian churches' worship, prayer, gatherings, content of sermons, and teaching of the Bible. The Christian Church and other religious bodies must be the defenders of conscience for the people; for destruction of conscience is a most demonic act. In defending the freedom of religious

belief against interference by the regime in Korea, Christian churches are also defending freedom of conscience for all people.

3) The dictatorship in Korea is using systematic deception, manipulation, and indoctrination to control the people. The mass media have been turned into the regime's propaganda machine to tell the people half-truths and outright lies, and to control and manipulate information to deceive the people. We believe that Christians are witnesses to truth, always struggling to break any system of deception and manipulation, for to tell the truth is the ultimate power that sets men free for God's Messianic Kingdom.

4) The dictatorship in Korea uses sinister and inhuman and at the same time ruthlessly efficient means to destroy political opponents, intellectual critics, and innocent people. The use of the Korean Central Intelligence Agency (CIA) for this purpose is somewhat similar to the evil ways of the Nazi Gestapo or the KGB of the Stalin era. People are physically and mentally tortured, intimidated and threatened, and sometimes even disappear completely. Such treatments are indeed diabolical acts against humanity.

We believe that God has created humans in body and soul. Body as well as soul will be resurrected at the day of judgment of the Messianic Kingdom. We believe especially in the sanctity of the human body; therefore any violation of it is equal to killing a man. It is a murderous act.

5) The present dictatorship is responsible for the economic system in Korea, in which the powerful dominate the poor. The people, poor urban workers and rural peasants, are victims of severe exploitation and social and economic injustice. So-called "economic development" in Korea turned out to be the conspiracy of a few rulers against the poor people, and a curse to our environment. We as Christians must struggle to destroy this system of extreme dehumanization and injustice; for we are witnesses to the ongoing movement of the Messianic Kingdom in history, in which the poor will be enriched, the oppressed will be vindicated, and peace will be enjoyed by the people.

6) The present regimes in the South and North are using the unification talks only to preserve their own power; and they are betraying the true aspirations of the people for the unification of their land.

We believe as Christians that the people deeply yearn for authentic community on the basis of true reconciliation. Without transcendence beyond the past experiences of bitter conflict and differences in ideological and politico-economic systems, and without transformation of our historical conditions of oppression, true unification cannot be realized.

A Call for Action and Support

1) *To the people in Korea:* Withdraw any form of recognition of the laws, orders, policies, and other political processes of dictatorship that have been wrought since October 17, 1972. Build various forms of solidarity among the people to struggle for the restoration of democracy in South Korea.

2) *To the Christians in Korea:* As preparation for the above struggle, we Christians should renew our churches by deepening our theological thinking, by our clear stance and solidarity with the oppressed and poor, by the relevant proclamation of the gospel of the Messianic Kingdom, and by praying for our nation; and we should prepare ourselves for martyrdom, if necessary, as our forefathers did.

3) *To the Christians of the world:* Most of all we need your prayers and solidarity, and we ask you to express our common bond through actions of encouragement and support.

Conclusion

Jesus the Messiah, our Lord, lived and dwelt among the oppressed, poverty-stricken, and sick in Judea. He boldly stood in confrontation with Pontius Pilate, a representative of the Roman Empire, and he was crucified in the course of his witness to the truth. He has risen from the dead to release the power of transformation which sets the people free.

We resolve that we will follow the footsteps of our Lord, living among our oppressed and poor people, standing against political oppression, and participating in the transformation of history, for this is the only way to the Messianic Kingdom.

May 20, 1973

(Source: *Theological Declaration by Christian Ministers in the Republic of Korea, 1973.* This document was smuggled out of Korea and circulated widely. The source of this copy is *Mission Trends No. 3*, ed. Gerald H. Anderson and Thomas F. Stransky [New York: Paulist Press, 1976], 227-32.)

54. *"Let My People Go,"* by Harvey Perkins, Harry Daniel, and Asal Simandjuntak

(Introduction by Gerald H. Anderson and Thomas F. Stransky.) Asking "What are the basic missionary concerns and strategies in Asia today?"—three executives of the Christian Conference of Asia (CCA; formerly the East Asia Christian Conference) discuss the issues in terms of liberation—"Let my people go"—as "the central theme of God's redeeming work." The issues are complex: cultural identity and theological integrity—evangelism and social justice—poverty and dependence— sending and receiving relationships—denominationalism and Christian unity—nation building and political oppression—to name a few. On the controversial question of a moratorium on foreign missionaries, the CCA—they point out—has not adopted the position of the All Africa Conference of Churches in favor of a moratorium. "Amid the diversity of Asia and of its Christian churches, such a stance would have little validity or significance. . . . There are alternatives to the total strategy of moratorium." They conclude: "Only a deeper identification with the responsibilities and priorities of mission will give clarity and freedom of judgement as to what the selfhood and mission of the Asian church requires." The CCA—an organ of continuing fellowship and cooperation among 16 member councils and 78 churches in 17 countries bounded by the Karachi-Sydney-Tokyo triangle—operates as a regional agency within the wider ecumenical movement. Its first assembly was at Prapat, Indonesia, in 1957; the seventh assembly at Manila in 1977. On the CCA executive staff with headquarters in Singapore, Harvey Perkins (Australia) is Development and Service Secretary, Harry Daniel (India) is Associate General Secretary, and Asal Simandjuntak

(Indonesia) is Mission and Evangelism Secretary. Though not an official CCA statement, the study document—issued in December 1974—has been widely circulated and discussed within the CCA membership.

A. In God's Mission in Asia, *"Let My People Go"*

1) This is a message and an invitation to share in a program in mission. We offer it to all those who work in committees of the CCA and to persons in positions of leadership in the member councils and churches throughout Asia.

We write with the conviction that the CCA should be seeking to enhance in the churches of Asia a sharp consciousness of mission. What are the basic missionary concerns and strategies in Asia today?

2) Mission belongs to God. His is the word. He is the word. His word is His action in creation and in redemption to restore His creation. God is a missionary God.

Because God is missionary, His Son Jesus Christ is His "sent one" or "anointed one"—His missionary. His people are called to be co-workers with Christ as the Son pursues the mission of the Father.

3) Our participation in mission is a humble one. The mission is not ours. To participate in His mission is our total calling. That calling is to discern God at work in the signs of our time. That is what shapes our missionary strategies. That calling is also to understand the situation of men and women and their societies—their need of God. That is what shapes our missionary concerns.

4) We have given our message the title "Let my people go." Let us explain why. With this cry, Moses demanded that his people be released from slavery. "Let go" is a call for liberation. From that time on, liberation has been the central theme of God's redeeming work.

The cry was also God's. Moses was His servant through whom He was calling a "people of God" into being. "I will be your God if you will be my people." From that time on, His people, His community have been called to be a liberated and a liberating community.

The creation story expresses how deep is that call. It is both a story of God's creative action and a story of the brokenness of His creation in the relationships of human beings with God and with each other. Then comes the Exodus story. God's redeeming action is toward the victims of His broken creation. He calls the victims to be His people. Through that people, He moves in mission to restore the wholeness of His creation.

5) In the missionary movement of the Father's Word, Jesus came. To people at the mercy of others, he offered the mercy of God, and called them into His community of mercy. For this he was anointed. To the broken and bruised, to the captive and those who could no longer see the way, he came with healing and liberty, deliverance and sight (Luke 4:18-19). Christians are those who know and confess His name, who bear it and proclaim Him. That is evangelism.

6) Our Asian consciousness begins in the awareness of being victims. The centuries of exploitation in the colonial days before our political independence, and today the continuing economic exploitation of our people and our resources, determine our present history. The Gospel is to us. We are called into the forefront of the missionary responsibility of the Christian church because it is of peoples such as ourselves that God's cry is made, "Let my people go." Liberation is the good news we receive from Christ. Liberation is the good news we are called to share with our fellows. The words of Moses and the declaration of Jesus' ministry at Nazareth declare both the situation within which the Asian mission is set and our Asian calling to that mission.

7) We hear the call to mission as part of the call of God to His people everywhere and also as His particular call to us who know Christ as the Redeemer in our particular Asian setting. God is one, the world is one and His call to mission is one. We give our obedience to that call in the context of our Asian setting and as Asian mission.

B. To Asian Responsibility in Mission, "Let My People Go"

8) Our Asian history, as part of the people of God called in Christ, makes it difficult for us to express our responsibility in mission. We have been "receiving" churches, and in many ways we still are. The word "mission" denotes to us something foreign, something which came to us in western missionaries and resources, something we received and responded to, rather than our calling which requires of us both response and responsibility. The missionary movement has come to us as something western, something which brings in its company the values of western society as if these values are the values of the Christian faith. With it, our ways of life have become western and our cultural roots have been loosened. Because it has been western, the missionary movement has been carried out with tremendous material resources, leaving unexamined the question whether those resources are really necessary for our participation in the mission of God. We often feel dependent in consequence, and act in a dependence which inhibits our imagination to see ways in which mission can proceed with our given scarcity of such resources. Even missionaries are mainly western because western resources are necessary for missionaries to be sent. Our poverty becomes what disqualifies us from participating in mission. "Let my people go."

9) From these facts arises the cry to "indigenize." The call to indigenization is not a primitive cry to revert to an earlier cultural state. Culture is itself dynamic and it is impossible to go back to a past that does not exist. But there are values and perspectives in our dynamic cultures which the word of God in Jesus Christ must meet, encounter and renew.

— To find expressions of faith and ways of life in which the word of God meets our culture, corrects and transforms it and produces the Christian style which belongs to us as the people we really are!
— To make that possible, claim some freedom with whatever sacrifice by relying less or not at all on western personnel and resources!
— To enter deeply into dialogue with people or other faiths in our midst!
— To read the Bible through our own cultural eyes and the eyes of our poverty rather than through the eyes of western culture and affluence!

— To engage ourselves in the struggle of the poor and the search for justice (righteousness) in our own societies, and challenge the structures of exploitation which oppress, both from the affluent world and within our own societies!

— To let "third world" theologies emerge!

— To seek a style of life in Christian community which is appropriate to our situations, which will be seen by others to whom we witness as a style which belongs and can be theirs.

— To build that style of life on our deeper sense of community and enrich it rather than feed upon the individualism of the western world!

— To find the dynamic of our life in sharing each other's burdens rather than in relying on western resources to relieve them or to make us privileged in the eyes of our fellows!

The call to indigenize is not inconsistent with the universality of the faith in God or of His call to mission. How western should our churches be? How important are our own cultural identities and expressions of faith and life? What does it mean to be indigenous in our societies which are being superimposed rather than transformed by western culture all the time?

10) Responsibility for mission lies primarily with the Christian community in each place. It is not a western missionary responsibility to evangelize the world. Our responsibility is set in the context of our situations, and that context is something with which we live and in which we can move as no foreigner whose life and faith is set in another context.

— The rise of national selfhood and the newly-found sense of national dignity is something to be recognised in the proclamation of the Gospel and to be addressed by it.

— The social and economic instability of our lives in our various national situations gives a depth of meaning to Jesus' proclamation of good news to the poor, which must be our proclamation too, and central to the context of mission in our hands.

— As there are tensions in our countries between the pressures for national unity and the demand for freedom, so in many situations within the churches there are tensions between the pressures for Christian unity in the national scene and the self-contained life of ethnic churches. In the struggle with these tensions, let us claim the new understandings and point to forms of community for our nations which western denominational divisions can never do.

— The ideological conflicts and political pressures in which our lives are set challenge us to seek in our context the meaning of liberation which the Gospel in its fulness offers.

— We also live usually as small Christian minorities in the midst of a plurality of religious allegiances. This fact requires us to recognise the deeply religious character of our peoples and to proclaim Jesus Christ, not as the leader of another religion, but as the Liberator of everyone. For this proclamation, "Let my people go."

C. For Asian Priorities in Mission, "Let My People Go"

11) This is the context of mission in which the CCA Executive Committee has suggested it is important that national consultations on the concerns of mission take place in Asian countries. It is important for us to define our priorities in mission. In these days, when there is talk about "moratorium," meaning temporary suspension of relationships with western mission boards which send personnel and resources, it is necessary to face, anew and radically, questions of priorities in mission. A moratorium on the past as a mental approach can release us to look into the future of mission and the priorities of mission in the future. Into new priorities "let my people go."

12) A few questions may stimulate us. We all recognise how much of our time, energy, and resources are spent in running our church administrations and institutions. Within them, we can close ourselves from what is going on around us and make decisions with the institutions primarily in mind—rather than the people, their lives, and their struggles. If we all try to put the interest of the institutions behind for a while, what are our real priorities in mission?

We claim one faith, but our ideas, even our ideologies and certainly our practices, differ. What provides us with our stance? That is often left unexamined. Jesus came to proclaim good news to the poor and release to the captives. What does it mean to be the community of the poor? What are the priorities in mission which follow?

We are facing heavy political pressures in many places. Such external pressures upon us often produce in us self-questioning and re-appraisal of our work. How do our contemporary situations make us think anew about the priorities of our missionary engagement?

13) CCA cannot determine priorities for the churches. What it can do and has done is to establish the priorities which will guide it as it facilitates the movements of people in mission between Asian countries. We share these again with you, because they may be suggestive and stimulating in your own considerations.

> *Evangelism*—to encourage new understandings, strategy and experiment in evangelism.
> *Mobilization of local congregations*—to build up congregations in new understanding of what it means to be the people of God, and how to participate in God's mission in a world of social change, living faiths and ideologies.
> *Social justice programmes*—to develop a new understanding of and commitment to justice and liberation.
> *Migration of people*—to care for people as they move into new situations in search of work and livelihood, and to help them as minority communities to participate more fully in the societies into which they move.
> *Understanding our neighbours*—to understand the histories and cultures of Asian countries and the life of churches in those contexts.

14) Listing areas of priority is comparatively easy. Making decisions about new priorities is much more difficult. We have traditional priorities which we have inherited from western missions, such as church growth, education and healing ministries. These priorities need to be reshaped for the sake of growth in quality; for more indigenous styles, content and objectives of education; for more community-oriented rather than insti-tution-centered approaches to healing. But they are entrenched in institutional approaches around churches, schools and hospitals and are difficult to change. It is also difficult to implement new priorities when so much of energy and resources are expended on these traditional and institutional priorities. Perhaps some examples will help to bring the CCA listing to life.

— There are a few situations in which the goal of evangelism has been the conversion of total village communities rather than of individuals within them. These programs reflect understanding of the communal character of village people, and express a strategy of seeking community allegiance to Christ. There are other situations where programs of village development have opened the way to very effective village evangelism.
— There are places where congregations have been renewed and mobilized as they have become involved in work with trade unions and industrial management, helping the poor to define their needs and methods of attaining their goals, and as they have supported the social service programs of groups adhering to other faiths in their midst as well as their own.
— In situations of political repression, there are churches which have found new life and understanding of the liberating Gospel they profess as they have become involved in vigilant action in defense of human rights and civil liberties.
— The recent conference on minorities has led to major changes of policy in one industrial firm in relation to employment of ethnic minorities in its midst.
— Those who have worked in Asian countries other than their own can testify to the understanding they have gained and which they have been able to share with their churches.

D. With Asian Resources for Mission, "Let My People Go"

15) When we look into these examples, we find that more limited resources from outside Asia have

been required. One problem with our traditional priorities is that they have been determined by others and have been developed in styles which are inherently dependent on personnel and resources from outside the Asian region. Today, they consume the limited resources of our own. Our action on new priorities must spring from our initiatives, reflect our agendas, implement our decisions. As we seek to review our understanding of the priorities of mission in the future, we need to relate our review to the question of greater reliance on our own resources, and greater use of external resources for our priorities.

16) One contributor to our discussion has recalled how Isaac first built his altar, then pitched his tent, and finally dug his well. All were necessary to his life and selfhood (Gen. 26:25). He compares the history of Asian churches and draws attention to how we have built our churches and developed our national church organizations but have done these things in foreign style and in heavy reliance on foreign resources. He suggests that is why we have not dug our wells very well, why we have not tapped our resources through the commitment of those who have joined the people of God. Isaac had to draw water in his own place. Our Asian churches need to dig our wells and draw our water in the life and the commitment of our local congregations. As we do so, we will find new strength as some of our churches have already found, for witness.

17) The question of resources arises in relation to both personnel and funds.

— How much do we rely on western personnel in our churches?
— How much do they affect our style and give us a foreign image which inhibits our identity, delays our indigenization, and impedes our proclamation?
— Do western workers help us to be, or hinder us from being, churches of the people?
— How much do they contribute to the gap between the urban and village styles of our churches?
— How acceptable to us is the gap between expatriate and local stipends in equivalent positions?
— Do we have clear views as to how we can use

western workers effectively for our chosen priorities?

18) There are also questions about how our people serve our priorities in mission.

— Does the gap between the urban and the village pastor divide the fellowship of our ministries?
— Do the modernized styles of our central and institutional church work produce false aspirations, jealousies, resentments and power struggles in our churches?
— As there is a question of what is the acceptable gap between expatriate and local stipends, have we faced the internal question of what is the acceptable gap between the highest and lowest levels of stipend in our ministries?

19) For years, the CCA has tried to encourage movements of persons in mission between Asian countries with the help of financial contributions of western mission boards to the Asian Missionary Support Fund. We help with only a few. It seems that more of our people in Asia go to the west than exchange with one another. We acknowledge that our missionary responsibility reaches to the western world and seek further opportunity to fulfill it. We acknowledge too that to work in other churches in any part of the world broadens experience and understanding. But we still have to ask why so few between Asian countries?

— Is it that there is more money and other factors in the west? If so, what does that say about our commitment in mission and our identification with the poor?
— Do we hesitate to replace western workers with our own people or with Christians from other Asian countries? If so, how important is it to us that the western worker is paid for by others?

20) So let us face questions too about financial resources.

— Does the extent to which we use foreign

funds hinder us from developing our own stewardship?

— Peoples' commitment is related to how we give ourselves, what we put into the cause, what it costs us to do it. Do foreign funds affect adversely the depth of commitment to the Christian cause among our people?
— Do they create a style of church life which is not ours and inappropriate to our situation?
— Do they create structures which we cannot maintain ourselves?
— Should we be more self-reliant and live more on the basis of our scarcity of resources?
— What are the guidelines which help us to be selective about how much of such resources we are ready to use and how we use them?

21) Many Asian churches are looking hopefully for capital investments in property and endowment funds to enable us to continue to live and work in the style which foreign resources have set for us. How does this enable us to be identified with the poor and to proclaim good news to the poor who have no such financial maneuverability? We already have wide gaps between the central and urban church style and the village style. But it is the village people who have strong cultural roots. How can we claim the cultural rootage of the poor for the identity of the whole church if church establishments continue along the rich man's way with the devices of property income and endowment funds?

22) Does our reliance upon foreign funds hinder us from sharing our own resources between our own churches, between richer and poorer congregations? The news that one mission board would need to reduce its grant to a national church recently led to a conversation in that church on how to develop its inter-regional sharing. Have we developed our own inter-church sharing programs within our own churches? Can we move the richer congregations to share more with poorer congregations in the fellowship?

23) In the CCA, we acknowledge that we too are heavily dependent on foreign funds. The question of our life-style is always with us. How can we, as well as, say, some national denominational offices be closer in style to the normal lifestyle of our churches insofar as that is possible in an international setting?

If dependence on foreign resources is what stops us from developing our own resources or another style more appropriate to our own resources, how serious do we regard that dependence to be? How radical must be our answer?

E. In Our Relationships with Others in Asian Mission, "Let My People Go"

24) Historically, many of our churches in Asia have been related over a long period of time with churches in North America, in the United Kingdom, Holland, Germany, and other countries of Western Europe. Within our own fellowship in the CCA, the relationship between "sending missions" and "receiving churches" is represented through the involvements of mission boards in Australia and New Zealand. Styles of relationship vary within the basic "sending and receiving" relationship. Some relationships began with pioneering missionary movements and have continued as relationships with autonomous churches in Asia. Other relationships developed later as church relationships through which smaller supplementary assistance is received. Some sending agencies rely on appeal methods and require a close identification of particular projects for their appeal purposes. Others secure their financial resources through a church budget system and so are able to use more general methods of funding. What styles of relationships do we really want to have, if any, with these agencies in the future? In what particular ways do we want them to change?

25) One mission board has recently changed its style of relating with churches overseas. It offers people in response to requests, and the requesting churches have the right to accept or decline the offer and are exercising that right. Persons so engaged are employed by the receiving churches rather than the sending mission board and the employing churches have the right to terminate as well as to engage and are exercising that right too. The employing churches have the right to set the field stipends for those whom it employs. In this way the employing church decides what

is the acceptable gap between payments to local and expatriate workers. The employing church is responsible to pay those whom it employs. The mission board makes an annual block grant to the budget of the receiving church and the church decides the use of its budget—how many expatriate workers will it employ, where it will seek them and what it will pay them. In this way the requesting church makes all the decisions about its strategies and priorities. How it uses expatriate personnel is one among the many questions of priority which the church has to decide.

26) This example leads to several questions which we may ask and which may suggest possible future patterns of relationship.

— Do we feel that sending mission boards and service agencies have too determinative a role in relationships with us, either by making unilateral decisions which affect us or influencing our own decisions too much?
— Do we want expatriate workers in our churches to be in our employment to the extent that we engage and terminate them, set their field payments at a level we consider appropriate in our national conditions and pay them?
— Do we wish to receive open grants as contributions to our Church budgets so that we have freedom to decide how all resources available to us are used according to our priorities?
— Do we operate on declining annual grants according to a schedule planned with our supporting bodies so that we are planning our growth in self-support?
— Have we developed personnel plans over some years ahead so that planned replacement of expatriate workers is possible and training programs to that end are also planned?
— Is it helpful for our freedom to seek the services of expatriate personnel through ecumenical rather than denominational channels?

27) We should also note the initiatives within Asia. There are indigenous missionary societies within our countries which serve in other areas of their own country or beyond it without using external resources. Some churches have missions departments which seek resources from their own congregations and through which bilateral movements are arranged with other churches.

Although the Asian Missionary Support Fund of the CCA operates with resources received from western mission boards, it facilitates movements by supporting the international costs of movements between Asian countries while the churches involved in each movement support at local salary levels and to meet family needs. Do not these examples point to styles of movement in mission toward which Asian churches should move as deliberate policy and in increasing measure?

F. Is Moratorium Necessary to "Let My People Go"?

28) Four years ago, the General Secretary of a church in Africa urged a moratorium on all western personnel and funds into the church of his country. It meant that all western personnel should leave, and none take their place. It also meant that no more funds should be received to support church work or its service in the community. He claimed that this was necessary for a time in order that the African church might find its real cultural identity, might change its style and determine its priorities freely. Moratorium does not mean moratorium on mission, a temporary suspension of mission. It means moratorium for mission, a temporary suspension of the flow of resources, so that the church may find how to obey its missionary calling in its own country and cultural reality and decide its own priorities and style of mission. The proposal envisages that relationships may be renewed after a reasonable period, but on the terms and for the purposes of the church within the priorities and style of mission which the African church has set in the meantime.

29) Since then, a debate on moratorium has developed in many parts of the world. The Ecumenical Sharing of Personnel (ESP) Committee of the World Council of Churches has become a focal point of debate. The argument for moratorium is that "True partnership and interdependence among

churches, in obedience to the Gospel, might better be achieved by pressing for independence through a period of search for selfhood rather than by modifying existing patterns of relationships in a more gradual way" (ESP 1972). Both sending and receiving churches need liberation from past patterns of domination and dependence if the response of each to God's mission is to be renewed.

30) In May 1974, the Assembly of the All Africa Conference of Churches (AACC) recommended to member churches a moratorium in Africa. It described the option as "the only potent means of coming to grips with being ourselves" and so sharing as an African church "in the redeeming work of Christ in our world." It recognised the tremendous effects such an option would exercise on the structures and programs of African churches, but saw also out of that option a new freedom in evangelism and a new drive for Christian unity in Africa. "To be truly redeemed," the report said, "one must die and be reborn"—African and viably African.

31) The Christian Conference of Asia has not taken such a stance. Amid the diversity of Asia and of its Christian churches, such a stance would have little validity or significance. In this paper, intended as message both to the committees and the member churches of CCA and to the ESP Committee of the WCC, we who write it have taken the position that we should engage each other in a process. The issues raised by the African call for moratorium are real. We have raised them as we share our concerns with you in this paper. But moratorium is a matter for each or any Asian church in its relationships with western churches and ecumenical agencies. Our task is to draw attention to the context which makes the option for moratorium important. Our task is also to stimulate an important process in which our churches need to engage—a process of reconsidering.

— What is the mission of God and what is our calling to participate in that mission as co-workers with Jesus Christ?
— What is the context of our missionary calling in Asia today and what are our priorities of mission in that context?
— How should resources of personnel and funds (Asian and external, if any) be used in serving those priorities? It is to stimulate

that process that we have written to a large extent in a self-questioning way. It is for that process that we seek earnest cooperation, and issue our invitation. Through that process, and in their own contexts, churches may find their own answers.

32) There are alternatives to the total strategy of moratorium. It is commonly agreed amongst us already that the first area for a "selective moratorium" is the salaries of local pastors. These should be the whole responsibility of the local congregation and the national church. In comments received from within national situations in Asia, one contributor who supports moratorium makes an exception in the case of service to the needy and destitute. Another would seek a moratorium on personnel only. Still another selective moratorium style would be to change our relationships with western boards and agencies so that we are free to seek the participation of expatriates from places we choose while maintaining an unearmarked financial resource flow on a declining basis. The Lausanne Covenant says that "a reduction of foreign missionaries and money in an evangelized country may sometimes be necessary to facilitate the national church's growth in self-reliance and to release resources for unevangelized areas." These are examples of partial or gradual approaches to moratorium such as AACC has declined to opt for.

33) We should take note of the fact that in the history of some of our churches in Asia, moratorium has been forced upon them. Some of our member churches experienced forced moratorium during the years of World War II. One contributor testifies to the renewal and new life of evangelism which was released in a church in his country as a result of this experience. National member churches in one country have been experiencing forced moratorium regarding personnel for many years and the values and problems of that experience need to be shared with us all.

One contributor has written in anticipation of a forced moratorium in the future in his country as a result of Government policy. He speaks of the need for staged moratorium regarding personnel; of the cooperation of government to enable local people to be trained for positions held by expatri-

167

ate personnel within a defined period; of policies of declining financial resource adopted in consultation with missionary societies; and of movements toward Church Union, encouraged by the pressure of political events regarded as inevitable.

34) Contributors from two other countries oppose the proposal totally. "The churches are interdependent. The question should be viewed from the point of view of growing togetherness and having common responsibility in mission and service." There lies the issue. Are the churches genuinely interdependent or is the prevailing situation one of dependence, one way? Does not interdependence involve a mutual responsibility toward each other, in which the doors of western churches are as open to our participation as are the doors of our churches to their participation? These are days in which we recognise that mission is in six continents, not three. The western world is passing through a deep crisis in faith. It is also involved in economic crisis and social sickness—the result of its acquisitive individualism and rapacious use of resources—ours as well as theirs—for their own profit. All the sickness of the affluent which Jesus described is apparent in western life. There are urgent missionary needs today in the countries from which the modern missionary enterprise originated.

35) Therefore there is another important question about moratorium. Would moratorium release the western church for new roles and new priorities in mission? Would it liberate a western church to see its mission among its exploited migrant communities and ethnic minorities or in a struggle in the seats of world power for a more just economic order in the world or in caring evangelism that people who have lost their way may find Him who is the way? We have been receivers for so long that we see our western brothers and sisters in Christ as "givers" rather than as churches with their own responsibility for mission in their places and with as many problems of missionary engagement as we have. Do we seek to understand their sense of mission? Do we acknowledge that they too have an option for moratorium as much as we have? In so far as moratorium for mission is on the past and for the future of mission, do we seek to share in their future tasks of mission? Will we offer to them in their life what we have received in faith and grace from God in Jesus Christ?

36) The immediate advantages of what we receive can benumb our judgements so that we are hardly capable of seeing the good that could come out of choosing a radical alternative to our present relationships. Only a deeper identification with the responsibilities and priorities of mission will give clarity and freedom of judgement as to what the selfhood and mission of the Asian church requires. Into that freedom, "let my people go."

(Source: "Let my People Go," Study Document of the Christian Conference of Asia, 1974. This document was not official, and was widely circulated. The source of this copy is *Mission Trends No. 3*, ed. Gerald H. Anderson and Thomas F. Stransky [New York: Paulist Press, 1976], 192-210.)

55. *"The Search for Freedom, Justice, and Fulfillment,"* by Samuel Escobar

(Introduction by Gerald H. Anderson and Thomas F. Stransky.) At the International Congress on World Evangelization in Lausanne, Switzerland, in July 1974, there was a strong emphasis—especially among "young evangelicals" and Third World participants—on the need to relate the Gospel to issues of social justice, and to see the inter-connection in Scripture between evangelization and the prophetic ministry of the Church. In his address to the Congress, Samuel Escobar said, "Jesus takes seriously the problems of property and power relationships. . . . He identified with the oppressed." Speaking from his Latin American experience to the 2,700 participants at Lausanne, Escobar argued: "The heart which has been made free with the freedom of Christ cannot be indifferent to the human longings for deliverance from economic, political, or social oppression." There is a continuing need, he said, for missionaries "ready to pioneer in areas of social justice and evangelism." Mr. Escobar—Peruvian by birth and now based in Cordoba, Argentina—is associate general secretary at large of the International Fellowship of Evangelical Students, and president of the Latin American Theological Fraternity.

This excerpt from his address first appeared in Engage/Social Action *for November 1974, published by the United Methodist Board of Church and Society in Washington, D.C. The full text is in* Let the Earth Hear His Voice, *the official reference volume for the Lausanne Congress, edited by J. D. Douglas and published in 1975 by World Wide Publications, Minneapolis, Minnesota.*

The first and most powerful answer to the social and political needs of human beings—to the search for freedom, justice, and fulfillment—is given by Jesus in his own work and in the church. Jesus takes seriously the problems of property and power relationships, which are essentially the problems that cause social and political maladjustment and injustice.

Jesus creates a new people, a new community, where social problems are dealt with under the Lordship of Christ. This is the community, *distinct from the rest of society,* that we find around Jesus first, then growing in Jerusalem, and then expanding into the world.

In this community there is a new attitude to money and property (Luke 6:29-31, 35; Acts 2:43-45; 4:34; 20:35; James 2:14-16; 1 John 3:16-17). In this community there is a new attitude to power and its exercise (Luke 22:23-27 and parallels in Matthew and Mark; 2 Corinthians 10:8; 12:10-15; 1 Peter 5:1-3). It is a community where human barriers and prejudices have been overcome under Christ's rule (Galatians 3:28; Colossians 3:11; Philemon 15-17). It is a community ready to suffer for justice and good (Matthew 5:10-12; Acts 7:51-60; Acts 16:16-24; 1 Peter 3:13-18).

The biblical model of evangelism includes the radically different community that calls people to faith in the crucified and resurrected Christ that has transformed their lives, and the new life in the Spirit that enables them to follow the example of Christ. Such a community has a revolutionary effect in changing a society.

Let us take a specific example. It is false, as some have written, that Paul did not do anything about the evil of slavery. He did at least three things.

First, he announced the gospel equally to masters and slaves. His own lifestyle and training added credibility to his message for both social classes.

Second, as part of his message he taught basic truths about the nature of man (Acts 17:26, a common origin for all persons) and the new type of relationship that human beings had under Christ (Galatians 3:28). These truths were contrary to the basic tenets of the then prevalent philosophy, in which slavery was based.

Third, he asked specifically for an application of his teaching in the context of the Christian community (Philemon). It has been demonstrated that by addressing himself to the slaves as moral agents (Col. 3:22-25; Eph. 6:5-8), Paul was doing something completely new in his day, treating them as responsible persons, not as things or animals, which was the way in those days. Moreover, Paul asked from masters in the same passage what not even the most advanced moralists or philosophers would have asked at that point.

Thus Paul, in his teaching and practice in the primitive church, was attacking slavery at its very base. The example and influence of the church in the first century, and later the active involvement of Christians in civil life, brought eventually the abolition of the system.

Later Christians and Slavery

When the south of Africa was discovered by the Portuguese in the fifteenth century, slavery soon appeared again, and in a matter of decades Christendom had accepted it. However, in 1774, in the wake of a spiritual revival, a great evangelist, John Wesley, published his short treatise, *Thoughts Upon Slavery.*

For Wesley, development without social justice was unacceptable. I pray that God will raise evangelists like Wesley, who also care about social evils enough to do research and write about them and throw the weight of their moral and spiritual authority on the side of the correction of injustices. Wesley, however, did more than write. He encouraged the political action that eventually was going to abolish slavery in England. Six days before his death, Wesley wrote to the famous evangelical politician William Wilberforce, encouraging him in the name of God to fight against slavery.

More than sixty years ago, a group called Peniel

Hall Society bought some land in Bolivia, in order to help Aymara peasants with a school and a hospital. As it was a practice until recent date in Latin America, the land was sold to them with 250 Aymara serfs who belonged to the estate. After a long period of failures and hesitations, the project in 1920 was handed to the Canadian Baptist Mission Board, which eventually brought an agricultural missionary. After the fruitless efforts of several years, it finally dawned on the missionaries that their position as land owners and serf masters was overriding every benevolent attempt to uplift the people.

Finally, in 1942, economic serfdom was abolished, the land was parceled and the Indians were given title of property to their plots. Norman Dabbs, the missionary martyr, comments: "Both missionaries and peons felt that a crushing weight had been lifted from their lives."

When ten years later a nationalist revolutionary government passed the desperately needed law of land reform, the pioneer experiment of the Baptists in Huatajata was recognized as a valid antecedent. The amazing fact is that the freedom of Indians and the distribution of land was immediately followed by church growth in the area; and also after the revolution of 1952 a wave of church growth started in Bolivia.

These examples are illustrations of how Christians can be obedient to God's word. We need a revival of life in our churches around the world, so that they again will be communities "distinct from the rest of society." We need evangelists who are also prophets like John Wesley. Where possible, we need Christian politicians like Wilberforce. We need imaginative missionaries, ready to pioneer in areas of social justice and evangelism.

Liberation Is Not Gospel Freedom

Please notice that the simple liberation from human masters is not the freedom of which the gospel speaks. Freedom in Christian terms means subjection to Jesus Christ as Lord, deliverance from bondage to sin and Satan (John 8:31-38), and consequently the beginning of new life under the law of Christ (1 Cor. 9:19), life in the family of the faith

where the old human master becomes also the new brother in Christ.

However, the heart which has been made free with the freedom of Christ cannot be indifferent to the human longings for deliverance from economic, political, or social oppression. And that is what many expect from the one who evangelizes. Not that he says: "I come to announce to you a spiritual freedom and because of that I do not care about your social, economic, or political oppression." But rather that he says: "I care for your oppression. I am with you in your search for a way out, and I can show you a deeper and most decisive deliverance that may help you also to find a better way out of your social and political oppression."

That is what Christ did. He identified with the oppressed. For instance, he became poor both by taking upon himself human limitations and by the social strata in which he chose to live when he came. When Jesus, who made himself poor, tells me "You always have the poor with you," I listen to him. He added to that, let us remember, "and whenever you will, you can do good to them" (Mark 14:7). But when a rich man tells me the same thing, I have the suspicion that he really means "You always have the rich with you . . . and that should not change."

Do We Stand with Rich or Poor?

What is the image that our missionary and evangelistic work projects? Do we stand with the rich or with the poor? Do we stand usually with oppressors or with the oppressed? What a contradiction it would be, says James, if not being rich, we would forget the poor and favour the rich (James 2:5-9). In my opinion the tough question is not "Are you rich?" The question is "Where do you stand when you preach the gospel?" "Where did your master stand?"

A dramatic example of this dilemma was recently presented to me by a missionary friend among a tribe in Latin America. He was torn apart by the dilemma of standing with his poor unknown tribe of "savages" or with the oil company that wanted to use him to move the Indians out of the area, getting them away in order to continue with exploration, thus eliminating "the Indian problem." Such hard decisions may increase in number, especially for those willing to reach parts of the so-called "fourth world," remote areas where the desperate search for raw materials and oil is going to center now. If these situations are not taken seriously by evangelists, in both their style and their message, the credibility of the gospel is at stake.

I do not think we can measure the effects that were registered in the conscience of evangelicals and of the hearers of the gospel by the firm stand that evangelist Billy Graham took on racial issues from the very beginning of his career. His refusal to preach to segregated audiences closed some doors and provoked disaffections. I think that it stems from his biblical convictions about the nature of man and God's design for him. I praise the Lord for it! He did not downgrade the demands of the gospel in order to have access to more numbers of hearers or in order to have the blessing of racists that consider themselves "fundamental Christians." A stance like this is already communicating something about the nature of the gospel that gives credibility to the gospel itself when it is announced. This is especially so for those who are the victims of injustice and are conscious of it.

Don't Reduce the Gospel!

In some societies and nations, there is desperate need for healing in the area of interracial relationships. In those cases, the Christian church might be the only place where the miracle of encounter, acceptance, and coexistence can happen because the redemptive power of Christ acts. To perpetuate segregation for the sake of numerical growth, arguing that segregated churches grow faster, is yielding to the sinfulness of society, refusing to show a new and unique way of life. It is an example of reducing the gospel to make it more palatable. Such "numerical growth" might not be the numerical growth of the church of Jesus Christ.

I wonder sometimes if taking into account the demonic forces at work behind racism, prejudice, oppression, corruption, and exploitation of the weak and the poor everywhere, and taking also into account evangelistic and missionary efforts that are totally unaware of those facts, the Lord

would not tell us: "Woe to you zealous evangelists, hypocrites, for you traverse sea and land to make a single proselyte, and when he becomes a proselyte, you make him twice as much a child of hell as yourselves" (Matthew 23:15).

It has been said that there is the danger that, if we concentrate on working out the social implications of the gospel, we will forget evangelism, and that history proves this fact. I do not believe that statement. I think that the Social Gospel, for instance, deteriorated because of poor theology. The sad thing is that those who have the right theology have not applied it to social issues. The practical answer must be seen in a different area. We have to rediscover the ministry of teaching in the church, the close link between evangelism and church life, and the role of the layman in the world.

In the life of our Lord, and in the life of the Apostles, there was no separation or gap between preaching and teaching. Both were very important and essential to their ministry. I think that the idea that you can "evangelize" and leave teaching for ten years later is antibiblical. Teaching is an indispensable part of the life of the body and, if it is not provided, a group called church can degenerate into nothing but a social club or a sect.

Part of the teaching is *how to live in the world as a Christian:* the ethics of the Kingdom. Laypersons then penetrate society by a *way of life* that is new in family relations, business, citizenship, and every area of daily life. Consequently, to mobilize laypersons is not only to teach them short summaries of the gospel, mini-sermons, and to send them to repeat these to their neighbors. It is also to teach them how to apply the teaching and example of Christ in their family life, in their business activities, in their social relationships, in their studies, and so forth.

Those who teach need to be solidly rooted in the word of God but also very aware of the world around them, so that they can help in the application. In societies that are increasingly hostile to Christianity, this task is more crucial and necessary, because you cannot take for granted that the value system and the social uses are "Christian." We desperately need this ministry in the Third World! We desperately need this ministry in the Western nations!

(Source: Samuel Escobar, "The Search for Freedom, Justice, and Fulfillment," *Engage/Social Action* [November 1974] [Washington, D.C.: United Methodist Board of Church and Society], 34-40.)

56. *"Evangelization and Cultural Liberation,"* by Segundo Galilea

(Introduction by Gerald H. Anderson and Thomas F. Stransky.) Defining the missionary as "one who leaves his culture in order to proclaim the Gospel in a different culture," Father Segundo Galilea, a pastoral theologian, maintains that the missionary must reject "both cultural domination and blind cultural assimilation." "Authentic mission," he says, "implies a cultural exchange, a giving and a receiving." In Latin America this calls for helping "to devise a radically Latin American way of development and liberation," together with evangelization, in the way proposed by Christ. This article is part of a longer essay that first appeared in English in Teaching All Nations *(1975/1 & 2), which is published in Manila, Philippines, by the East Asian Pastoral Institute.*

For the Third World, and particularly for Latin America (which belongs to the Western cultural family), one of the most disastrous consequences of the economic and eventually social and political dependence is cultural dependence and alienation. Unfortunately, the Medellín Conference (August 1968) did not pay enough attention to this matter. Such an oversight is reflected in subsequent currents of theological thinking and in the Christian concern vis-à-vis liberation and commitment. Moreover this lacuna was strongly influenced by political ideologies, especially Marxist, which neglect or even sacrifice the cultural dimension in favor of the socio-political or economic concern.

The growing cultural alienation in Latin America is obvious. Its most alarming symptoms seem to be the following:

1. The adoption of development patterns which are alien or unsuited to the social cultural reality of our peoples. Mainly through the mass media, such models are imposed by the "developed" countries

for the benefit of their economic imperialism. Such an imposition fosters pseudo-values, foreign to the local culture, and activates frustrating and alienating aspirations. This pseudo-development increases our dependence and does not foster growth in the proper cultural line. Instead it fosters growth along the lines of the capitalistic-bourgeois ideology in most cases. In the case of Cuba, it fostered growth along the lines of Marxist-Leninist ideology.

2. In other words, there is an ideological-cultural imposition accompanying the imposed model of development. Even in institutions which consider themselves popular, the peculiar way of the people is not being sufficiently discerned. By this we are criticizing the Latin-American Left and singling out an intrinsic cause for their failures. This also implies a negative criticism of strategic plans—such as armed subversion—and of certain serious neglect of "popular" ideologies. Popular religiosity is a case in point.

3. All this forces the Latin American people to life-styles which are both inconsistent and alienating. Their authentic values are not appreciated, become obsolete and the end-result is a loss of cultural and national identity.

4. In extreme cases—like that of indigenous tribes and other marginal minority races—this form of dependence is leading to a cultural genocide.

Confronted with this serious situation, it is necessary to devise a radically Latin American way of development and liberation. This imperative appears today all the more obvious because of the historical developments of the recent past in which there is a tendency to re-evaluate the cultural dimension. At the same time, politics, or rather political parties and their prestige are in real crisis. This is a fact almost without exception in the Latin American continent. There is also a "dead point" in the true participation in power by the people. Even in governments of a socialist orientation, the power of the state—increasingly more centralized—would at best be "at the service" of the people but without the people's decisively sharing in the power.

This political diagnosis applies both to the capitalistic and socialist systems—to the point of surprising convergence. In a more or less overt or subtle form, there is a tendency to form a dominant state which relies on the so-called "military-industrial complex," and at times also on a one-party system. The problem of power and the "idolatry of power" is a grave one in Latin America today both as a cultural question and as a requirement for liberation. From the point of view of this general trend, Brazil and Cuba—at the opposite extremes of the ideological spectrum—are astonishingly similar.

Faced with such a situation, the model of a just society in the continent is still to be devised. And for this task, the free expression and the appreciation of cultural values at all levels of society, especially those of the most oppressed and voiceless, appear as indispensable.

The quiet and native genius of these oppressed and silent peoples has already created a folklore, a popular religiosity. They have also been able to defend, no matter what, their own lifestyles. They will, we can be sure, use the same genius to create —within the context of their cultural liberation— new and viable social and political expressions towards a better and more equitable society.

This cultural liberation is perhaps all the more difficult, because it has to do with an "ethos" and with a change of mentality. There is nothing more sensitive about a culture than its growth through its own values, by self-criticism and self-transformation. There is nothing as difficult as liberating a mentality. This involves the whole problem of conscientization, which is often being caricatured or used as ideological politicization. Political imposition and cultural oppression remain permanent dangers threatening an authentic conscientization. This consists in passing from a mentality which is uncritical, conformist and characterized by a complex of cultural infidelity, to a creative attitude which is in contact with its own identity, conscious and critical of every subtle form of cultural or politico-ideological alienation.

Christianity—the Church—through the values which it transmits by evangelizing, possesses the ethical ingredient for genuine conscientization, and thus, for a true cultural liberation. This is the attitude of a people who take up their own changes and their historical vocation as their own task and project, using their own values as the *point of departure*. These values, and that vocation to liberate the creativity of a culture—the dream of a people—are stimulated by the Gospel. As the Gospel is

not tied to any particular cultural form or ideology, it is capable of accompanying from within the liberation of a culture, unifying it without alienation (*Gaudium et Spes*, 58).

This is evangelization at its ideal. For that, Catholicism itself must exercise a permanent self-critique in its historical context and in the concrete effects of its message, since there is a permanent temptation for it to identify itself with the dominant cultures and the existing ideologies. When this happens, decadent forms of Christianity are transmitted and enter into subtle complicity with those cultures or ideologies, slowing down liberation instead of stimulating it. This evokes the whole problem of liberating evangelization. The Latin American Church is today only too conscious of this task.

Such an authentic evangelization, by its very nature, will lend a special dynamism to people as free agents of their own Christian vocation along the lines of a given culture. Christianity communicates the ultimate and profound sense of the dignity and value of peoples and cultures by revealing the presence of Christ in each person and of the "seeds of the Word" in each culture. Further, in proclaiming that the salvation of individuals—and of cultures—takes place in history, it communicates to the peoples the fundamental reason for their historic responsibility, bringing them to a dynamism of growth and commitment. By criticizing the prevailing ideologies and cultures—to the extent that Christianity itself has managed to liberate itself from them— by criticizing power as well as the models and strategies of a materialistic and de-humanizing development, Christianity overcomes the radical obstacles. It thus paves the way for the cultural liberation of human beings.

Missionaries and Culture

The task of accompanying the growth of a culture with a purifying prophetic attitude both liberating and transforming is a very delicate enterprise. In fact, the history of the Christian mission shows us that the encounter of the Gospel with new cultures always resulted in something as paradoxical as it was astonishing. On the one hand evangelization assumed and respected—to a very relative degree according to the case—the new cultures. Catholicism is proof of this. But on the other hand, evangelization both baffled and unsettled the cultures. Surprisingly one could bring apparently contradictory accusations against the missionary activity. It has excessively acculturized Christianity (popular folkloric or syncretistic forms of the Indo-American Catholicism) and/or has demolished or dominated local culture (the various indigenous groups of the Caribbean).

That is why we are dealing with a delicate problem inasmuch as both results take place simultaneously and dialectically. A balanced approach to it must be sought in what we have already called the liberation of a culture "from within." This makes the problem all the more serious for the "evangelizers" who come from other cultures—as happens in the Third World countries. Today the cultural problem is the most acute for a missionary. We could even say that the very concept of missionary has changed: from the concept of someone who went to the pagans to that of one who leaves his culture in order to proclaim the Gospel in a different culture. This new view is overcoming—at least in the West—the old distinction between "mission territories" and "Christian countries." We can today speak about "mission among the workers," "mission in Catholic countries"—as it is in Latin America, "mission in the Andes" (even though all the indigenous people there may be Christians).

In the missionary who goes from one culture to another, the whole problematic of the Church vis-à-vis cultural liberation takes flesh in a concrete person. The abstract temptations of evangelization in any culture become in him personal temptations. The danger of his communicating his own ideals and his own cultural values as necessarily linked with Christianity, demands of him a form of conversion and of "kenosis." Such a conversion and "emptying" go far beyond his good-will and imply a special charism and a pastoral and cultural training. The tragedy of the missionary is that his action may well be a two-edged sword: he can do much good or much evil, depending on his attitude towards the local churches and cultures.

There is also the opposite temptation. That is, the missionary may completely abandon the values of his own culture and understand evangelization as an acculturation so radical, that he may end up assuming "the sins" (the defects) of the culture to which he is sent. And he may do this without bringing any prophetic and questioning element. In other words, the danger is that his cultural incarnation may eliminate the ultimate reason for his missionary presence. This is why I feel that the missionary-culture relationship is infinitely complex. What we as "cultures to be evangelized" reject in the name of the very nature of the Gospel is *cultural domination*. Very often such cultures are politically and sociologically weaker than those of the missionary. A typical example is the evangelization of America by Charles V's Spain. Cultural domination means that Christian forms that alienate an identity and hinder its liberation are imposed on a people. Further impositions in the form of ideologies of "development"—tending to become "ideological" Christianity—in the name and for the sake of human promotion may ensue. This amounts to a dominating and forced integration—which takes little account of the prevailing culture which may reject such a foreign transplant.

Authentic mission implies a *cultural exchange,* a giving and a receiving. Neither the culture of the missionary nor that of the "missionized" is perfect. Both have their values. Both are limited. Certainly both have complementary and mutually enriching aspects. The same must be said of the way in which Christianity is lived. Therefore, we can affirm with the assurance that the centuries-old missionary experience of the Church gives us, that there is no such thing as culturally pure local churches whose Christianity would be the result of their "locality" alone without any external influences. And we believe that this is positive and enriching both in the cultural as well as in the Christian level. Thus today, the Spanish Church is not "pure Spanish" but all the way from its conversion to Christianity it has undergone varied influence from the Gauls, Africans, the Nordics, Romans, and later Americans. The Church of Rome is not "Rome" but the result of Byzantine, Gaelic, Mozarabic, and other influences. The same has happened with the Latin American Church. The only difference is that in the Third World this interchange and mutually beneficial enrichment has been radically ambiguous since the process historically took place within a colonial context of cultural domination, which we are still trying to correct.

A typical case of this ambiguous interchange-domination is the phenomenon of the *evangelization of the Latin American popular religiosity*. In the foreign missionary we can detect two attitudes which have been very prominent especially in the pastoral context of the last 25 years. The first attitude—reinforced by many local people who have studied in Europe—is one of radical critique. He questions and discounts a form of Catholicism which is ritualistic, devotional, baroque, and without a sufficient social and temporal dimension (at least apparently). This is a religion, he feels, which alienates and encourages escapism from the task of development and liberation; a form of "religion of poverty." Pastorally speaking, he feels one should not bother with such a religiosity; it should be left to die a natural death, since, anyway, development and social revolution will do away with it. In contrast with such an attitude there is a consensus today among the evangelizers who are most lucid and who are truly one with the people in criticism of the previous position for its cultural Western and European bias and its "bourgeois Christian" point of departure. They see this as another form of cultural imposition and of domination by a European type of Christianity. Their own efforts, in the name of popular culture and of its autochthonous genius which has created that form of Catholicism as its own, are made to re-appreciate it—though critically—as the expression of a deeply respectable cultural identity. This understanding from within, elaborated in non-Western cultural categories, leads them to re-interpret many attitudes which at first glance seemed to be alienating and far from the movement of liberation. Thus, an evaluation of popular religiosity is emerging which does not proceed from "our" cultural categories or Christian expressions, but from "their" culture, meanings and scale of values.

Thus humanization and liberation of human beings in the way proposed by Christ become the criterion of such an evaluation, as it is the criterion of evangelization.

(Source: Segundo Galilea, "Evangelization and Cultural Liberation," *Teaching All Nations* [1975/1 & 2], Manila, Philippines, East Asian Pastoral Institute.)

57. *"Christianity Meets Traditional African Cultures,"* by Peter K. Sarpong

(Introduction by Gerald H. Anderson and Thomas F. Stransky, eds., Mission Trends No. 5 [New York: Paulist Press, 1981], 238.) In the judgment of the Roman Catholic Bishop of Kumasi, Ghana, "the Church has not become 'African' enough," and he hopes that the religious "symbols, imagery, signs, etc. that are clearly remnants of other cultures will be replaced by those comprehensible to the African." The African traditional cultures are deeply religious, even though they contain some objectionable elements which the Ashanti bishop lists. But areas of convergence are many and profound: godliness, fatherhood, and religious authority; veneration of ancestors; extolled virtues of respect, hospitality, purity, truth, and hard work; and liturgical sensitivity about the "life cycle" or rites of passage. Sensitive in dialogue with these traditions, the evangelist discovers that one need not preach "a new God" but "an old God who has been revealed to us positively by his Son." Indeed, "there is a vast Christian theological potential in Africa, not simply in spite of contemporary change, but because of it." The article from which these extracts are taken appeared in Worldmission *(vol. 30, no. 2, Summer 1979), a publication of the U.S. office of the Society for the Propagation of the Faith (366 5th Ave., New York, NY 10001).*

The ordinary African is not "logical" in the Western sense. By and large he has no interest in cause and effect but in actual happenings. Neither does he reason along strict syllogistic lines. This does not mean that he is not a thinker or that he is unintelligent. In fact, he is a philosopher in his own right. But he philosophizes in the concrete, not in the abstract.

The African can pursue a particular cause or act in a definite pattern for, say, 20 years and when the Westerner has concluded that he will continue to do so for the rest of his life, he suddenly goes off at a tangent. To the non-African this is illogical, but not to the African who on the whole does not accept absolutes. To his way of thinking, behavior must be related to his needs, to what he considers good. So it is not wrong to tell a "lie" for a good purpose. Baptism is a good thing; then it should be permissible to have a person unfit for Baptism receive the Sacrament by concealing the truth about him. . . .

I am not by any means suggesting that the African has no appreciation of what is true and what is a lie. I am only trying to explain that his understanding of these concepts is more pragmatic. . . . The Catholic Church is the true Church founded by Christ, but if my petition is unanswered when I go to Mass then there is nothing wrong in praying in a Spiritual Church or falling back on the traditional magico-religious ritual for help. After all, religion is worthwhile only inasmuch as it helps man to get rid of the many inevitable hazards of life—childlessness, illness, poverty, death, disgrace, hunger, etc. In some African languages there are no abstract terms and one has to seek a concrete image to convey the thought.

The African believes in God and spirits, but he is not interested in defining these realities, and most of the theological terms used in such an exercise mean nothing to him. His interest stops with how God and the spirits influence his life and what good or evil they mete out.

Much has to be accomplished in studying the culture and institutions of different African societies and endeavoring to harmonize the authentic teaching of Christ with the everyday lives of people.

To my mind, the Church has not become "African" enough. By "African" I am not referring to the skin or origin of people; I am not preaching racism. I am only expressing a concern that the Church truly become incarnated in the African soil, hoping that the symbols, imagery, signs, etc. that are clearly remnants of other cultures will be replaced by those comprehensible to the African.

The problem then is comprehending the unacknowledged and unanalyzed standpoints from which the African's views are taken.

The Vatican Propagation of the Faith in 1659 issued to missionaries in China and Indo-China the directives:

Put no obstacles in their way; and for no reason whatever should you persuade these people to change their rites, customs, and ways of life unless these are obviously opposed to religion and good morals. For what is more absurd than to bring France or Spain or Italy or any other part of Europe into China. It is not these that you should bring but the faith which does not spurn or reject any people's rites and customs, unless they are depraved, but, on the contrary, tries to keep them . . . admire and praise what deserves to be respected.

My contention is that like all other cultures, African traditional cultures contain several objectionable elements. This is not to say that they do not or did not fulfill a social function now or in the past. A careful examination of many an African custom, no matter how repulsive it may be to modern man, will reveal that it once played or even now plays a role in the social life of the people.

In the light of the Christian message one can hardly justify the reign of terror of some chiefs in Africa. The tests of endurance that young boys and girls have to undergo during their initiation ceremonies, and widows during the funeral celebration of their husbands, amount to objective cruelty. Those being initiated are sometimes subjected to circumcision and clitoridectomy, deep cuts on the forehead and other parts of the body, and forcible extraction of teeth—all with very crude instruments. Some bleed to death or die through infection of their wounds. Widows are sometimes placed in solitary confinement for days on end, made to sleep for weeks with stones as their pillow, or have pepper thrown into their eyes.

In the past, the atrocities committed through traditional secret societies were so horrifying that, as far back as the beginning of this century, the Colonial Powers had to proscribe societies, such as the Ogbonu in Nigeria, from the purely humanitarian point of view.

Traditional cultures' estimation of women, even in strictly matrilineal societies, has always been very low. Often the woman is considered only a second-class citizen, the mother of the man's children. The Christian teaching of the equality of all human beings would have taken many African cultures a very long time to appreciate.

Christianity insists on our loving everyone, even our enemies. Traditional cultures regard the downfall of the enemy a desirable thing to be sought vigorously. Love is the cornerstone of Christian religion. Traditional cultures emphasize fear as sufficient motivation for doing good and for avoiding evil. Traditionally, religion is useful because, and insofar as, it helps man to solve the many problems that beset him in life. A religion that prepares man mainly for a reward after death is, at best, of dubious utility.

In the context of traditional cultures, the African could never rise to the lofty heights of revelation attained by Christianity. The Trinity, the Incarnation, the Eucharist, and the Resurrection are theologically beyond the reach of "primitive revelations." Christianity gives meaning to suffering. Suffering has no place in traditional cultures except as the sign of the spirits' anger, the reward of man's inequity. Neither can traditional cultures understand the meaning of the virtue of humility. Traditionally, the African is by nature a proud person. He always feels more important than anyone else.

One could go on enumerating points of divergence between Christianity and traditional African cultures. Nevertheless, the areas of convergence appear to be many and profound. In fact, it looks as if the good Lord from all eternity has prepared the African soil for the reception of the Christian seed.

Godliness has always been part of the African tradition. Indeed the attributes of the African God are so "Christian" that many 19th-century ethnographers doubted their originality. It is true that besides the Supreme Being, Africans venerate or even worship other spirits, human and non-human, and have belief in totems, witches, magic, and taboos. But these are considered as manifestations of God, his functionaries who do his will. The preacher in Africa is therefore not preaching a new God; he is preaching an old God who has been revealed to us positively by his Son. If he studies and makes use of the belief of the Africans, then he is giving a new dimension to, rather than correcting, their religious conception. This belief is in fact basic to what is going to follow. As a matter of fact, in African traditional cultures there appears to be no distinction made between a person's religious practices and his other spheres of activity. Religion is a way of life, not a fashion. It permeates every aspect of a man's life, from cradle to grave. For the African, religion is not a subject to learn. Nor is it a subject for debate. Being part of ordinary life, it is accepted and absorbed in the normal cause of events. As an integral part of culture, it shares culture's compulsory, impersonal, objective, and universal nature. Religion is part of African society. . . .

The structure of African societies may and sometimes does have effects which may be inconsistent with Christian aspirations. For example, Christianity would insist that marriage is primarily an institution of love between a man and a woman for their mutual happiness and the well-being of their children. In many African cultures, however, marriage may be regarded as a social affair between two lineages which agree to hand over their people in marriage primarily for the benefit of the group. If an uncle or father can say: "I have arranged a marriage for my nephew or son," then there should be no wonder that they sometimes control the marriage, interfere with it, help it to last, or cause its disruption. . . .

The education of children may provide a serious point of conflict in African lineal cultures. Matrilineal fatherhood approaches the idea of the fatherhood of God more than the patrilineal fatherhood. For the matrilineal father has no juridical rights over his children and exercises authority over them only by virtue of a mystical bond that is supposed to exist between him and them. The patrilineal mother is in the same situation. Both love the children for the sake of the children. Here is love which does not ask for or expect something in return. It is love which is reminiscent of the words of the hymn: "My Lord, I love thee not because I hope for heaven thereby." But friction arises when Christianity advises that the education of the child is the responsibility of both parents. In African lineal cultures the responsibility falls on the lineage.

The patrilineal father and the matrilineal mother are the parents with authority over their children. They are not likely to neglect the training of their children. They guard and protect the children from harm. The children, in turn, develop the virtue of reverential fear towards them. However, parental or filial love of the kind expected between a Christian and God is strained. The son, especially the eldest son, is a sort of rival to his father for his property. In some African societies, the threat posed by an eldest son against his father is so feared that it is counter-balanced by a strict regulation making it illegal for a king's or chief's eldest son to succeed him. The absence of specialization of work which in Euro-American societies helps the child to become easily independent, coupled with the group sense which makes the child regard his father's possessions as his by right, makes him the potential "usurper" of his father. He is, therefore, looked upon askance by the father.

However, even here the concept of fatherhood is pregnant with "Christian" ideas. God indeed is our master, he possesses power and authority over us. He is provident, looking after us, guarding and protecting us from bodily as well as spiritual harm. He is jealous for our service and undivided loyalty. But his intolerance of man's infidelity is always altruistic, rather than egoistic. There can be no question of a strained relationship between us and God. His love for us increases precisely when we try to "inherit" his Kingdom.

Consequently, the very comparison and contrast between the two types of "African" fatherhood could be extremely useful in instructing catechumens. They project God's personality better on the catechetical screen.

Among other by-products of African social systems is the tendency to unfair play. Social structure alone cannot adequately explain the high incidence of bribery and corruption, nepotism and favoritism everywhere in Africa. However, in any society it should be difficult for a person conducting an interview not to give first consideration to ten candidates for whose education he feels responsible in some way. I would not like to be a judge in Ghana. The number of clansmen appearing before me expecting to be treated leniently, the number of the friends of these relatives in the same situation, not to count those on my wife's side, would leave very few people upon whom I could test my integrity!

But to be a little charitable to African social structures, let me explain that they do not always obstruct the practice of the Christian religion. On the contrary, they are capable of being used to promote the Christian cause. For one thing, the idea of authority in the lineage to whom lineage members look for direction and whom they willingly obey is a good example of the hierarchy in the Church. The communal spirit that ideally should reign supreme in a lineage and the mutual assistance given by and to members of the same lineage remind us of the early Christian communities described for us in the Acts of the Apostles, the spirit of which unfortunately appears to be found nowadays only among the Religious in their communities. Theoretically, no single person should die of hunger, nakedness, or lack of shelter. What belongs to one clansman belongs to another.

In African societies, terms like "father," "mother," "brother," and "sister," which, elsewhere, are employed to refer to strictly biological relations, have much wider practical and sociological connotation and application. At a time when so much is being said and recommended about "basic communities," a fresh look at African traditional cultures could point the way to the true salvation of mankind. . . .

The veneration of lineage tutelary gods and ancestors may be compared with our Christian cult of angels and saints. Here again we are strongly reminded of the doctrine of the Communion of Saints. African social structures well-utilized could afford us traditional ways of securing good relationships among members of our Christian communities. Their effects on marriage could be commendable, for loyalty to the lineage exercises a restraining influence on its married members.

African traditional cultures extol the values of respect, honor, hospitality, magnanimity, purity, truth, and hard work. Traditional cultures demand that all citizens have *character,* and live in conformity with their conscience. Without these, a person is not a human being. He is clothed only in the skin of a human being. If people in practice do not live up to the expectations of culture, this is because, as St. Paul tells us, they cannot understand their own behavior. They find themselves doing the very things they know they should not do. Moreover, African traditional religions lack the concept of grace, enabling weak and frail man to act in accordance with his nature and convictions, to do what is right.

The need to utilize the African's culture for the benefit of Christianity cannot be over-emphasized, especially in the area of the Liturgy. Africans want to enjoy a liturgical situation. They want to play an active and meaningful role in what is happening. Singing and dancing have always formed a constitutive part of their religious celebrations. What takes place must be relevant to their life. They seek room for spontaneous expressions of filial sentiments towards God. They desire the minister to be personally interested in them. To treat the individual as only one in a crowd, and as an impersonal, unnoticed, unacknowledged, and unaided spectator is to refuse to fulfill the innermost craving of his heart.

In reflecting on African cultures in relation to Christianity, one must mention the "life cycle" or rites of passage. These rites, which are very much religious in character, are found everywhere in Africa. Because of their varying complexity, my comments are based mainly on my Ashanti experience.

Until these rites of passage have been carefully analyzed and all their implications truly ascertained, we would do well to refrain from equating them with the Sacraments. The thought is tantalizing because the rites contain elements which on the surface are similar to features in the Sacraments. For instance, the rites are performed at crucial turning-points in a man's life—in particular at birth, puberty, and death. The same seems to be true for at least some of the Sacraments. Rites of passage are meant to produce what they symbolize. So also are the Sacraments. Each of the rites may be performed only once for any one person. Baptism, Confirmation, and the Priesthood too are received but once by any one individual. In the performance of the rites, material objects accompanied by words are employed, and the Sacraments, in scholastic terminology, are constituted of matter and form, and so on.

The two sets of ceremonies contain somewhat similar ideas indeed, but they are not therefore identical—the rites should not be regarded as some sort of primitive Sacraments, since the discrepancies between them are notable. Baptism, for Christians, is a new birth, which renders one a child of God, and an heir of his Kingdom. It produces its effects on the recipient alone. It is not necessarily received in babyhood—a 100-year-old man may be baptized just as validly as a one-day-old baby. Baptism, therefore appears to be different from

child-naming or outdooring ceremonies. The latter are not regarded as a new birth, but a "ratification" of the old. They are not thought to benefit the child alone, but its mother, father, and the whole community; and they cannot be postponed until adulthood.

The same view may be expressed on puberty or initiation rites. Their effects are not intended only for the novices. True, a girl neophyte is prayed for in order that she may be pleasing to the ancestors, have a happy and especially fruitful life, and grow old. But it would appear that the main motive behind her initiation is to change an alarming condition from a calm but unproductive girlhood to potentially dangerous but fertile adulthood. The adults in the community do not want to associate with an "unclean" girl at their level and thereby suffer from famine, plagues, child-death, etc. They cleanse her from her "impurity" before admitting her into their company. The rites are as important to them as to her. I therefore do not see which of the Sacraments can be favorably compared with initiation rites.

Funeral rites are probably the best example of ceremonies performed for the sake of community, and not those for whom ostensibly they are meant—the dead. In the first place they are rites of passage performed after the person has given up his soul. They are cautiously gone through lest the deceased become annoyed and visit the living with various calamities. Even when references are made to the dead, they are not necessarily meant to benefit them. The living are sorry that they no longer enjoy the good services of the dead; they petition them for things, ask them to protect them and so on. Therefore, one cannot by the wildest stretch of imagination claim that funeral obsequies are comparable to the Sacrament of the Sick, which is advantageous to the dying, not the dead. A close study of widowhood and other funeral rites will confirm this opinion.

So the Sacraments differ from rites of passage, but here again my intention is not to give the impression that they are so opposed that they cannot be reconciled. I want only to guard against the hasty and probably false hope that we have in Africa specimens of the Sacraments.

I am all for purifying the rites and then preserving them if only because of the good pragmatic effects they produce. They engender the spirit of solidarity in a community; funerals are attended by all and sundry and while in progress, disagreements and hatreds are buried. Puberty or nubility were once the mainstay of juvenile or premarital purity, not to say virginity. Even now it is the painful truth that the morally good girl or boy is more difficult to find among literate Christian children than among pagan children who still hold fast to their traditional beliefs. The same rites focussed attention on the girl, and gave her the publicity through which she hoped to attract a husband. They further served as an instrument of instruction in the qualities of a wife, in motherhood and in maternal attributes. Educators of children used them to maintain the accepted standards of morality and good behavior. They also acted as sanctions against bad husbands.

Another "African" theme of importance to Christianity is that of fecundity. Because of their fundamental humanity, Africans place a great value on physical generation, on life and the sharing of life. In the Western world, the "good life" is equated with proficiency in science and technology. It is a dehumanizing equation. Africa might assist in the process of revaluation.

Closely linked with the theme of fecundity is that of "man-in-community." Pope Paul VI, in his letter to Africa of 1967, pointed out that this has three characteristics: the spiritual view of life, the sense of the family, and the sense of community.

Finally, Africa has the potential to place a much-needed priority on a theology of relationships between human and spiritual beings, particularly between the living and the dead. As Aylward Shorter points out, this is a strong preoccupation of traditional religious systems in Africa and it could well provide an enrichment for the Christian idea of the Communion of Saints.

It is evident that there is a vast Christian theological potential in Africa, not simply in spite of contemporary change, but because of it. That is why it behooves Christianity in Africa to heed the exhortation:

Prudently and lovingly through dialogue and collaboration with the followers of other religions, and in witness of Christian faith and life, acknowledge, preserve, and promote the spiri-

tual and moral good found among these men, as well as the values in their society and culture. (Vatican Council II, *Nostra Aetate*, 2)

(Source: "Christianity Meets Traditional African Cultures," *Worldmission* 30, no. 2 [Summer 1979] [New York: U.S. Office of the Society for the Propagation of the Faith]; reprinted in *Mission Trends No. 5*, ed. Gerald H. Anderson and Thomas F. Stransky [New York: Paulist Press, 1981], 238-48.)

58. *"Change in the Church,"* by Manas Buthelezi

(Introduction by Gerald H. Anderson and Thomas F. Stransky, eds., Mission Trends *No. 1 [New York: Paulist Press, 1974], 195.) The socio-political dynamics in South Africa provide a critical testing ground for the Church as it seeks to engage in mission to the nation. Unfortunately, the voices of black Christians in that situation are not often heard. In this article, Dr. Buthelezi examined the urgent need for change in the church in South Africa, if the church is going to be faithful and effective in mission. Speaking of "the systematic apostasy of the white man," he says: "What has happened in this country is that the white man in his stewardship has violated the integrity of God's love and justice." This "spiritual vandalism on the part of the white man" leads the author to question "whether Christian love is safe at all in the hands of the white man." The same would apply, he says, to social justice. A few weeks after this article had been published in the August 1973 issue of the* South African Outlook *(Mowbray, Cape), the South African Minister of Justice issued a "banning order" against Dr. Buthelezi, prohibiting him from attending social, political, or educational gatherings and from teaching students. Under the "banning," however, no newspaper could publish what he said—or anything he has ever said in his life.*

To some people "change" and "Church" seem to be two irreconcilable concepts. The Church as an institution stands in sharp contrast to the transitoriness of the things of this world. While permanence and continuity describe the character of the Church to them, it is to worldly things that "change" relates.

In the Middle Ages "seculum," of which secularization and secularism are modern English variations, pointed to a category of time: it meant "age" or "century" as opposed to "eternity." It also came to designate those members of the clergy who ministered to people in their daily life in contrast to the members of the monastic orders. In "seculum" there was a notion of that which is passing away or temporal in contrast to that which is eternal.

Thus the secular was a realm of temporal political power, of labor and trade and natural law. This was in contrast to the Church which was a dispensary of grace that related man to the eternal. Timelessness and permanence was to the Church what change and transitoriness was to the world.

Heresies

Since the earliest times of Church history the category of antiquity was used to demonstrate the permanence and continuity of the Church vis-à-vis sects and heretical groups. The novelty of the sects and heretical groups stood in sharp contrast to the antiquity of the Church which dates back to the times of the apostles. Thus in his *Prescription Against Heretics,* Irenaeus challenges the heretics thus:

If there are many heresies which are bold enough to plant themselves in the midst of the apostolic age, that they may thereby seem to have been handed down by the apostles, because they existed in the time of the apostles, we can say: Let them produce the original records of their churches; let them unfold the roll of their bishops, running down in due succession from the beginning in such a manner that that first bishop of theirs shall be able to show for his ordainer and predecessor someone of the apostles or of apostolic men—a man, moreover, who continued steadfast with the apostles.

It is the wrong notion of what the Church stands for that causes many people here in South Africa

to find it difficult to see the Church as an instrument of social change and social process. To them that is social gospel. This poses the problem of the solidarity of the Church with the mass of people among whom it ministers. The issue at stake is whether the bridge between the Church and the secular world is just the mission of the Church to the world or whether this mission presupposes an already existing solidarity between the two.

Gustaf Wingren has made the observation that the salvation event which is the content of the message of the Church took place outside the religious center of Jerusalem. It took place in the world, in the sphere of the "secular." Not an apostle but a stranger, Simon of Cyrene, under compulsion, carried the cross of Christ. A criminal at Jesus' side and not a disciple received the promise of the kingdom. Both the death and resurrection were enacted before pagans, Roman soldiers, and not before a crowd of disciples who, as a matter of fact, had run away and were in hiding. Thus, this event in Jerusalem, which is to be proclaimed to all people "beginning from Jerusalem" is, as much as any could be, an event in the world.

From the beginning the Church is part of God's transforming social process in the world. Is there anything more transforming than the power of the Gospel to the lives and destinies of the peoples of the world? When Christ sent his disciples to make disciples of all nations, he was in effect prescribing that the Church should be an instrument of change in the historical destinies of those nations.

Structural Change

Therefore when we speak of change in the Church, it is not just a question of change in Church structures—even though that is also included—but also change in the role of the Church in the South African society. The Church does not exist for itself but for ministering to South Africa. Therefore what is of primary importance is not just structural change within the Church but how the Church projects itself as a catalyst in changing the thinking and behavior of South Africa's politicians, economists and citizens.

Let us take the question of social justice. There

are Christians who believe that the active promotion of social justice is outside the purview and competence of the Church. They believe that this is something that should safely be left in the hands of politicians. They forget that justice belongs to God and not to the discretion of politicians. There are people who believe that the social and political structures in South Africa radiate justice and fair play to all and that it is only political agitators and Communist-inspired churchmen who see the situation as problematic at all.

Talking about change, one of the things that should change is this type of thinking. Therefore there should be change within and through the Church.

Why There Is Need for Change

Rightly or wrongly the white man has been regarded as the standard-bearer of the mission of Christ in South Africa. He was the protector and watchdog of all the values that the Christian Gospel is designed to uphold.

We have, however, witnessed one of the greatest spectacles in the history of the Church in South Africa, namely, the systematic apostasy of the white man. Let me give a theological setting to this charge.

Justice and love are two concepts that are theological in the strict sense of the word. As far as the imperfect human language can go, "holy" and "love" are words which almost define the nature of God. We say that "God is holy" and "God is love."

The idea that God cares for his creation in general and for his people in particular is central in both the Old and New Testaments. In contrast to the gods of the Greek and Roman religious world, who were sometimes represented as jealous of and competing with man, the biblical God is characterized by his active interest in the welfare of his people: he loves and is just to them.

In one of the stories of Greek mythology it is told how sex came about among men. Man was originally a very beautiful being with four legs, four arms, and two heads. The gods became so jealous of his beauty that they clove him in half. Since then the two halves have been trying to come together in the form of man and woman.

Shepherd

When we encounter the "shepherd" of the psalms or that of St. John's Gospel, we not only get a glimpse of how a rural culture conceptualized its God, but, more important, we find an instance of what I shall call biblical oeconomia—that is, God not only produces the means of sustenance but he also distributes it equitably like a shepherd who tends his flock. The communism of the New Testament Church was a social extension of this biblical concept of "God's economics." The author of the Book of Acts portrays this social extension as a communal life of sharing, that is, a pooling together of God's gifts for common consumption.

The social extension of "God's economics" contains a moral element of stewardship. The story of Ananias and Sapphira dramatizes the moral accountability of the stewards of God's stewards. The point of reference is always how man's stewardship reflects God's justice and love.

What has happened in this country is that the white man in his stewardship has violated the integrity of God's love and justice.

It is common knowledge that in this country the active promotion of love between black and white is looked at with suspicion. Any fraternization between races, which should naturally develop from faith in Christ, instead of being a cause for praise, brings with it serious consequences, such as being visited by the security police or simple exposure to one form of censure or the other.

As a black Christian I have come in anguish to the conclusion that the white man, through his political and social governmental institutions, no longer services the promotion of God's love between black and white but is really doing his best to kill and frustrate it. This spiritual vandalism on the part of the white man has brought with it consequences so serious that it is no longer a theoretical possibility that Christians suffer just for the sake of promoting love and good will between black and white.

After the end of it all, South Africa will have a unique distinction of producing martyrs who suffered simply because they were trying to promote good will between the races.

Intriguing Question

The current and intriguing question is whether Christian love is safe at all in the hands of the white man. The same applies to social justice. As far as the question of the violation of social justice is concerned, there is a sense in which one can say that the black man has become a "Christ" to the white man: he has been "crucified" so as to bring security and social salvation to the white man. What counts for his insecurity means security to the white man; his poverty is the yardstick of the white man's affluence. In other words the white man would not be as affluent if the black man were less poor than he is.

The irony of all this is that Christianity in South Africa has a white image. This is in spite of the fact that almost all the major multi-racial churches are overwhelmingly black. "What the churches in South Africa are thinking" is very often identical to "what white people in South Africa are thinking." The voice of the black man has not yet been heard in the Church in any significant manner. Added to this is the fact that the white man has discredited himself as the protector of Christian values. The situation becomes very desperate indeed.

There must, therefore, be change in the Church in order to reflect a changed situation, namely, the white man's turning against that which promotes Christian love and justice. The Church must release its potential by promoting the reflection of its black constituency in both its structure and proclamation. The Church must cease to be sectarian in order to reflect the whole of the people of God. It must cease to be a satellite of white power politics in order to become a forum of communion for the whole people of God.

The Black Man Has Changed

The last three years have been characterized by the evolution of black consciousness in South Africa. This in turn called for the need to relate the Christian faith to the experience of the black man.

"But God, Why Did You Create Us?" was the title of an article published in a church periodical some years ago. The article as a whole reflects the mood of a black man who cries from the abyss of the shackles occasioned by the fact that he is black. He is seeking for meaning for and destiny in a life in which blackness is not a favorable intellectual point of orientation.

The theological meaning of this question cannot be appreciated in isolation from the whole gamut of social, political, and economic problems. This is not the place to discuss the content of the question as such since here we are discussing change in the Church in broad terms. I only wish to point to the reality of its existence as a primary pre-theological question. In other words there are certain questions which are suggested by the reality and mode of human existence. Any healthy theological reflection uses these questions as points of orientation.

In his critique against "kerygmatic theology," Paul Tillich cautions us against the danger of "throwing" the Christian message at those "in the situation." One need not follow all the turns and twists in his method of correlation in order to appreciate the validity of his caution. He defines the "situation" as follows: "Situation: one pole of all theological work does not refer to the psychological or sociological state in which individuals live. It refers to the scientific and artistic, the economic, political and ethical forms in which they express their interpretation of existence. . . . The situation to which theology must respond in a special period."

Paul Tillich asserts that the Christian message supplies answers correlated to the existential questions which arise from the human situation. The task of systematic theology, according to him, is to analyze the human situation from which the existential questions arise, and to demonstrate that "the symbols used in the Christian message are the answers to these questions."

When man—even an unbeliever—raises moral and existential questions about his life and environment, he is impelled by his condition of creatureliness. Gustaf Wingren argues that "men ask themselves questions like these because of the very fact that they are alive. They can ask them, even though they have no belief in God at all, but what they are really questioning is their relationship to God. For this relationship is given with life itself, and even when men have ceased to be related to him."

We can even go further and say that the preaching of the Word of God by missionaries in Africa did not serve to pull down God to the African situation, because he was already there protecting and sustaining life as Creator. All the preaching did was to bring the message of a God who was already there. The important soteriological motif out of which arises the question as to how man can be reconciled to God should not make us oblivious to the creation motif out of which arises the question of how God commands the situation in the fallen world. Neither should epistemological considerations, namely as to when man "graduates" from a lack of certain knowledge to ascertained knowledge of things divine, determine our conception of the temporal order of the events of God's active presence among sinful men.

From the above it follows that the existential questions which arise from the soul of the black man are the legitimate frame of reference for the Gospel which sums up God's design for the situation of man. If the Gospel is to save the black man, it must relate to such basic questions as: "Why did God create me black? What is the ultimate destiny of the black man in a world governed by the values of the white man?" It is the task of theology in Africa to use these questions as the frame of reference while it defines the content of the Gospel which is designed also to save the black man. The classical themes of theology and their formulation should only serve as starting points and not mark the final and ultimate points of the task of theologizing.

The so-called black theology is the intellectual arm of the spiritual awakening of the black man toward the message of the Gospel. The black man, for the first time, is beginning to hear the message directly from God's mount. For the first time he hears God from the depths of his existence as a black man.

The Church can no longer pretend that nothing has happened. It cannot close its ears forever toward the witness of faith—liberation by the majority of the South African believers. The Church must change so that the black man's witness to the Christian faith may also be heard. In a

eucharistic tone the black man is singing: "Out of the depths I cry unto thee, O Lord!" Who has the authority to silence the black man?

God Demands Change Now

This is the time of crises—the crises of Christian discipleship. South Africa urgently needs the Gospel of liberation, a Gospel that will liberate the whites from the bondage inherent in the South African way of life—a way of life that chokes brotherhood and fellowship between black and white. This is the Gospel which will liberate the white man into the realization of the fact that he is nothing but a fellow human being in relation to the black man, and a Gospel which will liberate the black man into the realization of the fact that he is nothing less than a human being.

South Africa urgently needs security—a security that results from fellowship between black and white, not a security created by distance between black and white, since the consciousness of distance does not lead to a feeling of security, but leads to fear and suspicion.

God demands that the white man repent of the political, economic, and social sins he has committed over the last three centuries. If the white man will be saved at all, the English and the Afrikaners of this country must say in unison: "Mea culpa, mea culpa, mea maxima culpa."

God is greater than the power which the white man wields today. The white man is nothing but the creature of God for whom Christ also died on the cross. The white man is guilty before God because he has manipulated his political and social institutions against the promotion of love between brothers and against justice toward brothers.

The Church must change because God demands it now. Both the white man and the black man must be liberated from the present bondage. That will be meaningful change because the whole Church, black and white, will have been instrumental in it.

(Source: Manas Buthelezi, "Change in the Church," *South African Outlook*, August 1973; reprinted in *Mission Trends No. 1*, ed. Gerald H. Anderson and Thomas F. Stransky [New York: Paulist Press, 1974], 195-204.)

59. *"Christian Missions and the Western Guilt Complex,"* by Lamin Sanneh

Lamin Sanneh's essay on the Western guilt complex indicates what would become the most sweeping movement in Christian mission in the latter part of the twentieth century, the rise of a critique of liberal Western missions for their growing disinterest in conversion, and with it strongly evangelical missionary movements arising in lands that were once the object of mission. Sanneh reminds the reader that guilt over colonialism and imperialism past and present does not grant missionaries and mission agencies the right to deny the value of conversion for the convert, or ignore the real contributions of Christianity to those lands into which it has come.

When at the age of 18 I approached a Methodist church in the Gambia with a request for baptism, thus signaling my conversion to Christianity from Islam, the resident senior minister, an English missionary, responded by inviting me to reconsider my decision. And, while I was at it, he said, I should also consider joining the Catholic Church. My conversion obviously caused him acute embarrassment, and I was mortified on account of it.

However, his imaginative solution of my linking up with the Catholic Church did not work out; after a year of vain attempts I returned to the English missionary. After assuring me that the baptism of the Methodists was recognized by the Catholics, he agreed in principle to receive me into the church.

At that stage of my life I would have joined the church on almost any condition, for I had this absurd idea that the gospel had marked me out for something, whether for reward, rebuke, or ridicule I did not know; whatever it was, I felt inexorably driven toward it. On the night of my baptism I was overcome with emotion, finding it hard to believe that my wish was being fulfilled. Not even the thousand tongues of Methodist hymnody could have given utterance to the avalanche of thoughts and feelings that erupted in me.

I make this extended autobiographical introduction to indicate how in the liberal Methodist tradition I first encountered the guilt complex about missions which I have since come to know so well after living more than two decades in the West. I have found Western Christians to be very embarrassed about meeting converts from Asia or Africa, but when I have repeated for them my personal obstacles in joining the church, making it clear that I was in no way pressured into doing so, they have seemed gratefully unburdened of a sense of guilt. Furthermore, when I have pointed out that missionaries actually made comparatively few converts, my Western friends have reacted with obvious relief, though with another part of their minds, they insist that missionaries have regularly used their superior cultural advantage to instill a sense of inferiority in natives.

It seems that for my Western Christian friends, if missionaries did not justify by their field labors the guilt the West carries about the mischief of the white race in the rest of the world, then other missionaries would have to be invented to justify that guilt.

It should provide food for thought that the church has succeeded in importing this guilt complex into Africa. I found the church there to be self-conscious about matters religious—especially matters involving God, death, judgment, the virgin birth, and miracles—which presumably the Enlightenment banished from rational debate. Consequently, the church was wary of embracing members tainted with the brush of conversion, for such new members would not have acquired the reservation deemed appropriate to religious subjects.

The church took further precautions against religious enthusiasm: for my catechism I was introduced to New Testament form criticism and to Reinhold Niebuhr, Paul Tillich. John Macmurray, John A. T. Robinson, Vincent Taylor, Oliver Chase Quick, and other "sensible" writers. On my own initiative I discovered the works of C. S. Lewis, whose brand of commonsense Christianity encouraged me no end. Nevertheless, the liberal strand was the dominant theme in my formation, hallowed with the refined ministration of writers like Bertrand Russell and Harold Nicolson.

The church's hesitant attitude about religious conversion in turn surprised, frustrated, dismayed, saddened, and confused me. Also, given the prominent place religion occupies in Africa, I was baffled by the apparent determination of my church superiors to keep religious subjects from all "decent" and "cultured" conversation. I realize now that this attitude is deep-rooted in Western liberal culture. However, before I left Africa for Europe I had no way of understanding it, for it had no analogue in my society, and, more important for me, it appeared to skirt the declared aims of a missionary church.

My business in this piece is not to linger on Memory Lane but to confront directly the guilt complex about missions that so often prevails in liberal counsels. I believe that the liberal claim to openmindedness about missions would be strengthened by a closer examination of what actually happened—and may still be happening—in the encounter between Western missionaries and non-Christian peoples.

Much of the standard Western scholarship on Christian missions proceeds by looking at the motives of individual missionaries and concludes by faulting the entire missionary enterprise as being part of the machinery of Western cultural imperialism. But missions in the modern era has been far more, and far less, than the argument about motives customarily portrays.

Missionaries of course went out with all sorts of motives, and some of them were clearly unwholesome. Yet if we were to try to separate good from bad motives, I daresay we would not, after a mountain of labor, advance the subject much beyond the molehill of stalemate. We might, for example, take a little out of the cultural imperialism bag and put it into the social-service category, and ascribe both phenomena to Western cultural conditioning. But that exercise would do little to further our understanding of the nature and consequences of cross-cultural missions.

Instead of examining motives, I propose that we focus on the field setting of missions, where local feedback exerted an influence all its own. And what stands out in particular about the field setting is the emphasis missionaries gave to translating Scripture into vernacular languages. Most Protestant missionary agencies embarked on the immense enterprise of vernacular translation with the enthusiasm, urgency, and commitment of first-timers, and they expended uncommon resources to make the vernacular dream come true. Today more than 1,800 languages have been involved in the worldwide translation movement. In Africa alone, the Bible has been translated into 522 vernacular languages, with texts in over 200 additional languages now under development. Catholic missions have been similarly committed to the transposition of the catechism into vernacular terms, with language study a crucial part of the enterprise. The importance of vernacular translation was that it brought the missionary into contact with the most intimate and intricate aspects of culture, yielding wide-ranging consequences for both missionary and native alike.

The translation enterprise had two major steps. One was the creation of a vernacular alphabet for societies that lacked a literary tradition. The other step was to shake the existing literary tradition free of its esoteric, elitist predilection by recasting it as a popular medium. Both steps stimulated an indigenous response and encouraged the discovery of local resources for the appropriation of Christianity. Local believers acquired a new interest not only in the vernacular but also in recording their history and collecting accounts of indigenous wisdom. One missionary whose work sparked such response was J. G. Christaller, who came from Basel to the Gold Coast (now Ghana). Between 1871 and 1881 he produced a Bible translation, a dictionary and a grammar of the Twi language, crowning his labors with a compilation of 3,600 Twi proverbs and axioms. He also helped found the *Christian Messenger* in 1883, a paper devoted to the promotion of Akan life and culture. His *Twi Dictionary* has been acclaimed as an "Encyclopaedia of Akan civilization" by the modern generation of Ghanaian scholars.

Often the outcome of vernacular translation was that the missionary lost the position of being the expert. But the significance of translation went beyond that. Armed with a written vernacular Scripture, converts to Christianity invariably called into question the legitimacy of all schemes of foreign domination—cultural, political, and religious. Here was an acute paradox: the vernacular Scriptures and the wider cultural and linguistic enterprise on which translation rested provided the means and occasion for arousing a sense of national pride, yet it was the missionaries—foreign agents—who were the creators of that entire process. I am convinced that this paradox decisively undercuts the alleged connection often drawn between missions and colonialism. Colonial rule was irreparably damaged by the consequences of vernacular translation—and often by other activities of missionaries.

Because of its concern for translations that employ the speech of the common workaday world, Christian proclamation has had a populist element. In many traditional societies, religious language has tended to be confined to a small elite of professionals. In extreme cases, this language is shrouded under the forbidding sanctions of secret societies and shrines, access to which is through induced trances or a magical formula. The Christian approach to translatability strikes at the heart of such gnostic tendencies, first by contending that the greatest and most profound religious truths are compatible with everyday language, and second, by targeting ordinary men and women as worthy bearers of the religious message. This approach introduced a true democratic spirit into hitherto closed and elitist societies, with women in particular discovering an expanded role.

For example, after George Pilkington, the English lay missionary, translated the Bible in Uganda, some 2,000 men and 400 women acted as colporteurs operating as far as the forests of the Congo. Pilkington's translated Bible sold 1,100 copies in the first year of publication, with an additional 4,000 New Testaments, 13,500 single Gospels, and 40,000 readers. Theodore Roosevelt, who visited Uganda in 1910, witnessed the scene and said it was nothing short of astounding.

The project of translation contains implications about the nature of culture itself. Translation destigmatizes culture—it denies that culture is "profane"—and asserts that the sacred message may legitimately be entrusted to the forms of everyday life. Translation also relativizes culture by denying that there is only one normative expression of the gospel; it results in a pluralism in which God is the relativizing center. The Christian insight into this phenomenon carries with it a profound ethical notion, for it opens culture up to the demand and need for change. A divinized, absolutized culture precludes the possibility of change.

The impact of the translation process is, indeed, incalculable. Suddenly hitherto illiterate populations were equipped with a written Scripture for the first time, and from the wonder and pride of possessing something new that is also strangely familiar, they burst upon the scene with confidence in the whos and whys of their existence. For example, the Luo tribesman Matthew Ajuoga was helping missionaries translate the Bible into his native language. He discovered that the missionaries translated the Greek word *philadelphia*, "brotherly love," into Luo as *hera*, and this experience caused him to protest, saying that "love" as the Bible explained it was absent from the missionaries' treatment of Africans. He subsequently founded an independent church, the Church of Christ in Africa, in 1957, which gained a considerable following across tribal divisions. Another example is the Zulu Bible, which enabled Zulu converts to respond to missionary criticism of the Zulu way of dressing. The Zulus said that they found in Genesis 27:16 sanction for their custom of dressing in skins, a practice the missionaries had attacked. In the eyes of the Zulus, it was the missionaries who were flouting the dress code. Thus it was that, confronted with the bewildering fact of Western intrusion, local populations used the vernacular to avert ultimate disenchantment, in this way utilizing the gains of mission to offset the losses to colonialism.

The evidence of the importance of translation in Christian missions is remarkably consistent. From the 16th century when Francis Xavier decided to cast his lot with the East against his own Western culture, to the 19th century when Christaller singlehandedly promoted Akan culture, to the 20th when Frank Laubach inveighed against the encroachments of American power in the Philippines, missionaries in the field have helped to promote indigenous self-awareness as a counterforce to Western cultural importation. Obviously missionaries wanted to proclaim the gospel because they believed it to be superior to any message others might offer. But it is really not consistent to blame missionaries for believing in what they preach. And we must note this salient, consistent feature of their work—namely, that they confidently adopted the language and culture of others as the irreplaceable vehicle for the transmission of the message. Whatever judgment missionaries brought with them, it certainly was not about the fitness of the vernacular to be the hallowed channel for communicating with God.

Besides the paradox of foreign missionaries establishing the indigenous process by which foreign domination was questioned, there is a theological paradox to this story: missionaries entered the missionary field to convert others, yet in the translation process it was they who first made the move to "convert" to a new language, with all its presuppositions and ramifications. Thus we have the example of Robert de Nobili (1577-1656), an Italian nobleman who went to India as a Jesuit missionary, arriving there in 1605. He passed for a guru, an Indian saintly figure, and even for a sannyasi, a wild, holy man, adopting Hindu customs and religious terminology to define his own personal piety. Two other examples were Matteo Ricci (1552-1610), who adopted the opposite path to de Nobili by assimilating into upper-class Chinese society during the Ming dynasty, coming to China in 1580, eventually undergoing a profound cultural transformation as a Confucian scholar; and Charles de Foucauld, who served in the French army in the Algerian war where he witnessed moving scenes of Muslim personal piety, leading him to regain his own Christian faith, and becoming in everything a Tuareg Bedouin nomad. Whether missionaries converted anybody else, there is no doubt that they were their own first converts.

It is also apparent that at least in Africa, Christian missions expanded and deepened pluralism—in language, social encounter, and ethnic participation in the Christian movement. Missions helped to preserve languages that were threatened by a rising lingua franca, extended the influence of the vernacular through careful methodical and systematic investigations in the field, and helped to establish connections within the wider family of languages. In their grammars, dictionaries, primers, readers, and systematic compilations of proverbs, axioms, customs, and other ethnographic materials, missionaries furnished the scientific documentation by means of which the modern study of cultures could begin. Whether missionaries translated well or badly—and there are masterpieces as well as outrageous parodies—they made

field criteria rather than the values of empire-building their operative standard.

Indeed, if there is any aspect of missionaries' motives I would want to pursue, it would be their desire to excel in whatever they undertook. They scrutinized their work in the hard and somber light of giving an account before God. Thus we find in their meticulous record-keeping, in the minutiae of account ledgers, in faithful official and family correspondence and in the assembling of petitions, an extraordinary concern for accuracy.

In examining missionary archives I am struck constantly by the missionaries' painstaking attention to detail. Inventiveness was a rather rare vice in that stern, austere world of missionary self-accounting. Thus, unwittingly, was laid the firm foundation of modern historiography in Africa and elsewhere. Even the nationalist point of view that came to dominate much historical writing about the new Africa was to a large extent molded by missionary exploration of indigenous societies.

When they succeeded in translation, missionaries inadvertently vindicated indigenous claims, and when they failed they called forth the criticism of local people. Furthermore, their success in translation merely hastened the day of their departure, while failure called into question their continuing presence. Words have impact, especially in the abundant surplus of their unintended consequences. Translation is no respecter of motives—which is why it should be detached from the question of motives and examined in its own right.

Missionary statesmen in the 19th century saw quite clearly where the vernacular principle was leading, and they welcomed it as the supreme reward of Christian discipleship. For example, Henry Venn of the Anglican Church Missionary Society said that "the marked national characteristics" that the vernacular principle fosters in the expression of the gospel, "in the overruling grace of God, will tend to its perfection and glory." He spoke vividly of "a euthanasia of mission" once the vernacular principle exerted its full force. He said the business of mission was "not to supply an European pastorate, but to prepare native pastors . . . and to fix the spiritual standard in such churches by securing for them a supply of Vernacular Scriptures" (*To Apply the Gospel: Selections from* the Writings of Henry Venn [Eerdmans, 1971]). Such an aim, he counseled, differed sharply from the goals of colonialism in perpetuating overseas dependencies.

The modern religious map of Africa reveals in a striking way the close connection between the growth of Christianity and the widespread employment of the vernacular. The converse also seems to hold: Christian growth has been slightest in areas where vernacular languages are weak—that is, where a lingua franca such as English, French, Portuguese, Arabic, or Swahili has succeeded in suppressing mother tongues.

To make the contrast even starker, we can point out that the reverse phenomenon appears in Islam, also a missionary religion, but one that does not translate its Scriptures for its canonical rites. Islam is strongest in societies where a lingua franca exists and weakest in places of vernacular preponderance. For example, Islamic gains in north Nigeria occurred at the hands of the Fulani reformers in the 19th century. In the process, the Fulani assimilated to an Islamized Hausa culture and lost their own Fulfulde language.

Islamic reform has nowhere to my knowledge made the perpetuation of the vernacular a concomitant of orthodox rectitude, and I know of no Muslim language institutes dedicated to the systematic study of the vernacular. Islam has succeeded brilliantly in its missionary enterprise, promoting at the same time a universal devotion to the sacred Arabic. In Africa, we see evidence of its considerable gains in spite of what we might regard as insuperable odds against a nontranslatable Scripture. For this reason the implications of Muslim success for pluralism are quite serious.

I will conclude, as I began, with a personal story, this one about the unexpected dynamics of translation. After completing my Islamic studies in the Middle East in 1969 I went to Yorubaland in Nigeria as a lay worker with the Methodist Church. I was immediately taken to the local market to purchase some bare essentials for my flat. My companion was a senior English missionary who had spent many years in Ibadan and knew his way around. He translated for me as we did the round of market stalls, with the stall keepers' curiosity naturally aroused by the missionary, in their eyes a stranger from beyond the stars.

Before we had picked our way through the market, a small crowd had gathered to marvel at the sight of a white man translating for an African in an African language. It was as if we had got our arrangement wrong and put the Western cart before the African horse. The image of "total stranger" the stall keepers had of the Western missionary was completely belied by this exposure.

Of the several lessons one can draw from this incident, one is particularly relevant to the Western guilt complex about missions. There is a widespread tendency in the West to see missions as destroyers of indigenous cultures or else as alien cultural agents from the West. Yet in the incident at the local market, my missionary companion came to be acknowledged by the stall keepers as an accomplished "native," one of themselves, on the basis of the vernacular rule that they normally used to determine the boundary between insiders and outsiders. In the act of translating, my missionary friend demonstrated that he had as much claim to being in Africa as he had to identifying with the West. His own Western cultural differences were no longer a barrier, nor even a useful evaluative standard, but an opportunity for cross-cultural interchange. This example suggests that Christian missions are better seen as a translation movement, with consequences for vernacular revitalization, religious change, and social transformation, than as a vehicle for Western cultural domination. Such an assurance should help alleviate some of the Western guilt complex about missions.

(Source: Lamin Sanneh, "Christian Missions and the Western Guilt Complex," Christian Century, April 8, 1987.)

9

Contemporary Documents of the Churches

Roman Catholic Mission Documents

The Decree Ad Gentes *was one of the key documents of the Second Vatican Council, held between 1962 and 1965 in Rome. Readers may wish to note the various ways in which mission is the work of the whole church and involves the whole life of the church—not least the celebration of the Eucharist as an eschatological sign. In two other documents,* Dominus Iesus *and* Christifideles Laici *the reader will see how late in the twentieth century the Roman Catholic Church continues to address the issues of competing ideologies, disunity among Christians, and growing concerns with the degradation of the environment.*

60. *Decree* Ad gentes, *On the Missionary Activity of the Church*

1. Divinely sent to the nations of the world to be unto them "a universal sacrament of salvation," the Church, driven by the inner necessity of her own catholicity, and obeying the mandate of her Founder (cf. Mark 16:16), strives ever to proclaim the Gospel to all men. The Apostles themselves, on whom the Church was founded, following in the footsteps of Christ, "preached the word of truth and begot churches." It is the duty of their successors to make this task endure "so that the word of God may run and be glorified" (2 Thess. 3:1) and the kingdom of God be proclaimed and established throughout the world.

In the present state of affairs, out of which there is arising a new situation for mankind, the Church, being the salt of the earth and the light of the world (cf. Matt. 5:13-14), is more urgently called upon to save and renew every creature, that all things may be restored in Christ and all men may constitute one family in Him and one people of God.

Therefore, this sacred synod, while rendering thanks to God for the excellent results that have been achieved through the whole Church's great-hearted endeavor, desires to sketch the principles of missionary activity and to rally the forces of all the faithful in order that the people of God, marching along the narrow way of the Cross, may spread everywhere the reign of Christ, Lord and overseer of the ages (cf. Eccl. 36:19), and may prepare the way for his coming.

2. The pilgrim Church is missionary by her very nature, since it is from the mission of the Son and the mission of the Holy Spirit that she draws her origin, in accordance with the decree of God the Father.

This decree, however, flows from the "fount-like love" or charity of God the Father who, being the "principle without principle" from whom the Son is begotten and Holy Spirit proceeds through the Son, freely creating us on account of His surpassing and merciful kindness and graciously calling us moreover to share with Him His life and His cry, has generously poured out, and does not cease to pour out still, His divine goodness. Thus He who created all things may at last be "all in all" (1 Cor. 15:28), bringing about at one and the same time His own glory and our happiness. But it pleased

God to call men to share His life, not just singly, apart from any mutual bond, but rather to mold them into a people in which His sons, once scattered abroad might be gathered together (cf. John 11:52).

3. This universal design of God for the salvation of the human race is carried out not only, as it were, secretly in the soul of a man, or by the attempts (even religious ones by which in diverse ways it seeks after God) if perchance it may contact Him or find Him, though He be not far from anyone of us (cf. Acts 17:27). For these attempts need to be enlightened and healed; even though, through the kindly workings of Divine Providence, they may sometimes serve as leading strings toward God, or as a preparation for the Gospel. Now God, in order to establish peace or the communion of sinful human beings with Himself, as well as to fashion them into a fraternal community, did ordain to intervene in human history in a way both new and finally sending His Son, clothed in our flesh, in order that through Him He might snatch men from the power of darkness and Satan (cf. Col. 1:13; Acts 10:38) and reconcile the world to Himself in Him (cf. 2 Cor. 5:19). Him, then, by whom He made the world, He appointed heir of all things, that in Him He might restore all (cf. Eph. 1:10). . . .

For Jesus Christ was sent into the world as a real mediator between God and men. Since He is God, all divine fullness dwells bodily in Him (Gal. 2:9). According to His human nature, on the other hand, He is the new Adam, made head of a renewed humanity, and full of grace and of truth (John 1:14). Therefore the Son of God walked the ways of a true Incarnation that He might make men sharers in the nature of God: made poor for our sakes, though He had been rich, in order that His poverty might enrich us (2 Cor. 8:9). The Son of Man came not that He might be served, but that He might be a servant, and give His life as a ransom for the many—that is, for all (cf. Mark 10:45). The Fathers of the Church proclaim without hesitation that what has not been taken up by Christ is not made whole. Now, what He took up was our entire human nature such as it is found among us poor wretches, save only sin (cf. Heb. 4:15; 9.28). For Christ said concerning Himself, He whom the Father sanctified and sent into the world (cf. John 10:36): "The Spirit of the Lord is upon me, because

He anointed me; to bring good news to the poor He sent me, to heal the broken-hearted, to proclaim to the captives release, and sight to the blind" (Luke 4:18). And again: "The Son of Man has come to seek and to save what was lost" (Luke 19:10).

But what the Lord preached that one time, or what was wrought in Him for the saving of the human race, must be spread abroad and published to the ends of the earth (Acts 1:8), beginning from Jerusalem (cf. Luke 24:27), so that what He accomplished at that one time for the salvation of all, may in the course of time come to achieve its effect in all.

4. To accomplish this, Christ sent from the Father His Holy Spirit, who was to carry on inwardly His saving work and prompt the Church to spread out. Doubtless, the Holy Spirit was already at work in the world before Christ was glorified. Yet on the day of Pentecost, He came down upon the disciples to remain with them forever (cf. John 14:16). The Church was publicly displayed to the multitude, the Gospel began to spread among the nations by means of preaching, and there was presaged that union of all peoples in the catholicity of the faith by means of the Church of the New Covenant, a Church which speaks all tongues, understands and accepts all tongues in her love, and so supersedes the divisiveness of Babel. For it was from Pentecost that the "Acts of the Apostles" took again, just as Christ was conceived when the Holy Spirit came upon the Virgin Mary, and just as Christ was impelled to the work of His ministry by the same Holy Spirit descending upon Him while He prayed.

Now, the Lord Jesus, before freely giving His life for the world, did so arrange the Apostles' ministry and promise to send the Holy Spirit that both they and the Spirit might be associated in effecting the work of salvation always and everywhere. Throughout all ages, the Holy Spirit makes the entire Church "one in communion and in ministering; He equips her with various gifts of a hierarchical and charismatic nature," a giving life, soul-like, to ecclesiastical institutions and instilling into the hearts of the faithful the same mission spirit which impelled Christ Himself. Sometimes He even visibly anticipates the Apostles' acting, just as He unceasingly accompanies and directs it in different ways.

5. From the very beginning, the Lord Jesus "called to Himself those whom He wished; and He caused twelve of them to be with Him, and to be sent out preaching" (Mark 3:13; cf. Matt. 10:1-42). Thus the Apostles were the first budding-forth of the New Israel, and at the same time the beginning of the sacred hierarchy. Then, when He had by His death and His resurrection completed once for all in Himself the mysteries of our salvation and the renewal of all things, the Lord, having now received all power in heaven and on earth (cf. Matt. 28:18), before He was taken up into heaven (cf. Acts 1:11), founded His Church as the sacrament of salvation and sent His Apostles into all the world just as He Himself had been sent by His Father (cf. John 20:21), commanding them: "Go, therefore, and make disciples of all nations, baptizing them in the name of the Father and of the Son and of the Holy Spirit; teaching them to observe all that I have commanded you" (Matt. 28:19 ff.). "Go into the whole world, preach the Gospel to every creature. He who believes and is baptized shall be saved; but he who does not believe, shall be condemned" (Mark 16:15ff.). Whence the duty that lies on the Church of spreading the faith and the salvation of Christ, not only in virtue of the express command which was inherited from the Apostles by the order of bishops, assisted by the priests, together with the successor of Peter and supreme shepherd of the Church, but also in virtue of that life which flows from Christ into His members; "From Him the whole body, being closely joined and knit together through every joint of the system, according to the functioning in due measure of each single part, derives its increase to the building up of itself in love" (Eph. 4:16). The mission of the Church, therefore, is fulfilled by that activity which makes her, obeying the command of Christ and influenced by the grace and love of the Holy Spirit, fully present to all men or nations, in order that, by the example of her life and by her preaching, by the sacraments and other means of grace, she may lead them to the faith, the freedom and the peace of Christ; that thus there may lie open before them a firm and free road to full participation in the mystery of Christ.

Since this mission goes on and in the course of history unfolds the mission of Christ Himself, who was sent to preach the Gospel to the poor, the Church, prompted by the Holy Spirit, must walk in the same path on which Christ walked: a path of poverty and obedience, of service and self-sacrifice to the death, from which death He came forth a victor by His resurrection. For thus did all the Apostles walk in hope, and by many trials and sufferings they filled up those things wanting to the Passion of Christ for His body which is the Church (cf. Col. 1:24). For often, the blood of Christians was like a seed.

6. This duty, to be fulfilled by the order of bishops, under the successor of Peter and with the prayers and help of the whole Church, is one and the same everywhere and in every condition, even though it may be carried out differently according to circumstances. Hence, the differences recognizable in this, the Church's activity, are not due to the inner nature of the mission itself, but rather to the circumstances in which this mission is exercised. . . .

Thus it is plain that missionary activity wells up from the Church's inner nature and spreads abroad her saving Faith. It perfects her Catholic unity by this expansion. It is sustained by her apostolicity. It exercises the collegial spirit of her hierarchy. It bears witness to her sanctity while spreading and promoting it. Thus, missionary activity among the nations differs from pastoral activity exercised among the faithful as well as from undertakings aimed at restoring unity among Christians. And yet these two ends are most closely connected with the missionary zeal because the division among Christians damages the most holy cause of preaching the Gospel to every creature and blocks the way to the faith for many. Hence, by the very necessity of mission, all the baptized are called to gather into one flock, and thus they will be able to bear unanimous witness before the nations to Christ their Lord. And if they are not yet capable of bearing witness to the same faith, they should at least be animated by mutual love and esteem.

7. This missionary activity derives its reason from the will of God, "who wishes all men to be saved and to come to the knowledge of the truth. For there is one God, and one mediator between God and men, Himself a man, Jesus Christ, who gave Himself as a ransom for all" (1 Tim. 2:45), "neither is there salvation in any other" (Acts 4:12). Therefore, all must be converted to Him, made known by the Church's preaching, and all must

be incorporated into Him by baptism and into the Church which is His body. For Christ Himself "by stressing in express language the necessity of faith and baptism" (cf. Mark 16:16; John 3:5), at the same time confirmed the necessity of the Church, into which men enter by baptism, as by a door. Therefore those men cannot be saved, who though aware that God, through Jesus Christ founded the Church as something necessary, still do not wish to enter into it, or to persevere in it. Therefore though God in ways known to Himself can lead those inculpably ignorant of the Gospel to find that faith without which it is impossible to please Him (Heb. 11:6), yet a necessity lies upon the Church (1 Cor. 9:16), and at the same time a sacred duty, to preach the Gospel. And hence missionary activity today as always retains its power and necessity. . . .

8. Missionary activity is closely bound up even with human nature itself and its aspirations. For by manifesting Christ the Church reveals to men the real truth about their condition and their whole calling, since Christ is the source and model of that redeemed humanity, imbued with brotherly love, sincerity, and a peaceful spirit, to which they all aspire. Christ and the Church, which bears witness to Him by preaching the Gospel, transcend every peculiarity of race or nation and therefore cannot be considered foreign anywhere or to anybody. Christ Himself is the way and the truth, which the preaching of the Gospel opens to all in proclaiming in the hearing of all these words of Christ: "Repent, and believe the Gospel" (Mark 1:15). Now, since he who does not believe is already judged (cf. John 3:18), the words of Christ are at one and the same time words of judgment and of grace, of death and of life. For it is only by putting to death what is old that we are able to approach the newness of life. This is true first of all about persons, but it holds also for the various goods of this world which bear the mark both of man's sin and of God's blessing: "For all have sinned and have need of the glory of God" (Rom. 3:23). No one is freed from sin by himself and by his own power, no one is raised above himself, no one is completely rid of his sickness or his solitude or his servitude. On the contrary, all stand in need of Christ, their model, their mentor, their liberator, their Savior, their source of life. The Gospel has truly been a leaven of liberty and progress in human history, even in the temporal sphere, and always proves itself a leaven of brotherhood, of unity and of peace. Not without cause is Christ hailed by the faithful as "the expected of the nations, and their Savior."

9. And so the time for missionary activity extends between the first coming of the Lord and the second, in which latter the Church will be gathered from the four winds like a harvest into the kingdom of God. For the Gospel must be preached to all nations before the Lord shall come (cf. Mark 13:10).

Missionary activity is nothing else and nothing less than an epiphany, or a manifesting of God's decree, and its fulfillment in the world and in world history, in the course of which God, by means of mission, manifestly works out the history of salvation. By the preaching of the word and by the celebration of the sacraments, the center and summit of which is the most holy Eucharist, He brings about the presence of Christ, the author of salvation. But whatever truth and grace are to be found among the nations, as a sort of secret presence of God, He frees from all taint of evil and restores to Christ its maker, who overthrows the devil's domain and wards off the manifold malice of vice. And so, whatever good is found to be sown in the hearts and minds of men, or in the rites and cultures peculiar to various peoples, not only is not lost, but is healed, uplifted, and perfected for the glory of God, the shame of the demon, and the bliss of men. Thus, missionary activity tends toward eschatological fullness. For by it the people of God is increased to that measure and time which the Father has fixed in His power (cf. Acts 1:7). To this people it was said in prophecy: "Enlarge the space for your tent, and spread out your tent cloths unsparingly" (Is. 54:2). By missionary activity, the mystical body grows to the mature measure of the fullness of Christ (cf. Eph. 4:13); and the spiritual temple, where God is adored in spirit and in truth (cf. John 4:23), grows and is built up upon the foundation of the Apostles and prophets, Christ Jesus Himself being the supreme corner stone (Eph. 2:20).

Mission Work Itself

10. The Church, sent by Christ to reveal and to communicate the love of God to all men and nations, is

aware that there still remains a gigantic missionary task for her to accomplish. For the Gospel message has not yet, or hardly yet, been heard by two billion human beings (and their number is increasing daily), who are formed into large and distinct groups by permanent cultural ties, by ancient religious traditions, and by firm bonds of social necessity. Some of these men are followers of one of the great religions, but others remain strangers to the very knowledge of God, while still others expressly deny His existence, and sometimes even attack it. The Church, in order to be able to offer all of them the mystery of salvation and the life brought by God, must implant herself into these groups for the same motive which led Christ to bind Himself, in virtue of His Incarnation, to certain social and cultural conditions of those human beings among whom He dwelt.

(Source: Vatican II, Document on the Mission Activity of the Church [*Ad Gentes*], www.vatican .va/archive/hist_councils/ii_vatican_council/ documents/vat-ii_decree_19651207_ad-gentes_ en.html; Reproduced by permission of Libreria Editrice Vaticana.)

61. *Declaration* Dominus Iesus, *On the Unicity and Salvific Universality of Jesus Christ and the Church*

This declaration of the Congregation for the Doctrine of the Faith (successor to the congregation once known as the "Congregation of the Holy Office of the Inquisition") became one of the most controversial documents of the Vatican from the moment it was published on August 6, 2000. Widely viewed as a critique of certain Catholic theologians' writings on the person of Christ and the relationship between Christ and the church and on the church's role in the universal economy of salvation, it was seen by many as a direct assault on the spirit of cordial ecumenism and interreligious relations brought about by Vatican Council II. It was also praised by many others, who saw in it a vigorous apology for the truth of Chris-

tianity in an age that Cardinal Ratzinger has characterized as ruled by a "dictatorship of relativism." As with many Vatican documents, the full richness of the document is revealed only when one refers to the dozens of notes that appear on every page. For the full text of Dominus Iesus, *including these notes, visit the Vatican's website.*

Introduction

4. The Church's constant missionary proclamation is endangered today by relativistic theories which seek to justify religious pluralism, not only *de facto* but also *de iure* (or in principle). As a consequence, it is held that certain truths have been superseded; for example, the definitive and complete character of the revelation of Jesus Christ, the nature of Christian faith as compared with that of belief in other religions, the inspired nature of the books of Sacred Scripture, the personal unity between the Eternal Word and Jesus of Nazareth, the unity of the economy of the Incarnate Word and the Holy Spirit, the unicity and salvific universality of the mystery of Jesus Christ, the universal salvific mediation of the Church, the inseparability—while recognizing the distinction—of the kingdom of God, the kingdom of Christ, and the Church, and the subsistence of the one Church of Christ in the Catholic Church.

I. The Fullness and Definitiveness of the Revelation of Jesus Christ

5. As a remedy for this relativistic mentality, which is becoming ever more common, it is necessary above all to reassert the definitive and complete character of the revelation of Jesus Christ. In fact, it must be firmly believed that, in the mystery of Jesus Christ, the Incarnate Son of God, who is "the way, the truth, and the life" (Jn 14:6), the full revelation of divine truth is given: "No one knows the Son except the Father, and no one knows the Father except the Son and anyone to whom the Son wishes to reveal him" (Mt 11:27); "No one has ever seen God; God the only Son, who is in the

bosom of the Father, has revealed him" (Jn 1:18); "For in Christ the whole fullness of divinity dwells in bodily form" (Col 2:9-10).

II. The Incarnate Logos and the Holy Spirit in the Work of Salvation

9. In contemporary theological reflection there often emerges an approach to Jesus of Nazareth that considers him a particular, finite, historical figure, who reveals the divine not in an exclusive way, but in a way complementary with other revelatory and salvific figures. The Infinite, the Absolute, the Ultimate Mystery of God would thus manifest itself to humanity in many ways and in many historical figures: Jesus of Nazareth would be one of these. More concretely, for some, Jesus would be one of the many faces which the Logos has assumed in the course of time to communicate with humanity in a salvific way.

Furthermore, to justify the universality of Christian salvation as well as the fact of religious pluralism, it has been proposed that there is an economy of the eternal Word that is valid also outside the Church and is unrelated to her, in addition to an economy of the incarnate Word. The first would have a greater universal value than the second, which is limited to Christians, though God's presence would be more full in the second.

10. These theses are in profound conflict with the Christian faith. The doctrine of faith must be firmly believed which proclaims that Jesus of Nazareth, son of Mary, and he alone, is the Son and the Word of the Father. The Word, which "was in the beginning with God" (Jn 1:2) is the same as he who "became flesh" (Jn 1:14). In Jesus, "the Christ, the Son of the living God" (Mt 16:16), "the whole fullness of divinity dwells in bodily form" (Col 2:9). He is the "only begotten Son of the Father, who is in the bosom of the Father" (Jn 1:18), his "beloved Son, in whom we have redemption. . . . In him the fullness of God was pleased to dwell, and through him, God was pleased to reconcile all things to himself, on earth and in the heavens, making peace by the blood of his Cross" (Col 1:13-14; 19-20). . . .

III. Unicity and Universality of the Salvific Mystery of Jesus Christ

13. The thesis which denies the unicity and salvific universality of the mystery of Jesus Christ is also put forward. Such a position has no biblical foundation. In fact, the truth of Jesus Christ, Son of God, Lord and only Saviour, who through the event of his incarnation, death, and resurrection has brought the history of salvation to fulfilment, and which has in him its fullness and centre, must be firmly believed as a constant element of the Church's faith. . . .

IV. Unicity and Unity of the Church

16. The Lord Jesus, the only Saviour, did not only establish a simple community of disciples, but constituted the Church as a salvific mystery: he himself is in the Church and the Church is in him (cf. Jn 15:1ff.; Gal 3:28; Eph 4:15-16; Acts 9:5). Therefore, the fullness of Christ's salvific mystery belongs also to the Church, inseparably united to her Lord. Indeed, Jesus Christ continues his presence and his work of salvation in the Church and by means of the Church (cf. Col 1:24-27), which is his body (cf. 1 Cor 12:12-13, 27; Col 1:18). And thus, just as the head and members of a living body, though not identical, are inseparable, so too Christ and the Church can neither be confused nor separated, and constitute a single "whole Christ." This same inseparability is also expressed in the New Testament by the analogy of the Church as the Bride of Christ (cf. 2 Cor 11:2; Eph 5:25-29; Rev 21:2, 9).

Therefore, in connection with the unicity and universality of the salvific mediation of Jesus Christ, the unicity of the Church founded by him must be firmly believed as a truth of Catholic faith. Just as there is one Christ, so there exists a single body of Christ, a single Bride of Christ: "a single Catholic and apostolic Church." Furthermore, the promises of the Lord that he would not abandon his Church (cf. Mt 16:18; 28:20) and that he would guide her by his Spirit (cf. Jn 16:13) mean, according to Catholic faith, that the unicity and the unity of the Church—like everything that belongs to the Church's integrity—will never be lacking.

The Catholic faithful are required to profess that there is an historical continuity—rooted in the apostolic succession—between the Church founded by Christ and the Catholic Church: "This is the single Church of Christ . . . which our Saviour, after his resurrection, entrusted to Peter's pastoral care (cf. Jn 21:17), commissioning him and the other Apostles to extend and rule her (cf. Mt 28:18ff.), erected for all ages as 'the pillar and mainstay of the truth' (1 Tim 3:15). This Church, constituted and organized as a society in the present world, subsists in [*subsistit in*] the Catholic Church, governed by the Successor of Peter and by the Bishops in communion with him." With the expression *subsistit in*, the Second Vatican Council sought to harmonize two doctrinal statements: on the one hand, that the Church of Christ, despite the divisions which exist among Christians, continues to exist fully only in the Catholic Church, and on the other hand, that "outside of her structure, many elements can be found of sanctification and truth," that is, in those Churches and ecclesial communities which are not yet in full communion with the Catholic Church. But with respect to these, it needs to be stated that "they derive their efficacy from the very fullness of grace and truth entrusted to the Catholic Church."

17. Therefore, there exists a single Church of Christ, which subsists in the Catholic Church, governed by the Successor of Peter and by the Bishops in communion with him. The Churches which, while not existing in perfect communion with the Catholic Church, remain united to her by means of the closest bonds, that is, by apostolic succession and a valid Eucharist, are true particular Churches. Therefore, the Church of Christ is present and operative also in these Churches, even though they lack full communion with the Catholic Church, since they do not accept the Catholic doctrine of the Primacy, which, according to the will of God, the Bishop of Rome objectively has and exercises over the entire Church.

On the other hand, the ecclesial communities which have not preserved the valid Episcopate and the genuine and integral substance of the Eucharistic mystery, are not Churches in the proper sense; however, those who are baptized in these communities are, by Baptism, incorporated in Christ and thus are in a certain communion, albeit imperfect, with the Church. Baptism in fact tends per se toward the full development of life in Christ, through the integral profession of faith, the Eucharist, and full communion in the Church.

"The Christian faithful are therefore not permitted to imagine that the Church of Christ is nothing more than a collection—divided, yet in some way one—of Churches and ecclesial communities; nor are they free to hold that today the Church of Christ nowhere really exists, and must be considered only as a goal which all Churches and ecclesial communities must strive to reach." In fact, "the elements of this already-given Church exist, joined together in their fullness in the Catholic Church and, without this fullness, in the other communities." "Therefore, these separated Churches and communities as such, though we believe they suffer from defects, have by no means been deprived of significance and importance in the mystery of salvation. For the spirit of Christ has not refrained from using them as means of salvation which derive their efficacy from the very fullness of grace and truth entrusted to the Catholic Church."

The lack of unity among Christians is certainly a wound for the Church; not in the sense that she is deprived of her unity, but "in that it hinders the complete fulfilment of her universality in history."

V. The Church: Kingdom of God and Kingdom of Christ

18. The mission of the Church is "to proclaim and establish among all peoples the kingdom of Christ and of God, and she is on earth, the seed and the beginning of that kingdom." On the one hand, the Church is "a sacrament—that is, sign and instrument of intimate union with God and of unity of the entire human race." She is therefore the sign and instrument of the kingdom; she is called to announce and to establish the kingdom. On the other hand, the Church is the "people gathered by the unity of the Father, the Son and the Holy Spirit," she is therefore "the kingdom of Christ already present in mystery" and constitutes its seed and beginning. The kingdom of God, in fact, has an eschatological dimension: it is a reality present in time, but its full realization will arrive only with the completion or fulfilment of history.

VI. The Church and the Other Religions in Relation to Salvation

20. From what has been stated above, some points follow that are necessary for theological reflection as it explores the relationship of the Church and the other religions to salvation.

Above all else, it must be firmly believed that "the Church, a pilgrim now on earth, is necessary for salvation: the one Christ is the mediator and the way of salvation; he is present to us in his body which is the Church. He himself explicitly asserted the necessity of faith and baptism (cf. Mk 16:16; Jn 3:5), and thereby affirmed at the same time the necessity of the Church which men enter through baptism as through a door." This doctrine must not be set against the universal salvific will of God (cf. 1 Tim 2:4); "it is necessary to keep these two truths together, namely, the real possibility of salvation in Christ for all mankind and the necessity of the Church for this salvation."

The Church is the "universal sacrament of salvation," since, united always in a mysterious way to the Saviour Jesus Christ, her Head, and subordinated to him, she has, in God's plan, an indispensable relationship with the salvation of every human being. For those who are not formally and visibly members of the Church, "salvation in Christ is accessible by virtue of a grace which, while having a mysterious relationship to the Church, does not make them formally part of the Church, but enlightens them in a way which is accommodated to their spiritual and material situation. This grace comes from Christ; it is the result of his sacrifice and is communicated by the Holy Spirit"; it has a relationship with the Church, which "according to the plan of the Father, has her origin in the mission of the Son and the Holy Spirit."

21. With respect to the way in which the salvific grace of God—which is always given by means of Christ in the Spirit and has a mysterious relationship to the Church—comes to individual non-Christians, the Second Vatican Council limited itself to the statement that God bestows it "in ways known to himself." Theologians are seeking to understand this question more fully. Their work is to be encouraged, since it is certainly useful for understanding better God's salvific plan and the ways in which it is accomplished. However, from what has been stated above about the mediation of Jesus Christ and the "unique and special relationship" which the Church has with the kingdom of God among men—which in substance is the universal kingdom of Christ the Saviour—it is clear that it would be contrary to the faith to consider the Church as one way of salvation alongside those constituted by the other religions, seen as complementary to the Church or substantially equivalent to her, even if these are said to be converging with the Church toward the eschatological kingdom of God.

Certainly, the various religious traditions contain and offer religious elements which come from God, and which are part of what "the Spirit brings about in human hearts and in the history of peoples, in cultures, and religions." Indeed, some prayers and rituals of the other religions may assume a role of preparation for the Gospel, in that they are occasions or pedagogical helps in which the human heart is prompted to be open to the action of God. One cannot attribute to these, however, a divine origin or an *ex opere operato* salvific efficacy, which is proper to the Christian sacraments. Furthermore, it cannot be overlooked that other rituals, insofar as they depend on superstitions or other errors (cf. 1 Cor 10:20-21), constitute an obstacle to salvation.

22. With the coming of the Saviour Jesus Christ, God has willed that the Church founded by him be the instrument for the salvation of all humanity (cf. Acts 17:30-31). This truth of faith does not lessen the sincere respect which the Church has for the religions of the world, but at the same time, it rules out, in a radical way, that mentality of indifferentism "characterized by a religious relativism which leads to the belief that 'one religion is as good as another.'" If it is true that the followers of other religions can receive divine grace, it is also certain that objectively speaking they are in a gravely deficient situation in comparison with those who, in the Church, have the fullness of the means of salvation. However, "all the children of the Church should nevertheless remember that their exalted condition results, not from their own merits, but from the grace of Christ. If they fail to respond in thought, word, and deed to that grace, not only shall they not be saved, but they shall be

more severely judged." One understands then that, following the Lord's command (cf. Mt 28:19-20) and as a requirement of her love for all people, the Church "proclaims and is in duty bound to proclaim without fail, Christ who is the way, the truth, and the life (Jn 14:6). In him, in whom God reconciled all things to himself (cf. 2 Cor 5:18-19), men find the fullness of their religious life."

In inter-religious dialogue as well, the mission *ad gentes* "today as always retains its full force and necessity." "Indeed, God 'desires all men to be saved and come to the knowledge of the truth' (1 Tim 2:4); that is, God wills the salvation of everyone through the knowledge of the truth. Salvation is found in the truth. Those who obey the promptings of the Spirit of truth are already on the way of salvation. But the Church, to whom this truth has been entrusted, must go out to meet their desire, so as to bring them the truth. Because she believes in God's universal plan of salvation, the Church must be missionary." Inter-religious dialogue, therefore, as part of her evangelizing mission, is just one of the actions of the Church in her mission ad gentes. Equality, which is a presupposition of inter-religious dialogue, refers to the equal personal dignity of the parties in dialogue, not to doctrinal content, nor even less to the position of Jesus Christ—who is God himself made man—in relation to the founders of the other religions. Indeed, the Church, guided by charity and respect for freedom, must be primarily committed to proclaiming to all people the truth definitively revealed by the Lord, and to announcing the necessity of conversion to Jesus Christ and of adherence to the Church through Baptism and the other sacraments, in order to participate fully in communion with God, the Father, Son and Holy Spirit. Thus, the certainty of the universal salvific will of God does not diminish, but rather increases the duty and urgency of the proclamation of salvation and of conversion to the Lord Jesus Christ.

Conclusion

23. The intention of the present Declaration, in reiterating and clarifying certain truths of the faith, has been to follow the example of the Apostle Paul,

who wrote to the faithful of Corinth: "I handed on to you as of first importance what I myself received" (1 Cor 15:3). Faced with certain problematic and even erroneous propositions, theological reflection is called to reconfirm the Church's faith and to give reasons for her hope in a way that is convincing and effective.

In treating the question of the true religion, the Fathers of the Second Vatican Council taught: "We believe that this one true religion continues to exist in the Catholic and Apostolic Church, to which the Lord Jesus entrusted the task of spreading it among all people. Thus, he said to the Apostles: 'Go therefore and make disciples of all nations baptizing them in the name of the Father and of the Son and of the Holy Spirit, teaching them to observe all that I have commanded you' (Mt 28: 19-20). Especially in those things that concern God and his Church, all persons are required to seek the truth, and when they come to know it, to embrace it and hold fast to it."

The revelation of Christ will continue to be "the true lodestar" in history for all humanity: "The truth, which is Christ, imposes itself as an all-embracing authority." The Christian mystery, in fact, overcomes all barriers of time and space, and accomplishes the unity of the human family: "From their different locations and traditions all are called in Christ to share in the unity of the family of God's children . . . Jesus destroys the walls of division and creates unity in a new and unsurpassed way through our sharing in his mystery. This unity is so deep that the Church can say with Saint Paul: 'You are no longer strangers and sojourners, but you are saints and members of the household of God'" (Eph 2:19).

The Sovereign Pontiff John Paul II, at the Audience of June 16, 2000, granted to the undersigned Cardinal Prefect of the Congregation for the Doctrine of the Faith, with sure knowledge and by his apostolic authority, ratified and confirmed this Declaration, adopted in Plenary Session and ordered its publication.

Rome, from the Offices of the Congregation for the Doctrine of the Faith, August 6, 2000, the Feast of the Transfiguration of the Lord.

Joseph Cardinal Ratzinger, Prefect

Tarcisio Bertone, S.D.B., Archbishop Emeritus of Vercelli, Secretary

62. *Apostolic Exhortation, On the Vocation and Mission of the Lay Faithful in the Church and the World,* by Pope John Paul II

In this document Pope John Paul II speaks specifically to the role of the laity in mission. The portions included in this text underscore the distinctive way in which the Roman Catholic Church views the world into which it is called in mission, and the challenges it faces as it articulates a Catholic view of the missional vocation (particularly with regard to the laity) in relation to that world. The final excerpts from the document relate to the roles of women and men, and address the particular challenge that contemporary views of gender bring to Roman Catholic views of the appropriateness of women for the priesthood. In Pope John Paul II's documents there are typically dozens of references to other church documents on every page. We omit those notes. To find them, the reader is advised to go to the Vatican's website for the full text.

To Bishops
To Priests and Deacons
To Women and Men Religious
and to All the Lay Faithful

Introduction

1. The lay members of Christ's Faithful People (*Christifideles Laici*), whose "Vocation and Mission in the Church and in the World Twenty Years after the Second Vatican Council" was the topic of the 1987 Synod of Bishops, are those who form that part of the People of God which might be likened to the labourers in the vineyard mentioned in Matthew's Gospel: "For the Kingdom of heaven is like a householder who went out early in the morning to hire labourers for his vineyard. After agreeing with the labourers for a denarius a day, he sent them into his vineyard" (Mt 20:1-2).

The gospel parable sets before our eyes the Lord's vast vineyard and the multitude of persons, both women and men, who are called and sent forth by him to labour in it. The vineyard is the whole world (cf. Mt 13:38), which is to be transformed according to the plan of God in view of the final coming of the Kingdom of God.

You Go into My Vineyard Too

2. "And going out about the third hour he saw others standing idle in the marketplace; and to them he said, 'You go into the vineyard too'" (Mt 20:3-4).

From that distant day the call of the Lord Jesus "You go into my vineyard too" never fails to resound in the course of history: it is addressed to every person who comes into this world.

In our times, the Church after Vatican II in a renewed outpouring of the Spirit of Pentecost has come to a more lively awareness of her missionary nature and has listened again to the voice of her Lord who sends her forth into the world as "the universal sacrament of salvation."

You go too. The call is a concern not only of Pastors, clergy, and men and women religious. The call is addressed to everyone: lay people as well are personally called by the Lord, from whom they receive a mission on behalf of the Church and the world. In preaching to the people Saint Gregory the Great recalls this fact and comments on the parable of the labourers in the vineyard: "Keep watch over your manner of life, dear people, and make sure that you are indeed the Lord's labourers. Each person should take into account what he does and consider if he is labouring in the vineyard of the Lord."

The Council, in particular, with its rich doctrinal, spiritual, and pastoral patrimony, has written as never before on the nature, dignity, spirituality, mission, and responsibility of the lay faithful. And the *Council Fathers, re-echoing the call of Christ, have summoned all the lay faithful, both women and men, to labour in the vineyard:* "The Council, then, makes an earnest plea in the Lord's name that all lay people give a glad, generous, and prompt response to the impulse of the Holy Spirit and to the voice of Christ, who is giving them an especially urgent invitation at this moment. Young people should feel that this call is directed to them in particular, and they should respond to it eagerly and magnanimously. The Lord himself renews his invitation to all the lay faithful to come closer to him every day, and with the recognition that what is his is also their own (Phil 2:5) they ought to associate themselves with him in his saving mission. Once again he sends them into every town and place where he himself is to come" (cf. Lk 10:1).

. . . At the same time, the Synod has pointed out that the post-conciliar path of the lay faithful has not been without its difficulties and dangers. In particular, two temptations can be cited which they have not always known how to avoid: the temptation of being so strongly interested in Church services and tasks that some fail to become actively engaged in their responsibilities in the professional, social, cultural, and political world; and the temptation of legitimizing the unwarranted separation of faith from life, that is, a separation of the Gospel's acceptance from the actual living of the Gospel in various situations in the world.

The Pressing Needs of the World Today: "Why Do You Stand Here Idle All Day?"

3. The basic meaning of this Synod and the most precious fruit desired as a result of it, is the *lay faithful's hearkening to the call of Christ the Lord to work in his vineyard,* to take an active, conscientious, and responsible part in the mission of the Church *in this great moment in history,* made especially dramatic by occurring on the threshold of the Third Millennium.

. . . The variety of situations and problems that exist in our world is indeed great and rapidly changing. For this reason it is all the more necessary to guard against generalizations and unwarranted simplifications. It is possible, however, to highlight *some trends that are emerging in present-day society.* The gospel records that the weeds and the good grain grew together in the farmer's field. The same is true in history, where in everyday life there often exist contradictions in the exercise of human freedom, where there is found, side by side and at times closely intertwined, evil and good, injustice and justice, anguish and hope.

Secularism and the Need for Religion

4. How can one not notice the ever-growing existence of *religious indifference* and *atheism* in its more varied forms, particularly in its perhaps most widespread form of *secularism?* Adversely affected by the impressive triumphs of continuing scientific and technological development and above all, fascinated by a very old and yet new temptation, namely, that of wishing to become like God (cf. Gen 3:5) through the use of a liberty without bounds, individuals cut the religious roots that are in their hearts; they forget God, or simply retain him without meaning in their lives, or outrightly reject him, and begin to adore various "idols" of the contemporary world.

The present-day phenomenon of secularism is truly serious, not simply as regards the individual, but in some ways, as regards whole communities, as the Council has already indicated: "Growing numbers of people are abandoning religion in practice." At other times I myself have recalled the phenomenon of de-Christianization that strikes long-standing Christian people and which continually calls for a re-evangelization.

Human longing and the need for religion, however, are not able to be totally extinguished. When persons in conscience have the courage to face the more serious questions of human existence—particularly questions related to the purpose of life, to suffering and to dying—they are unable to avoid making their own the words of truth uttered by Saint Augustine: "You have made us for yourself, O Lord, and our hearts are restless until they rest in you." In the same manner the present-day world bears witness to this as well, in ever-increasing and impressive ways, through an openness to a spiritual and transcendent outlook towards life, the renewed interest in religious research, the return to a sense of the sacred and to prayer, and the demand for freedom to call upon the name of the Lord.

The Human Person: A Dignity Violated and Exalted

5. We furthermore call to mind the *violations* to which the human person is subjected. When the individual is not recognized and loved in the person's dignity as the living image of God (cf. Gen 1:26), the human being is exposed to more humiliating and degrading forms of "manipulation," that most assuredly reduce the individual to a slavery to those who are stronger. "Those who are stronger" can take a variety of names: an ideology, economic power, political and inhumane systems, scientific technocracy, or the intrusiveness of the mass-media. Once again we find ourselves before many persons, our sisters and brothers, whose fundamental rights are being violated, owing to their exceedingly great capacity for endurance and to the clear injustice of certain civil laws: the right to life and to integrity, the right to a house and to work, the right to a family and responsible parenthood, the right to participation in public and political life, the right to freedom of conscience and the practice of religion.

Who is able to count the number of babies unborn because they have been killed in their mothers' wombs, children abandoned and abused by their own parents, children who grow without affection and education? In some countries entire populations are deprived of housing and work, lacking the means absolutely essential for leading a life worthy of a human being, and are deprived even of those things necessary for their sustenance. There are great areas of poverty and of misery, both physical and moral, existing at this moment on the periphery of great cities. Entire groups of human beings have been seriously afflicted.

But the *sacredness of the human person* cannot be obliterated, no matter how often it is devalued and violated because it has its unshakable foundation in God as Creator and Father. The sacredness of the person always keeps returning, again and again.

The sense of the dignity of the human person must be pondered and reaffirmed in stronger terms. A beneficial trend is advancing and permeating all peoples of the earth, making them ever more aware of the dignity of the individual: the person is not at all a "thing" or an "object" to be used, but primarily a responsible "subject," one endowed with conscience and freedom, called to live responsibly in society and history, and oriented towards spiritual and religious values.

It has been said that ours is the time of "humanism": paradoxically, some of its atheistic and secularistic forms arrive at a point where the human person is diminished and annihilated; other forms of humanism, instead, exalt the individual in such a manner that these forms become a veritable and real idolatry. There are still other forms, however, in line with the truth, which rightly acknowledge the greatness and misery of individuals and manifest, sustain, and foster the total dignity of the human person.

The sign and fruit of this trend towards humanism is the growing need for *participation,* which is undoubtedly one of the distinctive features of present-day humanity, a true "sign of the times" that is developing in various fields and in different ways: above all the growing need for participation regarding women and young people, not only in areas of family and academic life, but also in cultural, economic, social, and political areas. To be leading characters in this development, in some ways to be creators of a new, more humane culture, is a requirement both for the individual and for peoples as a whole.

Conflict and Peace

6. Finally, we are unable to overlook another phenomenon that is quite evident in present-day humanity: perhaps as never before in history, humanity is daily buffeted by *conflict.* This is a phenomenon which has many forms, displayed in a legitimate plurality of mentalities and initiatives, but manifested in the fatal opposition of persons, groups, categories, nations, and blocks of nations. This opposition takes the form of violence, of terrorism, and of war. Once again, but with proportions enormously widespread, diverse sectors of

humanity today, wishing to show their "omnipotence", renew the futile experience of constructing the "Tower of Babel" (cf. Gen 11:1-9), which spreads confusion, struggle, disintegration, and oppression. The human family is thus in itself dramatically convulsed and wounded.

On the other hand, totally unsuppressible is that human longing experienced by individuals and whole peoples for the inestimable good of *peace* in justice. The gospel beatitude: "Blessed are the peacemakers" (Mt 5:9) finds in the people of our time a new and significant resonance: entire populations today live, suffer, and labour to bring about peace and justice. The *participation* by so many persons and groups in the life of society is increasingly pursued today as the way to make a desired peace become a reality.

On this road we meet many lay faithful generously committed to the social and political field, working in a variety of institutional forms and those of a voluntary nature in service to the least.

Jesus Christ, the Hope of Humanity

7. This, then, is the vast field of labour that stands before the labourers sent forth by the "householder" to work in his vineyard.

In this field the Church is present and working, every one of us, Pastors, priests, deacons, religious, and lay faithful. The adverse situations here mentioned deeply affect the Church: they in part condition the Church, but they do not crush her, nor even less overcome her, because the Holy Spirit, who gives her life, sustains her in her mission.

Despite every difficulty, delay, and contradiction caused by the limits of human nature, by sin and by the Evil One, the Church knows that all the forces that humanity employs for communion and participation find a full response in the intervention of Jesus Christ, the Redeemer of man and of the world.

The Church knows that she is sent forth by him as "sign and instrument of intimate union with God and of the unity of all the human race."

Despite all this, then, humanity is able to hope. Indeed it must hope: the living and personal Gospel, *Jesus Christ himself, is the "good news" and the*

bearer of joy that the Church announces each day, and to whom the Church bears testimony before all people.

The lay faithful have an essential and irreplaceable role in this announcement and in this testimony: through them the Church of Christ is made present in the various sectors of the world, as a sign and source of hope and of love.

An Organic Communion: Diversity and Complementarity

20. Ecclesial communion is more precisely likened to an "organic" communion, analogous to that of a living and functioning body. In fact, at one and the same time it is characterized by a *diversity* and a *complementarity* of vocations and states in life, of ministries, of charisms and responsibilities. Because of this diversity and complementarity every member of the lay faithful is seen *in relation to the whole body* and offers a *totally unique contribution* on behalf of the whole body.

Saint Paul insists in a particular way on the organic communion of the Mystical Body of Christ. We can hear his rich teaching echoed in the following synthesis from the Council: "Jesus Christ"—we read in the Constitution *Lumen Gentium*—by communicating his Spirit to his brothers and sisters, called together from all peoples, made them mystically into his own body. In that body, the life of Christ is communicated to those who believe. . . . As all the members of the human body, though they are many, form one body, so also are the Faithful in Christ (cf. 1 Cor 12:12). Also, in the building up of Christ's body there is a diversity of members and functions. There is only one Spirit who, according to his own richness and the necessities of service, distributes his different gifts for the welfare of the Church (cf. 1 Cor 12:1-11). Among these gifts comes in the first place the grace given to the apostles to whose authority the Spirit himself subjects even those who are endowed with charisms (cf. 1 Cor 14). Furthermore it is this same Spirit, who through his power and through the intimate bond between the members, produces and urges love among the faithful. Consequently, if one member suffers anything, all the members suffer it too, and if one member is honoured, all members together rejoice" (cf. 1 Cor 12:26).

One and the same Spirit is always the dynamic principle of diversity and unity in the Church. Once again we read in the Constitution *Lumen Gentium,* "In order that we might be unceasingly renewed in him (cf. Eph 4:23), he has shared with us his Spirit who, existing as one and the same being in the head and in the members, gives life to, unifies and moves the whole body. This he does in such a way that his work could be compared by the Fathers to the function which the soul as the principle of life fulfills in the human body." And in another particularly significant text which is helpful in understanding not only the organic nature proper to ecclesial communion but also its aspect of growth toward perfect communion, the Council writes: "The Spirit dwells in the Church and in the hearts of the Faithful, as in a temple (cf. 1 Cor 3:16; 6:19). In them he prays and bears witness that they are adopted sons (cf. Gal 4:6; Rom 8:15-16, 26). Guiding the Church in the way of all truth (cf. Jn 16:13) and unifying her in communion and in the works of service, he bestows upon her varied hierarchical and charismatic gifts and adorns her with the fruits of his grace (cf. Eph 4:11-12; 1 Cor 12:4; Gal 5:22). By the power of the Gospel he makes the Church grow, perpetually renews her, and leads her to perfect union with her Spouse. The Spirit and the Bride both say to the Lord Jesus, 'Come!'" (cf. Rev 22:17).

Church communion then is a gift, a great gift of the Holy Spirit, to be gratefully accepted by the lay faithful, and at the same time to be lived with a deep sense of responsibility. This is concretely realized through their participation in the life and mission of the Church, to whose service the lay faithful put their varied and complementary ministries and charisms.

A member of the lay faithful "can never remain in isolation from the community, but must live in a continual interaction with others, with a lively sense of fellowship, rejoicing in an equal dignity and common commitment to bring to fruition the immense treasure that each has inherited. The Spirit of the Lord gives a vast variety of charisms, inviting people to assume different ministries and forms of service and reminding them, as he reminds all people in their relationship in the Church, that what distinguishes persons is *not an increase in dignity,* but *a special and complementary capacity for service. . . .* Thus, the charisms, the ministries, the different forms of service exercised by the lay faithful exist in communion and on behalf of communion. They are treasures that complement one another for the good of all and are under the wise guidance of their Pastors."

Ministries and Charisms, the Spirit's Gifts to the Church

21. The Second Vatican Council speaks of the ministries and charisms as the gifts of the Holy Spirit which are given for the building up of the Body of Christ and for its mission of salvation in the world. Indeed, the Church is directed and guided by the Holy Spirit, who lavishes diverse hierarchical and charismatic gifts on all the baptized, calling them to be, each in an individual way, active and co-responsible.

We now turn our thoughts to ministries and charisms as they directly relate to the lay faithful and to their participation in the life of Church-Communion.

Ministries, Offices and Roles

The ministries which exist and are at work at this time in the Church are all, even in their variety of forms, a participation in Jesus Christ's own ministry as the Good Shepherd who lays down his life for the sheep (cf. Jn 10:11), the humble servant who gives himself without reserve for the salvation of all (cf. Mk 10:45). The Apostle Paul is quite clear in speaking about the ministerial constitution of the Church in apostolic times. In his First Letter to the Corinthians he writes: "And God has appointed in the Church first apostles, second prophets, third teachers . . ." (1 Cor 12:28). In his Letter to the Ephesians we read: "But the grace was given to each of us according to the measure of Christ's gift. . . . And his gifts were that some should be apostles, some prophets, some evangelists, some pastors and teachers, to equip the saints for the work of ministry, for building up the body of Christ, until we all attain to the unity of the faith and of the knowledge of the Son of God, to mature manhood, to the measure of the stature of the fullness of Christ" (Eph 4:7, 11-13; cf. Rom 12:4-8). These and other New Testament texts indicate the diversity of ministries as well as of gifts and ecclesial tasks.

The Ministries Derived from Holy Orders

22. In a primary position in the Church are the *ordained ministries,* that is, the ministries *that come from the Sacrament of Orders.* In fact, with the mandate to make disciples of all nations (cf. Mt 28:19), the Lord Jesus chose and constituted the apostles—seed of the People of the New Covenant and origin of the Hierarchy—to form and to rule the priestly people. The mission of the Apostles, which the Lord Jesus continues to entrust to the Pastors of his people, is a true service, significantly referred to in Sacred Scripture as *diakonia,* namely, service or ministry. The ministries receive the charism of the Holy Spirit from the Risen Christ, in uninterrupted succession from the apostles, through the Sacrament of Orders: from him they receive the authority and sacred power to serve the Church, acting in *persona Christi Capitis* ("in the person of Christ, the Head") and to gather her in the Holy Spirit through the Gospel and the Sacraments.

The ordained ministries, apart from the persons who receive them, are a grace for the entire Church. These ministries express and realize a participation in the priesthood of Jesus Christ that is different, not simply in degree but in essence, from the participation given to all the lay faithful through Baptism and Confirmation. On the other hand, the ministerial priesthood, as the Second Vatican Council recalls, essentially has the royal priesthood of all the faithful as its aim and is ordered to it.

For this reason, so as to assure and to increase communion in the Church, particularly in those places where there is a diversity and complementarity of ministries, Pastors must always acknowledge that their ministry is fundamentally ordered to the service of the entire People of God (cf. Heb 5:1). The lay faithful, in turn, must acknowledge that the ministerial priesthood is totally necessary for their participation in the mission in the Church.

The Ministries, Offices and Roles of the Lay Faithful

23. The Church's mission of salvation in the world is realized not only by the ministers in virtue of the Sacrament of Orders but also by all the lay faithful; indeed, because of their Baptismal state and their specific vocation, in the measure proper to each person, the lay faithful participate in the priestly, prophetic and kingly mission of Christ.

The Pastors, therefore, ought to acknowledge and foster the ministries, the offices and roles of the lay faithful that find their *foundation in the Sacraments of Baptism and Confirmation,* indeed, for a good many of them, *in the Sacrament of Matrimony.*

When necessity and expediency in the Church require it, the Pastors, according to established norms from universal law, can entrust to the lay faithful certain offices and roles that are connected to their pastoral ministry but do not require the character of Orders. The Code of Canon Law states: "When the necessity of the Church warrants it and when ministers are lacking, lay persons, even if they are not lectors or acolytes, can also supply for certain of their offices, namely, to exercise the ministry of the word, to preside over liturgical prayers, to confer Baptism, and to distribute Holy Communion in accord with the prescriptions of the law." However, *the exercise of such tasks does not make Pastors of the lay faithful:* in fact, a person is not a minister simply in performing a task, but through sacramental ordination. Only the Sacrament of Orders gives the ordained minister a particular participation in the office of Christ, the Shepherd and Head, and in his Eternal Priesthood. The task exercised in virtue of supply takes its legitimacy formally and immediately from the official deputation given by the Pastors, as well as from its concrete exercise under the guidance of ecclesiastical authority.

The recent Synodal Assembly has provided an extensive and meaningful overview of the situation in the Church on the ministries, offices, and roles of the baptized. The Fathers have manifested a deep appreciation for the contribution of the lay faithful, both women and men, in the work of the apostolate, in evangelization, sanctification, and the Christian animation of temporal affairs, as well as their generous willingness to supply in situations of emergency and chronic necessity.

Following the liturgical renewal promoted by the Council, the lay faithful themselves have acquired a more lively awareness of the tasks that they fulfill in the liturgical assembly and its preparation, and have become more widely disposed to fulfill them: the liturgical celebration, in fact, is a sacred action not simply of the clergy, but of the entire assembly. It is, therefore, natural that the tasks not proper to the ordained ministers be fulfilled by the lay faithful. In this way there is a natural transition from an effective involvement of the lay faithful in the liturgical action to that of announcing the word of God and pastoral care.

In the same Synod Assembly, however, a critical judgment was voiced along with these positive elements, about a too-indiscriminate use of the word "ministry," the confusion and the equating of the common priesthood and the ministerial priesthood, the lack of observance of ecclesiastical laws and norms, the arbitrary interpretation of the concept of "supply," the tendency towards a "clericalization" of the lay faithful and the risk of creating, in reality, an ecclesial structure of parallel service to that founded on the Sacrament of Orders.

Precisely to overcome these dangers the Synod Fathers have insisted on the necessity to express with greater clarity, and with a more precise terminology, both *the unity of the Church's mission* in which all the baptized participate, and the substantial *diversity of the ministry* of Pastors which is rooted in the Sacrament of Orders, all the while respecting the other ministries, offices and roles in the Church, which are rooted in the Sacraments of Baptism and Confirmation.

. . . In the context of Church mission, then, the Lord entrusts a great part of the responsibility to the lay faithful, in communion with all other members of the People of God. This fact, fully understood by the Fathers of the Second Vatican Council, recurred with renewed clarity and increased vigor in all the works of the Synod: "Indeed, Pastors know how much the lay faithful contribute to the welfare of the entire Church. They also know that they themselves were not established by Christ to undertake alone the entire saving mission of the Church towards the world, but they understand that it is their exalted office to be shepherds of the lay faithful and also to recognize the latter's services and charisms that all according to their proper roles may cooperate in this common undertaking with one heart."

Proclaiming the Gospel

33. The lay faithful, precisely because they are members of the Church, have the vocation and mission of proclaiming the Gospel: they are prepared for this work by the sacraments of Christian initiation and by the gifts of the Holy Spirit.

In a very clear and significant passage from the Second Vatican Council we read: "As sharers in the mission of Christ, priest, prophet and king, the lay faithful have an active part to play in the life and activity of the Church. . . . Strengthened by their active participation in the liturgical life of their community, they are eager to do their share in apostolic works of that community. They lead to the Church people who are perhaps far removed from it; they earnestly cooperate in presenting the Word of God, especially by means of catechetical instruction; and offer their special skills to make the care of souls and the administration of the temporal goods of the Church more efficient."

The entire mission of the Church, then, is concentrated and manifested in *evangelization*. Through the winding passages of history the Church has made her way under the grace and the command of Jesus Christ: "Go into all the world and preach the gospel to the whole creation" (Mk 16:15) ". . . and lo, I am with you always, until the close of the age" (Mt 28:20). "To evangelize," writes Paul VI, "is the grace and vocation proper to the Church, her most profound identity."

Through evangelization the Church is built up into a *community of faith:* more precisely, into a community that *confesses* the faith in full adherence to the Word of God which is *celebrated* in the Sacraments, and *lived* in charity, the principle of Christian moral existence. In fact, the "good news" is directed to stirring a person to a conversion of heart and life and a clinging to Jesus Christ as Lord and Saviour; to disposing a person to receive Baptism and the Eucharist and to strengthen a person in the prospect and realization of new life according to the Spirit.

Certainly the command of Jesus: "Go and preach the Gospel" always maintains its vital value and its ever-pressing obligation. Nevertheless, the *present situation,* not only of the world but also of many parts of the Church, *absolutely demands that the word of Christ receive a more ready and generous obedience.* Every disciple is personally called by name; no disciple can withhold making a response: "Woe to me, if I do not preach the gospel" (1 Cor 9:16).

The Hour Has Come for a Re-Evangelization

34. Whole countries and nations where religion and the Christian life were formerly flourishing and capable of fostering a viable and working community of faith are now put to a hard test, and in some cases, are even undergoing a radical transformation, as a result of a constant spreading of an indifference to religion, of secularism and atheism. This particularly concerns countries and nations of the so-called First World, in which economic well-being and consumerism, even if coexistent with a tragic situation of poverty and misery, inspires and sustains a life lived "as if God did not exist." This indifference to religion and the practice of religion devoid of true meaning in the face of life's very serious problems are not less worrying and upsetting when compared with declared atheism. Sometimes the Christian faith as well, while maintaining some of the externals of its tradition and rituals, tends to be separated from those moments of human existence which have the most significance, such as birth, suffering, and death. In such cases, the questions and formidable enigmas posed by these situations, if remaining without responses, expose contemporary people to an inconsolable delusion or to the temptation of eliminating the truly humanizing dimension of life implicit in these problems.

On the other hand, in other regions or nations many vital traditions of piety and popular forms of Christian religion are still conserved; but today this moral and spiritual patrimony runs the risk of being dispersed under the impact of a multi-

plicity of processes, including secularization and the spread of sects. Only a re-evangelization can assure the growth of a clear and deep faith, and serve to make these traditions a force for authentic freedom.

Without doubt a mending of the Christian fabric of society is urgently needed in all parts of the world. But for this to come about what is needed is to *first remake the Christian fabric of the ecclesial community itself* present in these countries and nations.

At this moment the lay faithful, in virtue of their participation in the prophetic mission of Christ, are fully part of this work of the Church. Their responsibility, in particular, is to testify how the Christian faith constitutes the only fully valid response—consciously perceived and stated by all in varying degrees—to the problems and hopes that life poses to every person and society. This will be possible if the lay faithful will know how to overcome in themselves the separation of the Gospel from life, to again take up in their daily activities in family, work and society, an integrated approach to life that is fully brought about by the inspiration and strength of the Gospel.

. . . In the case of coming generations, the lay faithful must offer the very valuable contribution, more necessary than ever, of a *systematic work in catechesis.* The Synod Fathers have gratefully taken note of the work of catechists, acknowledging that they "have a task that carries great importance in animating ecclesial communities." It goes without saying that Christian parents are the primary and irreplaceable catechists of their children, a task for which they are given the grace by the Sacrament of Matrimony. At the same time, however, we all ought to be aware of the "rights" that each baptized person has to being instructed, educated, and supported in the faith and the Christian life.

Go into the Whole World

35. While pointing out and experiencing the present urgency for a re-evangelization, the Church cannot withdraw from *her ongoing mission of bringing the gospel to the multitudes*—the millions and millions of men and women—*who as yet do not know Christ*

the Redeemer of humanity. In a specific way this is the missionary work that Jesus entrusted and again entrusts each day to his Church.

The activity of the lay faithful, who are always present in these surroundings, is revealed in these days as increasingly necessary and valuable. As it stands, the command of the Lord "Go into the whole world" is continuing to find a generous response from laypersons who are ready to leave familiar surroundings, their work, their region or country, at least for a determined time, to go into mission territory. Even Christian married couples, in imitation of Aquila and Priscilla (cf. Acts 18; Rom 16:3 ff.), are offering a comforting testimony of impassioned love for Christ and the Church through their valuable presence in mission lands. A true missionary presence is exercised even by those who for various reasons live in countries or surroundings where the Church is not yet established and bear witness to the faith.

However, at present the missionary concern is taking on such extensive and serious proportions for the Church that only a truly consolidated effort to assume responsibility by all members of the Church, both individuals and communities, can lead to the hope for a more fruitful response.

The invitation addressed by the Second Vatican Council to the particular Church retains all its value, even demanding at present a more extensive and more decisive acceptance: "Since the particular Churches are bound to mirror the universal Church as perfectly as possible, let them be fully aware that they have been sent also to those who do not believe in Christ."

The Church today ought to take *a giant step forward* in her evangelization effort, and enter into *a new stage of history* in her missionary dynamism. In a world where the lessening of distance makes the world increasingly smaller, the Church community ought to strengthen the bonds among its members, exchange vital energies and means, and commit itself as a group to a unique and common mission of proclaiming and living the Gospel. "So-called younger Churches have need of the strength of the older Churches and the older ones need the witness and impulse of the younger, so that individual Churches receive the riches of other Churches."

In this area, younger Churches are finding that an essential and undeniable element in the *founding of Churches* is the formation not only of local clergy but also of a mature and responsible lay faithful: in this way the community which itself has been evangelized goes forth into a new region of the world so that it too might respond to the mission of proclaiming and bearing witness to the Gospel of Christ.

The Synod Fathers have mentioned that the lay faithful can favour the relations which ought to be established with followers of *various religions* through their example in the situations in which they live and in their activities: "Throughout the world today the Church lives among people of various religions. . . . All the Faithful, especially the lay faithful who live among the people of other religions, whether living in their native region or in lands as migrants, ought to be for all a sign of the Lord and his Church, in a way adapted to the actual living situation of each place. Dialogue among religions has a preeminent part, for it leads to love and mutual respect, and takes away, or at least diminishes, prejudices among the followers of various religions and promotes unity and friendship among peoples."

What is first needed for the evangelization of the world are *those who will evangelize.* In this regard everyone, beginning with the Christian family, must feel the responsibility to foster the birth and growth of *vocations,* both priestly and religious as well as in the lay state, *specifically directed to the missions.* This should be done by relying on every appropriate means, but without ever neglecting the privileged means of prayer, according to the very words of the Lord Jesus: "The harvest is plentiful, but the labourers are few; pray therefore the Lord of the harvest to send out labourers into his harvest!" (Mt 9:37, 38).

To Live the Gospel Serving the Person and Society

36. In both accepting and proclaiming the Gospel in the power of the Spirit the Church becomes at one and the same time an "evangelizing and evangelized" community, and for this very reason she is made the *servant of all.* In her the lay faithful par-

ticipate in the mission of service to the person and society. Without doubt the Church has the Kingdom of God as her supreme goal, of which "she on earth is its seed and beginning," and is therefore totally consecrated to the glorification of the Father. However, the Kingdom is the source of full liberation and total salvation for all people: with this in mind, then, the Church walks and lives, intimately bound in a real sense to their history.

Having received the responsibility of manifesting to the world the mystery of God that shines forth in Jesus Christ, *the Church likewise awakens one person to another,* giving a sense of one's existence, opening each to the whole truth about the individual and of each person's final destiny. From this perspective the Church is called, in virtue of her very mission of evangelization, to serve all humanity. Such service is rooted primarily in the extraordinary and profound fact that "through the Incarnation the Son of God has united himself in some fashion to every person."

For this reason the person "is the primary route that the Church must travel in fulfilling her mission: the individual is the *primary and fundamental way for the Church,* the way traced out by Christ himself, the way that leads invariably through the mystery of the Incarnation and Redemption."

Promoting the Dignity of the Person

37. *To rediscover and make others rediscover the inviolable dignity of every human person* makes up an essential task, in a certain sense, the central and unifying task of the service which the Church, and the lay faithful in her, are called to render to the human family.

Among all other earthly beings, *only a man or a woman is a "person,"* a conscious and free being and, precisely for this reason, the "center and summit" of all that exists on the earth.

The dignity of the person is *the most precious possession* of an individual. As a result, the value of one person transcends all the material world. The words of Jesus, "For what does it profit a man, to gain the whole world and to forfeit his life?" (Mk 8:36) contain an enlightening and stirring statement about the individual: value comes not from

what a person "has" even if the person possessed the whole world!—as much as from what a person "is": the goods of the world do not count as much as the good of the person, the good which is the person individually.

The dignity of the person is manifested in all its radiance when the person's origin and destiny are considered: created by God in his image and likeness as well as redeemed by the most precious blood of Christ, the person is called to be a "child in the Son" and a living temple of the Spirit, destined for the eternal life of blessed communion with God. For this reason every violation of the personal dignity of the human being cries out in vengeance to God and is an offence against the Creator of the individual.

In virtue of a personal dignity the human being is *always a value as an individual,* and as such demands being considered and treated as a person and never, on the contrary, considered and treated as an object to be used, or as a means, or as a thing.

The dignity of the person constitutes *the foundation of the equality of all people among themselves.* As a result all forms of discrimination are totally unacceptable, especially those forms which unfortunately continue to divide and degrade the human family, from those based on race or economics to those social and cultural, from political to geographic, etc. Each discrimination constitutes an absolutely intolerable injustice, not so much for the tensions and the conflicts that can be generated in the social sphere, as much as for the dishonour inflicted on the dignity of the person: not only to the dignity of the individual who is the victim of the injustice, but still more to the one who commits the injustice.

Just as personal dignity is the foundation of equality of all people among themselves, so it is also *the foundation of participation and solidarity of all people among themselves:* dialogue and communion are rooted ultimately in what people "are," first and foremost, rather than on what people "have."

The dignity of the person is the indestructible property of *every human being.* The force of this affirmation is based on the *uniqueness and irrepeatibility of every person.* From it flows that the individual can never be reduced by all that seeks to crush and to annihilate the person into the anonymity that comes from collectivity, institutions, structures, and systems. As an individual, a person is not a number or simply a link in a chain, nor even less, an impersonal element in some system. The most radical and elevating affirmation of the value of every human being was made by the Son of God in his becoming man in the womb of a woman, as we continue to be reminded each Christmas.

Respecting the Inviolable Right to Life

38. In effect the acknowledgment of the personal dignity of every human being demands *the respect, the defence, and the promotion of the rights of the human person.* It is a question of inherent, universal, and inviolable rights. No one, no individual, no group, no authority, no State, can change—let alone eliminate—them because such rights find their source in God himself.

The inviolability of the person which is a reflection of the absolute inviolability of God finds its primary and fundamental expression in the *inviolability of human life.* Above all, the common outcry, which is justly made on behalf of human rights—for example, the right to health, to home, to work, to family, to culture—is false and illusory if *the right to life,* the most basic and fundamental right and the condition for all other personal rights, is not defended with maximum determination.

The Church has never yielded in the face of all the violations that the right to life of every human being has received, and continues to receive, both from individuals and from those in authority. The human being is entitled to such rights, *in every phase of development,* from conception until natural death; and in *every condition,* whether healthy or sick, whole or handicapped, rich or poor. The Second Vatican Council openly proclaimed: "All offences against life itself, such as every kind of murder, genocide, abortion, euthanasia, and willful suicide; all violations of the integrity of the human person, such as mutilation, physical, and mental torture, undue psychological pressures; all offences against human dignity, such as subhuman living conditions, arbitrary imprisonment, deportation, slavery, prostitution, the selling of women

and children, degrading working conditions where men are treated as mere tools for profit rather than free and responsible persons; all these and the like are certainly criminal: they poison human society; and they do more harm to those who practice them than those who suffer from the injury. Moreover, they are a supreme dishonour to the Creator."

If, indeed, everyone has the mission and responsibility of acknowledging the personal dignity of every human being and of defending the right to life, some lay faithful are given a particular title to this task: such as *parents, teachers, health workers, and the many who hold economic and political power.*

. . . The enormous development of *biological and medical science,* united to an amazing *power in technology,* today provides possibilities on the very frontier of human life which imply new responsibilities. In fact, today humanity is in the position not only of "observing" but even "exercising a control over" human life at its very beginning and in its first stages of development.

. . . Today maximum vigilance must be exercised by everyone in the face of the phenomenon of the concentration of power and technology. In fact such a concentration has a tendency to manipulate not only the biological essence but the very content of people's consciences and life styles, thereby worsening the condition of entire peoples by discrimination and marginalization.

Free to Call upon the Name of the Lord

39. Respect for the dignity of the person, which implies the defence and promotion of human rights, demands the recognition of the religious dimension of the individual. This is not simply a requirement "concerning matters of faith," but a requirement that finds itself inextricably bound up with the very reality of the individual. In fact, the individual's relation to God is a constitutive element of the very "being" and "existence" of an individual: it is in God that we "live, move and have our being" (Acts 17:28). Even if not all believe this truth, the many who are convinced of it have the right to be respected for their faith and for their life-choice, individual and commu-

nal, that flows from that faith. This is the *right of freedom of conscience and religious freedom,* the effective acknowledgment of which is among the highest goods and the most serious duties of every people that truly wishes to assure the good of the person and society. "Religious freedom, an essential requirement of the dignity of every person, is a cornerstone of the structure of human rights, and for this reason an irreplaceable factor in the good of individuals and of the whole of society, as well as of the personal fulfillment of each individual. It follows that the freedom of individuals and of communities to profess and practice their religion is an essential element for peaceful human coexistence. . . . The civil and social right to religious freedom, inasmuch as it touches the most intimate sphere of the spirit, is a point of reference for the other fundamental rights and in some way becomes a measure of them."

The Family: Where the Duty to Society Begins

40. The human person has an inherent social dimension which calls a person from the innermost depths of self to *communion* with others and to the *giving* of self to others: "God, who has fatherly concern for everyone, has willed that all people should form one family and treat one another in a spirit of brotherhood." Thus *society* as a fruit and sign of the *social nature* of the individual reveals its whole truth in being a *community of persons.*

Thus the result is an interdependence and reciprocity between the person and society: all that is accomplished in favour of the person is also a service rendered to society, and all that is done in favour of society redounds to the benefit of the person. For this reason the duty of the lay faithful in the apostolate of the temporal order is always to be viewed both from its meaning of service to the person founded on the individual's uniqueness and irrepeatibility as well as on the meaning of service to all people which is inseparable from it.

The first and basic expression of the social dimension of the person, then, is *the married couple and the family:* "But God did not create man a solitary being. From the beginning 'male and female

he created them'" (Gen 1:27). This partnership of man and woman constitutes the first form of communion between persons. Jesus is concerned to restore integral dignity to the married couple and solidity to the family (Mt 19:3-9). Saint Paul shows the deep rapport between marriage and the mystery of Christ and the Church (cf. Eph 5:22-6:4; Col 3:18-21; 1 Pt 3:1-7).

The *lay faithful's duty to society primarily begins* in marriage and in the family. This duty can only be fulfilled adequately with the conviction of the unique and irreplaceable value that the family has in the development of society and the Church herself.

Charity: The Soul and Sustenance of Solidarity

41. Service to society is expressed and realized in the most diverse ways, from those spontaneous and informal to those more structured, from help given to individuals to those destined for various groups and communities of persons.

The whole Church as such, is directly called to the service of charity: "In the very early days the Church added the *agape* to the Eucharistic Supper, and thus showed herself to be wholly united around Christ by the bond of charity. So too, in all ages, she is recognized by this sign of love, and while she rejoices in the undertakings of others, she claims works of charity as her own inalienable duty and right. For this reason, mercy to the poor and the sick, works of charity and mutual aid intended to relieve human needs of every kind, are held in special honour in the Church." *Charity towards one's neighbor,* through contemporary forms of the traditional spiritual and corporal works of mercy, represent the most immediate, ordinary and habitual ways that lead to the Christian animation of the temporal order, the specific duty of the lay faithful.

Through charity towards one's neighbor, the lay faithful exercise and manifest their participation in the kingship of Christ, that is, in the power of the Son of man who "came not to be served but to serve" (Mk 10:45). They live and manifest such a kingship in a most simple yet exalted manner, possible for everyone at all times because charity is the highest gift offered by the Spirit for building up the Church (cf. 1 Cor 13:13) and for the good of humanity. In fact, *charity gives life and sustains the works of solidarity that look to the total needs of the human being.*

Public Life: For Everyone and by Everyone

42. A charity that loves and serves the person is never able to be separated from *justice.* Each in its own way demands the full, effective acknowledgment of the rights of the individual, to which society is ordered in all its structures and institutions.

In order to achieve their task directed to the Christian animation of the temporal order, in the sense of serving persons and society, the lay faithful *are never to relinquish their participation in "public life,"* that is, in the many different economic, social, legislative, administrative, and cultural areas, which are intended to promote organically and institutionally the *common good.* The Synod Fathers have repeatedly affirmed that every person has a right and duty to participate in public life, albeit in a diversity and complementarity of forms, levels, tasks, and responsibilities. Charges of careerism, idolatry of power, egoism, and corruption that are oftentimes directed at persons in government, parliaments, the ruling classes, or political parties, as well as the common opinion that participating in politics is an absolute moral danger, does not in the least justify either skepticism or an absence on the part of Christians in public life.

Placing the Individual at the Center of Socio-Economic Life

43. Service to society on the part of the lay faithful finds its essence in the *socio-economic question,* which depends on the organization of *work.* The basis for the social doctrine of the Church is the principle of *the universal destination of goods.* According to the plan of God the goods of the earth are offered to all people and to each individual as a means towards the development of a truly human life. At the service of this destination of goods is

private property, which—precisely for this purpose—possesses an *intrinsic social function.* Concretely the *work* of man and woman represents the most common and most immediate instrument for the development of economic life, an instrument that constitutes at one and the same time a right and a duty for every individual.

Once again, all of this comes to mind in a particular way in the mission of the lay faithful. The Second Vatican Council formulates in general terms the purpose and criterion of their presence and their action: "In the socio-economic realm the dignity and total vocation of the human person must be honoured and advanced along with the welfare of society as a whole, for man is the source, the center, and the purpose of all socio-economic life."

In the context of the transformations taking place in the world of economy and work which are a cause of concern, the lay faithful have the responsibility of being in the forefront in working out a solution to the very serious problems of growing unemployment; to fight for the most opportune overcoming of numerous injustices that come from organizations of work which lack a proper goal; to make the workplace become a community of persons respected in their uniqueness and in their right to participation; to develop new solidarity among those that participate in a common work; to raise up new forms of entrepreneurship and to look again at systems of commerce, finance and exchange of technology.

To such an end the lay faithful must accomplish their work with professional competence, with human honesty, and with a Christian spirit, and especially as a way of their own sanctification, according to the explicit invitation of the Council: "By work an individual ordinarily provides for self and family, is joined in fellowship to others, and renders them service; and is enabled to exercise genuine charity and be a partner in the work of bringing divine creation to perfection. Moreover, we know that through work offered to God an individual is associated with the redemptive work of Jesus Christ, whose labour with his hands at Nazareth greatly ennobled the dignity of work."

Today in an ever-increasingly acute way, the *so-called "ecological" question* poses itself in relation to socio-economic life and work. Certainly humanity has received from God himself the task of "dominating" the created world and "cultivating the garden" of the world. But this is a task that humanity must carry out in respect for the divine image received, and, therefore, with intelligence and with love, assuming responsibility for the gifts that God has bestowed and continues to bestow. Humanity has in its possession a gift that must be passed on to future generations, if possible, passed on in better condition. Even these future generations are the recipients of the Lord's gifts: "The dominion granted to humanity by the Creator is not an absolute power, nor can one speak of a freedom to 'use and misuse,' or to dispose of things as one pleases. The limitation imposed from the beginning by the Creator himself and expressed symbolically by the prohibition not to 'eat of the fruit of the tree' (cf. Gen 2:16-17) shows clearly enough that, when it comes to the natural world, we are subject not only to biological laws but also to moral ones, which cannot be violated with impunity. A true concept of development cannot ignore the use of the things of nature, the renewability of resources and the consequences of haphazard industrialization—three considerations which alert our consciences to the *moral dimension* of development."

Evangelizing Culture and the Cultures of Humanity

44. Service to the individual and to human society is expressed and finds its fulfillment through *the creation and the transmission of culture,* which especially in our time constitutes one of the more serious tasks of living together as a human family and of social evolution. In light of the Council, we mean by "culture" all those "factors which go to the refining and developing of humanity's diverse spiritual and physical endowments. It means the efforts of the human family to bring the world under its control through its knowledge and its labour; to humanize social life both in the family and in the whole civic community through the improvement of customs and institutions; to express through its works the great spiritual experiences and aspirations of all peoples throughout the ages; finally, to communicate and to preserve them to be an inspiration for the progress of many, indeed of the whole human race." In this sense, culture must be held as the common good of every people, the expression of its dignity, liberty, and creativity, and the testimony of its course through history. In particular, only from within and through culture does the Christian faith become a part of history and the creator of history.

Women and Men

49. The Synod Fathers gave special attention to the status and role of women, with two purposes in mind: to themselves acknowledge and to invite all others to once again acknowledge the indispensable contribution of women to the building up of the Church and the development of society. They wished as well to work on a more specific analysis of women's participation in the life and mission of the Church.

Making reference to Pope John XXIII, who saw women's greater consciousness of their proper dignity and their entrance into public life as signs of our times, the Synod Fathers, when confronted with the various forms of discrimination and marginization to which women are subjected simply because they are women, time and time again strongly affirmed the urgency to defend and to promote the *personal dignity of woman,* and consequently, her equality with man.

. . . In particular when speaking of *active and responsible participation in the life and mission of the Church,* emphasis should be placed on what has already been stated and clearly urged by the Second Vatican Council: "Since in our days women are taking an increasingly active share in the whole life of society, it is very important that they participate more widely also in the various fields of the Church's apostolate."

The awareness that women with their own gifts and tasks have *their own specific vocation,* has increased and been deepened in the years following the Council and has found its fundamental inspiration in the Gospel and the Church's history. In fact, for the believer the Gospel, namely, the word and example of Jesus Christ, remains the necessary and decisive point of reference. In no other moment in history is this fact more fruitful and innovative.

Though not called to the apostolate of the Twelve, and thereby, to the ministerial priesthood, many women, nevertheless, accompanied Jesus in his ministry and assisted the group of Apostles (cf. Lk 8:2-3), were present at the foot of the Cross (cf. Lk 23:49), assisted at the burial of Christ (cf. Lk 23:55), received and transmitted the message of resurrection on Easter morn (cf. Lk 24:1-10), and prayed with the apostles in the Cenacle awaiting Pentecost (cf. Acts 1:14).

Anthropological and Theological Foundations

50. The condition that will assure the rightful presence of woman in the Church and in society is a more penetrating and accurate consideration of the *anthropological foundation for masculinity and femininity* with the intent of clarifying woman's personal identity in relation to man, that is, a diversity yet mutual complementarity, not only as it concerns roles to be held and functions to be performed, but also, and more deeply, as it concerns her make-up and meaning as a person.

The Synod Fathers have deeply felt this requirement, maintaining that "the anthropological and theological foundations for resolving questions about the true significance and dignity of each sex require deeper study."

Through committing herself to a reflection on the anthropological and theological basis of femininity, the Church enters the historic process of the various movements for the promotion of woman, and, in going to the very basic aspect of woman as a personal being, provides her most precious contribution. But even before this the Church intends, in such a way, to obey God, who created the individual "in his image," "male and female he created them" (Gen 1:27) and who intended that they would accept the call of God to come to know, reverence and live his plan. It is a plan that "from the beginning" has been indelibly imprinted in the very being of the human person—men and women—and, therefore, in the make-up, meaning and deepest workings of the individual. This most

wise and loving plan must be explored to discover all its richness of content—a richness that "from the beginning" came to be progressively manifested and realized in the whole history of salvation, and was brought to completion in "the fullness of time," when "God sent his Son, born of a woman" (Gal 4:4). That "fullness" continues in history: God's plan for woman is read and is to be read within the context of the faith of the Church, and also, in the lives lived by so many Christian women today. Without forgetting the help that can come from different human sciences and cultures, researchers because of an informed discernment will be able to help gather and clarify the values and requirements that belong to the enduring essential aspects of women and those bound to evolve in history. The Second Vatican Council reminds us: "The Church maintains that beneath all changes there are many realities which do not change; these find their ultimate foundation in Christ, who is the same yesterday, and today, and forever" (cf. Heb 13:8). The Apostolic Letter on the Dignity and Vocation of Woman gives much attention to the anthropological and theological foundation of woman's dignity as a person. The document seeks to again treat and develop the catechetical reflections of the Wednesday General Audiences devoted over a long period of time to the "theology of the body," while at the same time fulfilling a promise made in the Encyclical *Redemptoris Mater* and serving as a response to the request of the Synod Fathers.

May the reading of the Apostolic Letter *Mulieris Dignitatem,* in particular, as a biblical theological meditation, be an incentive for everyone, both women and men, and especially for those who devote their lives to the human sciences and theological disciplines, to pursue on the basis of the personal dignity of man and woman and their mutual relationship, a critical study to better and more deeply understand the values and specific gifts of femininity and masculinity, not only in the surroundings of social living but also and above all in living as Christians and as members of the Church.

This meditation on the anthropological and theological foundations of women ought to enlighten and guide the Christian response to the most frequently asked questions, oftentimes so crucial, on *the "place" that women can have and ought to have in the Church and in society.*

It is quite clear from the words and attitude of Christ, which are normative for the Church, that no discrimination exists on the level of an individual's relation to Christ, in which "there is neither male nor female; for you are all one in Christ Jesus" (Gal 3:28) and on the level of participation in the Church's life of grace and holiness, as Joel's prophecy fulfilled at Pentecost wonderfully attests: "I will pour out my spirit on all flesh; your sons and daughters shall prophecy" (Joel 3:1; cf. Acts 2:17ff.). As the Apostolic Letter on the Dignity and Vocation of Woman reads: "Both women and men . . . are equally capable of receiving the outpouring of divine truth and love in the Holy Spirit. Both receive his salvific and sanctifying 'visits.'"

Mission in the Church and in the World

51. In speaking about participation in the apostolic mission of the Church, there is no doubt that in virtue of Baptism and Confirmation, a woman—as well as a man—is made a sharer in the threefold mission of Jesus Christ, Priest, Prophet, and King, and is thereby charged and given the ability to fulfill the fundamental apostolate of the Church: *evangelization.* However, a woman is called to put to work in this apostolate the "gifts" which are properly hers: first of all, the gift that is her very dignity as a person exercised in word and testimony of life, gifts therefore, connected with her vocation as a woman.

In her participation in the life and mission of the Church a woman cannot receive the *Sacrament of Orders,* and therefore, cannot fulfill the proper function of the ministerial priesthood. This is a practice that the Church has always found in the expressed will of Christ, totally free and sovereign, who called only men to be his apostles; a practice that can be understood from the rapport between Christ, the Spouse, and his Bride, the Church. Here we are in the area of *function,* not of *dignity* and *holiness.* In fact, it must be maintained: "Although the Church possesses a 'hierarchical' structure, nevertheless this structure is totally ordered to the holiness of Christ's members."

However, as Paul VI has already said, "We cannot change what our Lord did, nor his call to women; but we can recognize and promote the role of women in the mission of evangelization and in the life of the Christian community."

Above all the *acknowledgment in theory* of the active and responsible presence of woman in the Church must be *realized in practice.* With this in mind this Exhortation addressed to the lay faithful with its deliberate and repeated use of the terms "women and men," must be read. Furthermore the revised Code of Canon Law contains many provisions on the participation of women in the life and mission of the Church: they are provisions that must be more commonly known and, according to the diverse sensibilities of culture and opportuneness in a pastoral situation, be realized with greater timeliness and determination.

The Presence and Collaboration of Men Together with Women

52. Many voices were raised in the Synod Hall expressing the fear that excessive insistence given to the status and role of women would lead to an unacceptable omission, that, in point, regarding *men.* In reality, various sectors in the Church must lament the absence or the scarcity of the presence of men, some of whom abdicate their proper Church responsibilities, allowing them to be fulfilled only by women. Such instances are participation in the liturgical prayer of the Church, education and, in particular, catechesis of their own sons and daughters and other children, presence at religious and cultural meetings, and collaboration in charitable and missionary initiatives.

Therefore, the coordinated presence of both men and women is to be pastorally urged so that the participation of the lay faithful in the salvific mission of the Church might be rendered more rich, complete, and harmonious.

The fundamental reason that requires and explains the presence and the collaboration of both men and women is not only, as it was just emphasized, the major source of meaning and efficacy in the pastoral action of the Church, nor even less is it the simple sociological fact of sharing a life together as human beings, which is natural for man and woman. It is, rather, the original plan of the Creator who from the "beginning" willed the human being to be a "unity of the two," and willed man and woman to be the prime community of persons, source of every other community, and, at the same time, to be a "sign" of that interpersonal communion of love which constitutes the mystical, intimate life of God, One in Three.

Given at Rome, in St. Peter's, on 30 December, the Feast of the Holy Family of Jesus, Mary and Joseph, in the year 1988, the eleventh of my Pontificate.

(Source: On the Vocation and the Mission of the Lay Faithful in the Church and in the World (*Christifideles Laici*), http://www.vatican.va/holy_father/john_paul_ii/apost_exhortations/documents/hf_jp-ii_exh_30121988_christifideles-laici_en.html. Reproduced by permission of Libreria Editrice Vaticana.)

Orthodox Mission Documents

The next two documents are not official Orthodox statements on mission, but come rather from two Orthodox scholars explaining the Orthodox theology of Missions. The reason for using these articles rather than the Orthodox equivalent of papal encyclicals or Conciliar documents is twofold. First, as Petros Vassiliadis points out, it is only in the 1920s after the last encyclical of the Orthodox Patriarchs of Istanbul/Constantinople that Orthodox fully began to engage the modern world represented by other documents in this section. Second, as it engaged that world the Orthodox churches joined the World Council of Churches, and hence are likewise represented in the WCC documents in the next section.

63. The Universal Claims of Orthodoxy and the Particularity of Its Witness in a Pluralistic World, by Petros Vassiliadis

Orthodoxy as an Ecclesial Category, and Its Eschatological Dimension

Orthodoxy is normally defined in confessional or denominational terms, that is, as the Eastern branch of Christianity, which was separated from the West around the beginning of the second millennium C.E. This is at least how the *Oxford Dictionary of the Christian Church* describes the Orthodox Church, as "a family of churches, situated mainly in Eastern Europe: each member Church is independent in its internal administration, but all share the same faith and are in communion with one another, acknowledging the honorary primacy of the Patriarch of Constantinople." This definition no longer holds true. According to its most serious interpreters, Orthodoxy refers to the wholeness of the people of God who share the right conviction [i.e., *orthē doxa*, "right opinion"] concerning the event of God's salvation in Christ and his Church,

and the right expression (*orthopraxid*) of this faith. *Orthodoxia* leads to the maximum possible application in *orthopraxia* of charismatic life in the freedom of the Holy Spirit, in all aspects of daily public life, social and cosmic alike. Everybody is invited by Orthodoxy to transcend confessions and inflexible institutions without necessarily denying them. The late Nikos Nissiotis has reminded us that Orthodoxy is not to be identified only with us Orthodox in the historical sense and with all our limitations and shortcomings:

> We should never forget that this term is given to the one, (holy, catholic and) apostolic church as a whole over against the heretics who, of their own choice, split from the main body of the Church. The term (Orthodoxy) is exclusive for all those, who willingly fall away from the historical stream of life of the One Church but it is inclusive for those who profess their spiritual belonging to that stream.[1]

The term "Orthodoxy," therefore, has more or less ecclesial rather than confessional connotations.[2]

This ecclesial understanding of Orthodoxy was first put forward by the late George Florovsky who, speaking at an ecumenical meeting in the name of the one Church, declared, "The Church is first of all a worshipping community. Worship comes first, doctrine and discipline second. The *lex orandi* has a privileged priority in the life of the Christian Church. The *lex credendi* depends on the devotional experience and vision of the Church."[3]

Elsewhere,[4] I have argued that out of the three main characteristics that generally constitute Orthodox theology, namely its "eucharistic," "trinitarian," and "hesychastic" dimensions, only the first one can bear a universal and ecumenical significance. If the last dimension and important feature marks a decisive development in Eastern Christian theology and spirituality after the final schism between East and West, a development that has determined, together with other factors, the mission of the Orthodox Church in recent history; and if the trinitarian dimension constitutes the supreme expression of Christian theology ever produced by human thought in its attempt to grasp the mystery of God, after Christianity's dynamic encounter with the Greek culture; it was, nevertheless, only because of the eucharistic experience, the matrix of all theology and spirituality of Christianity, that all theological and spiritual climaxes in our Church have been actually achieved.

And the eucharist, heart and centre of Christian liturgy, is always understood in its authentic perception as a proleptic manifestation of the kingdom of God, as symbol and image of an alternative reality, which was conceived before all creation by God the Father in his mystical plan (the *mysterion* in the biblical sense), was inaugurated by our Lord, and is permanently sustained by the Holy Spirit. What is, nevertheless, of paramount and undisputed importance is that this kingdom is expected to culminate at the *eschata*. This, in fact, brings us to the eschatological dimension of the Church.[5] Eschatology constitutes the central and primary aspect of ecclesiology, the beginning of the Church, that which gives her identity, sustains and inspires her in her existence. Hence the priority of the kingdom of God in all ecclesiological considerations. Everything belongs to the kingdom. The Church in her institutional expression does not administer all reality; she only prepares the way to the kingdom, in the sense that she is an image if it. That is why, although to the eyes of the historian and the sociologist the Church is yet another human institution, to the theologian she is primarily a mystery, and we very often call her an icon of the kingdom to come.

Eschatology, however, constitutes also the starting-point of the Church's witness to the world. It is to the merits of modern Orthodox theologians,[6] who reaffirmed the paramount importance of eschatology for Christian theology, although very little has been written about the relationship between the Church's (eschatological) identity and her (historical) mission.[7] The mission of the Church is but a struggle to witness and to apply this eschatological vision of the Church to the historical realities and to the world at large. Christian theology, on the other hand, is about the right balance between history and eschatology. We should never forget that theology and the Church exist not for themselves, but for the world. The tension, therefore, between eschatology and history, or, to put it more sharply, the relationship between the ecclesial community and our pluralistic society, is one of the most important chapters in the Church's witness today.[8]

However, if for Christian theology the Church's ecumenicity and her universal claims are quite simple to establish,[9] it is not at all an easy task to determine her witness in today's pluralistic context, especially in view of her eschatological particularity. In the remaining space I will focus on three areas, in an effort to shed light on the issue we are discussing: (a) the Church's attitude towards modernism,[10] and the whole range of the achievements of the Enlightenment, especially within the framework of post-modernity; (b) the understanding of universalism in Christian mission theology; and (c) the present understanding and application of eschatology and the importance of the rediscovery of the Church's authentic eschatological identity.

Pluralism as a "Modern" Phenomenon and "Post-Modernity"

Pluralism is definitely related to, and for most scholars is the result of, "modernism," the most tangible outcome of the Enlightenment that prevailed in Europe and dominated all aspects of the public life of our Western civilization after the disastrous religious wars in the 17th century that ended with the famous peace of Westphalia in 1648. In my view, modernism has arisen from a certain perspective on the so-called external mission of Christianity. Having been deprived of privileged status and dominant and exclusive presence in the public domain, Christianity set out to conquer the world. In this way, the modernist revolution had a lasting and catalytic, though indirect, effect on the religious life of the Christian world on both sides of the Atlantic. The real consequence of modernism in Christian mission has not yet been given the attention it deserves, although pluralism has been focused upon and correctly assessed in ecumenical reflections by the missionary movement.[11]

In order to define properly the present context of the Church's witness, it is necessary to locate pluralism within the framework of modernism and dialectics between modernism and post-modernism. For this reason, I have chosen to tackle the issue through a reference to the contrast between pre-modernity, modernity, and post-modernity.[12]

In the pre-modern world, the sacred cosmic stories of all religions provided, each for its own culture, the most public and certain knowledge human beings believed they had about reality. After the Enlightenment, that is, in modernity, secular science replaced religion as the most public and certain knowledge that human beings believed they had of their world, whereas religious stories were reduced to matters of personal belief and opinion. The ideal of modernism was the separation of the Church from the state (or religion from society), the relegation of religion to the private or personal realm, and the declaration of the public realm as secular, in other words free from all religious influence. Pluralism was, therefore, established as the necessary context for the welfare of a civilized society. During almost the entire period of modernity, Christianity was reserved, if not hostile, to both pluralism and the principles of modernism. This is more evident in Eastern Christianity, whereas in the West the opposite path was followed, that of an almost complete surrender, especially in Protestantism.

"Post-modernity" is an ambiguous term used to name an ambiguous time of transition in history. The post-modern period has its beginnings in the emergence of the social sciences, which at its earlier stages undermined the authority of religion and their public presence, and contributed to the secularization of society. When, however, the same techniques of sociological and historical criticism were finally applied to science itself, including the social sciences, it was discovered that scientific knowledge was also an imaginative interpretation of the world. For some, this discovery was more shocking than the discovery that the earth was not the centre of the universe.[13] Suddenly, all our world-views, including the so-called scientific ones, were relativized. This made people aware that their respective (modern) views of the world could not automatically be assumed to be objective descriptions. As a result, pluralism has been highlighted more in post-modernity than in modernity itself.[14] All these developments have brought religion, and the Church in particular, back into the public domain. This made theology adopt a new approach and articulate what is generally called "public theology."[15]

Having said all this, it is important to reaffirm what sociologists of knowledge very often point out, that is, that modernism, counter- (alternative) modernism, post-modernism, and even de-modernism, are always simultaneous processes.[16] Otherwise post-modernism can easily end up and evaporate to a neo-traditionalism, and at the end to a neglect or even negation of the great achievements of the Enlightenment and the ensuing scholarly critical "paradigm." The rationalistic sterility of modern life has turned to the quest for something new, something radical, which nevertheless is not always new, but very often the old recycled: such as neo-romanticism, neo-mysticism, or naturalism.[17]

I firmly believe that the Church cannot exercise her mission in today's pluralistic world in a meaningful and effective way without a reassessment of the present context, without a certain encounter with modernism.[18] By and large, there still exists an aloofness between Christianity and modernity[19] which is caused not only by the former's rejection of the latter, and the negative attitude towards the whole range of the achievements of the Enlightenment, but also by the obstinate persistence of the adherents of modernism—and of course the democratic institutions that come out of it—to allow historic and diachronic institutions, like the Church, to play a significant role in public life, without being either absorbed or alienated by it, with the simple argument that they derive their origin in the pre-modern era. If today this encounter is possible, and even desirable despite the tragic events of 11 September 2001, this is because of the undisputed transition of our culture to a new era, the post-modern era that brought with it the resurgence of religion.

Earlier we pointed out that post-modernity is inconceivable without some reference to modernism as such. In the past, Peter Berger tried to describe the attitude of the Church towards the modernist revolution, and the pluralistic condition that entailed, in terms of two opposite positions: accommodation and resistance.[20] In my view both these positions are inadequate from a theological point of view (more precisely, from an Orthodox theological point of view).

Resistance is no longer suggested as a practical solution, because of the progress made in the theology of mission, as we will see later.[21] As to accommodation, the impossibility of its application derives from a theological and ecclesiological ground.[22] For the Church and her theology are incompatible with at least three cornerstones of modernism: (1) secularism, (2) individualism, and (3) privatization.

If the Church accommodates to modernism and accepts secularism, then automatically her role, her nature and mission are all exhausted in her institutional expression. The Church will become yet another institution of this world, which can of course be welcomed, and even become a desirable player, by the dominant modern paradigm in the public domain, but she will lose her prophetic, and above all her eschatological, character. The Church, drawing her *esse* and identity neither from what she is at the present, nor from what it was given to her in the past, but from what she will become in the *eschaton,* must not only avoid acting as an institution of this world, she must also critically respond to and prophetically challenge all institutional and unjust structures.

With regard to individualism, it is quite obvious that the Church as a communion of faith, a *koinonia* of free people (and not as an oppressive communitarian system that ignores individual human rights),[23] is incompatible with any system that has as a basic principle the individual being and not his or her relations with the "other," any other, and of course God, the "Ultimate Other."

Finally, the relegation and extrusion of the Church exclusively to the private domain contradicts her identity, and above all nullifies her responsibility and imperative duty to evangelize, to take the good news to the end of the world. This mission, of course, should not have an expansional character with imperialistic attitude and behaviour, as happened in the past,[24] nor should it aim "at the propagation or transmission of intellectual convictions, doctrines, moral commands etc., but at the transmission of the life of communion, that exists in God."[25]

If, nevertheless, neither resistance nor accommodation of the Church to the modern critical paradigm is legitimate on theological grounds, there is a third solution that has been applied by the Church on grounds of her missionary responsibility during the golden era of the 4th century C.E., that of social integration, the famous Byzantine synthesis, when the Church took the risk to embrace the "empire" and practically reject the "desert."[26] At that critical moment in her history the Church had not only integrated with contemporary society of the Roman empire—one could *mutatis mutandis* call it "modern"; she had not only shown respect to what was earlier called "Whore of Babylon" (Rev. 17:5); but she had even included the empire—certainly a "secular" institution—in her liturgical tablets. The only thing she preserved intact was her identity (and this not without difficulties and risks) and her prophetical voice over the historical process. In other words, she followed in this respect the example of St Paul and not the radical stance of the seer/prophet of the Apocalypse.[27]

The Understanding of Universalism in the Theology of Christian Mission

The essence of what has been briefly presented has been on the ecumenical agenda of world mission, the turning-point of which was the 1963 world mission conference in Mexico. It was there that ecumenical theology of mission replaced the negative assessment of modernism by a more positive one. Since then, most of the earlier models of evangelization of the whole world, as well as of mission as proclamation and conversion in their literal sense, were enriched by a new understanding of mission mostly represented by a variety of terms like "witness" or *martyria*, "public presence," "dialogue" and "liberation."[28]

This is not to say that churches no longer organize evangelical campaigns or revival meetings; in fact, many Christians are still asked to take up conversion as their top mission priority. What I mean is that all churches on the institutional level are coping in one way or the other with the questions of many contexts, many religions, many cultures and systems of values—what we call pluralism or the effects of globalization. Rather than proclamation alone, all churches are exploring in their own ways a different understanding of "Christian witness." In addition to the earlier models of evangelization of the whole world, as well as of mission as proclamation and conversion in their literal sense—that is, besides preaching Jesus as "the way, the truth, and the life" (John 14:6), as the sole saviour of human sin—the Church began to address human sin in the structural complexities of our world, and started ministering to the socially poor and marginalized of our societies in their contexts, and above all entering into a constructive dialogue with pluralism, and at the end of the road with modernism or post-modernism, thus making her presence visible in society.

Of crucial importance at this stage was the reassessment of the concept of universalism which, according to some analysts, is the primary cause of all religious, social, and even ethnic conflicts. It was then that we rediscovered that the early Church understood her mission in a broad variety of ways.[29] Following Martin Goodman's analysis,[30] I have argued elsewhere that following the steps of Judaism, Christianity, in fact, developed an informative, educational, apologetic, and proselytizing mission to propagate its faith.[31] However, this pluralistic understanding has gradually given place more or less to a universalistic understanding, a universal proselytizing mission, which during the Constantinian period became dominant through its theological validation by

the great ancient Christian historian Eusebius. However, it never became entirely dormant in the undivided Church,[32] with a very few exceptions of course.

Universal proselytizing mission was actually promoted in a systematic way only in the second millennium, during which the concept of universalism was developed. With the theological articulation of Christocentric universalism the old idea of "Christendom" has determined to a considerable degree the shaping of our understanding of mission.[33] Universal proselytizing mission was given fresh life by the discovery of the New World, and by the prospect of christianizing the entire inhabited earth. It reached its peak with the so-called African and Asian Christian missions during the last century.[34] This concept of "Christendom" however, carried with it other non-Christian elements to such an extent that eventually industrialized development of bourgeois society in Europe and America, as well as colonialism and expansionism of any sort, walked hand in hand with Christian mission.

It has been rightly argued that during that "old ecumenical paradigm" Christians felt that they were called "to convey to the rest of humanity the blessings of Western (i.e. bourgeois) Christian civilization. . . . The slogan 'the evangelization of the world in this generation' emphasizes the missionary consciousness of this early movement, in which genuine missionary and evangelistic motives were inextricably combined with cultural and social motives."[35]

It was for these reasons that Christian theology on the world mission scene adopted a more holistic view, and with the contribution—among others—of Orthodox theology, suggested a radical shift to a "new paradigm," away from "Christocentric universalism," towards a "trinitarian" understanding of the divine reality and towards an *oikoumene* as the one household of life.[36] For mission theology, these meant abandoning the primary importance of proselytism, not only among Christians of other denominations, but even among peoples of other religions. "Dialogue" was suggested as a new term parallel to, and in some cases in place of, the old missiological terminology.[37] Nowadays, the problem of reconciliation in the religious field has become not simply a social necessity but a legitimate theological imperative.[38] In the *Guidelines on Dialogue with People of Living Faiths and Ideologies,* published some 25 years ago by the WCC, the people of the other faiths are for Christians "no longer the objects of (their) discussions but partners in (their mission)."[39]

Thus, the Christian theology of mission no longer insists on the universal proselytizing mission, but on the authentic witness of the Church's eschatological experience. This was, in fact, made possible by the fundamental assumption of trinitarian theology, "that God in God's own self is a life of communion and that God's involvement in history aims at drawing humanity and creation in general into this communion with God's very life."[40] Taken a little further, this understanding of Christian witness suggests that the problem of ethics, that is, the problem of overcoming the evil in the world—at least for Christianity—is not only a moral and social issue; it is also—and for some even exclusively—an ecclesial one, in the sense that the moral and social responsibility of Christians, their mission in today's pluralistic world, is the logical consequence of their ecclesial (i.e., eschatological) self-consciousness.

Today in the field of world mission we speak for the "oikoumene which is to come" . . . according to the terminology of Hebrews (2:5; cf. 13:14ff.), as it is described in the book of Revelation (chs. 21 and 22), as an open society, where an honest dialogue between existing living cultures can take place. The world pluralistic society can and must become a *household* (*oikos*), where everyone is open to the "other" (as they are open to the Ultimate Other, i.e., God), and where all can share a common life, despite the plurality and difference of their identity. In modern missiology the term *oikoumene* and its derivatives (ecumenism, etc.) no longer describe a given situation. When we talk about the *oikumene* we no longer exclusively refer to an abstract universality, such as the entire inhabited world, or the whole human race, or even a united universal Church. What we actually mean are substantial—and at the same time threatened—relations between churches, between cultures, between people and human societies, and at the same time between humanity and the rest of God's creation.

The Importance of the Rediscovery of the Authentic Prophetic Eschatological Vision of the Church

This eschatological perspective on the understanding of the Church's witness, and view of the Orthodox eschatological identity, makes a reassessment of the prophetic eschatological vision of the Church an absolute imperative. For the ineffectiveness of Christian witness in today's pluralist world is partly due to the distortion of the eschatological vision of the Church. And it is not only Western Christianity, but Eastern Orthodoxy as well, that gradually lost the proper and authentic understanding of eschatology.[41] Throughout the medieval and post-medieval periods the strong eschatological vision of the early Church was almost completely lost.[42] It was only in the liturgy, and more particularly in the eucharistic tradition of Christianity, and especially and much more clearly in Eastern Orthodoxy, that it never disappeared completely.

Of course, even the liturgy was not preserved intact, as was shown by social and cultural anthropological analysis. As we indicated earlier, it was through the social sciences, and especially through cultural anthropology,[43] that the importance of liturgy for the identity of all religious systems and societies was actually reinforced in academic discussions. I have argued elsewhere[44] that there are two major understandings of liturgy. According to the first one, the liturgy is understood as a private act, functioning as a means to meet some particular religious needs: i.e., both the need of the community to exercise its power and supervision on its members, and the need of the individual for personal "sanctification." I will call this understanding of the liturgical act juridical. According to a second understanding, however, the liturgy functions as a means for the up-building of the religious community, which is no longer viewed in institutional terms or as a cultic organization, but as a communion and as a way of living. And this is what I call "communal" understanding of liturgy.

The juridical understanding of liturgy encourages and in effect promotes a sharp distinction between the various segments of the religious society (clergy and laity, etc.), thus underlining the dimensions of super- and sub-ordination within the ritual, and contributing to the maintenance of social structure not only within the religious community itself, but also by extension within wider social life. This juridical understanding of liturgy, in addition, develops separation and certain barriers, sometimes even hostility, between members of different religious systems, thus intensifying phenomena of intolerance and fanaticism. With such an understanding of liturgy there is no real concern for history, social life, and public presence of the Church, nor any acceptance of pluralism.

At the other end, the communal understanding of liturgy discourages all distinctions between the various segments, not only within the religious communities themselves but also, by extension, within wider social life. This understanding of liturgy dissolves barriers between members of different religious systems, thus promoting religious tolerance and peace, and accepts pluralism as a God-given context of mission. In modern Orthodox contexts both these attitudes have been experienced and expressed. And this phenomenon has puzzled Church historians, when they tried to evaluate the public presence of Orthodoxy.

However, even outside the liturgy of the Church—which as we pointed out is closely related to, and in fact determines, her eschatological dimension—in the course of history Christianity has reflected upon an "applied eschatology"; but articulated different, sometimes contradicting, in some cases even distorted, types of eschatology. John Meyendorff distinguishes three such types in the Church's life, which cover all aspects of Christian ethics, the application of which in a sense determines the variety of Christian attitudes towards pluralism and modernism.[45]

The first one is the apocalyptic version of eschatology. According to this version the kingdom of God is coming soon, and therefore there is not anything to expect from history. Christians can do nothing to improve human reality. No real mission or social responsibility or public presence or culture is possible or even desirable. God is seen alone as the Lord of history, acting without any cooperation or synergy (cf. 1 Cor. 3:9). The New Jerusalem is expected to come from heaven all prepared (Rev. 21:2), and we have nothing to contribute to it. This view, which was rejected by the ancient Church,

allows only repentance and ascetic life to combat the passions.

The second type, which stands in opposition to the first, is humanistic eschatology. This eschatology has an optimistic understanding of history, and has been dominant in Western society since the time of the Enlightenment. In the Orthodox realm this kind of eschatology has taken the form of a revival of the old paradigm of the Byzantine synthesis, this time in the narrow limits of nationalistic religious entities: Holy Russia, Great Serbia, the chosen Greek Orthodoxy, etc. are some expressions, which taken even further envisage a dangerous development of an Orthodox axis, which will conquer the faithless, or even heretic, West!

The third type of eschatology is prophetic eschatology. It is the only acceptable type of eschatology, and it is based on the biblical concept of prophecy, which in both the Old and the New Testaments does not simply forecast the future or announce the inevitable, but also places humans before an option, a choice between two types of personal or social behaviour. The people of God are free to choose, but the prophet has informed them of the consequences; and the consequences today are the realities of the pluralistic (post)modern world.

With the exception of some diaspora (or better "Western") and newly established missionary communities—modern Orthodoxy in its historical expression finds itself in a rather strange situation. Our metropolitan "mother" churches are in fact struggling between two poles, quite opposite or at least unrelated to each other: on the one hand, the ideal of the later hesychastic movement—of course wrongly interpreted and applied—has given rise to an individualistic understanding of salvation, which only partially takes history and pluralism seriously into account; on the other hand, a completely secularized approach is adopted in dealing with historical developments. As in the Old Testament, in later and even recent Judaism, the splendour of the Davidic kingdom usually overshadowed the more authentic desert and prophetic vision of a wandering people of God, so in contemporary Orthodoxy the famous "Byzantine synthesis" seems to be the only model—again unsuccessfully envisioned or applied—which almost all national autocephalic Orthodox churches constantly refer to.

It is not a surprise, therefore, that in contemporary Orthodoxy—and I would also add in the Church universal—the creative tension between history and the *eschaton* has almost disappeared. No one preaches about the reality of the kingdom drastically entering into our pluralistic reality. Even our modern church buildings have ceased to reflect the kingdom reality, having rather become imitations, and sometimes even caricatures, of traditional (but meaningful) edifices. Again, only in the eucharistic liturgy is there something to remind us, that when we offer our "reasonable worship" we offer it "for the life of the world," remembering not only past events, but also future realities, in fact the (eschatological) reality *par excellence:* Christ's "second and glorious Coming."[46] Naturally, then, only those Orthodox communities which have undergone liturgical and eucharistic renewal are able to experience or rediscover a proper understanding of eschatology. The rest are struggling to overcome today's real challenges of globalization by a retreat to the glorious past, despite their strong pneumatological and eschatological tradition. But thus they become vulnerable at best to a kind of traditionalism and at worst to an anti-ecumenical, nationalistic, and intolerant fundamentalism, attitudes of course totally alien and unacceptable to the Orthodox ethos.

To sum up: Orthodoxy—like the Church Universal—in order to effectively witness to the gospel in today's pluralistic context, in addition to an affirmation of her ecclesial rather than confessional identity, desperately needs a new relation with modernism, a new and dynamic understanding of universalism and a rediscovery of the authentic perception of eschatology.

Notes

1. N. Nissiotis, "Interpreting Orthodoxy," *The Ecumenical Review,* 14, 1961, p. 26. Cf. also the notion of *sobornicitatea* (open catholicity) advanced by D. Staniloae, *Theology and the Church,* p. 7. More on this in N. Mosoiu, *Taina prezentei lui Dumnezeu în viata umană. Viziunea creatoare a Părintelui Profesor Dumitru Stăniloae,* Pitesti/Brasov/Cluj-Napoca 2000, pp. 246ff.

2. For this reason one can safely argue that the fundamental principles of Christian spirituality, of the Christian mission, are the same in the East and in the West. What I am going to say, therefore, applies to the entire Christian faith, to the one, holy, catholic and apostolic Church. In what follows, therefore, I will freely alternate the terms "Orthodoxy" and "Christianity," avoiding as much as possible any reference to the canonical boundaries of the term "Church."

3. G. Florovsky, "The Elements of Liturgy," in G. Patelos, ed., *The Orthodox Church in the Ecumenical Movement,* WCC, 1978, pp. 172-82, 172.

4. Cf. my "The Eucharistic Perspective of the Church's Mission," in P. Vassiliadis, *Eucharist and Witness: Orthodox Perspectives on the Unity and Mission of the Church,* WCC Publications/Holy Cross Orthodox Press, Geneva/Brookline MA, 1998, pp. 49-66, 50.

5. The early Christian tradition stresses, in one way or another, the eschatological and not the historical dimension of the Church. Even the episcopocentric structure of the Church was understood eschatologically. The bishop, e.g., as *primus inter pares* presiding in love over the eucharistic community, was never understood (except very late under the heavy influence of scholasticism) as a vicar, representative, or ambassador of Christ, but as an image of Christ. So with the rest of the ministries of the Church: they are not parallel to, or given by, but identical with those of, Christ. That is also why the whole of Orthodox theology and life, especially as this latter is expressed in Sunday's liturgical offices, are centred around the resurrection. The Church exists not because Christ died on the cross, but because he is risen from the dead, thus becoming the *aparche* of all humanity. See J. Zizioulas, *Being as Communion: Studies in Personhood and the Church,* New York, St Vladimir's Seminary Press, 1985; also *idem,* "The Mystery of the Church in Orthodox Tradition," in *One in Christ,* 24, 1988, pp. 294-303.

6. Almost all prominent Orthodox theologians of the recent past (G. Florovsky, S. Agouridis, J. Meyendorff, A. Schmemann, J. Zizioulas, to name just few) have underlined the eschatological dimension of Orthodoxy. Cf. also E. Ciapsis's doctoral dissertation, *Eschatology and the Unity of the Church: The Impact of the Eschatology in Ecumenical Thought,* Ann Arbor MI, U.M.I., 1988; also his "Eschatology," in the *Dictionary of the Ecumeni-*

cal Movement, N. Lossky et al. eds., WCC, 2002, pp. 361a-64a.

7. Cf. my *Eucharist and Witness, passim,* also "L'eschatologie dans la vie de l'Eglise: Une perspective chretienne orthodoxe et son impact sur la vie de la société," in *Irenikon,* 73, 2000, pp. 316-34.

8. Cf. Staniloae's strong criticism of the trend in contemporary Orthodoxy to identify Orthodox spirituality with a disregard for everyday life, a phenomenon described in his own words as "a premature eschatologism." D. Staniloae, *Ascetica si mistica orthodoxa,* Alba Iulia, 1993, p. 28 (in Romanian).

9. More on this in (Archbishop of Albania) Anastasios Yannoulatos, *Universality and Orthodoxy,* Athens, 2000 (in Greek); also in T. FitzGerald, "Orthodox Theology and Ecumenical Witness: An Introduction to Major Themes," in *St Vladimir's Theological Quarterly,* 42, 1998, pp. 339-61, 360.

10. In this essay I use the terms "modernism" (and "pre- or post-modernism") as an ideological, spiritual, cultural category or paradigm, and "modernity" (and "pre- or post-modernity") as the discrete period in history in which this paradigm circulated.

11. See W. A. Visser't Hooft, "Pluralism—Temptation or Opportunity?" *The Ecumenical Review,* 18, 1966, pp. 129-49. For an early Orthodox response, see Metropolitan George Khodre, "Christianity in a Pluralistic World—The Economy of the Holy Spirit," in *The Ecumenical Review,* 23, 1971, pp. 118-28.

12. From Nancey Murphy's three-fold approach to the subject (philosophy of language, epistemology, philosophy of science) I will concentrate only on the last one (*Anglo-American Postmodernity: Philosophical Perspectives on Science, Religion and Ethics,* Boulder CO, Westview, 1997). Cf. also Rodney L. Petersen, ed., *Christianity and Civil Society,* Boston, Boston Theological Institute, 1995; and Jacob Neusner, ed., *Religion and the Political Order,* Atlanta, Scholars, 1996.

13. Darrell Fasching, "Judaism, Christianity, Islam: Religion, Ethics, and Politics in the (Post) modern World," in Neusner, ed., *Religion and the Political Order,* pp. 291-99. Also idem, *The Ethical Challenge of Auschwitz and Hiroshima: Apocalypse or Utopia?* Albany NY, State Univ. of New York Press, 1993.

14. According to Stanley Grenz (*A Primer on Postmodernism,* Grand Rapids MI, Eerdmans, 1996, esp. pp. 161-74) the hallmark of postmodernity is "centreless pluralism."

15. Cf. E. Ciapsis, "The Orthodox Church in a Pluralistic World," *Orthodoxy in Conversation: Orthodox Ecumenical Engagements,* WCC Publications/Holy Cross Orthodox Press, Geneva/Brookline MA, 2000, pp. 127-50.

16. Jürgen Habermas, "Die Moderne—Ein unvollendetes Projekt," in W. Welsch, ed., *Wege aus der Moderne: Schlüsseltexte der postmodernen Diskussion,* Weinheim, Wiley, 1988, pp. 177-92; Jean-Francois Lyotard, "An Interview," in *Theory, Culture and Society,* 5, 1989, pp. 277-309, esp. p. 277; idem, *The Postmodern Condition,* Minneapolis MN, Minnesota UP, 1984; Hayden White, *Metahistory: The Historical Imagination in 19th Century Europe,* Baltimore, Johns Hopkins UP, 1973; I. Petrou, "Παράδοση και πολιτισμική προσαρμογή στη δεύτερη νεωτερικότητα," *Σύναξη,* 75, 2000, pp. 25-35; W. Welsch, *Unsere postmoderne Moderne,* Weinheim, VCH Acta humaniora, 1988, σελ, 7.

17. Post-modernity's responses and reactions to the modern project of the Enlightenment to ground knowledge or "reason" as a timeless, universal construct, immune from the corrosive forces of history, has very seldom gone to the extreme. The enduring dream of modernity should not be minimized or dismissed out of hand, and the many achievements it has realized, such as a concern for universal human rights, and justice and equality, all deserve commendation and praise from the Church.

18. Cf. my recent book, *Postmodernity and the Church: The Challenge of Orthodoxy,* Athens, Akritas, 2002.

19. The first positive assessment of modernism within Orthodoxy I was exposed to was in (Archbishop) Demetrios Trakatellis's paper at the third conference of Orthodox theological schools in Boston ("The Gospel in a Secular Context," *Greek Orthodox Theological Review,* 38, 1993, pp. 45-55). For a detailed analysis see also Stanley S. Harakas, *Wholeness of Faith and Life: Orthodox Christian Ethics,* Brookline MA, Holy Cross Orthodox Press, 1999.

20. Peter Berger, *The Sacred Canopy: Elements*

of a Sociological Theory of Religion, New York, Doubleday, 1967, pp. 156ff.; also pp. 106ff.

21. F. J. Verstraelen et al. eds., *Missiology: An Ecumenical Introduction,* Grand Rapids, MI, Eerdmans, 1995; also K. Raiser, *Ecumenism in Transition: A Paradigm Shift in the Ecumenical Movement,* WCC, 1991 (trans. with modifications from the German original *Ökumene im Übergang,* München, C. Kaiser, 1989, pp. 54ff.

22. What follows comes from my *Postmodernity and the Church,* pp. 38ff.

23. Cf. Kostas Delikostantis, *Human Rights: A Western Ideology or an Ecumenical Ethos?* Thessaloniki, 1995 (in Greek).

24. Cf. my article "Beyond Christian Universalism: The Church's Witness in a Multicultural Society", in Επιστημονική Επετηρίδα Θεολογογιχής Σχολής. Τιμητιχό αψιέρωμα στον Ομότιμο Καθηγητή Αλέζανδρο Γουσίδη, n.s. Τμήμα Θεολογίας, 9, 1999, pp. 309-20.

25. Bria ed., *Go Forth in Peace,* WCC Publications, 1986, p. 3.

26. G. Florovsky, "Antinomies of Christian History: Empire and Desert," in *Christianity and Culture: The Collected Works of Georges Florovsky,* vol. II, Belmont CA, Nordland, 1974, pp. 67-100.

27. Cf. my "Orthodox Christianity," in J. Neusner, ed., *God's Rule: The Politics of World Religions,* Washington D.C., Georgetown UP, 2003. Also "Σχέσεις Εχχλησίας-Πολιτείας: Η θεολογία της χοινωνιχής ενσωμάτωσης (Σχόλιο στο Ρωμ. 13,1)," in *Επίχαιρα Αγιογραφιχά Θέματα. Αγία Γραφή χαι Ευχαριστία,* BB 15, Thessaloniki, Pournars, 2000, pp. 75-82.

28. Cf. *Common Witness: A Joint Document of the Working Group of the Roman Catholic Church and the WCC,* WCC Mission Series, 1982; the document *Common Witness and Proselytism;* also I. Bria ed., *Martyria-Mission,* WCC, 1980. Even *Mission and Evangelism—An Ecumenical Affirmation,* WCC Mission Series, 1982, 1985 (2nd ed.), is an attempt correctly to interpret the classical missionary terminology. Cf. also the most recent agreed statement of the Dorfweil/Germany consultation of CEC with the European Baptist Federation and the European Lausanne Committee for World Evangelization (12-13 June 1995) with the title: "Aspects of Mission and Evangelization in Europe Today." We must confess, however, that the traditional terminology (mission, conversion, evangelism or evangelization, christianization) still has an imperative validity and is retained as the *sine qua non* of the Christian identity of those Christian communities which belong to the "evangelical" stream of the Christian faith. A comprehensive presentation of the present state of the debate is J. Matthey, "Milestones in Ecumenical Missionary Thinking from the 1970s to the 1990s," in *International Review of Mission,* 88, 1999, pp. 291-304.

29. D. J. Bosch, *Transforming Mission: Paradigm Shifts in Theology of Mission,* New York, Orbis 1991, has described through the "Paradigm shift theory" the development of Christian understanding of mission down to the most recent ecumenical era.

30. "Mission and Proselytism: An Orthodox Understanding," in *Eucharist and Witness,* pp. 29ff.

31. Martin Goodman, in his book *Mission and Conversion: Proselytizing in the Religious History of the Roman Empire,* Oxford, Clarendon, 1994, has discerned four different uses of the word "mission" in modern scholarship of the history of religions, and consequently four different understandings of what has come to be labelled as "Christian mission": (1) *The informative mission.* The missionaries of this type felt "that they had a general message which they wished to impart to others. Such disseminators of information may have had no clear idea of the reaction they desired from their auditors.... [The aim of this attitude] was to tell people something, rather than to change their behaviour or status" (p. 3). (2) *The educational mission.* "Some missionaries did intend to change recipients of their message by making them more moral or contented. ... Such a mission to educate is easily distinguished from a desire to win converts" (ibid.). (3) *The apologetic mission.* "Some missionaries requested recognition by others of the power of a particular divinity without expecting their audience to devote themselves to his or her worship. Such a mission was essentially apologetic. Its aim was to protect the cult and beliefs of the missionary" (p. 4). Finally, (4) *The proselytizing mission.* According to Goodman, "information, education, and apologetic might or might not coexist within any one religious system, but all three can individually be distinguished from what may best

be described a proselytizing . . . [the aim of which was] to encourage outsiders not only to change their way of life but also to be incorporated within their group" (ibid.).

32. Ibid., p. 7.

33. Cf. the characteristic work of W. A. Visser 't Hooft, *No Other Name: The Choice between Syncretism and Christian Universalism,* London, SCM Press, 1963. More in Bosch, *Transforming Mission.*

34. It was the conviction that the "decisive hour of Christian mission" had come that impelled John R. Mott to call the world mission conference of 1910, with the primary purpose of pooling resources and developing a common strategy for the "world's conquest" for Christ. The task of "taking the gospel to all the regions of the world" was seen to be of paramount importance. On the recent history of Christian mission see J. Verkuyl, *Contemporary Missiology: An Introduction,* Engl. trans. Grand Rapids MI, Eerdmans, 1978.

35. Raiser, *Ecumenism in Transition,* p. 34.

36. Ibid., pp. 79ff.

37. This development is a radical reinterpretation of Christology through pneumatology (cf. Zizioulas, *Being as Communion,* through the rediscovery of the forgotten trinitarian theology of the undivided Church (cf. A. I. C. Heron, ed., *The Forgotten Trinity,* London, 1991).

38. For an Orthodox contribution to the debate see (Archbishop of Albania) Anastasios Yannoulatos, *Various Christian Approaches to the Other Religions (A Historical Outline),* Athens, 1971.

39. *Guidelines on Dialogue with People of Living Faiths and Ideologies,* WCC, 1990 (4th printing). Cf. Stanley J. Samartha, ed., *Faith in the Midst of Faiths: Reflections on Dialogue in Community,* WCC, 1977.

40. Bria, ed., *Go Forth in Peace,* p. 3.

41. Cf. my "Eucharistic and Therapeutic Spirituality," in *Greek Orthodox Theological Review,* 1997, pp. 1-23.

42. Of course, the process started with the voluntary incorporation of Christianity within the Roman empire in the 4th century C.E., but the eschatological vision survived, though obscured, thanks to the theological reflection of some great ecclesiastical figures such as Maximus the Confessor.

43. P. L. Berger and T. Luckmann, *The Social Construction of Reality: A Treatise in the Sociology of Knowledge,* New York, Doubleday, 1966; C. Geertz, *The Interpretation of Cultures: Selected Essays,* New York, Basic Books, 1973, pp. 126-41. One of the most imaginative insights of modern cultural anthropologists is their conviction that *ritual,* and the *liturgical life* in general, is a form of communication, a "performative" kind of speech, instrumental in creating the essential categories of human thought (E. Durkheim, *The Elementary Forms of the Religious Life,* trans. J. W. Swain, New York, Free Press, 1965 reprint, p. 22). They communicate the fundamental beliefs and values of a community, outlining in this way its "world view" and its "ethos." The rituals do not only transmit culture, but they also "create a reality which would be nothing without them. It is not too much to say that ritual is more to society than words are to thought. For it is very possible to know something and then find words for it. But it is impossible to have social relations without symbolic acts" (M. Douglas, *Purity and Danger: An Analysis of the Concepts of Pollution and Taboo,* London, Routledge & Kegan Paul, 1966, p. 62).

44. Petros Vassiliadis, "Sanctus and the Book of Revelation. Some Anthropological and Theological Insights on the Communal and Historical Dimension of Christian Liturgy," in L. Padovese, ed., *Atti del VII Simposio di Efeso su S. Giovanni Apostolo,* Rome, 1999, pp. 143-56.

45. What follows comes from J. Meyendorff, "Does Christian Tradition Have a Future?," *St Vladimir's Theological Quarterly,* 26, 1982, pp. 140ff.

46. It is quite characteristic that in the Byzantine liturgies of both St Basil and St Chrysostom, just before the *epiclesis,* the faithful "remember" not only the past events of the divine economy ("those things which have come to pass for us: the cross, the tomb, the resurrection on the third day, the ascension into heaven, the sitting at the right hand"), but in addition future eschatological realities (Christ's "second and glorious coming").

(Source: Petros Vassiliadis, "The Universal Claims of Orthodoxy and the Particularity of Its Witness in a Pluralistic World," *The Orthodox Churches in a Pluralistic World* [Geneva: WCC Publications; Brookline, MA: Holy Cross Orthodox Press, 2004].)

64. *The Missionary Imperative in the Orthodox Tradition*

(Introduction by Daniel B. Clendenin.) While the preceding document gives the lie to the characterization of Orthodoxy as non-missionary, it is nonetheless the case, as this essay points out, that the contribution of Orthodox missions and missiology were little appreciated among Catholics and Protestants in the West. In an era still dominated by attempts to disentangle mission from colonialism Orthodox theology offers what will be for non-Orthodox readers a fresh approach to understanding the complex relationship of church, world, and gospel.

Born in Estonia, Alexander Schmemann (1921-83) was educated in France, first at the University of Paris, and later at the Saint Sergius Orthodox Theological Institute. After graduation in 1945 he taught for six years at Saint Sergius. In 1951 Schmemann moved to the United States to join St. Vladimir's Orthodox Theological Seminary as professor of church history and liturgical theology, where he was later appointed dean (1962-83). In addition, Schmemann taught as an adjunct professor in Columbia University's Slavic department. The best known among his many works include Introduction to Liturgical Theology *and* Historical Road of Eastern Orthodoxy.

Until quite recently the Eastern Orthodox Church was regarded in the West as a nonmissionary church. It was an opinion commonly held that the great missionary movement which marked so deeply the Christian West during the last centuries bypassed somehow the static Christianity of the East. Today this view seems to have lost some of its strength: new historical research has made it quite clear that the Orthodox achievements in the field of mission, although somewhat different from those of the West, are nonetheless important and impressive. Our purpose in this brief essay, however, is not to present a historical or statistical survey of the Orthodox missionary expansion. It is much more important to try to understand and to

analyze—be it only tentatively and partially—the missionary imperative in the Orthodox tradition, or, in other terms, the relation in it between mission, on the one hand, and the faith, the life, and the whole spiritual vision of Orthodoxy on the other hand.

A theology of mission is always the fruit of the total being of the church and not a mere speciality for those who receive a particular missionary calling. But for the Orthodox church there is a special need to reflect upon its basic missionary motivations, because its presumably nonmissionary character has been too often explained by, and ascribed to, the very essence, the "holy of holies" of Orthodoxy: its sacramental, liturgical, mystical ethos. Even now, as the study of Orthodox missions seems to correct the traditional view, there remains the temptation to explain these missions as a marginal epiphenomenon in the history of Orthodoxy, as something that happened in spite of its general tendencies and trends (Josef Glazik, *Die Russisch-Orthodoxe Heidenmission seit Peter dem Grossen: Ein missions geschichtlicher Versuch nach russischen Quellen und Darstellungen* [Münster: Aschendorff, 1954]; idem, *Die Islammission der Russisch-Orthodoxen Kirche* [Münster: Aschendorff, 1959]). This is why a theological clarification is necessary. Can a church whose life is centered almost exclusively on the liturgy and the sacraments, whose spirituality is primarily mystical and ascetical, be truly missionary? And if it is, where in its faith are the deepest motivations of the missionary zeal to be found? In somewhat simplified terms this is the question addressed, explicitly or implicitly, to the Orthodox church by all those for whom "ecumenical" means necessarily and unescapably "missionary."

Obstacles to Understanding the Orthodox Approach to Missions

It is without any doubt in Orthodox ecclesiology, that is, in the doctrine and experience of the church, that we find the basic elements of an answer. To formulate them, however, is not an easy task. It must be kept in mind that the Orthodox church has never been challenged by an ecclesiological or doctrinal crisis comparable to the Reformation or Counter-Reformation. And because of this it had no compelling reason to reflect upon itself, upon the traditional structures of its life and doctrine. There was no theological elaboration of the doctrine of the church, this doctrine having been never questioned or opposed.

It was in the ecumenical encounter with the West, an encounter whose beginnings must be traced back to the twenties (Stockholm, 1925, and Lausanne, 1927), that for the first time the Orthodox were requested not only to state their ecclesiological beliefs, but also to explain them, that is, to express them in consistent theological terms. But at this point there appeared an additional difficulty which has remained ever since as the major difficulty of the Orthodox participation in the ecumenical movement. A dialogue presupposes necessarily an agreement on the terms that are being used, a common language. Yet from the Orthodox point of view it was precisely the rupture in theological understanding, the theological alienation of the West from the East, that, first, made the schism so deep and, then, all attempts to heal it—from 1054 to the Council of Florence in 1438-39—so hopelessly inadequate. Therefore, in the ecumenical encounter, the Orthodox church had to face a Christian world with several centuries of autonomous theological and spiritual development behind it, with a mind and thought forms radically different from those of the East. The questions asked of the Orthodox were formulated in Western terms, were conditioned very often by specifically Western experience and developments. The Orthodox answers were classified according to Western patterns, reduced to categories familiar to the West, but hardly adequate to Orthodoxy. This situation, although years of contacts and conversations have no doubt improved it, is still far from being overcome completely. The catholic language has not yet been recovered. All this, in addition to basic dogmatical differences, explains the agony of Orthodox participation in the ecumenical movement and constitutes a very real obstacle not only to an agreement, but to a simple understanding. One must remember this when trying to grasp the Orthodox approach to missions.

Orthodox Doctrine and Experience of the Church

"Heaven on earth": this formula familiar to every Orthodox expresses rather well the fundamental Orthodox experience of the church. The church is first of all and before everything else a God-created and God-given reality, the presence of Christ's new life, the manifestation of the new eon of the Holy Spirit. An Orthodox in his contemplation of the church sees it as the divine gift before he thinks of the church as human response to this gift. One can rightly describe the church as an eschatological reality, for its essential function is to manifest and to actualize in this world the eschaton, the ultimate reality of salvation and redemption. In and through the church the kingdom of God is made already present, is communicated to men. And it is this eschatological, God-given fullness of the church (not any juridical theory of mediation) that constitutes the root of the ecclesiological absolutism of Eastern Orthodoxy, absolutism which is so often misunderstood and misinterpreted by the Protestants.

The church as a whole is a means of grace, the sacrament of the kingdom. Therefore its structure—hierarchical, sacramental, liturgical—has no other function but of making the church ever capable of fulfilling itself as the body of Christ, as the temple of the Holy Spirit, to actualize its very nature as grace. For the God-given fullness of the church, or rather the church as fullness—and this is an essential aspect of Orthodox ecclesiology—cannot be manifested outside these ecclesiastical structures. There is no separation, no division, between the church invisible (*in statu patriae*) and the visible church (*in statu viae*), the latter being the expression and the actualization of the former, the sacramental sign of its reality. Hence the unique, the central ecclesiological significance of the Eucharist, which is the all-embracing sacrament of the church. In the Eucharist "the church becomes what it is," fulfils itself as the body of Christ, as the divine parousia—the presence and the communication of Christ and of his kingdom. Orthodox ecclesiology is indeed eucharistic ecclesiology. For in the Eucharist the church accomplishes the passage from this world into the world to come, into the eschaton; participates in the ascension of its Lord and in his messianic banquet; tastes of the joy and peace of the kingdom. "And thou didst not cease to do all things until thou hadst brought us back to heaven, and hadst endowed us with thy kingdom . . ." (eucharistic prayer in the Liturgy of John Chrysostom). Thus the whole life of the church is rooted in the Eucharist, is the fruition of this eucharistic fullness in the time of this world whose "image passeth by. . . ." This is indeed the mission of the church.

The church is also *human response* to the divine gift, its acceptance and appropriation by humanity. If the order of the church is shaped and conditioned by the eschatological fullness of the gift, is its sacramental sign, it is the acceptance of the gift and the growth into its fullness that are the purpose of the Christian community. The church is fullness, and the church is also increase and growth in faith and love, knowledge and *koinonia*. This response has two aspects, neither of which can be separated from the other, because they condition each other and together constitute the dynamics of Christian life and action.

The first aspect of the church as response is *God-centered:* it is the sanctification, the growth in holiness, of both the Christian individual and the Christian community, the "acquisition by them of the Holy Spirit," as the ultimate goal of Christian life was defined by one of the last and the greatest Orthodox saints, Seraphim of Sarov (d. 1833). It is the slow transformation of the old Adam in us into the new one, the restoration of the pristine beauty, which was lost in sin, the illumination with the noncreated light of Mount Tabor. It is also the slow victory over the demonic powers of the cosmos, the joy and peace which *hic et nunc* make us partakers of the kingdom and of life eternal. The Orthodox spiritual tradition has always stressed the mystical nature of Christian life, as life hidden with Christ in God. And the great monastic movement which started in the fourth century after the church was officially recognized by the Roman Empire, and given a status in this world, was nothing else but a new expression of the early Christian eschatologism, the affirmation of Christianity as belonging ontologically to the life of the world to come, the negation of any permanent home and identification in this world.

The second aspect of the church as response is *man- or world-centered.* It is the understanding of the church as being left in this world, in its time, space, and history, with a specific task or mission: "to walk in the same way in which he walked" (1 John 2:6). The church is fullness and its home is in heaven. But this fullness is given to the world, sent into the world as its salvation and redemption. The eschatological nature of the church is not the negation of the world, but, on the contrary, its affirmation and acceptance as the object of divine love. Or, in other terms, the whole other-worldliness of the church is nothing but the sign and the reality of the love of God for this world, the very condition of the church's mission to the world. The church thus is not a self-centered community but precisely a missionary community, salvation not from, but of, the world. In the Orthodox experience and faith it is the church-sacrament that makes possible the church-mission.

The Missionary Imperative

We can try now to formulate with more precision the various aspects of the missionary imperative as implied in the Orthodox experience of the church. This imperative is the essential expression of the church as gift and fullness, its projection in time and space of this world. For if, on the one hand, nothing can be added to the church—its fullness is that of Christ himself—the manifestation and the communication of this fullness constitute, on the other hand, the very life of the church in this eon. On the day of Pentecost, when the fullness of the church was realized once for all, began the time of the church, the last and the crucial segment of the history of salvation. Ontologically the only newness and, therefore, the only soteriological content of this segment is precisely mission: the proclamation and the communication of the eschaton, which is already the being of the church and indeed its only being. It is the church as mission that gives to this time its real significance and to history its meaning. And it is mission that gives to the human response in the church its validity, makes us real co-workers in the work of Christ.

Nothing reveals better the relation between

the church as fullness and the church as mission than the Eucharist, the central act of the church's *leiturgia,* the sacrament of the church itself. There are two complementary Eastern Orthodox Theology movements in the eucharistic rite: the movement of ascension and the movement of return. The Eucharist begins as an ascension toward the throne of God, toward the kingdom. "Let us put aside all earthly care," says the hymn of offertory, and we prepare ourselves to ascend into heaven with Christ and in Christ, and to offer in him his Eucharist. This first movement, which finds its fulfillment in the consecration of the elements, the sign of the acceptance by God of our Eucharist, is, to be sure, already an act of mission. The Eucharist is offered "on behalf of all and for all"; it is the fulfillment by the church of its priestly function: the reconciliation of the whole creation with God, the sacrifice of the whole world to God, the intercession for the whole world before God. All this in Christ, the God-man, the unique priest of the new creation, the "one who offers and the one who is offered. . . ." This is accomplished by a total separation of the church from the world ("The doors, the doors!" proclaims the deacon as the eucharistic prayer begins), by its ascension to heaven, its entrance into the new eon.

And then, precisely at the moment when this state of fullness has been reached and consummated at the table of the Lord in his kingdom, when "we have seen the true Light and partaken of the Holy Spirit," the second movement begins—that of the return into the world. "Let us depart in peace," says the celebrant as he leaves the altar and leads the congregation outside the temple—and this is the last, the ultimate, commandment. The Eucharist is always the end, the sacrament of the parousia; and yet it is always the beginning, the starting point: now the mission begins. "We have seen the true Light, we have enjoyed life eternal," but this life, this Light, are given us in order to transform us into Christ's witnesses in this world. Without this ascension into the kingdom we would have had nothing to witness to; now, having once more become his people and his inheritance, we can do what Christ wants us to do: "you are witnesses of these things" (Luke 24:48). The Eucharist, transforming the church into what it is, transforms it into mission.

The Objects of Mission

What are the objects, the goals, of mission? The Orthodox church answers without hesitation: these objects are man and world. Not man alone in an artificially religious isolation from the world, and not world as an entity of which man would be nothing but a part. Man not only comes first, but is indeed the essential object of mission. And yet the Orthodox idea of evangelism is free from individualistic and spiritualistic connotations. The church, the sacrament of Christ, is not a religious society of converts, an organization to satisfy the religious needs of man. It is new life and redeems therefore the whole life, the total being of man. And this whole life of man is precisely the world in which and by which he lives. Through man the church saves and redeems the world. One can say that this world is saved and redeemed every time a man responds to the divine gift, accepts it, and lives by it. This does not transform the world into the kingdom or the society into the church. The ontological abyss between the old and the new remains unchanged and cannot be filled in this eon. The kingdom is yet to come and the church is not of this world. And yet this kingdom to come is already present and the church is fulfilled in this world. They are present not only as proclamation, but in their very reality; and through the divine *agape,* which is their fruit, they perform all the time the same sacramental transformation of the old into the new; they make possible a real action, a real "doing" in this world.

All this gives the mission of the church a cosmical and a historical dimension that in the Orthodox tradition and experience are essential. State, society, culture, nature itself, are real objects of mission and not a neutral milieu in which the only task of the church is to preserve its own inner freedom, to maintain its religious life. It would require a whole volume to tell the story of the Orthodox church from this point of view: of its concrete participation in societies and cultures of whose whole existence Orthodoxy became the total expression; of its identification with nations and peoples, yet without betrayal of its otherworldliness, of the eschatological communion with the heavenly Jerusalem. It would require a long theological analysis to express adequately the Orthodox idea of the sanctification of matter, or precisely the cosmical aspect of its sacramental vision. Here we can state only that all this is the object of Christian mission, because all this is assumed and offered to God in the sacrament. In the world of incarnation nothing neutral remains, nothing can be taken away from the Son of man.

(Source: Alexander Schmemann, "The Missionary Imperative in the Orthodox Tradition," in *Eastern Orthodox Theology: A Contemporary Reader,* 2nd ed., ed. Daniel B. Clendenin [Grand Rapids, MI: Baker Academic, 2003]; also in Gerald H. Anderson, ed., *The Theology of the Christian Mission* [New York: McGraw-Hill, 1961], 250-57.)

Patriarchal Encyclicals and Other Official Documents of the Orthodox Church

The first two of the following four documents trace Orthodox thinking about mission in the twentieth century. The final two documents highlight the distinctive voice of Orthodoxy within the ecumenical movement.

65. *Encyclical Letter of the Patriarch of Constantinople, Joachim III, 1902*

Encyclical of H.H. Joachim III, Patriarch of Constantinople, to all local Orthodox Churches (1902)

To their Beatitudes and Holinesses the Patriarchs of Alexandria and Jerusalem, and to the most holy autocephalous sister-Churches in Christ, in Cyprus, Russia, Greece, Romania, Serbia, and Montenegro.

Whereas the most holy presidents of the venerable autocephalous Orthodox Churches have written to us in Irenical Letters in reply to our announcement of our election (by God's pleasure) and elevation to the most holy apostolic and patriarchal Ecumenical Throne, we are happy to observe the ancient and unbreakable bond, manifested with all haste and great warmth, and the words of evangelical love so warmly expressed and the ardent prayers addressed to God on behalf of this senior holy and Great Church of Christ, their sister most ready in faith and hope and love.

This appearance of brethren praying together in Christ and united in a sacred harmony stirs our soul and warms us to a more continuous effectual fellowship; and it has excited in us greater hopes of a more fruitful cultivation of mutual relations among Churches sharing in the same opinion, with a view to a more splendid and abundant religious harvest. We declare ourselves full of most excellent intentions and we gladly take up the sincere assurances of

the holy Churches, among whom our most holy sister who bears the honours among the Churches in Orthodox States (we speak of the Orthodox Church of All the Russias) has brought us great consolation by addressing herself as follows:

"The summons to peace and fraternal love and lively mutual fellowship, which you addressed to us and to the other autocephalous Churches, will find an echo and a sympathy in the hearts of all Orthodox Christians, who are sincerely devoted to their mother Church. Divided by reasons of history and differences of language and nationality, the local holy Churches of God find their unity in mutual love and their courage in close fellowship with one another; and they derive power to make progress in faith and devotion, rejecting the crafts of hostility and proclaiming the Gospel universally." The same spirit of brotherly love and unity derived from the divine source of the Gospel breathes vitally through similar words and expressions in the esteemed letters from all the other sister-Churches: they give us courage and strength, and they afford happy opportunities for us, following the good custom (which dates from time immemorial) of exchanging fraternal greetings and love, to seek also their wise counsel on matters on which both common study and judgement could be considered opportune by the Churches and also the successful achievement of good works to the benefit of the local Churches as well as of the whole Church, whose head is Christ.

Happily encouraged, then, by such brotherly support to the Corinthians and to all in all ages who believe in Christ: "I beseech you, brethren, through the name of our Lord Jesus Christ, that you all speak the same thing, and that there be no division among you; but that you be perfected together in the same mind and in the same judgement," we decided to suggest to our Holy Synod for deliberation a plan which we judged to be right and holy and worthy of serious consideration. With a view to a clearer formulation and easier study of certain topics of a religious nature and of great importance, we communicated that plan to our venerable and dear synodical brothers in Christ; and we asked them whether our holy and Great Church of Christ considered it opportune to seek an exchange of views with the holy patriarchs and most reverend presidents of the auto-cephalous Churches on these topics.

After expert study and preparation, they have agreed by a unanimous synodical resolution of our dear brother-bishops gathered around us in the Holy Synod; but standing firm to the custom prevailing in the primitive Church (according to which the bishops and pious guardians of the Churches acquainted each other by letter of their problems and of their solutions, diligently and fraternally being careful to seek after a common mind in word and deed), we are proceeding to outline the questions which have been approved synodically: they do not raise any new matters, but put forward matters which have for some time been the subjects of common study, with the object of mutual enlightenment of the local holy Orthodox Churches of God. They, motivated (of course) by similar intentions for the general good, will gladly (we believe) accept and judge opportune such research into the cycle of spiritual intercommunion in overseeing: it is not only to be perceived pragmatically but is also commanded by the calling with which all of us who have been called in Christ, by the favour and grace of God, to guard His holy Churches by giving heed to themselves and to be concerned for the salvation of all men.

It is, indeed, necessary that those who are set over the faithful for their spiritual government should pay attention to the greater good of all Christians, in order that the most precious crown of love might be enabled to bear more fruit according to the divine will. Wherefore, we consider that what should first of all be examined is whatever the venerable presidents of the holy autocephalous Orthodox Churches deem would be beneficial to

do but which is not being done; and what henceforward should and could be done, towards bringing together the Orthodox peoples in the unity of faith and in mutual love and common purpose; and what thereafter should be done to strengthen further our holy and Orthodox faith, and to defend more strongly the holy Churches of God against the assault of the contrary spirit of these days.

It is, moreover, pleasing to God, and in accordance with the Gospel, to seek the mind of the most holy autocephalous Churches on the subject of our present and future relations with the two great growths of Christianity, viz., the Western Church and the Church of the Protestants. Of course, the union of them and of all who believe in Christ with us in the Orthodox faith is the pious and heart-felt desire of our Church and of all genuine Christians who stand firm in the evangelical doctrine of unity, and it is the subject of constant prayer and supplication; but at the same time we are not unaware that this pious desire comes up against the unbroken persistence of these Churches in doctrines on which, having taken their stand as on a base hardened by the passage of time, they seem quite disinclined to join a road to union, such as is pointed out by evangelical and historical truth; nor do they evince any readiness to do so, except on terms and bases on which the desired dogmatic unity and fellowship is unacceptable to us. It is a truism that the holy catholic and apostolic Church is founded upon the Apostles and preserved by the divine and inspired Fathers in the Ecumenical Councils, and that her head is Christ the great shepherd, who bought her with his own blood; and that according to the inspired and heaven-bound Apostle she is the pillar and ground of the truth and the body of Christ: this holy Church is indeed one in identity of faith and similarity of manners and customs, in unison with the decisions of the seven Ecumenical Councils, and she must be one and not many, differing from each other in dogmas and fundamental institutions of ecclesiastical government. If, as in every matter which is impossible with men but possible with God, we cannot yet hope for the union of all as ever being a possibility, yet because divine grace is constantly active and men are being guided in paths of evangelical love and peace, one must consider very carefully whether it might be possible to prepare the (at present) anomalous way which leads to such a goal and to find points of encounter and contact, or even to turn a blind eye to certain irregularities until the completion in due course of the whole task, whereby might be fulfilled to our joint satisfaction and benefit our Lord and God and Saviour Jesus Christ's saying about one flock and one shepherd. Wherefore, if it might be acceptable to the holy brethren to follow up this suggestion, we are bold to add this fraternal question: whether the present is judged to be the right time for a preliminary conference on this, to prepare a level ground for a fraternal approach and to determine, by common agreement of members of the whole of our Orthodox Church, what might be considered the best bases, ways, and means.

Clearly relevant to Christian unity are the questions concerning those Western Christians who recently separated from the Roman Church and call themselves Old Catholics, and who say that they accept the teachings of the undivided Church down to the 9th century and the decrees of the seven holy Ecumenical Councils: they claim that they are already in the Orthodox Church as a whole, and they seek union and communion with her as the remaining task of formal regularization. The impetuous zeal for Christian truth and evangelical love on the part of these pious Christians is all together praiseworthy, and in their fine struggle they proved themselves to be filled with it. Their conferences' resolutions and acts are well known to the Christian world, as are their dogmatic and liturgical teaching through their catechetical and symbolical books.

A clear and agreed opinion as to their professed confession of faith does not yet prevail among us, but various opinions about it are expressed by our churchmen, both by those who have known them at close quarters and also by those who have studied them at a distance: some of them have decided that on important dogmatic points this confession is still far from perfect Orthodoxy, and others on the contrary consider it not to contain essential differences which would preclude unity of faith and ecclesiastical communion but to be a well-nigh complete acceptance by them of the complete healthy Orthodox teaching and tradition. We think it good, therefore, to invite the pious and fraternal views of the holy Orthodox sister-Churches on this important matter, as to whether they deem it opportune (and what way would be good and

acceptable) to facilitate the realization of the desire of these Christians for complete union with us, as an auspicious first-fruit of the hoped-for and longed-for unity of all Christians.

Worthy of no less attention, in our opinion, is the question of a common calendar, already for some time spoken and written about, especially the proposed methods of reforming the Julian Calendar which has prevailed in the Orthodox Church for centuries, or the acceptance of the Gregorian: the former is more defective scientifically, the latter more exact, considering also the change of our ecclesiastical Easter after the necessary agreement. In the studies on this topic, we see that the opinions which are held by Orthodox who have made a special investigation of it are divided. Some of them consider our ancient inheritance as alone fitting in the Church, having been handed down from the fathers and always having had the Church's authority; not only do they think that there is very little need for change, but they would rather avoid it, for the reasons which they elaborate. Others, champions of the Westerners' calendar and its introduction by us, suggest the greatest possible chronometric accuracy, or even the new usage of uniformity; and they advocate the practice of the Western Church as being reasonable, perhaps in expectation of possible religious benefits, in their own opinion. So, in our times, the discussion has been intensified, various and stimulating assertions being propounded by either side, both of a scientific and of a religious nature, on both of which in some Orthodox countries a certain inclination is evident of adherence to the notion of changing our Orthodox calendar or of some reform of it; and, inasmuch as this question (for all its obvious scientific form) has an ecclesiastical importance, it seems right to us to exchange with the other Orthodox Churches the relevant information in order that on this too a common mind might be reached among them, and a single opinion and decision of the whole Orthodox Church expressed. For, to her alone belongs the judgement on this matter and the research (if necessary) for a way of uniting (so far as is possible) the hoped-for scientific accuracy with the desired maintenance of hallowed ecclesiastical decrees.

So, then, our Great Church of Christ considers this exchange of views on the above-mentioned points to be a simple indication of spiritual and practical intercommunion, and as cementing the unity which should be maintained on all common questions and which is most effective in Orthodoxy; and she cherishes high hopes that her fraternal concern in this matter, and her earnest prayer for holy and evangelical conclusions, will find a sympathetic echo in the hearts of the venerable sister-Churches in Christ and have the approval of their brotherly love, so that on each matter the views of those who reverently preside over the Churches may be made known. We think, too, that as well as the common benefits expected from the mutual exchanges the great moral strength of the holy Orthodox Church of Christ may be demonstrated once again to the world; for its source is her possession of the unchanging truth, and its strong lever is the unbreakable unity of the local Churches. With such hopes and convictions, which we base upon the inspired zeal of those venerable presidents who govern the holy Churches of God and of the Holy Synods, that their Churches may be glorious and steadfast, we pray to the Lord with all our heart that all the Orthodox faithful may be preserved and sheltered by His invincible shield, and that He will vouchsafe great happiness and health and long life to Your Beatitude and Holiness, who are much beloved and cherished by us.

—Joachim of Constantinople

(Source: Joachim of Ephesus, Nathanael of Proussa, Alexander of Neocaesarea, Basil of Smyrna, Constantine of Chios, Polycarpos of Varna, Joachim of Xanthi, Nicodemus of Vodena, Nicephoros of Lititsa, Tarasios of Helioupolis, Hieronytnos of Kallioupolis, *The Orthodox Church in the Ecumenical Movement: Documents and Statements,* 1902-1975, ed. Constantin G. Patelos [Geneva: World Council of Churches, 1978].)

66. *Encyclical of the Patriarch of Constantinople, 1920, "Churches throughout the World"*

"Love one another earnestly from the heart."
—*1 Peter 1:22*

Our own church holds that rapprochement between the various Christian churches and fellow-ship among them is not excluded by the doctrinal differences which exist among them. In our opinion such a rapprochement is highly desirable and necessary. It would be useful in many ways for the real interest of each particular church and of the whole Christian body, and also for the preparation and advancement of that blessed union which will be completed in the future in accordance with the will of God. We therefore consider that the present time is most favourable for bringing forward this important question and studying it together.

Even if in this case, owing to antiquated prejudices, practices, or pretensions, the difficulties which have so often jeopardized attempts at reunion in the past may arise or be brought up, nevertheless, in our view, since we are concerned at this initial stage only with contacts and rapprochement, these difficulties are of less importance. If there is good will and intention, they cannot and should not create an invincible and insuperable obstacle.

Wherefore, considering such an endeavour to be both possible and timely, especially in view of the hopeful establishment of the League of Nations, we venture to express below in brief our thoughts and our opinion regarding the way in which we understand this rapprochement and contact and how we consider it to be realizable; we earnestly ask and invite the judgment and the opinion of the other sister churches in the East and of the venerable Christian churches in the West and everywhere in the world.

We believe that the two following measures would greatly contribute to the rapprochement which is so much to be desired and which would be so useful, and we believe that they would be both successful and fruitful:

First, we consider as necessary and indispensable the removal and abolition of all the mutual mistrust and bitterness among the different churches which arise from the tendency of some of them to entice and proselytize adherents of other confessions. For nobody ignores what is unfortunately happening today in many places, disturbing the internal peace of the churches, especially in the East. So many troubles and sufferings are caused by other Christians and great hatred and enmity are aroused, with such insignificant results, by this tendency of some to proselytize and entice the followers of other Christian confessions.

After this essential re-establishment of sincerity and confidence among the churches, we consider,

Secondly, that above all, love should be rekindled and strengthened among the churches, so that they should no more consider one another as strangers and foreigners, but as relatives, and as being a part of the household of Christ and "fellow heirs, members of the same body and partakers of the promise of God in Christ" (Eph. 3:6).

For if the different churches are inspired by love, and place it before everything else in their judgments of others and their relationships with them, instead of increasing and widening the existing dissensions, they should be enabled to reduce and diminish them. By stirring up a right brotherly interest in the condition, the well-being and stability of the other churches; by readiness to take an interest in what is happening in those churches and to obtain a better knowledge of them, and by willingness to offer mutual aid and help, many good things will be achieved for the glory and the benefit both of themselves and of the Christian body. In our opinion, such a friendship and kindly disposition towards each other can be shown and demonstrated particularly in the following ways:

- By the acceptance of a uniform calendar for the celebration of the great Christian feasts at the same time by all the churches.
- By the exchange of brotherly letters on the occasion of the great feasts of the churches' year as is customary, and on other exceptional occasions.
- By close relationships between the representatives of all churches wherever they may be.
- By relationships between the theological schools and the professors of theology; by the exchange of theological and ecclesiastical reviews, and of other works published in each church.
- By exchanging students for further training among the seminaries of the different churches.
- By convoking pan-Christian conferences in order to examine questions of common interest to all the churches.

- By impartial and deeper historical study of doctrinal differences both by the seminaries and in books.
- By mutual respect for the customs and practices in different churches.
- By allowing each other the use of chapels and cemeteries for the funerals and burials of believers of other confessions dying in foreign lands.
- By the settlement of the question of mixed marriages among the confessions.
- Lastly, by wholehearted mutual assistance for the churches in their endeavours for religious advancement, charity, and so on.

Such a sincere and close contact among the churches will be all the more useful and profitable for the whole body of the Church, because manifold dangers threaten not only particular churches, but all of them. These dangers attack the very foundations of the Christian faith and the essence of Christian life and society. For the terrible world war which has just finished brought to light many unhealthy symptoms in the life of the Christian peoples, and often revealed great lack of respect even for the elementary principles of justice and charity. Thus it worsened already existing wounds and opened other new ones of a more material kind, which demand the attention and care of all the churches. Alcoholism, which is increasing daily; the increase of unnecessary luxury under the pretext of bettering life and enjoying it; the voluptuousness and lust hardly covered by the cloak of freedom and emancipation of the flesh; the prevailing unchecked licentiousness and indecency in literature, painting, the theatre, and in music, under the respectable name of the development of good taste and cultivation of fine art; the deification of wealth and the contempt of higher ideals; all these and the like, as they threaten the very essence of Christian societies, are also timely topics requiring and indeed necessitating common study and cooperation by the Christian churches. Finally, it is the duty of the churches which bear the sacred name of Christ not to forget or neglect any longer his new and great commandment of love. Nor should they continue to fall piteously behind the political authorities, who, truly applying the spirit of the Gospel and the teaching of Christ, have under happy auspices already set up the so-called League of Nations in order to defend justice and cultivate charity and agreement among the nations.

For all these reasons, being ourselves convinced of the necessity for establishing a contact and league (fellowship) among the churches and believing that the other churches share our conviction as stated above, at least as a beginning we request each one of them to send us in reply a statement of its own judgment and opinion on this matter so that, common agreement or resolution having been reached, we may proceed together to its realization, and thus "speaking the truth in love, may grow up into him in all things, which is the head, even Christ; from whom the whole body fitly joined together and compacted by that which every joint supplieth, according to the effectual working in the measure of every part, maketh increase of the body unto the edifying of itself in love" (Eph. 4:15-16).

In the Patriarchate of Constantinople the month of January in the year of salvation 1920

(Source: *The Orthodox Church in the Ecumenical Movement: Documents and Statements,* 1902-1975, ed. Constantin G. Patelos [Geneva: World Council of Churches, 1978].)

67. *The Evangelistic Witness of Orthodoxy Today, Bucharest 1974*

An Orthodox consultation on "Confessing Christ Today" was held in Bucharest, Romania, June 4-8, 1974, as follow-up to the Bangkok Conference on "Salvation Today" and as part of the preparations for Section One on "Confessing Christ Today" at the Fifth Assembly of the World Council of Churches in Nairobi, Kenya, in November 1975. The following report is one of four working documents prepared by the consultation.

1. What Is the Evangelistic Witness?

a) The evangelistic witness is not the whole mission of the Church. It has many other dimensions. Evangelistic witness is understood to be restricted to the communication of Christ to those who do not consider themselves Christian, wherever these people may be found. This includes the need of the Church to witness to some of its own nominal members.

b) The evangelistic witness is a call to salvation, which means the restoration of the relationship of God and man as understood in the Orthodox Christian teaching of theosis. This message has its source in the Scriptures, which witness to the redemption of mankind in Christ Jesus, yet it also includes a world-view that locates man vis-à-vis God and vis-à-vis his fellow-man as individual and society, as well as his own personhood and destiny. It includes both the God-and-man (vertical) relationship and the human-being-to-fellow-human-being (horizontal) relationship.

c) By its nature, however, evangelistic witness is first of all and primarily a confrontation of man by the message, judgment, love, presence, redemption, command, and transfiguring power of the energies of the one holy and undivided trinity.

d) Evangelistic witness brings to man the true response to his essential need *qua* human being. It is the bringing of the Divine response to the real need of persons as individuals and of persons in community. It is the message of human restoration and the divinization of the human. As such it speaks to the most profound human need, yet it also meets and overcomes the felt needs of human beings in more specific and concrete dimensions.

e) Because man is fallen, the evangelistic witness will also appear to him to have an element of foolishness (*moria*) and will always contain within it an element of *skandalon*, simply because the wisdom of man cannot fully comprehend the transcendent wisdom of God. Yet the evangelistic witness does more than provide a message of divine dimensions; it also conveys a way of living applicable in full within the community of believers, the Church, and in part in the world at large.

2. Why Are We Required to Make Evangelistic Witness?

a) We do not have the option of keeping the Good News to ourselves. Sharing the Word and communicating the Word and confessing the Faith once given to the saints is an integral part of fulfilling the image and likeness of God and the achievement of theosis. Like St. Paul the believer must be able to say about all who do not know the life in Christ what he said about his fellow-countrymen: "My heart's desire and prayer to God for them is that they may be saved" (Rom. 10:1). The uncommunicated Gospel (Good News) is a patent contradiction.

b) The goal of evangelistic witness—though it may pass through many stages and pause at many intermediate places—is conversion from a life characterized by sin, separation from God, submission to evil, and the unfulfilled potential of God's image to a new life characterized by the forgiveness of sins, obedience to the commands of God, renewed fellowship with God in Trinity, growth in the restoration of the Divine image and the realization among us of the prototype of the love of Christ. More briefly and succinctly put, the final goal of evangelistic witness is conversion and baptism. Conversion is a willful turning from sin, death, and evil to true life in God. Baptism is the reception of a new member into the new life of the community of God's people, the Church.

c) Though the conversion and baptism of all is the final goal of evangelistic witness, there is a need to identify many intermediate goals. The increase of love among Christians and non-Christians, entry into dialogue and brotherly conversation, the formulation of the Gospel message into the language and thought-forms of the non-Christian neighbor, the interpenetration of the structures of society, the promulgation of the will of God in reference to injustice among us and the prophetic challenge to the world's values share in the task of evangelistic witness and in part serve as a motive to speak the word of Christ to all men.

3. In What Manner Do We Make Our Evangelistic Witness?

a) It is the task of evangelistic witness to lead persons to the acknowledgement of God's saving power in their lives. "He is Lord of all and bestows his riches upon all who call upon Him." Yet "how are men to call upon Him in whom they have not believed? And how are they to believe in Him of whom they have never heard? And how are they to hear without a preacher? And how can men preach unless they are sent?" (Rom. 10:12, 14-15). After two thousand years this Pauline injunction retains its urgency and its timeliness.

b) Yet those same intervening years require of us a review of our conceptions of the methods of evangelistic witness. On the one hand it is clear that the proclamation alone is not the only way in which the evangelistic witness is made. Further, in this day and age mere preaching may no longer be the most effective way of evangelistic witness. Paul does not tell us what we are to do when the Gospel has been proclaimed and rejected, or even worse, simply ignored! Yet of one thing we are sure: We are sent by Christ to bear witness to him and his saving truth for all of mankind.

c) How is it to be done today? In the first instance this question must be directed to the attitudes and motives of "those who are sent." Those who are sent must be first conscious of their own repentance, conversion, and salvation. Those who are fully aware of the new life of Grace in the community of the Holy Trinity and in the reality of the community of the Church alone are able to communicate the saving witness. This above all comes about with the knowledge that nothing we do is of effect without the energizing power of the Trinity. No matter what it is that we do in evangelistic witness we know that it is "God making his appeal through us" (2 Cor. 5:20).

d) As difficult and beyond our capabilities as the work of evangelistic witness may seem, then, we undertake the task with the spirit not of fear or of inadequacy or of insufficiency—though all these in truth exist in us—but with hope that through our meager efforts it may be stored up and empowered by the gracious energies of the Triune God in whose name we undertake the task.

e) And so it is that "those who are sent" to be evangelistic witnesses do so as ones having experienced the redemption of God and who then work with the full understanding of their own insufficiency, fully expecting the grace of God to "provide the growth." Thus it is in a constant spirit of metanoia (repentance), with a full sense of our own limitations that we make our evangelistic witness.

f) How is this evangelistic witness to be made today objectively? The chief means of witness for the Church today is not the bold announcement of Christ as Saviour to a world that has already heard the words and still remains unresponsive. The first and chief method of evangelistic witness is the same as that of the early Church. Pagans saw the quality of life of those early believers and were so attracted by its power and beauty that they sought to find its power and its source (e.g., Epistle of Diognetus; Libanius' praise of Chrysostom's mother).

g) The first method of evangelistic witness is the sharing of love by those who have acknowledged the love of God for them. "We love because he first loved us" (1 John 4:19). It was an injunction to evangelistic witness when the apostle of Love instructed: "Beloved, let us love one another; for love is of God, and he who loves is born of God and knows God" (1 John 4:7).

h) More specifically the same apostle says: "This is the love of God, that we keep His commandments . . . this is the victory that overcomes the world, our faith" (1 John 5:3-4). Our obedience to his will is equally a powerful form of evangelistic witness. We have cheapened the Gospel in the past by much talking and little practice. Our obedience to God's will must now be the vehicle for our message.

i) Though the Divine liturgy is essentially and primarily the realization of the unity of the Church with Christ, and as such is in and of itself a manifestation of the reality of the Church, it may have consequences for the evangelistic witness of the Church. From all parts of the world we bring witness to the transforming and evangelizing power of the Divine liturgy.

j) Evangelistic witness wherever possible must be made to the unchurched. But this witness must be understood in the broadest manner. Certainly, it will include personal witnessing of the power of God in the individual life of the believer. The stories of the saints, the synaxaria, and the writings of the Fathers encourage the living Christian to speak of the power of the Holy Spirit in his or her own life.

k) But the Word of God cannot be contained only in the personal sphere. Evangelistic witness must also be made before the social and the political tribunal. Christians must speak the Word of God to contemporary issues of justice with all available means. Evangelistic witness will keep a vigilant eye upon all emergent social movements and concerns (women's liberation, racial consciousness, sexual

freedom, demonology), to speak the word of truth. But it will seek to do its task of evangelization towards and in these phenomena not by parroting words of another age, but by reformulating the unchanging truth with an eye to its contemporization. Certainly in doing this it will also respond creatively in the patristic spirit to the ever-new and ever-changing phenomena of our times.

l) This it will do in the honored spirit of the indigenization of the Orthodox faith in reference to national cultures. Orthodoxy is proud of its foreign missionary tradition, which has not been carried out in a spirit of colonialism but rather with the intent of adapting the faith to the manners, language, traditions and life-styles of the people to whom it brings the Gospel. Wherever Orthodoxy is now active in such mission it must retain and expand that method.

m) At this time in our history, however, most Orthodox Churches find it very difficult to speak of foreign missions. It certainly is not a live option for many of the national Orthodox Churches. Their duty remains primarily within the churches and the nations in which they find themselves. Yet other Orthodox Churches are to be challenged for having both the opportunity and the resources, yet not responding to the charge "Go therefore and make disciples of all nations, baptizing them in the name of the Father and of the Son and of the Holy Spirit, teaching them to observe all that I have commanded you" (Matt. 28:19). The same may be said in reference to inter-Orthodox assistance, especially to the newer Orthodox in Africa, Alaska, and the Far East.

4. For Whom Is the Evangelistic Witness?

a) The preceding section implies the answer to the title question of this section. Yet perhaps it would be good to articulate it. It would be true to say that the evangelistic witness is directed towards all of the *ktisis* that groans and travails in search of adoption and redemption (Rom. 8:22). But what specifically does this mean?

b) In the first case the Church's evangelistic witness is for the Christian who is not a Christian. There are many who have been baptized and yet have put off Christ, either deliberately or through indifference. Often such people still find it possible sociologically or culturally or ethnically to relate in some manner to the Christian community. The re-Christianization of Christians is an important task of the Church's evangelistic witness.

c) The evangelistic witness is consequently also directed to those who superficially identify Orthodox Christianity with their national culture. We cannot be content with a process of indigenization that leaves much of our national and cultural lives untouched by the spirit of the Gospel. The transfiguring power of the Holy Trinity is meant to reach into every nook and cranny of our national life. Those who live in or come from the traditional Orthodox lands are especially sensitive to this challenge of evangelistic witness.

d) The evangelistic witness will also speak to the structures of this world, its economic, political, and societal institutions. Especially necessary is the witness of social justice in the name of the poor and the oppressed. We must relearn the patristic lesson that the Church is the mouth and voice of the poor and oppressed in the presence of the powers that be. In our own way we must learn once again "how to speak to the ear of the King" on the people's behalf.

e) Finally, the evangelistic witness is directed to the new secularized man in an ever more secularized world. The forces of technology, scientific success, and control over the environment have provided mankind with an enviable control over the conditions of his life. Yet that control has had many undesirable consequences. It has taught man to think of himself as fully sufficient; he now conceives of himself primarily as consumer; he is *homo economicus*; his circumscribed goals of life require no transcendent referent, no forgiveness, no restoration of relationship, no sacramental life, no theosis, no God. Yet exactly because he sits in that darkness, he is the object of the Church's evangelistic witness.

5. Who Performs the Task of Evangelistic Witness?

a) The most true and profound response to this question would be that it is God, through the power of the Holy Spirit, who does the work of evangelistic witness. We are made *diakonoi* of the Gospel "according to the gift of God's grace which was given [us] by the working of his power" (Eph. 3:7). In a further sense, it is the whole community of God that does this work. For it is "through the Church" that "the manifold wisdom of God [is] now made known to the principalities and powers" (Eph. 3:10).

b) More particularly, three groups or classes of Christians are charged, each in its own way, with the task of evangelistic witness. First are those ordained to the Lord's service. The chief evangelizer of the Church is the bishop, with his presbyterion and diaconate as well as the monastic establishment. In the history of the Church, these "professionals" of evangelical witness have carried on the work of the Church with great success. And inasmuch as they still lead the conduct of worship, preach the Word of God, visit the oppressed and suffering, speak the word of truth in the tribunals of power, proclaim the Gospel before vast audiences electronically present, communicate the Orthodox truth through the printed word, or walk the foreign mission trails, they continue to carry it. Yet we are all too conscious of our lethargy and deafness to the Divine commission. Theological schools at all levels are challenged to heal that deafness through proper and full education for evangelical witness of the candidates for holy orders. There is need to restore the claim of evangelical witness upon the priestly conscience of the servants of God.

c) The second group specifically charged with the work of evangelistic witness is the laity. We have just rediscovered the theology of the laity in the Orthodox Church. Laity are part of the "royal priesthood" of the Church. We are all—clergy and laity—called to be "a holy priesthood, to offer spiritual sacrifices acceptable to God through Christ" (1 Pet. 2:5). As such, we are all "a chosen race, a royal priesthood, a holy nation, God's own people." Thus the laity shares in the whole work of the Church, including that of evangelistic witness. Part of the task of the clergy is to "raise the consciousness" of the laity regarding their roles in the fulfillment of the work of the Church. As we have noted, the primary means of evangelistic witness today is the authentic Christian life, to which every lay person is called. So also is the vital and living participation in the Divine liturgy, the personal witness of faith, the Christian involvement of the believer in the social, political, educational, cultural, and intellectual life of his nation and society. Orthodoxy of doctrine, combined with evangelical behavior are the conditions of true evangelistic witness by the laity.

d) Then there are those among us called against our will to mission. Some of us become evangelistic witnesses suddenly, when the principalities and powers of the age force us into situations of martyrdom, when compromise and accommodation are not possible. Today, the ancient experience of expropriation, prison, and arena is frequently repeated. When called, we must be ready for the special witness of martyrdom. Others of us are called from among the members of the Body of Christ to evangelistic witness because of the special gifts of the Holy Spirit. Throughout the ages persons have been touched by the Holy Spirit and provided with gifts of unique character. These persons may do the work of evangelistic witness. However it is incumbent upon them to do so always from within the faith and truth of the body of the Church. In turn, the Church must look upon these brethren seized of the Holy Spirit with the wisdom of Gameliel.

e) The difficult and thorny question of the renewal of foreign mission by the Church cannot be met or solved by any one of the particular Orthodox churches. We cannot deny the goal. Yet a unified and organized Orthodox approach is needed, lest we harm and do disservice to our fellow Orthodox. This certainly is an important element in our understanding of our total mission in the world today, from a pan-Orthodox perspective. Part of our mission is also to protect and preserve Orthodoxy where it is found today. An honest recognition of our limitations and existential restrictions is also required.

(Source: "The Evangelistic Witness of Orthodoxy Today," Draft Report No. 4 from the Orthodox Consultation in Bucharest, 1974, published in *St. Vladimir's Theological Quarterly* 18, no. 4 [1974] [Crestwood, N.Y.: St. Vladimir's Orthodox Theological Seminary].)

68. *Encyclical, For the Day of the Protection of Natural Environment, September 1, 2006,* by Ecumenical Patriarch Bartholomew

Beloved brothers and children in the Lord,

Our merciful God Who loves mankind created the world to be beautiful and functional, sufficient to meet all human needs. He granted to man, the crown and king of creation, the enjoyment of everything in the world that is necessary for life.

God instilled in every beneficial relationship between man and creation feelings of joy and pleasure. Furthermore, He imbued man with a sense of longing when in genuine need, and a sense of satiety to protect against abuse by excess. Man, therefore, is equipped by God with an instinctual awareness of the proper measure of things, of the difference between what is necessary and beneficial and what is excessive and harmful. Endowed as well with free will, man has the ability to act on his instinctual understanding of the boundaries of these two conditions, so that he can either set new boundaries of self-deprivation for purposes of spiritual exercise, or can set them aside altogether through willful acts of self-aggrandizement.

In the latter case, we are dealing either with covetousness, which the Apostle Paul characterizes as idolatry, or with a hostile loathing of the God-given gifts of life and the things of this world. Both such attitudes are equally condemnable for they oppose God's perfect plan that the life of man be full of joy and gladness.

Unfortunately, man refused to comply with God's directives regarding the measured use of natural resources according to his needs, nor did he preserve and protect the world entrusted to him, and thus he estranged himself from the governing grace of God. As a result, man acts toward his surrounding environment in rapacious and destructive ways, as a ruler rather than a steward, disrupting the natural harmony and balance that are from God. Nature in turn has reacted to man's abuse in unbalanced ways, inflicting upon humanity a series of natural catastrophes. Recent unusual temperature fluctuations, hurricanes, earthquakes, storms, the pollutions of rivers and seas and numerous other occurrences that hurt both the environment and man are the results of human actions, whether carried out openly or executed in secret. The ultimate cause of all this destructive behavior is man's egocentrism, an expression of his self-willed alienation from God and his effort to make himself god.

Because of this egocentrism, the relationship of man and nature intended by the Creator has degenerated into one of insolent and arrogant subjugation of natural forces and their use for the killing or subjection of our fellow human beings rather than for the preservation of life and freedom, or for the satisfaction of excessive pleasures, without care of the consequences of overuse.

The use of atomic and nuclear forces of nature for war is an insult to creation and Creator, as is over-consumption of any kind, which burdens the natural environment with pollutants, which leads to climate change and global warming and an imbalance in the natural order, with all that implies. The immense consumption of energy for purposes of war and the excessive consumption of contemporary humanity far beyond its needs are two areas where the responsibilities of political leaders and common citizens are interwoven in such a way so that each of us has the power to contribute to the betterment of the general condition.

Beloved brothers and sisters in the Lord, let us all make every effort possible, each from where God has placed us, to rein in our reckless over-consumption, so that the harmonious workings of this planet, our common home, may be restored, and that we and our children may enjoy in peace all the good things which God in His love for us has created and offers to all men and women. Amen.

—Bartholomew of Constantinople beloved, brother in Christ and fervent intercessor before God.

(Source: Encyclical of Ecumenical Patriarch Bartholomew for the Day of the Natural Environment, September 1, 2006; online at http://www.oikoumene .org/gr/resources/documents/wcc-programmes/ justice-diakonia-and-responsibility-for-creation/ climate-change-water/01-09-06-encyclical-of- ecumenical-patriarch-bartholomew.html.)

World Council of Churches Mission Documents

69. *Preparatory Paper No. 1 on Evangelism and Mission*

The preparatory paper below gives a historical overview of the major concerns of the WCC as it considers the relationship between ecumenism and mission. It was published in preparation for the WCC Conference on Mission and Evangelism in Athens, 2005. The document "Towards a Common Witness" takes up in particular the issue of proselytism, which is of special concern to the Orthodox at a time when Protestant evangelists are flooding into the dominantly Orthodox countries of the former Soviet Union, Eastern Europe, and the Middle East. The third document is a news release indicating the ways in which the World Council of Churches, World Evangelical Fellowship,
and the Roman Catholic Church have begun to reach a common mind on issues related to evangelism and conversion. Two declarations from the WCC follow—AGAPE Consultations on Poverty, Wealth, and Ecology—one arising from the Latin American context and the other from South Africa. They illustrate some of the ways in which the conciliar movement has come to understand the sources and impact of globalization and ecological concerns.

This is the first of a series of papers which will be published at irregular intervals, first on the Web, then for some also in printed version. The paper "Mission and Evangelism in Unity Today" was adopted by the WCC Commission on World Mission and Evangelism in 2000 as a study document to be used during the preparations for the next world mission conference.

Introduction

1. The ecumenical movement has its origins in the missionary movement, for the contemporary search for the unity of the church was initiated within the framework of the mission endeavor. The missionaries were among the first to look for ways and styles of witness in unity, recognizing that the scandal of Christian divisions and denominational rivalries hindered greatly the impact of their message.

2. The concern for mission and evangelism in unity has been constantly on the ecumenical agenda, especially since 1961 when the International Missionary Council merged with the World Council of Churches. In this context, the then Commission on World Mission and Evangelism issued in 1982 "Mission and Evangelism: An Ecumenical Affirmation." This statement summed up, in a comprehensive way, a number of the most important aspects and facets of mission, including diverse understandings of mission and its biblical and theological basis. Appropriating understandings already reached in the debates of the previous decade and enlarging them in a wider perspective, that document articulated ecumenical affirmations on mission and evangelism in the context of the world of the early 1980s.

3. The 1982 statement, which was approved by the WCC Central Committee, was received warmly and widely by the churches. It has been used by mission agencies, theological schools, local congregations, and individual Christians. It has fermented, during these decades, new understandings of mission and evangelism and has inspired, provoked, and strengthened the longing for witness in unity. It has reached far beyond the frontiers of the member churches of the WCC.

4. Since 1982 many of the world's realities have changed, confronting the churches with new mission challenges. Two world mission conferences have been held under WCC auspices, in San Antonio, USA (1989), and Salvador, Brazil (1996). Important mission issues were raised also in the WCC Seventh Assembly in Canberra, Australia (1991). In the context of the new world situation and fresh missiological insights and learnings, a number of WCC member churches requested that a new statement on mission and evangelism be elaborated to assist the churches together to respond with an appropriate and meaningful mission praxis.

5. In response to such requests, the WCC decided to undertake the development of a further statement to assist Christians and the churches in their task of mission and evangelism in unity at the turn of the millennium. The present text, which has been adopted in March 2000 by the WCC's Commission on World Mission and Evangelism (CWME) as a Study Document is offered in the hope that it will stimulate reflection on the nature, content, and implications of the gospel of Jesus Christ in the varied but inter-related contexts of their life and faithful witness to the gospel, to the end that all people everywhere may have the opportunity to hear and to believe.

6. The present document does not replace the 1982 statement; neither does it promote a theology of mission different from what was agreed upon ecumenically in that statement. It has an identity of its own. It attempts to articulate anew the churches' commitment to mission and evangelism in unity within the context of the challenges facing them today.

7. *Use of terminology.* For some Christians and churches the terms "mission" and "evangelism," although related, are perceived and used differently; for others the two are virtually identical in both meaning and content. In the present document the two terms are used with some differentiation.

a. "Mission" carries a holistic understanding: the proclamation and sharing of the good news of the gospel by word (*kerygma*), deed (*diakonia*), prayer and worship (*leiturgia*) and the everyday witness of the Christian life (*martyria*); teaching as building up and strengthening people in their relationship with God and each other; and healing as wholeness and reconciliation into *koinonia*—communion with God, communion with people, and communion with creation as a whole.

b. "Evangelism," while not excluding the different dimensions of mission, focuses on explicit and intentional voicing of the gospel, including the invitation to personal conversion to a new life in Christ and to discipleship.

8. The expression "mission in unity" refers to the search for ways of witnessing together in unity and cooperation—despite differing ecclesiologies—within the context of the burning challenges facing churches everywhere today "so that the world may believe" (John 17:21), avoiding any form of confessional rivalry or competition. This does not imply an unrealistic super-church ecclesiology; neither does it deny the intrinsic relationship between mission and ecclesiology.

Mission and Evangelism in Unity: An Imperative and Vocation

9. Mission is central to Christian faith and theology. It is not an option but is rather an existential calling and vocation. Mission is constitutive of and conditions the very being of the church and of all Christians.

10. The God revealed by the scriptures is not static but rather relational and missionary: a God who has always been manifested as the Lord of history, leading God's people towards fullness of life through the covenants, the law, and the prophets who voiced God's will and interpreted the signs of the times; a God who came into the world through the incarnated Son, our Lord Jesus Christ, who, taking human flesh, shared our human condition and became one of us, died on the cross and rose from the dead; a God who, in the power of the Holy Spirit, loves, cares for, and sustains humanity and the whole of creation, leading them towards salvation and transfiguration.

11. The mission of God (*missio Dei*) has no limits or barriers; it has been addressed to and has been at work within the entire human race and the whole of creation throughout history. Jesus' parables of the good Samaritan and the sheep and the goats and his dialogue with the Syro-Phoenician woman clearly point in that direction. The early church apologists, in the framework of the dialogue with the people of their time, developed this idea further. On the basis of John 1, they explained that the Logos (Word), God's co-eternal and consubstantial Son, was and is present with the Father and the Holy Spirit in all God's acts, and that through the Word the world was created: God spoke, and "the Spirit swept over the face of the waters" (Gen. 1:2). In the Holy Spirit, they said, God spoke clearly and explicitly through the Word not only to the prophets of the Old Testament but also (though in a different way) to people of other nations and religions. When the fullness of time had come (Gal. 4:4), the very same Word "became flesh and lived among us" (John 1:14), coming to "his own" (John 1:11).

12. A trinitarian approach to the *missio Dei* is therefore important. On the one hand, this promotes a more inclusive understanding of God's presence and work in the whole world and among all people, implying that signs of God's presence can and should be identified, affirmed, and worked with even in the most unexpected places. On the other hand, by clearly affirming that the Father and the Spirit are always and in all circumstances present and at work together with the Word, the temptation to separate the presence of God or the Spirit from the Son of God, Jesus Christ, will be avoided.

13. The mission of God (*missio Dei*) is the source of and basis for the mission of the church, the body of Christ. Through Christ in the Holy Spirit, God indwells the church, empowering and energizing its members. Thus mission becomes for Christians an urgent inner compulsion, even a powerful test and criterion for authentic life in Christ, rooted in the profound demands of Christ's love, to invite others to share in the fullness of life Jesus came to bring (John 10:10). Participating in God's mission, therefore, should be natural for all Christians and all churches, not only for particular individuals or specialized groups. The Holy Spirit transforms Christians into living, courageous, and bold witnesses (cf. Acts 1:8). "We cannot keep from speaking about what we have seen and heard" (Acts 4:20) was the response of Peter and John when they were ordered to keep silent about Jesus; or, in Paul's words: "If I proclaim the gospel, this gives me no ground for boasting, for an obligation is laid on me, and woe betide me if I do not proclaim the gospel!"(1 Cor. 9:16).

14. Christians are called through metanoia to "have the mind of Christ" (1 Cor. 2:16), to be agents of God's mission in the world (Matt. 28:19-20;

Mark 16:15), to identify the signs of God's presence, affirming and promoting them by witnessing to and cooperating with all people of good will, and to be co-workers with God (1 Cor. 4:1) for the transfiguration of the whole of creation. Thus, the goal of mission is "a reconciled humanity and renewed creation," and "the vision of God uniting all things in Christ is the driving force of its life and sharing." "The church is sent into the world to call people and nations to repentance, to announce forgiveness of sin and a new beginning in relations with God and with neighbours through Jesus Christ."

15. The mission of the church in the power of the Spirit is to call people into communion with God, with one another, and with creation. In so doing, the church must honour the intrinsic and inseparable relationship between mission and unity. The church has the responsibility to live out the unity for which Jesus prayed for his people: "that they may all be one . . . so that the world may believe" (John 17:21). This conviction must be proclaimed and witnessed to in the community into which people are invited.

16. Mission in Christ's way is holistic, for the whole person and the totality of life are inseparable in God's plan of salvation accomplished in Jesus Christ. It is local—"the primary responsibility for mission, where there is a local church, is with that church in its own place." It is also universal, that is, to all peoples, beyond all frontiers of race, caste, gender, culture, nation—to "the ends of the earth" in every sense (cf. Acts 1:8; Mark 16:15; Luke 24:47).

17. "To tell the story [of Jesus Christ] is the specific privilege of the churches within God's overall mission." Evangelism includes explication of the gospel—"accounting for the hope that is in you" (1 Pet. 3:15)—as well as an invitation to believe in the triune God, become a disciple of Christ, and join the community of an existing local church. "Proclamation of Jesus Christ requires a personal response. The Living Word of God is never external, unrelational, disconnected, but always calling for personal conversion and relational communion. Such a conversion is more than appropriation of a message: it is a commitment to Jesus Christ, imitating his death and resurrection in a very visible and tangible way. That which begins with a personal commitment must, however, immediately lead into a relationship with other members of the body of Christ, the local witnessing community."

Context of Mission Today: Contemporary Trends

18. A major facet of the contemporary context of mission is that of globalization—a relatively recent phenomenon having to do with economic developments, changes in means of global communication and the consequent imposition of a new monoculture and a related set of values on most societies. These trends are of course not totally new; but the political changes at the end of the 1980s allow them now to influence the whole world unhindered by any global counter-force. . . .

23. Through processes of globalization, the values of post-modernity, rooted in Western cultures, are spreading rapidly across the globe. The very identities of people are in danger of being diluted or weakened in the melting-pot of the powerfully tempting and attractive monoculture and its new set of values. The very notion of nationhood itself is severely challenged. Individualism is preferred to life in community. Traditional values which formerly were lived as public values are today being privatized. Even religion is treated as merely a private matter. Personal experience takes the place of reason, knowledge, and understanding. Images are preferred to words and have a greater impact on people in terms of advertising, promoting, or conveying "truths" and goods. The importance of the present moment is emphasized; the past and future do not really matter. People are persuaded to believe that they are masters of their own lives and are therefore free to pick and choose what suits themselves. . . .

25. The centripetal forces of globalization are accompanied by centrifugal forces of fragmentation, which are being felt ever more acutely. This fragmentation is being experienced at personal, national, and international levels. Traditional family patterns are breaking down. Divorces have reached an unprecedented rate and the number of one-parent families is growing in many places. At the national level, in the vacuum created by

the collapse of the totalitarian regimes in Eastern Europe and the ramifications of that collapse in the rest of the world, turmoil, tensions, and fragmentation have arisen among and within the somewhat artificial statal units inherited from the pre-1989 period. New states have emerged along ethnic and tribal lines. Peoples who have lived together for generations can no longer stand one another. Cultural and ethnic identities are being used to oppress other identities. "Ethnic cleansing" and genocides are taking place in many parts of the world, bringing immense suffering, increasing hatred, and setting the stage for further violence towards humankind and creation.

26. The contemporary context of mission includes trends within the churches as well. In many parts of the world, churches are growing dramatically. This is true of churches—including so-called mainline churches—in disadvantaged communities, Pentecostal or African instituted churches and charismatic renewal movements, especially but not exclusively in the South. Even in the wealthier countries, where post-modernity is influencing attitudes and beliefs, new ways of "being church" in terms of community life and worship are experienced. And a growing number of strong missionary movements reaching out to other parts of the world are based in the South.

27. Some but not all of these churches appear to be striving for holistic witness to the gospel. Indeed, the highly competitive environment of the free market is reinforcing many churches and para-church movements in their perception of mission as the effort to attract and recruit new "customers," while retaining the old ones. Their programmes and doctrines are presented as "religious products," which must be appealing and attractive to potential new members. They evaluate the success of their mission in terms of growth, of numbers of converts or of newly planted churches. Unfortunately, very often their "new members" already belonged to other churches. Thus proselytism (as competition and "sheep-stealing") is one of the sharp contemporary issues facing the churches....

29. Finally, new religious movements of various kinds are proliferating everywhere, recruiting their adherents from traditionally Christian families, even from among active church members. The churches and their teachings are often attacked and denounced while new, modern, more attractive messages are promoted.

30. The above brief description of the overall context does not, of course, take into consideration the important variations and even opposite emphases in different regions and local situations. Nevertheless, this is the "world" in which the churches are called to give clear, authentic witness to the gospel and to develop viable alternatives for the future which are faithful to mission in Christ's way.

Mission Paradigms for Our Times

Called to Participate in God's Mission for Fullness of Life

31. The rapidly spreading processes of globalization, expressed in the savage and uncontrolled free-market economy and in high technology which reduces the value of the whole of reality to economic and financial categories, confronts the mission of the church with the growing phenomenon of dehumanization. In contexts of poverty and inhuman exploitation this is experienced as a daily struggle for the most elementary basics of life, even for life itself. In other contexts, within a framework of hopelessness, discouragement, and estrangement—experienced as lack of meaning in the present and lack of hope for the future—the suicide rate (especially among young people) is growing and apathy is becoming fashionable. In all cases, the church is called to proclaim the good news of Jesus Christ with boldness and to participate in God's mission for fullness of life. It is the mission of the church to reaffirm with courage and persistence the unique and eternal value of each human person as being created in the image of the holy, mighty, and immortal God....

Called to Life in Community

37. Another great challenge facing Christian mission in our time, especially in the North, is individualism, which penetrates and influences all spheres of life. The individual seems to be considered the sole norm of reality and existence. Society and community are losing their traditional, his-

torical meaning and value. This trend in human relationships also affects the traditional understanding of the relationship between Christians and the church in the process of salvation. Many perceive salvation as a matter between an individual and God, and do not see the role of the community of faith, the church. They may affirm faith in God, but may severely challenge or even deny the significance of the church as an instrument for relationship to God, other people, and the whole of creation, as well as the concept of salvation in and through community.

38. In the face of such a trend, which is affecting the very fabric of human society in general and of Christian community in particular, the church is called to proclaim God's will and intention for the world. Created in the image of the triune God—who is by definition an eternal communion of life and love—human beings are by nature relational. The relational dimension of human life is a given, ontological reality. Any authentic anthropology, therefore, must be relational and communitarian. . . .

Called to Incarnate the Gospel within Each Culture

45. "Culture shapes the human voice that answers the voice of Christ," said the Bangkok world mission conference in 1973. Recent developments have again placed the inseparable relation between the gospel and human cultures on the mission agenda. At the Canberra assembly (1991) and in other circles there have been heated debates about inculturation theologies and attempts to articulate the gospel in terms very different from the traditions of some of the historical churches. Experiences shared during the Ecumenical Decade of Churches in Solidarity with Women demonstrated how cultures have sometimes been misused for power purposes and become oppressive. During the 1990s the world has witnessed an increasing affirmation of local identities, often leading to violent conflicts and persecution on ethnic and cultural grounds, sometimes with direct or indirect support by Christians or churches. Such a context

makes it urgent for mission reflection to take up afresh the challenge of inculturation.

46. The Salvador conference strongly affirmed that "there is no way of being human without participating in culture, for it is through culture that identity is created." Culture is interpreted both as a result of God's grace and as an expression of human creativity. In any actual context, it must be stressed that culture is intrinsically neither good nor bad, but has the potential for both—and is thus ambiguous. . . .

49. When the gospel interacts authentically with a culture, it becomes rooted in that culture and opens up biblical and theological meaning for its time and place. The gospel will affirm some aspects of a culture, while challenging, critiquing, and transforming others. Through such processes, cultures may be transfigured and become bearers of the gospel. At the same time, cultures nourish, illuminate, enrich, and challenge the understanding and articulation of the gospel.

50. The gospel challenges aspects of cultures which produce or perpetuate injustice, suppress human rights or hinder a sustainable relationship towards creation. There is now need to go beyond certain inculturation theologies. Cultural and ethnic identity is a gift of God, but it must not be used to reject and oppress other identities. Identity should be defined not in opposition to, in competition with, or in fear of others, but rather as complementary. "The gospel reconciles and unites people of all identities into a new community in which the primary and ultimate identity is identity in Jesus Christ (Gal. 3:28)."

51. The debate over the inter-relation between the gospel and cultures has specific significance for indigenous peoples, who suffered greatly from missionary endeavours and colonial conquest, in the course of which their cultures and religions were described mostly as "pagan," in need of the gospel and "civilization." Later the terminology changed, but indigenous peoples were still considered mainly as "objects" of the churches' witness, as "poor" in need of economic or development aid. In more recent theologies, which affirmed "God's preferential option for the poor," marginalized people were indeed considered as bearers—that is, subjects—of a new mission movement from the so-called periphery to the centre. But these theologies

still functioned on the basis of socio-economic categories, neglecting people's religious heritage. Now, indigenous peoples are challenging the churches to recognize the richness of their culture and spirituality, which emphasizes interconnectedness and reciprocity with the whole creation. They are asking the churches to work in real partnership with them, doing mission together as equals, in mutual sharing. . . .

Called to Witness and Dialogue

56. The phenomenon of religious pluralism has become one of the most serious overall challenges to Christian mission for the coming century. Witness in multifaith societies has traditionally been considered a concern primarily of churches and missionaries in Africa, Asia, the Middle East, and other parts of the world. In recent years, however, through increased migration, religious pluralism has become a global reality. In some places Christians enjoy freedom and live and cooperate with others in a spirit of mutual respect and understanding. In other places, however, there is growing religious intolerance. . . .

61. In mission there is place both for the proclamation of the good news of Jesus Christ and for dialogue with people of other faiths. According to the situation and the charisms of Christians in that situation, the emphasis may differ. Many would claim, however, that the only proper mode of living in community is dialogical. Reaffirming the evangelistic mandate of Christians, the San Antonio conference pointed out that "our ministry of witness among people of other faiths presupposes our presence with them, sensitivity to their deepest faith commitments and experiences, willingness to be their servants for Christ's sake, affirmation of what God has done and is doing among them, and love for them. . . . We are called to be witnesses to others, not judges of them." If mission is to be in Christ's way, there cannot be evangelism without openness to others and readiness to discover his presence also where it is not expected. . . .

Called to Proclaim the Truth of the Gospel

63. One of the great challenges of our times—and one which touches the very heart of the Chris-

tian message—is the growing phenomenon of relativism, as developed especially among Western philosophers and scientists. In post-modern thinking, the notion of absolute and universal truth, whether in the political, social, economic, or even religious realm, is drastically questioned or rejected. Truth is rather seen as a matter of individual discernment through a personal "pick-and-choose" preference, experience, and decision. Rather than objective, universal, and absolute "truth," there are "truths" parallel to and cohabiting with one another. . . .

66. In the ecumenical field, notions such as "unity," "consensus," and "apostolic truth" are questioned and, for some, have even acquired a pejorative connotation. A more recent ecumenical vision includes the search for a new paradigm and image which could accommodate a diversity of truths under the same roof without diluting or annihilating any in the process of trying to bring them into convergence, for the sake of reaching one common and binding apostolic truth.

67. Glimpses of directions and partial responses to the challenges raised by relativism have been proffered; sharper and more coherent responses are still needed. What is the relationship between the truth of the gospel that Christians are called to proclaim concerning the uniqueness of Jesus Christ, "the way, and the truth, and the life" (John 14:6), and the truth of "the gospel before the gospel," and what are the consequences for the unity of the church?

Called to Witness in Unity

68. In recent decades the churches have become ever more aware of the necessity to engage in mission together, in cooperation and mutual accountability: hence mission partnerships have been established, some international mission structures transformed, and common projects undertaken. The same period, however, has seen an escalation of confessional rivalries and competition in mission in many parts of the world. These realities compel the ecumenical family to re-examine issues of mission in unity, cooperation among the churches, common witness and proselytism, and to work towards more responsible relationships in mission. . . .

76. *Convictions*

a. Mission begins in the heart of the triune God. The love which binds together the persons of the Holy Trinity overflows in a great outpouring of love for humankind and all creation.

b. God calls the church in Jesus Christ and empowers it by the Holy Spirit to be a partner in God's mission, bearing witness to the gospel of the love of God made clear in the life, death, and resurrection of Jesus Christ, and inviting people to become disciples of Christ.

c. Christian mission involves a holistic response through evangelistic and diaconal work to reach out to people in their experience of exclusion, brokenness, and meaninglessness. It involves the empowerment, affirmation, and renewal of people in their hope for fullness of life.

d. All baptized Christians are commissioned to bear witness to the gospel of Christ and all are accountable to the body of Christ for their witness; all need to find a home in a local worshipping community through which to exercise their accountability to the body.

77. *Commitments*

a. Impelled by the love of Christ, we commit ourselves to work to ensure that all our neighbours in every place, near and far, have the opportunity to hear and respond to the gospel of Jesus Christ.

b. We acknowledge that the primary responsibility for mission in any place rests with the church in that place.

c. Where missionaries or funds are sent by our church to a place where there is already a Christian church, that will be done in a negotiated, mutually acceptable, respectful arrangement, with equal participation of all parties in the decision-making process.

d. We acknowledge that in our partnerships all partners have gifts to offer and all have need to learn, receive, and be enriched by the relationship; so the relationship must allow for the reciprocal sharing of both needs and gifts.

e. We acknowledge that all the churches' resources belong to God, and that the wealth of the rich has often been derived from the exploitation of others.

f. We commit ourselves to make the relationship on all sides as transparent as possible concerning finance, theology, personnel, struggles, dilemmas, fears, hopes, ideas, stories—an open sharing that builds trust.

g. We recognize that nearly every intercultural encounter between churches is marked with an unequal distribution of power. Money, material possessions, state connections, history, and other factors affect the way churches relate to each other. In entering into relationships in mission, we commit ourselves to guard against misuse of power and to strive for just relationships.

h. We recognize that it is important not to create dependency. Partnerships must lead to interdependence. We will seek through our partnerships to enable the emergence of authentic local cultural responses to the gospel in terms of liturgies, hymns, rituals, structures, institutions, theological formulations.

i. We believe that mission and unity are inseparably related. We therefore commit ourselves to encourage collaboration and structural unity between our mission agencies and our own church, between mission agencies, and between mission agencies and our partner churches. Where several churches already exist in a given area we commit ourselves to deliberately fostering a council of churches.

j. We recognize that mission and evangelism have been carried on almost entirely along denominational lines. We commit ourselves to undertake mission ecumenically, both locally and abroad, wherever possible.

k. In developing international partnerships in mission, we commit ourselves to giving priority to building solidarity with excluded and suffering people and communities in their struggles for fullness of life.

70. *Towards Common Witness: A Call to Adopt Responsible Relationships in Mission and to Renounce Proselytism (on Evangelism and Proselytism), by the World Council of Churches*

This document of the World Council of Churches represents what might be called an internal settlement among its members on what constitutes best practices in evangelism, particularly in relation to new Protestant missions in areas where there are long-established Christian churches. The news release following this document shows how the drive to address issues of appropriate evangelism has become a concern well beyond the WCC.

Preface

Within the ecumenical movement and the World Council of Churches the concern for common witness and the unity of the churches has always been a priority, and proselytism has been recognized as a scandal and counterwitness. Ecumenical statements have repeatedly expressed the need for the clearer practice of responsible relationships in mission, a sharper commitment to witness in unity and renunciation of all forms of proselytism. Yet during these almost 50 years of ecumenical fellowship in the WCC, proselytism has continued to be a painful reality in the life of the churches. . . .

This statement is presented in the conviction that it is both timely and important for churches in all parts of the world. Its genesis also reflects the spirit of the WCC's "Common Understanding and Vision" document, in that it has provided space for wider participation in ecumenical discussions.

Introduction

Dramatic developments in different parts of the world in recent years have compelled the ecumenical family to re-examine issues related to common witness and proselytism in greater depth. For the WCC the situation is made even more urgent by the fact that complaints of proselytistic activities are being made against some of its own member churches as well as churches and groups outside its fellowship.

Among present-day realities damaging the relationships between churches in different parts of the world and thus requiring the urgent attention of the ecumenical family are:

- competitive missionary activities, especially in Central and Eastern Europe, Africa, Asia, and Latin America, carried out independently by foreign missionary groups, churches, and individuals, often directed at people already belonging and committed to one of the churches in those countries, and often leading to the establishment of parallel ecclesial structures;
- the re-emergence of tensions between the Orthodox and the Roman Catholic Church concerning the Eastern Rite Catholic churches.
- a sharp increase in the number of new mission agencies based in the South working independently in other parts of the world, often without contact with the churches in those countries;
- growing frustration among churches, especially in the South, whose members are being lured to other churches by offers of humanitarian aid;
- the humanitarian work done among immigrants, poor, lonely, and uprooted people in big cities intended to influence them to change their denominational allegiance;
- the growth of religious fundamentalism and intolerance;
- the growing impact of sects and new religious movements in many parts of the world;
- the discrediting of established minority Christian churches in multifaith communities.

The aims of this statement are: (1) to make churches and Christians aware of the bitter reality of proselytism today; (2) to call those involved in proselytism to recognize its disastrous effects on church unity, relationships among Christians and the credibility of the gospel and, therefore, to renounce it; and (3) to encourage the churches and mission agencies to avoid all forms of competition in mission and to commit themselves anew to witness in unity.

I. Christian Witness and Religious Freedom

1. The Mission Imperative

Christian mission is primarily and ultimately God's mission—the *missio Dei*. It is centred in the loving and eternal purpose of the triune God for humankind and all of creation, revealed in Jesus Christ. Central to God's mission is the life-giving presence of the Holy Spirit, who continues the mission of Christ through the church and remains the source of its missionary dynamism. The WCC Canberra assembly (1991) described a vision of mission in unity: "A reconciled humanity and renewed creation (cf. Eph. 1:9-10) is the goal of the mission of the church. The vision of God uniting all things in Christ is the driving force of its life and sharing."

As the body of Christ, constituted, sustained and energized by the life-giving presence of the Holy Spirit, the church is missionary by nature. It proclaims that in Jesus Christ the incarnate Word, who died and rose from the dead, salvation is offered to all as God's gift of love, mercy, and liberation.

Participating in God's mission is an imperative for all Christians and all churches, not only for particular individuals or specialized groups. It is an inner compulsion, rooted in the profound demands of Christ's love, to invite others to share in the fullness of life Jesus came to bring (cf. John 10:10).

Mission in Christ's way is holistic, for the whole person and the totality of life are inseparable in God's plan of salvation accomplished in Jesus Christ. It is local—"the primary responsibility for mission, where there is a local church, is with that church in its own place." It is also universal, that is, to all peoples, beyond all frontiers of race, caste, gender, culture, nation to "the ends of the earth" in every sense (cf. Acts 1:8; Mark 16:15; Luke 24:47).

2. Common Witness: Mission in Unity

Numerous WCC documents have recalled the intrinsic relation between the credibility of the mission of the church in the world and the unity among Christians—underscored in the prayer of Jesus "that they all may be one . . . so that the world may believe" (John 17:21) and historically realized among the apostles in Jerusalem already on the day of Pentecost. Common witness is "the witness that the churches, even while separated, bear together, especially through joint efforts, by manifesting whatever divine gifts of truth and life they already share and experience in common." It may be thought of as "'a eucharistic vision of life' which gives thanks for what God has done, is doing, and will do for the salvation of the world through acts of joyous self-offering." . . .

3. Mission in the Context of Religious Freedom

God's truth and love are given freely and call for a free response. Free will is one of the major gifts with which God has entrusted humans. God does not force anyone to accept God's revelation and does not save anyone by force. On the basis of this notion, the International Missionary Council and the World Council of Churches (in process of formation) developed a definition of religious freedom as a fundamental human right. This definition was adopted by the WCC First Assembly in Amsterdam (1948), and at the suggestion of the WCC's Commission of the Churches on International Affairs it was subsequently incorporated in the Universal Declaration of Human Rights: "Everyone has the right to freedom of thought, conscience and religion. This right includes the freedom to change his/her religion or belief, and freedom, either alone or in community with others, in public or in private, to manifest his/her religion or belief, in teaching, practice, worship and observance." The same principle is to be applied in mission work.

II. Proselytism—A Counterwitness

While the word "proselyte" was originally used to designate a person who became a member of the

Jewish community by believing in Yahweh and respecting the Law of Moses, and subsequently, in early Christian times, for a person of another faith who converted to Christianity, proselytism in later centuries took on a negative connotation due to changes in the content, motivation, spirit, and methods of "evangelism."

"Proselytism" is now used to mean the encouragement of Christians who belong to a church to change their denominational allegiance, through ways and means that "contradict the spirit of Christian love, violate the freedom of the human person and diminish trust in the Christian witness of the church."

Proselytism is "the corruption of witness." On the surface, proselytism may appear as genuine and enthusiastic missionary activity; and some people involved in it are genuinely committed Christians who believe that they are doing mission in Christ's way. It is the aim, spirit, and methodology of this activity which make it proselytism.

Some of the characteristics which clearly distinguish proselytism from authentic Christian witness are:

- Unfair criticism or caricaturing of the doctrines, beliefs, and practices of another church without attempting to understand or enter into dialogue on those issues. Some who venerate icons are accused of worshipping idols; others are ridiculed for alleged idolatry towards Mary and the saints or denounced for praying for the dead.
- Presenting one's church or confession as "the true church" and its teachings as "the right faith" and the only way to salvation, rejecting baptism in other churches as invalid and persuading people to be rebaptized.
- Portraying one's own church as having high moral and spiritual status over against the perceived weaknesses and problems of other churches.
- Taking advantage of and using unfaithfully the problems which may arise in another church for winning new members for one's own church.
- Offering humanitarian aid or educational opportunities as an inducement to join another church.

- Using political, economic, cultural, and ethnic pressure or historical arguments to win others to one's own church.
- Taking advantage of lack of education or Christian instruction which makes people vulnerable to changing their church allegiance.
- Using physical violence or moral and psychological pressure to induce people to change their church affiliation. This includes the use of media techniques profiling a particular church in a way that excludes, disparages, or stigmatizes its adherents, harassment through repeated house calls, material and spiritual threats, and insistence on the "superior" way to salvation offered by a particular church.
- Exploiting people's loneliness, illness, distress, or even disillusionment with their own church in order to "convert" them.

Common witness is constructive: it enriches, challenges, strengthens, and builds up solid Christian relationships and fellowship. Through word and deed, it makes the gospel relevant to the contemporary world. Proselytism is a perversion of authentic Christian witness and thus a counterwitness. It does not build up but destroys. It brings about tensions, scandal and division, and is thus a destabilizing factor for the witness of the church of Christ in the world. It is always a wounding of koinonia, creating not fellowship but antagonistic parties.

Nevertheless, it must be acknowledged that some people may move from one church to another out of true and genuine conviction, without any proselytistic pressure or manipulation, as a free decision in response to their experience of the life and witness of another church.

The churches must continually assess their own internal life to see whether some of the reasons people change church allegiance may lie with the churches themselves. . . .

Conclusion

With the Salvador world mission conference, "we decry the practice of those who carry out their endeavours in mission and evangelism in ways which destroy the unity of the body of Christ, human dignity and the very lives and cultures of those being evangelized; we call on them to confess their participation in and to renounce proselytism."

Called to one hope, we commit ourselves to our common call to mission and to work towards mission in unity. We actively seek a new era of "mission in Christ's way" at the dawn of the third millennium, enriched by one another's gifts and bound together in the Holy Spirit.

> As you, Father, are in me and I am in you, may they also be in us, so that the world may believe that you have sent me. The glory that you have given me I have given them, so that they may be one, as we are one, I in them and you in me, that they may become completely one, so that the world may know that you have sent me and have loved them even as you have loved me. (John 17:20-23)

Recommendations

In addition to commending the document "Towards Common Witness" to the churches for their reflection and action, Central Committee approved the following recommendations to facilitate the implementation of the document:

1. That the churches and related agencies:
a. make greater efforts to educate their own faithful in local congregations, Sunday schools, training centres, and seminaries to respect and love members of other churches as sisters and brothers in Christ;
b. actively promote knowledge of the heritages and contributions of other churches that, despite differences, confess the same Jesus Christ as God and Saviour, worship the same triune God, and are engaged in the same witness in the world;
c. promote efforts towards reconciliation by addressing historical wounds and bitter memories;
d. initiate (with the assistance of the WCC when necessary) encounter and dialogue at the local, national, and regional levels with those engaging in mission work that is per-

ceived as proselytism, in order to help them understand their motivations, make them aware of the negative impact of their activities, and promote responsible relationships in mission;
e. seek opportunities for working together with other churches on pastoral and social issues that affect local communities and countries as a whole, and be open to authentic cooperation with others in addressing the needs of the people being served;
f. together renounce proselytism as a denial of authentic witness and an obstruction to the unity of the church, and urge support for common witness, unity and understanding among the churches proclaiming the gospel;
g. continue to pray together for Christian unity, allowing God's Spirit to lead the churches into fuller truth and faithfulness.

2. That the World Council of Churches:
a. strengthen its emphasis on ecumenical formation using all resources of its education sector, in view of the growing trend towards confessionalism and confessional rivalries;
b. undertake a study on ecclesiology and mission, since many of the points of tension and division in relation to common witness stem from conflicting understandings in these areas.

Although it is recognized that the main responsibility for implementing the "Towards Common Witness" document lies with the churches, the WCC should play a facilitating role in stimulating the dialogue within and among the churches.

(Source: World Council of Churches, "Towards Common Witness: A Call to Adopt Responsible Relationships in Mission and to Renounce Proselytism," http://www.oikoumene.org/gr/resources/documents/wcc-commissions/mission-and-evangelism/19-09-97-towards-common-witness.html.)

71. Christian Code of Conduct

The following headline and news release indicates the growing ecumenical consen-

sus that methods of evangelism and those toward whom evangelistic efforts should be directed have become a concern for all the major Christian bodies. In a world characterized by globalization and pluralism, models of mission based on a "free religious market" approach are seen increasingly as neither tenable nor desirable, regardless of one's evangelistic zeal.

The World Evangelical Alliance (WEA) is ready to join the World Council of Churches (WCC) and the Vatican in supporting a code of conduct to guide activities seeking converts to Christianity.

The WEA general secretary Rev. Dr Geoff Tunnicliffe "gave his full approval" to the organization's involvement in the process so far sponsored by the WCC and the Vatican, said Rev. Dr. Thomas Schirrmacher, head of the organization's International Institute for Religious Freedom. The WEA is an association of organizations and churches with a membership of some 420 million Christians worldwide.

Schirrmacher was one of the speakers at an 8-12 August consultation held in Toulouse, France, where some 30 Catholic, Orthodox, Protestant, Pentecostal, and Evangelical theologians and church leaders from Europe, Asia, Africa, and the United States gathered to outline the content of the code of conduct, which is expected to be finalized by 2010. . . .

Taking Shape

Among the issues identified by the participants as elements upon which the code of conduct should be based are: common understandings of conversion, witness, mission, and evangelism, and concern for human dignity; a distinction between aggressive proselytizing and evangelism; the balance between the mandate to evangelize and the right to choose one's religion. . . .

The complexity of the issue was highlighted at the consultation by contributions reflecting very diverse experiences in different contexts: from living as a Christian minority in India, to preaching the gospel to Turks in Austria, to having to turn down people asking for baptism in Zanzibar; from being a Lutheran missionary to Muslim Nigeria, to being an Anglican priest in a British city where Hindus have bought and worship in a former Christian church, or to being a US Pentecostal struggling with the fact that Pentecostals "are indeed ecumenical but just don't know it."

The code of conduct should on the one hand establish what all the partners agree needs to be banned when it comes to Christian mission, a daunting task given the many different contexts involved. On the other hand, it should hopefully provide guidelines as to how to deal with complicated issues, like interreligious marriages.

Its promoters expect the code of conduct to fulfil several goals: be an advocacy tool in discussions with governments considering anti-conversion laws, to help to advance the cause of religious freedom, address other religions' concerns about Christian proselytism and inspire them to consider their own codes of conduct, and also help to ease intra-Christian tensions.

None of the partners involved intend—nor have the means—to impose the code of conduct on their constituencies, but they all trust that it will be able to "impact hearts and minds" and allow for "moral and peer pressure."

The next step in this study project jointly undertaken by the Pontifical Council for Interreligious Dialogue and the WCC's programme on inter-religious dialogue will be a meeting in 2008 in which the code of conduct will be drafted, building upon the findings of the Toulouse consultation. Launched in May 2006 in Lariano/Velletri, near Rome, the project bears the name: "An interreligious reflection on conversion: From controversy to a shared code of conduct."

(Source: World Council of Churches, "Christian Code of Conduct on Religious Conversion Wins Broader Backing," http://www.oikoumene.org/en/news/news-management/eng/a/article/1634/christian-code-of-conduct.html.)

72. AGAPE Consultation: Linking Poverty, Wealth, and Ecology: Ecumenical Perspectives in Latin America and the Caribbean

This document and the one that follows give insight into how WCC-related churches are evaluating relationships with a world in which economic and ecological crisis are overwhelming all other considerations in how Christians, particularly those from wealthy countries with high levels of consumption, engage their neighbors.

The Guatemala Declaration, Guatemala, October 6-10, 2008

An AGAPE Consultation on *Linking Poverty, Wealth, and Ecology: Ecumenical Perspectives in Latin America and the Caribbean* took place on 6-10 October 2008 at the La Salle University Residence Centre in Guatemala City. The meeting was convened by the World Council of Churches, the Latin America Council of Churches, and the Christian Ecumenical Council of Guatemala.

The consultation began with a pre-meeting in which men and women of the faith, from the Youth, Women, and Gender Justice and Indigenous Peoples pastoral services, responding to the gospel of justice, shared experiences about the situation we are living through in Latin America and the Caribbean, with regard to Poverty, Wealth, and Ecology.

We approached and discussed the following issues from a faith perspective:

I. The Global Situation

The Climate Crisis

The climate crisis has been caused by human beings, especially by the industries of the countries of the North, which are mainly responsible for the greenhouse effect. Some countries have signed the Kyoto Protocol and other European Community agreements, but some countries do not have the political will to commit themselves to reducing carbon dioxide emissions. Some of these agreements have set medium- and long-term targets for the implementation of their policies, which is not enough to stop damage to the environment.

The ecological debt is due to the destruction of ecosystems for purposes of human consumption, especially irresponsible consumption in the North. This destruction is caused by oil, gas, mining, and timber companies, hydroelectricity mega projects, agribusiness, and others that exploit natural resources to sustain a model that endangers local communities and the planet as a whole. The international financial institutions also bear a lot of responsibility because they finance this extraction of resources while paying little attention to its social and environmental consequences. The situation is made more acute by the water crisis. Major and unprecedented droughts and floods have caused a lack of access to drinking water and sanitation.

There has been a marked increase of migration from rural to urban areas and abroad because of the lack of local opportunities to make a living. Political persecution is partly to blame. The result is broken families, violence, and the uprooting of people from their cultures.

As a result of their forms of production and consumption, the mainly Northern post-industrial countries and the institutions that reproduce patriarchal models in our countries owe a social and ecological debt to humanity and the Earth. This debt has accumulated in the course of centuries of looting and depredation that have caused destruction, death, and poverty. It has imposed on us a system that puts the market at the centre rather than human beings and nature, and this system is having a devastating impact on us.

"Food Crisis"

Although the world exports agricultural produce valued at $500,000 million per year, eight million people die every year from starvation and diseases associated with hunger, and 840 million people, including farmers and agricultural workers, suffer from a lack of food. During 2007, world production of grains increased four per cent in comparison with 2006. The problem of hunger in the world is not therefore due to a lack of food but rather to the fact that millions of human beings cannot buy it. The central problem (high production of food and increases in the price of food) results from the increasingly monopolistic concentration of the world agricultural-food industry.

At the same time, transnational companies are trying to control the other element that is essential to the cycle of life—water—increasingly presenting this as something normal and inevitable.

The search for non-fossil fuels has led to the increasing use of wheat, soya, and corn for the production of agrofuels, which increases the price of grains and reduces the population's access to grains for consumption.

Financial Crisis

The origin of the global financial crisis lies in the usury and endless accumulation that are in the very nature of capitalism. Exacerbated by neoliberalism, this system has had serious negative global consequences. According to the experts, the cost of the $700,000 million (or even more) United States rescue package for the banks will be borne by the people because of the capacity of transnational capitalism to transfer its crises to the system's peripheral countries. This domination by finance capital is unprecedented and goes hand-in-hand with speculation and the indebtedness of peripheral countries, from which the central countries extract immense flows of resources, thereby limiting social investment in, for example, health, education, housing, roads, and drinking water.

Distribution of Wealth

World per capita income has currently reached $6,954, which is eight times more than the poverty line and would comfortably satisfy basic needs and eliminate world poverty if there were an adequate social redistribution of wealth. However, 2,600 million people, equivalent to 40% of the world population, are living in poverty, and among them, 1,000 million of these are living in extreme poverty. Far from easing, this profound inequity has increased on a world scale, reducing the share of developing regions, except for China and India. In particular, Latin America and Africa have seen their share of world income fall. The increasing social inequality in the world has been accentuated by globalization

and the implementation of neoliberal policies on a planetary scale.

Latin America and the Caribbean

In addition to the inequality between countries, there are major social differences between people within these same countries. Latin America and the Caribbean are considered to be the regions with the greatest social inequality in the world and the evidence confirms that these inequalities have tended to become more acute in recent decades.

Imposition of the neoliberal model, which gives pride of place to individuals and capital accumulation, has increased inequalities between the few who are rich and the millions who are poor. This model has looted and destroyed creation with the only goal being excessive accumulation. This model has become a great machine to produce poverty and misery. Governments are also responsible for promoting the interests of capital and the economic power groups, to the detriment of the majority of peoples. Encouraged by the "developed" countries, transnational companies and governments have created administrative and legal structures that sustain the system, coordinate corruption, and promote their own interests.

The neoliberal model promotes a drastic reduction of the state's role in the economy, fiscal austerity, privatization, the adoption of policies favourable to the free market, and the opening up of the international economy.

There are 100 million young people between the ages of 15 and 24 in Latin America. Ten million of these young people are unemployed, 22 million neither study or work for various reasons, and more than 30 million work in the informal economy in precarious conditions.

The neoliberal economic model and its policies affect communities as a whole but have a greater impact on women, whose poverty is exacerbated by the privatization of health and education services, unequal pay, increased working hours, and the increasing price of basic goods, as well as the destruction of their livelihoods. Their invisible and unrecognized domestic work subsidizes the global economic model.

In addition, the work-production-domination system results in various forms of exploitation, with human beings at the service of production rather than production at the service of human beings. Proclaimed by the Bible as a gift and source of human fulfilment, work has been diminished in terms of its dignity and spiritual content.

Despite all these processes of social, economic, religious, and political exclusion, people continue to resist and provide alternatives for satisfying their goal of living well. Governments have emerged that defend national and popular interests and this tendency has become more pronounced in the region.

We long for the birth of a new world founded on: 1) The indigenous view of the world, which sees the Earth as a mother rather than as a collection of resources to be exploited and which sees human beings as part of creation. 2) The feminist principles that promote non-hierarchical decision-making models and gender justice. 3) The energy, enthusiasm and creative activity of youth.

To this end, we want to highlight the signs of hope in Latin America. In recent years, we have noted the gradual retreat of neoliberalism, which can be observed in: 1) The increasing strength of the movements of indigenous peoples, peasants, and women, who are fighting for social, economic, and ecological justice, especially for food sovereignty and who demand that their governments be made accountable. 2) The emergence of democratic governments in Bolivia, Ecuador, Venezuela, and Paraguay and of others who call for the economic independence of their countries and who promote social policies aimed at eradicating poverty and inequity in the region. 3) The development of regional initiatives that show an increase in South-South co-operation and solidarity between the countries of Latin America and the Caribbean, such as the Bank of the South (*Banco del Sur*), the Fund of the South (*Fondo del Sur*) and the Bolivarian Alternative for the Americas (ALBA).

II. Our Alternatives and Commitments

1. Implement food sovereignty and promote the solidarity and community economy, which values and promotes good living conditions, and in which surpluses are produced for the benefit of those involved rather than to make a profit.

2. Create alliances with organizations who also want to promote cooperation and strengthen the dialogue between churches and social organizations with a view to increasing our impact in society.

3. Create institutional forums in which women, indigenous peoples, youth, and people with different capacities can actively participate in decision-making. Recognize their capacity to contribute to promoting just alternatives. Promote their role as political actors and strengthen them so they can transform their family, church, and social environment.

4. Promote the integration of people with different capacities into the life of the churches and society.

5. Denounce the local and global ecological impact of transnational companies in the mining, oil, and other sectors, which are destroying our livelihoods and making our communities ever poorer.

6. Call for the unconditional cancellation of the External Debt and the implementation of audits in all indebted countries. Recognize that the external debt has been one of the mechanisms used by multilateral institutions (World Bank, IMF) and their allies to loot our countries, provoking the climate crisis and other disasters and also building up a social and ecological debt to our peoples.

7. Announce and proclaim a gospel of justice and peace for all human beings and Creation.

From the Perspective of Women

8. Use Latin American and Caribbean feminist pastoral theology to dismantle all the religious myths that perpetuate and justify the historic inequality between men and women.

9. Give resolute support to the actions taken by women in the fight for their rights, and vigorously reject everything that generates any kind of violence against women.

10. Delegitimize the fundamentalist discourse

and practice of those who intervene in public affairs to punish, proscribe, and prohibit sexual health initiatives, particularly those for women, as this has a major impact on reproductive health and increases the incidence of HIV/AIDS.

From the Perspective of Indigenous Peoples

11. Organize a world conference of indigenous people's churches to plan strategies to build a more just and solidarity-based model based on the perspective of indigenous peoples.
12. Encourage the development of a national and international legal framework, including implementation of ILO (International Labour Organization) Convention 169, the United Nations Declaration on the Rights of Indigenous Peoples and national constitutions, laws, and regulations that guarantee collective rights.
13. Raise the awareness of the churches about the need to support the return of ancestral lands and cultural property, and to commit themselves to denouncing the massacres and genocides suffered by indigenous peoples.

From the Perspective of Youth

14. Raise the awareness of youth and churches with a view to generating responsible and healthy attitudes, moving from an attitude of protest to an attitude of making constructive solidarity-based proposals for action and accompaniment.
15. Develop a consensus on new values that allows us to promote a new civilizing and communitarian model of thinking for young people.
16. Promote the implementation of legal and institutional frameworks for youth by governments, social organizations and churches.
17. Let Jesus, who restores the dignity of all creatures who are indebted, impoverished, or who have suffered violence, maintain our commitment until the day when we can see "the new skies and the new earth." Let the Holy Spirit, which encourages hope and promotes solidarity, strengthen the certainty of this prophetic vision. Let God, who encourages all efforts aimed at achieving the integral fullness of Life, make us fight tirelessly for the construction and installation of his Reign.

III. Recommendations to the Churches

The Churches face a major challenge, starting with their first task of explaining the predatory and anti-civilization characteristics of the neoliberal model. Until people are clear about the inhuman and predatory nature of this model, they will not have the tools they need to try and change it.

The Churches should actively accompany the people's resistance to attacks on their rights. This resistance is expressed in the various ways in which they defend their economic, social, cultural, political, and environmental rights. It is expressed in the communities' defence of water, in their resistance against mining, in their defence of forests and rivers, in the resistance of the women's movement, the indigenous peoples' movement, the youth movement, and the many social and civil society organizations. The diversity of resistance to the neoliberal model requires the Churches to develop strategies to accompany and participate in it, given the great dispersion of struggles and processes.

The Churches should disseminate the results of studies on the inevitable ethical, economic, and ecological limitations of capital accumulation.

The Churches should convert all their ethical and spiritual capital into instruments to promote the wide-ranging mobilization and coordination of social movements and actors that will allow them to find a path towards the construction of another kind of logic for the reproduction of life.

In the name of the faith that links us through love and makes us a single community, living in the world created by God, we challenge the Churches to raise their prophetic voice, denounce injustice and announce the Good News.

Participants came from the following countries:

- Bolivia
- Brazil
- Cuba

- Ecuador
- El Salvador
- Guatemala
- Honduras
- Jamaica
- Mexico
- Nicaragua
- Peru
- Uruguay
- Canada
- United States
- Tanzania
- Cote d'Ivoire
- South Africa
- India
- Philippines
- Australia
- Fiji
- Germany
- Slovakia

73. The Dar es Salaam Statement on Linking Poverty, Wealth, and Ecology in Africa, Alternative Globalisation Addressing People and Earth (AGAPE) Consultation on Linking Poverty, Wealth and Ecology: Africa Ecumenical Perspectives, November 7-9, 2007, Dar es Salaam, Tanzania

Preamble

We, African people of faith, youth, women, men, activists, theologians, and church leaders, in the spirit of community and critical discernment, have convened in Dar es Salaam, Tanzania, from 05-09 November 2007 to: Share the perspectives of women and youth on the links between poverty, wealth, and ecology in the context of Africa; Develop African theological bases for studying these issues; and Formulate ecumenical strategies and actions for addressing the interlinked problems of poverty, excessive wealth, and ecological degradation in Africa as part of the AGAPE process.

Linking Poverty, Wealth, and Ecology in Africa

Africa is endowed with rich communities of people, bountiful resources, and diverse ecology. Yet, African children die of hunger, malnutrition, and preventable diseases because of neoliberal trade policies and patent systems that force Africa to produce cash crops for export and that refuse poor people access to medicines and healthcare.

Young people are denied the right to education and forced to migrate to unfriendly lands by debt conditionalities that oblige governments to privatise educational systems.

Women die in childbirth, are pushed into insecure work in the informal economy, and are trafficked into new forms of slavery because of desperate economic conditions produced by systemic trade deficits, external indebtedness, and structural adjustment.

African men, deprived of the dignity of decent work by neoliberal economic policies, are driven to violence and war over resources.

African communities are forced away from their land and blocked off from the basics of life by multinational resource extractive industries and the construction of mega-dams.

Africa's monetary wealth continues to flow out of the continent in the form of debt and interest payments, profit repatriation of multinational corporations, and capital flight.

The ecological fabric of Africa—the source and means to life, food, water, fuel, and medicine—is systematically destroyed to fuel production for production's sake and to sustain the consumerist lifestyles of rich, northern countries.

We have come to the crucial recognition that impoverishment, enrichment, and ecological destruction are interlinked. Transatlantic slavery and 500 years of colonialism had instituted a system of plunder of human and natural resources that enriched colonial powers at the cost of decimating and dehumanising African people. Moreover, the current context of neoliberal economic globalisation, in complicity with patriarchal structures and militarisation, has further undermined African sovereignty, wresting away African people's communal ownership and control over productive means, natural and biotic resources. In concentrating these resources, especially capital, in the hands of powerful nations, international financial institutions and multinational corporations working in collusion with African elites—the agents of empire—the socio-economic disparities between Africa and rich nations continue to widen at alarming rates. Driven by motives of endless economic expansion and profit maximisation—rather than provisioning for life and care of community and ecology—neoliberal models of wealth creation are threatening the entire web of life.

We, therefore: Denounce neoliberal economic globalisation; Remind the countries of the North of the wealth that was built and sustained on the continued extraction and plunder of Africa's resources as well as on the exploitation of African people; Reclaim African communities' sovereignty over decision-making processes, productive means, and resources; and Affirm that African people are creditors of a tremendous economic, socio-cultural, and ecological debt.

Theological Bases of Linking Poverty, Wealth, and Ecology

God has created the household of life (*oikos*) and human beings to live in community with one another (Psalm 115:16 and Genesis 1-2). We are created in God's own image and likeness and have the responsibility to take care of God's good creation. The Christian notion of *oikos* resonates with the African understanding of *ubuntu/botho/uzima* (life in wholeness) and *ujamaa* (life in community). They embrace among others, the values of fullness of life, full participation in all life processes including in the economy and ecology. It further entails the just care, use, sharing, and distribution of resources and elements of life. Where the above and life-affirming relationships have been violated, the institution of restorative, redistributive and rectificatory (wisdom) justice are necessary. These principles of justice, reparation, restoration and reconciliation, forgiveness, mutual love, and dignity for all God's creation ought to be promoted ecumenically as bases for constructive critique of global capitalism, which increasingly violates life-in-abundance (John 10:10).

We confess that the churches, understood as the body of Christ, have not been faithful in bearing just witness to the questions of justice in the economy, ecology, and relationships amongst the peoples. Churches have often neglected to challenge the death-dealing effects of the degradation of God's creation and the unjust sharing of God's resources. This failure to address the structural sins of greed, exploitation, racism, dehumanization, and inequitable sharing of power which persist in economy and ecology, results in trivialization of poverty where the poor are blamed for their plight.

Churches have not always offered balanced theologies and praxes on stewardship of (or caring for) life. They have often promoted narrow perspectives which place ecological issues at the periphery of daily life and have neglected to proclaim in truth the promised wholesome abundance for all (John 8:32). God calls us to care for creation (Psalm 148), requiring a new understanding which affirms that caring for creation is mandatory, not optional.

Churches have not adequately exercised their prophetic call to challenge people, companies, institutions, and countries which are the benefactors and beneficiaries of neoliberal economic globalization.

If we affirm ourselves to be a worldwide community that respects and honours the web of life and human dignity, the life-denying relationships and practices which create poverty in the midst of wealth and dehumanize people must be challenged.

We, therefore, call upon churches to bear prophetic witness to: Speak truth to power (Amos 8:4-6) and condemn systems of domination in relations, international trade, and debt systems that enslave people (Nehemiah 5); Criticise greed as the cause and manifestation of empire (Isaiah 5:7-10). We understand the empire to mean "the convergence of economic, political, cultural, military, and religious power, in a system of domination that imposes the flow of benefits from the vulnerable to the powerful. Empire crosses all boundaries, distorts identities, subverts cultures, subordinates nations-states, and either marginalize or co-opts religious communities" (World Alliance of Reformed Churches 2005/6). Greed violates wholeness that God created and expects. It also contradicts *ubuntu/botho/ujamaa* which affirm dignity and wholeness in community (*uzima*); Remind the world that greed cuts off individuals, communities, and whole countries from the richness of life (Matthew 5) and *ubuntu;* Condemn the imperial ideologies and praxes that present neoliberal economic globalisation as the only way of life, denying the ecological and human diversity that exist in life; and Condemn patriarchal collusion with injustices in the economy and ecology.

We, therefore, declare: Structures of domination and exploitation based on class, gender, race/ethnicity are sinful; and Greed and its negative manifestations (as stated above), overproduction and over-consumption are sinful and require radical transformation (*metanoia*).

This is the *kairos*—a moment for change and repentance, reparations, justice, forgiveness, reconciliation, wellbeing, and peace. Radical transformation derives power and inspiration from the seeds of hope rooted in African heritage and spirituality; and requires us to re-envision and re-create life in the context of these challenges.

Seeds of Hope

In building creative and practical alternatives to, and resisting the neoliberal economic paradigm, we obtain immense hope and inspiration from: The spiritualities and theologies of life that place community, sharing, justice, and care of life and creation at the centre; The ecumenical movement's historical engagement for justice, peace and integrity of creation; African liberation and justice-seeking movements that continue to work for freedom from colonial and neo-colonial powers; and Social movements in Africa of peoples struggling for life and dignity—especially youth and women's movements—that are mobilizing women and men for just wages and decent work, defending food sovereignty, responding to the HIV-AIDS pandemic and other epidemics, demanding accountability from their governments and multinational corporations, resisting mining and logging activities, and advocating at the international and national levels for just trade and debt cancellation.

Towards **Metanoia** *(Radical Transformation)*

We invite and challenge Church and society, ecumenical partners, and our brothers and sisters in the North to: Acknowledge the privileges deriving from complicity—through their production and consumption patterns—in systems of domination and exploitation that dehumanise and destroy life in Africa; Stop silencing and trivialising the voices of African people as they seek to expose the negative impacts and contradictions of neoliberal economic globalisation in Africa. African people's realities, experiences, and rich intellectual resources place them in the best position to critically understand their own socio-economic conditions; Transform institutions and conduct that perpetuate injustices in the economy and ecology; and seek and engage in a radical spirituality of solidarity manifested in sharing, reparation, and justice.

We call on those who collude with systems of domination in economy and ecology—including African government leaders and elites—to recognise, confess, repent, and engage in restorative, distributive and transformative justice.

We commit ourselves to: Life-affirming theologies in the economy and ecology; Connect theologies with struggles for life; Strengthen the spaces for churches in partnership with social movements to jointly formulate strategies to overcome poverty, redefine wealth, protect the environment, and to build alternatives to neoliberal economic globalisation; Promote and affirm gender justice and feminist non-hierarchical models of relating (Joel 2: 28) and the care economy; Consolidate the movement for AGAPE economy and ecology in Africa and in the world and dialogue with other disciplines and faiths; Call on the northern churches to repent for the African holocaust, which killed over 10 million Africans; and to intensify their efforts toward reparations; and Call on northern churches to examine their financial resources and investments and how these impact on poverty.

We are committed to advancing work on the AGAPE process on linking poverty, wealth, and ecology and to ensure that these are translated into concrete and life-affirming actions.

(Source: World Council of Churches, "The Dar es Salaam Statement on Linking Poverty, Wealth, and Ecology in Africa: Alternative Globalisation Addressing People and Earth (AGAPE) Consultation on Linking Poverty, Wealth and Ecology: Africa Ecumenical Perspectives, November 7-9, 2007, Dar es Salaam, Tanzania," http://www

.oikoumene.org/gr/resources/documents/wcc-programmes/public-witness-addressing-power-affirming-peace/poverty-wealth-and-ecology/ neoliberal-paradigm/09-11-07-dar-es-salaam-statement-on-linking-poverty-wealth-and-ecology.html.)

Evangelical Mission Documents

The documents below arise from a series of meetings first hosted by the Billy Graham Association, beginning at Lausanne, Switzerland, in 1992. Their significance may be found by comparison with the WCC documents, particularly as they describe the human situation, but also in what they choose as the beginning point for making their affirmations, and what they choose to affirm that other statements do not. It is also useful to compare the Lausanne Covenant from 1974 with the Iguassu Declaration of 1999.

74. The Lausanne Covenant (1974)

Introduction

We, members of the Church of Jesus Christ, from more than 150 nations, participants in the International Congress on World Evangelization at Lausanne, praise God for his great salvation and rejoice in the fellowship he has given us with himself and with each other. We are deeply stirred by what God is doing in our day, moved to penitence by our failures and challenged by the unfinished task of evangelization. We believe the Gospel is God's good news for the whole world, and we are determined by his grace to obey Christ's commission to proclaim it to all mankind and to make disciples of every nation. We desire, therefore, to affirm our faith and our resolve, and to make public our covenant.

1. The Purpose of God

We affirm our belief in the one-eternal God, Creator and Lord of the world, Father, Son, and Holy Spirit, who govern all things according to the purpose of his will. He has been calling out from the world a people for himself, and sending his people back into the world to be his servants and his witnesses, for the extension of his kingdom, the building up of Christ's body, and the glory of his name. We confess with shame that we have often denied our calling and failed in our mission, by becoming conformed to the world or by withdrawing from it. Yet we rejoice that even when borne by earthen vessels the gospel is still a precious treasure. To the

task of making that treasure known in the power of the Holy Spirit we desire to dedicate ourselves anew (Isa. 40:28; Matt. 28:19; Eph. 1:11; Acts 15:14; John 17:6, 18; Eph 4:12; 1 Cor. 5:10; Rom. 12:2; 2 Cor. 4:7).

2. The Authority and Power of the Bible

We affirm the divine inspiration, truthfulness, and authority of both Old and New Testament Scriptures in their entirety as the only written word of God, without error in all that it affirms, and the only infallible rule of faith and practice. We also affirm the power of God's word to accomplish his purpose of salvation. The message of the Bible is addressed to all men and women. For God's revelation in Christ and in Scripture is unchangeable. Through it the Holy Spirit still speaks today. He illumines the minds of God's people in every culture to perceive its truth freshly through their own eyes and thus discloses to the whole Church ever more of the many-colored wisdom of God (2 Tim. 3:16; 2 Pet. 1:21; John 10:35; Isa. 55:11; 1 Cor. 1:21; Rom. 1:16, Matt. 5:17, 18; Jude 3; Eph. 1:17, 18; 3:10, 18).

3. The Uniqueness and Universality of Christ

We affirm that there is only one Saviour and only one gospel, although there is a wide diversity of evangelistic approaches. We recognise that everyone has some knowledge of God through his general revelation in nature. But we deny that this can save, for people suppress the truth by their unrighteousness. We also reject as derogatory to

Christ and the gospel every kind of syncretism and dialogue which implies that Christ speaks equally through all religions and ideologies. Jesus Christ, being himself the only God-man, who gave himself as the only ransom for sinners, is the only mediator between God and people. There is no other name by which we must be saved. All men and women are perishing because of sin, but God loves everyone, not wishing that any should perish but that all should repent. Yet those who reject Christ repudiate the joy of salvation and condemn themselves to eternal separation from God. To proclaim Jesus as "the Saviour of the world" is not to affirm that all people are either automatically or ultimately saved, still less to affirm that all religions offer salvation in Christ. Rather it is to proclaim God's love for a world of sinners and to invite everyone to respond to him as Saviour and Lord in the wholehearted personal commitment of repentance and faith. Jesus Christ has been exalted above every other name; we long for the day when every knee shall bow to him and every tongue shall confess him Lord (Gal. 1:6-9; Rom. 1:18-32; 1 Tim. 2:5, 6; Acts 4:12; John 3:16-19; 2 Pet. 3:9; 2 Thess. 1:7-9; John 4:42; Matt. 11:28; Eph. 1:20, 21; Phil. 2:9-11).

4. The Nature of Evangelism

To evangelize is to spread the good news that Jesus Christ died for our sins and was raised from the dead according to the Scriptures, and that as the reigning Lord he now offers the forgiveness of sins and the liberating gifts of the Spirit to all who repent and believe. Our Christian presence in the world is indispensable to evangelism, and so is that kind of dialogue whose purpose is to listen sensitively in order to understand. But evangelism itself is the proclamation of the historical, biblical Christ as Saviour and Lord, with a view to persuading people to come to him personally and so be reconciled to God. In issuing the gospel invitation we have no liberty to conceal the cost of discipleship. Jesus still calls all who would follow him to deny themselves, take up their cross, and identify themselves with his new community. The results of evangelism include obedience to Christ, incorporation into his Church and responsible service in the world (1 Cor. 15:3, 4; Acts 2:32-39; John 20:21;

1 Cor. 1:23; 2 Cor. 4:5; 5:11, 20; Luke 14:25-33; Mark 8:34; Acts 2:40,47; Mark 10:43-45).

5. Christian Social Responsibility

We affirm that God is both the Creator and the Judge of all people. We therefore should share his concern for justice and reconciliation throughout human society and for the liberation of men and women from every kind of oppression. Because men and women are made in the image of God, every person, regardless of race, religion, colour, culture, class, sex, or age, has an intrinsic dignity because of which he or she should be respected and served, not exploited. Here too we express penitence both for our neglect and for having sometimes regarded evangelism and social concern as mutually exclusive. Although reconciliation with other people is not reconciliation with God, nor is social action evangelism, nor is political liberation salvation, nevertheless we affirm that evangelism and socio-political involvement are both part of our Christian duty. For both are necessary expressions of our doctrines of God and man, our love for our neighbour and our obedience to Jesus Christ. The message of salvation implies also a message of judgment upon every form of alienation, oppression, and discrimination, and we should not be afraid to denounce evil and injustice wherever they exist. When people receive Christ they are born again into his kingdom and must seek not only to exhibit but also to spread its righteousness in the midst of an unrighteous world. The salvation we claim should be transforming us in the totality of our personal and social responsibilities. Faith without works is dead (Acts 17:26, 31; Gen. 18:25; Isa. 1:17; Psa. 45:7; Gen. 1:26, 27; Jas. 3:9; Lev. 19:18; Luke 6:27, 35; Jas. 2:14-26; John 3:3, 5; Matt. 5:20; 6:33; 2 Cor. 3:18; Jas. 2:20).

6. The Church and Evangelism

We affirm that Christ sends his redeemed people into the world as the Father sent him, and that this calls for a similar deep and costly penetration of the world. We need to break out of our ecclesiastical ghettos and permeate non-Christian society. In the Church's mission of sacrificial service evangelism is primary. World evangelization requires the whole Church to take the whole gospel to the whole world. The Church is at the very centre of God's cosmic purpose and is his appointed means of spreading the gospel. But a church which preaches the cross must itself be marked by the cross. It becomes a stumbling block to evangelism when it betrays the gospel or lacks a living faith in God, a genuine love for people, or scrupulous honesty in all things including promotion and finance. The church is the community of God's people rather than an institution, and must not be identified with any particular culture, social or political system, or human ideology (John 17:18; 20:21; Matt. 28:19, 20; Acts 1:8; 20:27; Eph. 1:9, 10; 3:9-11; Gal. 6:14, 17; 2 Cor. 6:3, 4; 2 Tim. 2:19-21; Phil. 1:27).

7. Cooperation in Evangelism

We affirm that the Church's visible unity in truth is God's purpose. Evangelism also summons us to unity, because our oneness strengthens our witness, just as our disunity undermines our gospel of reconciliation. We recognize, however, that organisational unity may take many forms and does not necessarily forward evangelism. Yet we who share the same biblical faith should be closely united in fellowship, work, and witness. We confess that our testimony has sometimes been marred by a sinful individualism and needless duplication. We pledge ourselves to seek a deeper unity in truth, worship, holiness, and mission. We urge the development of regional and functional cooperation for the furtherance of the Church's mission, for strategic planning, for mutual encouragement, and for the sharing of resources and experience (John 17:21, 23; Eph. 4:3, 4; John 13:35; Phil. 1:27; John 17:11-23).

8. Churches in Evangelistic Partnership

We rejoice that a new missionary era has dawned. The dominant role of western missions is fast disappearing. God is raising up from the younger churches a great new resource for world evangelization, and is thus demonstrating that the responsibility to evangelise belongs to the whole body of Christ. All churches should therefore be asking God and themselves what they should be doing both to reach their own area and to send missionaries to other parts of the world. A reevaluation of our missionary responsibility and role should be continuous. Thus a growing partnership of churches will develop and the universal character of Christ's Church will be more clearly exhibited. We also thank God for agencies which labor in Bible translation, theological education, the mass media, Christian literature, evangelism, missions, church renewal, and other specialist fields. They too should engage in constant self-examination to evaluate their effectiveness as part of the Church's mission (Rom. 1:8; Phil. 1:5; 4:15; Acts 13:1-3; 1 Thess. 1:6-8).

9. The Urgency of the Evangelistic Task

More than 2,700 million people, which is more than two-thirds of all humanity, have yet to be evangelised. We are ashamed that so many have been neglected; it is a standing rebuke to us and to the whole Church. There is now, however, in many parts of the world an unprecedented receptivity to the Lord Jesus Christ. We are convinced that this is the time for churches and para-church agencies to pray earnestly for the salvation of the unreached and to launch new efforts to achieve world evangelization. A reduction of foreign missionaries and money in an evangelised country may sometimes be necessary to facilitate the national church's growth in self-reliance and to release resources for unevangelised areas. Missionaries should flow ever more freely from and to all six continents in a spirit of humble service. The goal should be, by all available means and at the earliest possible time, that every person will have the opportunity to hear, understand, and to receive the good news. We cannot hope to attain this goal without sacrifice. All of us are shocked by the poverty of millions and disturbed by the injustices which cause it. Those of us who live in affluent circumstances accept our duty to develop a simple life-style in order to contribute more generously to both relief and evangelism (John 9:4; Matt. 9:35-38; Rom. 9:1-3; 1 Cor.

9:19-23; Mark 16:15; Isa. 58:6, 7; Jas. 1:27; 2:1-9; Matt. 25:31-46; Acts 2:44, 45; 4:34, 35).

10. Evangelism and Culture

The development of strategies for world evangelization calls for imaginative pioneering methods. Under God, the result will be the rise of churches deeply rooted in Christ and closely related to their culture. Culture must always be tested and judged by Scripture. Because men and women are God's creatures, some of their culture is rich in beauty and goodness. Because they are fallen, all of it is tainted with sin and some of it is demonic. The gospel does not presuppose the superiority of any culture to another, but evaluates all cultures according to its own criteria of truth and righteousness, and insists on moral absolutes in every culture. Missions have all too frequently exported with the gospel an alien culture and churches have sometimes been in bondage to culture rather than to Scripture. Christ's evangelists must humbly seek to empty themselves of all but their personal authenticity in order to become the servants of others, and churches must seek to transform and enrich culture, all for the glory of God (Mark 7:8, 9, 13; Gen. 4:21, 22; 1 Cor. 9:19-23; Phil. 2:5-7; 2 Cor. 4:5).

11. Education and Leadership

We confess that we have sometimes pursued church growth at the expense of church depth, and divorced evangelism from Christian nurture. We also acknowledge that some of our missions have been too slow to equip and encourage national leaders to assume their rightful responsibilities. Yet we are committed to indigenous principles, and long that every church will have national leaders who manifest a Christian style of leadership in terms not of domination but of service. We recognise that there is a great need to improve theological education, especially for church leaders. In every nation and culture there should be an effective training programme for pastors and laity in doctrine, discipleship, evangelism, nurture, and service. Such training programmes should not rely on any stereotyped methodology but should be developed by creative local initiatives according to biblical standards (Col. 1:27, 28; Acts 14:23; Tit. 1:5, 9; Mark 10:42-45; Eph. 4:11, 12).

12. Spiritual Conflict

We believe that we are engaged in constant spiritual warfare with the principalities and powers of evil, who are seeking to overthrow the Church and frustrate its task of world evangelization. We know our need to equip ourselves with God's armour and to fight this battle with the spiritual weapons of truth and prayer. For we detect the activity of our enemy, not only in false ideologies outside the Church, but also inside it in false gospels which twist Scripture and put people in the place of God. We need both watchfulness and discernment to safeguard the biblical gospel. We acknowledge that we ourselves are not immune to worldliness of thoughts and action, that is, to a surrender to secularism. For example, although careful studies of church growth, both numerical and spiritual, are right and valuable, we have sometimes neglected them. At other times, desirous to ensure a response to the gospel, we have compromised our message, manipulated our hearers through pressure techniques, and become unduly preoccupied with statistics or even dishonest in our use of them. All this is worldly. The Church must be in the world; the world must not be in the Church (Eph. 6:12; 2 Cor. 4:3, 4; Eph. 6:11, 13-18; 2 Cor. 10:3-5; 1 John 2:18-26; 4:1-3; Gal. 1:6-9; 2 Cor. 2:17; 4:2; John 17:15).

13. Freedom and Persecution

It is the God-appointed duty of every government to secure conditions of peace, justice, and liberty in which the Church may obey God, serve the Lord Jesus Christ, and preach the gospel without interference. We therefore pray for the leaders of nations and call upon them to guarantee freedom of thought and conscience, and freedom to practise and propagate religion in accordance with the will of God and as set forth in The Universal

Declaration of Human Rights. We also express our deep concern for all who have been unjustly imprisoned, and especially for those who are suffering for their testimony to the Lord Jesus. We promise to pray and work for their freedom. At the same time we refuse to be intimidated by their fate. God helping us, we too will seek to stand against injustice and to remain faithful to the gospel, whatever the cost. We do not forget the warnings of Jesus that persecution is inevitable (1 Tim. 1:1-4; Acts 4:19; 5:29; Col. 3:24; Heb. 13:1-3; Luke 4:18; Gal. 5:11; 6:12; Matt. 5:10-12; John 15:18-21).

14. The Power of the Holy Spirit

We believe in the power of the Holy Spirit. The Father sent his Spirit to bear witness to his Son; without his witness ours is futile. Conviction of sin, faith in Christ, new birth, and Christian growth are all his work. Further, the Holy Spirit is a missionary spirit; thus evangelism should arise spontaneously from a Spirit-filled church. A church that is not a missionary church is contradicting itself and quenching the Spirit. Worldwide evangelization will become a realistic possibility only when the Spirit renews the Church in truth and wisdom, faith, holiness, love, and power. We therefore call upon all Christians to pray for such a visitation of the sovereign Spirit of God that all his fruit may appear in all his people and that all his gifts may enrich the body of Christ. Only then will the whole world become a fit instrument in his hands, that the whole earth may hear his voice (1 Cor. 2:4; John 15:26, 27; 16:8-11; 1 Cor. 12:3; John 3:6-8; 2 Cor. 3:18; John 7:37-39; 1 Thess. 5:19; Acts 1:8; Psa. 85:4-7; 67:1-3; Gal. 5:22, 23; 1 Cor. 12:4-31; Rom. 12:3-8).

15. The Return of Christ

We believe that Jesus Christ will return personally and visibly, in power and glory, to consummate his salvation and his judgment. This promise of his coming is a further spur to our evangelism, for we remember his words that the gospel must first be preached to all nations. We believe that the interim period between Christ's ascension and return is to be filled with the mission of the people of God, who have no liberty to stop before the end. We also remember his warning that false Christs and false prophets will arise as precursors of the final Antichrist. We therefore reject as a proud, self-confident dream the notion that people can ever build a utopia on earth. Our Christian confidence is that God will perfect his kingdom, and we look forward with eager anticipation to that day, and to the new heaven and earth in which righteousness will dwell and God will reign forever. Meanwhile, we rededicate ourselves to the service of Christ and of people in joyful submission to his authority over the whole of our lives (Mark 14:62; Heb. 9:28; Mark 13:10; Acts 1:8-11; Matt. 28:20; Mark 13:21-23; John 2:18; 4:1-3; Luke 12:32; Rev. 21:1-5; 2 Pet. 3:13; Matt. 28:18).

Conclusion

Therefore, in the light of this our faith and our resolve, we enter into a solemn covenant with God and with each other, to pray, to plan, and to work together for the evangelization of the whole world. We call upon others to join us. May God help us by his grace and for his glory to be faithful to this our covenant! Amen, Alleluia!

(Source: "The Lausanne Covenant," http://www.lausanne.org/covenant.)

75. Iguassu Affirmation of the World Evangelical Fellowship, 1999

Preamble

We have convened as 160 mission practitioners, missiologists, and church leaders from 53 countries, under the World Evangelical Fellowship Missions Commission in Foz de Iguassu, Brazil, on October 10-15, 1999, to: (1) Reflect together on the challenges and opportunities facing world missions at the dawn of the new millennium; (2) Review the different streams of twentieth-century evangelical missiology and practice, especially since the 1974

Lausanne Congress; (3) Continue developing and applying a relevant biblical missiology which reflects the cultural diversity of God's people.

We proclaim the living Christ in a world torn by ethnic conflicts, massive economic disparity, natural disasters, and ecological crises. The mission task is both assisted and hindered by technological developments that now reach the remotest corners of the earth. The diverse religious aspirations of people, expressed in multiple religions and spiritual experimentation, challenge the ultimate truth of the Gospel.

In the twentieth century, missiology witnessed unprecedented development. In recent years, reflection from many parts of the church has helped missions to continue shedding paternalistic tendencies. Today, we continue to explore the relationship between the Gospel and culture, between evangelism and social responsibility and between biblical mandates and the social sciences. We see some international organizations—among them the World Evangelical Fellowship, the Lausanne Committee for World Evangelization, and the AD 2000 and Beyond Movement—that have begun a promising process of partnership and unity.

Increased efforts at partnership have been catalyzed by an emphasis on methodologies involving measurable goals and numerical growth. Flowing from a commitment to urgent evangelization these methodologies have shown how our task might be accomplished. However these insights must be subject to biblical principles and growth in Christlikeness.

We rejoice in diverse missiological voices emerging around the world, but we confess that we have not taken them all into our theory and practice. Old paradigms still prevail. Participation by and awareness of the global church, as well as mission from people of all nations to people of all nations, are needed for a valid missiology in our time.

Our discussions have invited us to fuller dependence on the Spirit's empowering presence in our life and ministry as we eagerly await the glorious return of our Lord Jesus Christ.

In the light of these realities, we make the following declarations:

Declarations

Our faith rests on the absolute authority of the God-breathed Scriptures. We are heirs of the great Christian confessions handed down to us. All three Persons of the Godhead are active in God's redeeming mission. Our missiology centers on the overarching biblical theme of God's creation of the world, the Father's redeeming love for fallen humanity as revealed in the incarnation, substitutionary death, and resurrection of our Lord Jesus Christ, and ultimately of the redemption and renewal of the whole creation. The Holy Spirit, promised by our Lord, is our comforter, teacher, and source of power. It is the Spirit who calls us into holiness and integrity. The Spirit leads the Church into all truth. The Spirit is the agent of mission, convicting of sin, righteousness, and judgment. We are Christ's servants, empowered and led by the Spirit, whose goal is to glorify God.

We confess the following themes as truths of special importance in this present age. These themes are clearly attested to in the whole of the Scriptures and speak to the desire of God to provide salvation for all people.

1. *Jesus Christ is Lord of the Church and Lord of the Universe.* Ultimately every knee will bow and every tongue confess that Jesus is Lord. The lordship of Christ is to be proclaimed to the whole world, inviting all to be free from bondage to sin and the dominion of evil in order to serve the Lord for His glory.

2. *The Lord Jesus Christ is the unique revelation of God and the only Savior of the world.* Salvation is found in Christ alone. God witnesses to Himself in creation and in human conscience, but these witnesses are not complete without the revelation of God in Christ. In the face of competing truth claims, we proclaim with humility that Christ is the only Savior, conscious that sin as well as cultural hindrances often mask Him from those for whom He died.

3. *The good news of the salvation made possible by the work of Jesus Christ must be expressed in all the languages and cultures of the world.* We are commanded to be heralds of the Gospel to every creature so that they can have the opportunity to confess faith in Christ. The message must come to them in a language they can understand and in a

form that is appropriate to their circumstances. Believers, led by the Holy Spirit, are encouraged to create culturally appropriate forms of worship and uncover biblical insights that glorify God for the benefit of the whole church.

4. *The Gospel is good news and addresses all human needs.* We emphasize the holistic nature of the Gospel of Jesus Christ. Both the Old Testament and the New Testament demonstrate God's concern with the whole person in the whole of society. We acknowledge that material blessings come from God, but prosperity should not be equated with godliness.

5. *Opposition to the spread of the Gospel is foremost a spiritual conflict involving human sin and principalities and powers opposed to the Living God.* This conflict is manifested in different ways, e.g., fear of spirits or indifference to God. We recognize that the defense of the truth of the Gospel is also spiritual warfare. As witnesses of the Gospel, we announce that Jesus Christ has power over all powers and is able to free all who turn to Him in faith. We affirm that in the cross God has won the victory.

6. *Suffering, persecution and martyrdom are present realities for many Christians.* We acknowledge that our obedience in mission involves suffering and recognize that the church is experiencing this. We affirm our privilege and responsibility to pray for those undergoing persecution. We are called to share in their pain, do what we can to relieve their sufferings, and work for human rights and religious freedom.

7. *Economic and political systems deeply affect the spread of God's kingdom.* Human government is appointed by God, but all human institutions act out of fallenness. The Scriptures command that Christians pray for those in authority and work for truth and justice. Appropriate Christian response to political and economic systems requires the guidance of the Holy Spirit.

8. *God works in a variety of Christian traditions and organizations, for His glory and the salvation of the world.* For too long believers, divided over issues of church organization, order, and doctrine—such as the gifts and ministry of the Holy Spirit—have failed to recognize each other's work. We affirm, bless, and pray for authentic Christian witness wherever it is found.

9. *To be effective witnesses of the holy God, we need to demonstrate personal and corporate holiness, love, and righteousness.* We repent of hypocrisy and conformity to the world, and call the church to a renewed commitment to holy living. Holiness requires turning from sin, training in righteousness, and growing in Christlikeness.

Commitments

We commit ourselves to continue and deepen our reflection on the following themes, helping one another to enrich our understanding and practice with insight from every corner of the world. Our hearts' desire is the discipling of the nations through the effective, faithful communication of Christ to every culture and people.

1. Trinitarian Foundation of Mission

We commit ourselves to a renewed emphasis on God-centered missiology. This invites a new study of the operation of the Trinity in the redemption of the human race and the whole of creation, as well as to understand the particular roles of Father, Son, and Spirit in mission to this fallen world.

2. Biblical and Theological Reflection

We confess that our biblical and theological reflection has sometimes been shallow and inadequate. We also confess that we have frequently been selective in our use of texts rather than being faithful to the whole biblical revelation. We commit ourselves to engage in renewed biblical and theological studies shaped by mission, and to pursue a missiology and practice shaped by God's Word, brought to life and light by the Holy Spirit.

3. Church and Mission

The Church in mission is central to God's plan for the world. We commit ourselves to strengthen our ecclesiology in mission, and to encourage the global church to become a truly missionary community in which all Christians are involved in mission. In the face of increasing resistance and opposition from political powers, religious fundamentalism and secularism, we commit ourselves to encourage and challenge the churches to respond with a deeper level of unity and participation in mission.

4. Gospel and Culture

The Gospel is always presented and received within a cultural context. It is therefore essential to clarify the relationship between Gospel and Culture, both in theory and practice, recognizing that there is both good and evil in all cultures. We commit ourselves to continue to demonstrate the relevance of the Christian message to all cultures, and ensure that missionaries learn to wrestle biblically with the relationship between Gospel and culture. We commit ourselves to serious study of how different cultural perspectives may enrich our understanding of the Gospel as well as how all worldviews have to be critiqued and transformed by it.

5. Pluralism

Religious pluralism challenges us to hold firmly to the uniqueness of Jesus Christ as Savior even as we work for increased tolerance and understanding among religious communities. We can not seek harmony by relativizing the truth claims of religions. Urbanization and radical political change have bred increased interreligious and ethnic violence and hostility. We commit ourselves to be agents of reconciliation. We also commit ourselves to proclaim the Gospel of Jesus Christ in faithfulness and loving humility.

6. Spiritual Conflict

We welcome the renewed attention given in recent decades to the biblical theme of spiritual conflict. We rejoice that power and authority is not ours but God's. At the same time we must ensure that the interest in spiritual warfare does not become a substitute for dealing with the root issues of sin, salvation, conversion, and the battle for the truth. We commit ourselves to increase our biblical understanding and practice of spiritual conflict

while guarding against syncretistic and unbiblical elements.

7. Strategy in Mission

We are grateful for many helpful insights gained from the social sciences. We are concerned that these should be subject to the authority of Scripture. Therefore we call for a healthy critique of mission theories that depend heavily on marketing concepts and missiology by objectives.

8. Globalized Missiology

The insights of every part of the church are needed and challenges encountered in every land must be addressed. Only thus can our missiology develop the richness and texture reflected in the Scriptures and needed for full obedience to our risen Lord. We commit ourselves to give voice to all segments of the global church in developing and implementing our missiology.

9. Godly Character

Biblical holiness is essential for credible Christian witness. We commit ourselves to renewed emphasis on godly living and servanthood, and we urge training institutions, both missionary and ministerial, to include substantive biblical and practical training in Christian character formation.

10. The Cross and Suffering

As our Lord called us to take up our crosses, we remind the church of our Lord's teaching that suffering is a part of authentic Christian life. In an increasingly violent and unjust world with political and economic oppression, we commit to equip ourselves and others to suffer in missionary service and to serve the suffering church. We pursue to articulate a biblical theology of martyrdom.

11. Christian Responsibility and the World Economic Order

In a world increasingly controlled by global economic forces, Christians need to be aware of the corrosive effects of affluence and the destructive effects of poverty. We must be aware of ethnocentrism in our view of economic forces. We commit ourselves to address the realities of world poverty and oppose policies that serve the powerful rather than the powerless. It is the responsibility of the church in each place to affirm the meaning and value of a people, especially where indigenous cultures face extinction. We call all Christians to commit themselves to reflect God's concern for justice and the welfare of all peoples.

12. Christian Responsibility and the Ecological Crisis

The earth is the Lord's and the Gospel is good news for all creation. Christians share in the responsibility God gave to all humanity to care for the earth. We call on all Christians to commit themselves to ecological integrity in practicing responsible stewardship of creation, and we encourage Christians in environmental care and protection initiatives.

13. Partnership

As citizens of the Kingdom of God and members of Christ's body, we commit ourselves to renewed efforts at cooperation because it is our Lord's desire that we be one and that we work in harmony in His service so that the world will believe. We acknowledge that our attempts have not always been as equals. Inadequate theology, especially in respect to the doctrine of the church, and the imbalance of resources has made working together difficult. We pledge to find ways to address this imbalance and to demonstrate to the world that believers in Christ are truly one in their service of Christ.

14. Member Care

Service of the Lord in cross-cultural environments exposes missionaries to many stresses and criticisms. While acknowledging that missionaries also share the limitations of our common humanity and have made errors, we affirm that they deserve love, respect, and gratitude. Too often, agencies, churches, and fellow Christians have not followed biblical guidelines in dealing with cross-cultural workers. We commit ourselves to support and nur-

ture our missionary workers for their sakes and for the Gospel witness.

Pledge

We, the participants of the Iguassu Missiological Consultation, declare our passion as mission practitioners, missiologists, and church leaders for the urgent evangelization of the whole world and the discipling of the nations to the glory of the Father, the Son, and the Holy Spirit.

In all our commitments we depend on the Lord who empowers us by the Holy Spirit to fulfill His mission. As evangelicals, we pledge to sustain our biblical heritage in this ever-changing world. We commit ourselves to participate actively in formulating and practicing evangelical missiology. Indwelt by the Spirit, we purpose to carry the radical good news of the Kingdom of God to all the world. We affirm our commitment to love one another and to pray for one another as we struggle to do His will.

We rejoice in the privilege of being part of God's mission in proclaiming the Gospel of reconciliation and hope. We joyfully look to the Lord's return and passionately yearn to see the realization of the eschatological vision when people from every nation, tribe, and language shall worship the Lamb.

To this end may the Father, the Son and the Holy Spirit be glorified. Hallelujah!

Amen.

(Source: World Evangelical Fellowship Missions Commission, "Iguassu Affirmation," *Evangelical Review of Theology* 24, no. 3 (2000): 200-206; http://www.worldevangelicals.org/igua_affirm.html.)

76. The Sandy Cove Covenant and Invitation, June 28-30, 2004

We are a gathering of evangelical Christians who provide institutional, pastoral, and intellectual leadership in a wide variety of life settings. We have come together at Sandy Cove, Maryland, in order to pray, reflect, and learn together about our role as stewards of God's creation. We are convinced that

God has moved among us in our time together over these three days.

We represent a variety of perspectives and varying levels of expertise about environmental issues. Some of us have given our entire lives to caring for all of God's creation, while for others the issue is a new one. For all of us, this meeting has resulted in a deepening of our concern about God's creation, a joyful sense of community, and a desire to work together on these issues in days ahead. In reflecting on Scripture and on the pressing environmental problems that beset our world, we are persuaded that we must not evade our responsibility to care for God's creation. We recognize that there is much more we need to learn, and much more praying we need to do, but that we know enough to know that there is no turning back from engaging the threats to God's creation.

We feel called of God to covenant together to move the work of creation-care ahead in a variety of ways. Therefore:

We covenant together to make creation-care a permanent dimension of our Christian discipleship and to deepen our theological and biblical understanding of the issues involved. We covenant together to draw upon the very best and most trustworthy resources that can help us understand the particular environmental challenges we face today, as well as promising solutions, as fully and accurately as possible.

We covenant together to share our growing knowledge and concern about these issues with other members of our constituencies. We invite our brothers and sisters in Christ to engage with us the most pressing environmental questions of our day, such as health threats to families and the unborn, the negative effects of environmental degradation on the poor, God's endangered creatures, and the important current debate about human-induced climate change. We covenant together to engage the evangelical community in a discussion about the question of climate change with the goal of reaching a consensus statement on the subject in twelve months.

Our continuing goal is to motivate the evangelical community to fully engage environmental issues in a biblically faithful and humble manner, collaborating with those who share these concerns, that we might take our appropriate place in the healing of God's creation, and thus the advance of God's reign.

Signatories (Please Note: Institutional affiliation provided for information purposes only. Signatories do so as individuals and not as representatives of their institutions.)

Rev. Peter Borgdorff, Executive Director, Christian Reformed Church

Rev. Paul Cedar, Chair, Mission America

Rev. Richard Cizik, VP of Governmental Affairs, National Association of Evangelicals

Andy Crouch, Columnist, Christianity Today

Dr. Cal DeWitt, President, Au Sable Institute of Environmental Studies

Rev. Barrett Duke, VP for Public Policy & Research, Southern Baptist Ethics Commission

Adrienne Gaines, News Editor, Charisma magazine

Dr. Dave Gushee, Professor, Union University

Rev. Ted Haggard, President, National Association of Evangelicals

Rev. Dave Holdren, General Superintendent, Wesleyan Church

Sir John Houghton, Chairman, John Ray Initiative

Dr. Cheryl Johns, Professor, Church of God Theological Seminary

Jennifer Jukanovich, Founder & Chairperson, The Vine

Rev. Jo Anne Lyon, Executive Director, World Hope

Dr. Ron Mahurin, VP for Campus Programs & Communications, Council for Christian Colleges and Universities

Rev. Dwight McKissic, Senior Pastor, Cornerstone Baptist Church

Rev. Brian McLaren, Emergent

David Neff, Editor, Christianity Today

Shelly Ngo, Dir. of Publications, World Vision

Michael Nyenhuis, President, MAP International

Rev. Paul Risser, Former President, FourSquare Church

Rev. Ron Sider, President, Evangelicals for Social Action

Mark Smith, Dir. of Disaster Response, World Relief

Dr. Howard Snyder, Prof., Asbury Seminary

Rev. Roy Taylor, Stated Clerk, Presbyterian Church in America

Rev. Bob Wenz, VP of Natl. Ministries, National Association of Evangelicals

Bruce Wilkinson, VP of International Programs, World Vision

John Wilson, Editor, Books & Culture, Christianity Today

Rev. Jim Ball, Ex. Dir., Evangelical Environmental Network

(Source: Christianity Today—National Association of Evangelicals—Evangelical Environmental Network Conference on Creation-Care, June 28-30, 2004. http://www.creationcare.org/conference.)

77. *I Was Hungry and You Gave Me Food,* by Ronald J. Vos

The document below is excerpted from a larger document on holistic mission prepared for a 2004 forum of the Lausanne Committee on World Evangelism in Thailand by the Issue Group on Holistic Mission. Other sections focused on Economic Justice, The Church and Health, and Christians in Response to Uprooted People. The overall introduction by C. René Padilla sets the tone of the entire document on holistic Mission and the reading below, insisting that Christian mission must include social as well as evangelistic responsibility if it is to be faithful to the command of Jesus in Matthew 28:20. And, as the document shows, social responsibility demands social analysis and listening to the voices of the poor and marginalized.

Approximately 40,000 people die each day from starvation or hunger-related causes. [Estimates range. *Justpeace News,* 2:1, January 2004 used the figure of 34,000 under the age of five. Others including the United Nations Food and Agriculture Organization have used numbers as high as 54,000. Regardless of the estimate, it is unacceptably too large. This figure is much higher than the number that reportedly die each day from HIV/AIDS. There is a correlation between those dying of HIV/AIDS and hunger because many of the food providers are dying and this adds to the hunger problem.] Yet in developed countries there is a surplus of food in the form of cereal grains. In some regions even potable drinking water is often lacking. In this paper the group has decided to focus on agriculture. Water is intrinsically linked to sanitation and irrigation, and as an issue of global importance should be discussed in another paper. [Fresh water is a very precious commodity. Approximately 97% of all the earth's water is saline. Most of the remainder of the 3% of fresh water is tied up in glaciers or ice caps of mountains, too deep in the earth to extract, or is tied up in soil. In fact, only 0.003% of all the earth's water is available for consumption and agricultural production. Annually renewable freshwater supplies on land account for only 0.000008% of all water on earth. While this many seem to be a small amount, estimates show that with proper care there is adequate water for all people and other creatures living on earth. The problems arise due to unequal distribution and frequency of rainfall, location of population centres that are demanding water that exceeds supply, and salination and siltation due to irrigation. For more information see "Water Conservation and the Politics of Irrigation," by Laura E. Powers and Robert McSorly in *Ecological Principles of Agriculture,* Delmar Thomson Learning, 2000, and *The Conquest of Land over Seven Thousand Years* by Lowdermilk (http://www.soilandhealth.org/01aglibrary/010119lowdermilk.usda/cls.html).]

Worldview Issues

How we regard creation, how we practice agriculture, all depends upon how we view the world. A worldview can be described as the basic assumptions that one holds either consciously or unconsciously about the makeup of the world and how the world works. A worldview has been described as the pair of spectacles through which we view the world. If you believe that the earth is given to humans to be used for what humans ultimately deem is appropriate, then a logical conclusion is that you will use it for human profit and ignore consequences to the rest of creation. A biblical worldview is necessary to understand appropriate responses to agriculture.

People's view of the nonhuman creation will ultimately affect how agriculture is practiced.

Depending on our worldview, either God (theocentric), the rest of creation (biocentric), or humans (anthropocentric) are exalted. [Roger W. Elmore, "Our Relationship with the Ecosystem and Its Impact on Sustainable Agriculture," *Journal of Production Agriculture*, 9:1, 1996.] We are not passive observers of the ecosystem, but constantly have an impact on it, and the impact we have is dependent on our worldview.

A biocentric worldview elevates the ecosystem over humans. Humans are subservient to the earth and are often seen as a pathogen that threatens the health of the planet. [Biologist E. O. Wilson stated back in 1945, "The human species is our own home-grown asteroid."] While exalting the rest of the creation may appear unselfish, people who believe this either tend to worship creation or believe in the elimination of humans in order to conserve the ecosystem. [James Lovelock, *The Gaia Hypothesis*, 1979.] This view is typically held by New Age followers and some traditional religions.

Animism is the belief that "the physical world is animated by spirits or gods." Because certain natural objects are worshiped they cannot be used for food or fibre by humans. Animists will often starve while certain edible plants and animals surround them because appropriate use of these plants or animals would be considered sacrilegious. The Animist's fear of offending the spirits keeps people in ignorance of the blessings of creation.

The danger for Christians in rejecting the biocentric view is to swing to the opposite extreme of over-valuing human power over the natural world and thus fall into the error of anthropocentrism. The anthropocentric worldview exalts humans over the rest of creation; humans are considered dominators of creation. Anthropocentrism assumes that people are accountable to no higher authority for their treatment of the rest of natural world. Everything is there for humans and nothing has intrinsic or God-given value. One direct result of this worldview is the tendency to view the natural world simply in terms of price. This results in a focus on short-term actions and often near-sighted approaches to land and natural resources. Land is worth only the amount of income it will produce for its owner. Therefore, the best use of land is what brings in the most income. If land can be sold for a purpose that brings more money than

it would bring if it were being used for agricultural purposes, then it should be converted to the most profitable use. Urban sprawl is a simple example of "developers" being able to pay more for land than people involved in agriculture. Other examples are factory farming and genetically modified crops. Most of the present-day use of land and agriculture in Western countries is a result of this anthropocentric view.

An anthropocentric worldview assumes that forests or prairies only have value when humans can utilize them. Thus forests or prairies should be preserved because they can provide us with a plentiful supply of oxygen or because there may be some plant species that could serve as future sources of medicine or food for humans. The anthropocentric view puts the forests' and prairies' economic value above any intrinsic or God-given value. A result of this philosophy is that all technology is initially embraced as good technology because it hastens the human exploitation of creation for human benefit. Only if there is overwhelming evidence that humans can be affected negatively is such technology called into question. There is little regard for non-human effects.

Sadly some Christians have interpreted God's granting "rule" (Genesis 1:28) over the natural world to humankind as the sort of "rule" found in the anthropocentric view. Christians who recognize that humans are created in God's image often misinterpret this passage and think this gives them the right to use their power to do as they please, rather than practicing the servant ruler model as exemplified in Jesus Christ. [Ronald J. Vos, "Social Principles for 'Good' Agriculture," in *Biblical Holism and Agriculture: Cultivating our Roots*, ed. David J. Evans, Ronald J. Vos, and Keith P. Wright, William Carey Library, 2003.]

Because human beings are by nature selfish the anthropocentric view leads to some demanding so much of the natural world's benefits that others are left with nothing. Some come to possess vast tracts of land while others are left landless (Isaiah 58). Here again land is viewed in terms of its price for the few without any regard for its value for the many. God condemns such exploitation in no uncertain terms and legislated against the inequality of land holding in the law of Jubilee (Leviticus 25). [Some critics like Berkeley historian Lynn White Jr. often blame Christians for the environmental crisis and the exploitation of creation. See "The Historical Roots of Our Ecological Crisis," *Science* 155, 1967, pp. 1203-07.] This accusation is the result of a misinterpretation of the biblical message. Severe environmental problems in the Former Soviet Union demonstrate that tremendous problems exist in non-Christian societies.

The anthropocentric view does not promote an agriculture that is sustainable for the long term. Under this view, some people, but not all, will have food; some people, but not all, will have a reasonable quality of life and some, but not all, agricultural producers will be economically viable. This is considered a normal economic process because there is a survival-of-the-fittest mentality driving this worldview. Standards of justice are the result of what a majority of humans decide is just. This is a worldview that, if unchecked and carried to its logical end, breeds cutthroat competition as well as the destruction of creation because it is driven by human greed and selfishness. [The selfishness of humans is illustrated by Garrett Hardin, professor of biology, in an animal-grazing example. Hardin's concept has become known as the Tragedy of the Commons. (See "The Tragedy of the Commons," *Science* 162, 1968, pp. 1243-48.) In a grazing area that is open to all herders, everyone will work together for their mutual benefit until the carrying capacity of the land is reached. At that point each herder may consider the cost and benefit of adding one more animal to his herd. One person may soon discover that his benefit is the addition of one more animal but that the cost of adding another animal is divided among all herders. As each individual herder seeks to add more animals, the commons becomes ruined and tragedy ultimately results. "Ruin is the destination toward which all men rush, each pursuing his own interest in a society that believes in the freedom of the commons. Freedom in a commons brings ruin to all" (Hardin, 1968, p. 1244).]

Christians who believe that salvation is only a matter of saving individual souls are in danger of adopting by default an anthropocentric view of the natural world. [Wendell Berry, "Christianity and the Survival of Creation," in *The Art of the Commonplace,* Shoemaker and Hoard, 2002.] This leads to an exclusive focus on personal morality and neglecting the teaching in God's word regarding creation. The world's way of practicing agriculture is accepted without question, resulting in adding to environmental degradation. Views of the end of the world that emphasize the destruction of the earth rather than its regeneration also lead to a neglect of environmental ethics and seeing no value in the natural world beyond exploiting it for human gain or using it to prove the existence of God. Failure to understand the delight that God takes in His creation (see Genesis 1 and Job 38-42, for example) and failure to realize that because He is sovereign, He upholds and provides for His creation, inevitably results in humankind misusing God's creation.

Theocentrism: Creation, Fall, Redemption, and Consummation

Human beings are directly involved in the ecosystem and like the rest of creation are created by God. We derive our food and the air we breathe from the ecosystem; we add wastes to it and ultimately our present bodies return as dust to it. Interaction with creation cannot be avoided; it is a holistic activity that must be brought with the rest of life under the Lordship of Christ.

The Bible teaches that the earth is God's creation, that He declares it good, and that the pinnacle of His creative activity is the Sabbath when He rested from His work and delighted in what He had made (Genesis 1-2:3). As a reflection of who He is, the creation declares God's glory to anyone who chooses to see it (Psalm 19; Romans 1:20). In contrast to the biocentric view, God is seen as separate from His creation. In contrast to the anthropocentric view, humankind is seen as the crown of God's creation, but in the context of the rest of creation which is given intrinsic value by God. God also upholds the creation over which he is sovereign (Job 38-42; Psalm 104, 148, 150; Isaiah 55; Luke 12; Matthew 6). As mentioned previously, God delights in the creation that He has made. To diminish a part of God's creation is to diminish what God delights in and prevents that part from praising God.

God is the first agriculturalist. This fact has great implications for how we practice agriculture.

Since God is the first farmer all those who work in agriculture are engaged in a dignified and holy vocation. God upholds and delights in the great diversity that He has made (Genesis 2:8-9).

Human beings, both female and male, were appointed as rulers of the rest of creation under the authority of God (Genesis 1:28). This concept is further explained in Genesis 2:15 where God puts Adam in the garden and commands him to realize the potential of (*abad*) and conserve (*shamar*) the creation. This servant kingship is fully revealed in Jesus Christ the servant king, who will usher in the new heaven and earth.

An old but rich concept that expresses the biblical concept of how humankind can use the earth and its fruits is that of "usufruct." Usufruct literally means "to use the fruits of." It is the right to utilize and enjoy the profits and advantages of something belonging to another so long as the property is not damaged. [As author, professor, and farmer Wendell Berry, in a letter read by Wes Jackson at a Theology of the Land Conference, Collegeville, Minnesota in 1986 stated: "To receive the gift of Creation and then to hasten directly to practical ways of exploiting that gift for maximum production without regard to long term impacts is at best ingratitude and at worse blasphemy (the act of claiming for oneself the attributes and rights of God)."] This concept should be a guiding principle in how we should practice agriculture and how we approach issues related to hunger. [Richard Bauckham, "Human Authority in Creation," in *God and the Crisis of Freedom: Biblical and Contemporary Perspectives,* Louisville, Westminster John Knox Press, 2002.]

Even though God created everything good, humankind rejected God's authority and destroyed the perfect relationship that existed between them. Yet the destruction of this relationship also involved destroying the relationship between themselves and the rest of creation. However, because He loved the world (*cosmos*) (John 3:16) that He had made, God in the person of Jesus Christ came into this world to pay the penalty for all sin. Through his suffering, death, resurrection, and ascension, Christ has redeemed his people and all of creation (Colossians 1:15-20; Ephesians 1:9-10). In gratitude we are called to spread this good news and with the help of the Holy Spirit to reform human activities to be in accord with God's original mandate. [Charles Colson and Nancy Pearcy, *How Now Shall We Live*, Tyndale House, 1999, p. 296. "Salvation does not consist simply of freedom from sin; salvation also means being restored to the task that we were given in the beginning: the job of creating culture. . . . Christians are saved not only from something (sin) but to something (Christ's lordship over all life)."]

God has not discarded His creation. As a result of the fall, every part of creation was subjected to frustration and bondage to decay (Romans 8:20-21). Yet God graciously established a covenant with humankind and the rest of creation that He would never destroy the world again with a flood (Genesis 9:8-11, 22). This covenant demonstrated God's continued delight and concern for all of his creation. This covenantal understanding is in stark contrast to the utilitarian economic view that the value of creation is determined solely by how humankind benefits. This places great responsibility on Christians in how we interact with creation.

While the natural world obeys God's laws without any choice in the matter, humankind was given the responsibility to rule over and care for this natural world. Because of sin, cultures and social institutions are often damaging to the natural world. It is not surprising that agriculture may be detrimental to God's creation.

The covenant which was fulfilled in Christ's death and resurrection has cosmic consequences for creation as well as personal consequences for believing Christians. As Fred Van Dyke (et al.) states in the book *Redeeming Creation*: "God's saving grace through Christ not only pays the price for people, but redeems an oppressed cosmos. This does not demean the work of Christ, but rather amplifies it. Just as the sin of Adam affected all creation, so the sacrifice of Christ begins the redemption of it." [Fred Van Dyke, David C. Mahan, Joseph K. Sheldon, Raymond H. Brand, *Redeeming Creation: The Biblical Basis for Environmental Stewardship*, InterVarsity Press, 1996, p. 86.] That redemption is not just for humans, but all God's creation as shown in Romans 8:19-21: "the creation itself will be liberated from the bondage of decay." Colossians 1:15-20 describes Christ holding everything together in creation, everything was made for and by Christ; everything holds together in Christ and everything will be reconciled by Christ. Redemption at the end of time is not an end to the creation, but the beginning of a purified new heaven and a new earth. God will make all things new (Revelation 21:5).

In summary, theocentrism exalts God over creation, including human beings. But if we follow the example of Christ as servant leader, we have the ability to put others above self and to become caretakers of creation accountable to God. This view results in the blessing of sustainable agriculture and will promote good environmental stewardship and sufficient food production for a long period of time. It aims for a quality of life based on sufficiency rather than excess and leads to the long-term sustainability of creation.

Implications Related to Agriculture

From a biblical perspective, holistic mission—where agriculture is concerned—means focusing on stewardship under God and sustainability. The industrial model of agriculture is very prominent in Western culture and many Christians are involved in its practice. This model is being exported around the world. In some ways it can be considered a success because it relies on few people and large amounts of purchased inputs to produce a lot of food. However, the social and environmental costs that accompany this type of agriculture are often ignored. Some of the well known, but often ignored, negative results of this type of agriculture are: environmental degradation, depleted aquifers, polluted ground and surface water, diminished genetic diversity, and heavy reliance on limited fossil fuels.

Our view of plants and animals is also different from the world's view if we accept a theocentric worldview. For example: weeds are not some evil plants that have been planted by the devil, but plants that are growing in places in which humans wish they were not growing. A weed is simply a plant that is out of place from a human viewpoint. This plant still functions as God intended. It prevents soil erosion by anchoring itself to the soil with its roots. It reduces the impact of raindrops on soil by intercepting the rain with its leaves. It

produces carbohydrates as a result of photosynthesis, and can serve as a source of food and protection for non-human creatures. Domestic animals are not just objects that produce something to be utilized by humans. Animals are part of God's creation and their diversity gives Him great pleasure. An animal gives praise to God when it is allowed to be the animal that God intended it to be. Humans must remember this fact as we raise our animals for food and fibre. Christians especially need to remember that they are dealing with something that is not theirs. Creation is a gift given them by the Creator Himself. This fact should instil a sense of awe and respect in Christians.

Sustainable agriculture is economically viable, resource efficient, environmentally sound, promotes justice to both the human and non-human creation, and builds community while providing food and fibre for humans for long periods of time. [Ron Vos and Del Vander Zee, "Trends in Agriculture: Sustainability," in *Pro Rege*, March, 1990.] Sustainable agriculture may involve many different practices. There is no one method that can be applied as a panacea. Agricultural practice has to be tailored to the local soils, topography, growing season, livestock, rainfall, etc. Diversity and adaptation to local conditions are the keys for successful sustainable agriculture. Land and soil cannot be managed well by mass-produced mono-technologies but by wisdom and local insight.

A sustainable model of agriculture must mimic the creational model of the ecosystem it replaces because in reality agricultural systems are highly modified ecosystems. [An ecosystem is "a system of interacting organisms in a particular habitat" (*The Concise Oxford Dictionary*).] Ecosystems are systems of "communities" of living things (biotic communities) that have the following features.

- They use solar energy, which is like a stream of income, to produce local products which recycle raw materials locally and are not exported to a faraway place as if they were mined. (For example, solar energy degrades animal waste so that it can be used as a fertilizer.)
- They depend on local plants that hold the soil and nutrients in place.

- Species diversity is encouraged rather than relying on one single species for income.
- Local resources are kept in place as much as possible instead of being mined for a distant country.
- If changes and displacements occur they occur at a rate and scale that is compatible with maintaining internal integrity. Social and ecological impact is minimized.

A sustainable agriculture will be characterized by the following. Agroecosystems:

- that are less dependent on fossil fuel and manufactured items (such as fertilizers) and more dependent on local renewable resources. Efficiency is measured in terms of energy not money because solar energy is like an income stream whereas fossil fuels are like a savings deposit that is gone forever once spent;
- that have little or no adverse environmental impact (for example, on ground water, downstream watersheds, and local wetlands);
- that depend on local wisdom instead of following a centralized command that does not know the local system as intimately as those who live and work in it;
- that values diversity in creation;
- that allows room for wild creatures in addition to domestic creatures;
- that encourages local and natural methods of pest control instead of purchased pesticides;
- that grows plants and animals in regions to which they are adapted. For example, rice should not be grown in a desert just because it is technologically possible to do so;
- that produces agricultural products primarily for sale in the region in which they are produced with only the surplus being used to earn income, rather than producing for a country a long distance away while neighbours may be starving because the product grown for sale is not used locally.

Sustainable agriculture is something to strive for. To implement the characteristics listed will require local knowledge, wisdom, and care by local people and will thus support community. [Ron Voss and Del Vander Zee, "Sustainable Agriculture," in *Signposts of God's Liberating Kingdom*, Potchefstroome University Press, 1998.] These characteristics outline a sustainable holistic approach to land, creatures, water, and people. Implementation is not going to be possible without active support from church and mission leaders around the globe. Practical help is also available from sources such as *Footsteps*, a magazine produced by Tearfund (UK) dealing with various issues including agriculture and available in English, French, Portuguese, and Spanish from footsteps@tearfund.org or on the web at www.tilz.info.

We cannot ignore the long-term implications of our actions while immersing ourselves in a personal piety that ignores the full impact of the gospel on how we live out our faith before the face of God. Such piety reinforces a non-biblical but often practiced dichotomy of the sacred and secular. Instead, Christians should heed the wisdom of theologian, educator, and diplomat Abraham Kuyper.

"Wherever a person may stand, whatever anyone may do, in agriculture, in commerce, and in industry, or whatever one may do in one's mind, in the world of art, or in science, everyone is, in whatsoever it may be, constantly standing before God. Each person should see him/herself employed in the service of God, responsible to obey God and above all, to aim to give glory to God." [Abraham Kuyper, *Lectures on Calvinism*, Grand Rapids, Eerdmans, 1983, p. 7.]

Action Plan for the Church

In a world in which many millions die annually because of inadequate nutrition, agriculture should be clearly a matter of vital interest to everyone, including Christians. As already discussed, God is interested in agriculture—in the way food is produced. What type of agriculture we practice and endorse as Christians is, therefore, an important element of our witness to the kingdom that has been ushered in by our Lord Jesus Christ. In a world where the majority of its peoples will soon be living in cities there is an urgent need for strong holistic biblical teaching on agriculture. We suggest the following actions:

Education

1. Christian schools, colleges and universities should teach all students the fundamental principles of holistic agriculture and where possible provide courses either in agriculture or closely allied fields such as agricultural economics, horticulture and ecology, or environmental studies.
2. Seminaries and Bible colleges should teach the principles of holistic agriculture in courses focusing on both the theology of creation and ethics.
3. Many Christian educational establishments have land, which more often than not is kept as decoration. Some of this land could easily be used to practice the principles of holistic agriculture.

Church Leaders

1. Church leaders should embrace and understand the principles of holistic agriculture and begin to preach and live them out in their churches and communities. This could range from encouraging farmers in the congregation to practice holistic agriculture to Bible exposition encouraging the purchase of locally grown food. Church leaders could even grow some of their own food holistically.
2. Church leaders should encourage church members that are knowledgeable in holistic agriculture to teach their congregations.

Churches and Individual Christians

1. All Christians—rural, urban, and suburban—should grow at least some of their own food so that they can better understand the connection between the land and the food they eat, and to give praise to God who is the First Farmer.
2. The church should come alongside and support farmers who desire to adopt more creation-friendly agricultural practices. Examples of this would be supporting farmers who decided to switch to organic farming or getting involved with Community Supported Agriculture (CSA). [For a brief description of how CSA works see "Social Principles for 'Good' Agriculture," by Ronald J. Vos in *Biblical Holism and Agriculture: Cultivating Our Roots*, ed. David J. Evans, Ronald J. Vos, and Keith P. Wright, William Carey Library, 2003, p. 57.]
3. The church should take advantage of planting and harvest festivals to celebrate God's gifts and to educate members about holistic agriculture.
4. Church members should be educated to understand that God cares for the earth and is actively involved in sustaining it and in providing for all its creatures including human beings. It is therefore appropriate to pray God's blessing on crops and animals.
5. The church should educate its members about purchasing and using fair trade agricultural goods.

Campaigning and Advocacy

1. The church should actively support the UN Millennium Development Goals that relate to and reinforce holistic agriculture. This can be done through supporting the Micah Challenge, a joint initiative of the Micah Network and the World Evangelical Alliance to campaign for the fulfillment of the Millennium Development Goals.
2. Access to land to produce food because most of the land is in the possession of a few very wealthy families is still a major problem for many rural people. There is still a need to advocate on behalf of the landless.
3. Lands that have been cared for in a sustainable way by indigenous people are

being threatened by logging companies and *campesinos* in many countries. It is our Christian duty to work with and on behalf of these traditional farmers.

Materials

1. There is a growing body of theological and practical material on holistic agriculture. However, there is a need to produce more material and to disseminate such material to pastors, churches, and farmers.
2. Some of the Lausanne Holistic Mission issue group participants in the agriculture sector will:

   a. network in this area to discover what is available for use by pastors, churches, and farmers.
   b. develop up-to-date descriptions of best practice models for publication and dissemination to those working in the agricultural sector.

(Source: Ronald J. Vos, "I Was Hungry and You Gave Me Food," in *Holistic Mission*, Lausanne Occasional Paper No. 33, published by David Claydon, ed., in *A New Vision, A New Heart, A Renewed Call*, vol. 1 [Pasadena: William Carey Library, 2005], 248-55. Produced by the Issue Group on Holistic Mission, 2004 Forum for World Evangelization hosted by the Lausanne Committee for World Evangelization.)

Index